AF607814

MATERIALITIES OF RITUAL IN THE BLACK ATLANTIC

BLACKS IN THE DIASPORA

Materialities of Ritual in the Black Atlantic

EDITED BY

Akinwumi Ogundiran and Paula Saunders

Indiana University Press
Bloomington & Indianapolis

This book is a publication of
Indiana University Press
Office of Scholarly Publishing
Herman B Wells Library 350
1320 East 10th Street
Bloomington, Indiana 47405 USA

iupress.indiana.edu

Telephone 800-842-6796
Fax 812-855-7931

♾ The paper used in this publication meets the minimum requirements of the American National Standard for Information Sciences —Permanence of Paper for Printed Library Materials, ANSI Z39.48–1992.

Manufactured in the United States of America

Library of Congress
Cataloging-in-Publication Data

Materialities of ritual in the Black Atlantic / edited by Akinwumi Ogundiran and Paula Saunders.
page cm. — (Blacks in the diaspora)
Includes bibliographical references and index.
ISBN 978-0-253-01386-6 (cloth) — ISBN 978-0-253-01391-0 (ebook) 1. African diaspora. 2. Blacks—Material culture—Atlantic Ocean Region. 3. Blacks—Material culture—Caribbean Area. 4. African Americans—Material culture. 5. Material culture—Atlantic Ocean Region. 6. Material culture—Caribbean Area. 7. Material culture—United States. 8. Ritual—Atlantic Ocean Region. 9. Ritual—Caribbean Area. 10. Ritual—United States. I. Ogundiran, Akinwumi, editor of compilation, author. II. Saunders, Paula V., editor of compilation, author. III. Series: Blacks in the diaspora.
DT16.5.M37 2014
306.45096—dc23

2014010218

1 2 3 4 5 19 18 17 16 15 14

Robert Farris Thompson (b. 1932)

Ogun, the pathfinder in Black Atlantic Studies,
and

Otegbeye (ca. 1840–1890)

Orphan of the Middle Passage, gentle warrior of Ibadan,
Ogun-Osoosi, the restorer of memory
—AO

AND

Many people in the Black Atlantic world who have and continue to engage in ritual: your practice has not gone unnoticed.
—PS

CONTENTS

PREFACE

Broadly, the human experience of material—things, objects, and their contexts—in ritual domains is the subject of this book, with emphasis on the everyday rituals that define human conditions in the Black Atlantic. There are indeed many studies that have examined different aspects of spiritual and religious traditions of African-descended populations in the Atlantic world. This current book is different in its focus on the material dimensions of quotidian rituals. The overriding question that guides the volume is how objects, places, and landscapes are mobilized to fulfill their communicative, symbolic, and semiotic roles in the rituals of everyday life dealing with the different ramifications of human conditions, including birth, death, healing, wellness, social preservation, self-realization, memory, and identity formation, and the consequences for forging meaningful human existence.

We have sought to answer this question across different temporal and spatial planes. In the process, the contributors offer important insights into the agentive action of the material life on the cultural formation processes through which rituals were invented and mobilized in the making of modern black subjectivities. They take us out of the synchronic boundaries of meanings that have dominated the literature to the open field of meaningfulness that highlight Black Atlantic rituals as innovative cultural processes and products enmeshed in sociopolitical and economic realities as well as spiritual and power relations. This collection of integrated essays also examines how the entanglement of the African-descended peoples in different spheres of the Atlantic encounters—commerce, commodification, slavery, Middle Passage, colonialism, and post-emancipation—shaped the forms, contents, and meanings of ritual practices; and how, through rituals, the Africana peoples created different understandings of their material conditions in the Atlantic world.

This book is a sequel to *Archaeology of the Atlantic Africa and the African Diaspora* (Indiana University Press 2007, paperback 2010), co-edited by one of us. This earlier work is an introductory volume on the subject of Black Atlantic archaeology in general. The current book, *Materialities of Ritual in the Black Atlantic,* offers a more focused theme. It centers on what rituals do in individualized contexts and community settings, as meaningful representations of social realities in the modern world. It showcases the materials with which everyday ritual practices were constituted as a set of actions through which thought is realized. It also highlights how the material practices in ritual are thoughtful processes through which action is constituted and made meaningful. Hence, in seventeen chapters, the contributors privilege materiality as a conceptual and empirical starting point for investigating ritual practice in the Africana world. They inject the variegated African and African Diaspora experiences into the bourgeoning literature on ritual and materiality as critical sites for investigating human conditions. Each chapter is a product of original research that taps into two or more evidentiary sources including archaeological, archival, mythistorical, folklore, mortuary, and ethnographic studies. We, however, foreground archaeological perspectives in the questions and thematic priorities that constitute the substantive focus of the volume. Hence, the book highlights the archaeological resonances of some of the issues that are increasingly becoming vital in material, ritual, and religious studies. The book also showcases the kinds of interdisciplinary dialogues that need to take place between archaeology and other disciplines in Black Atlantic studies, especially history and cultural anthropology.

It is not possible to cover all of the geographical and thematic scopes for the dense topic we have taken up in this volume. Many chapters demonstrate circumatlantic and transatlantic perspectives in their multisited empirical, conceptual, and comparative pursuits across the ocean and within particular Atlantic regions, while others are cisatlantic—focusing on particular places in the Atlantic world (Armitage 2002). Overall, the volume concentrates on four areas: the Gold Coast, the Bight of Benin, and their hinterlands; the U.S. eastern seaboard; the Caribbean; and the northern coastlands of South America. There is also secondary reference to the Bight of Biafra and West Central Africa. We hope the conceptual issues raised and the methodological paths pursued in these case studies open new directions for engaging materialities of ritual in the wider terrains of Atlantic Africa and the African Diaspora, while also serving as a springboard for exploring new questions about cultural formation, materiality, and ritual process in general.

Most of the chapters in this book evolved from papers presented in the symposium on "Materialities and Meanings of Rituals in Atlantic Africa and the African Diaspora" at the Society of Historical Archaeology conference held in Toronto, 6–9 January 2009. We thank the participants—presenters, discussants, and audience members, including Andrew Apter, James Davidson, and Jamie Brandon, for the success of the all-day session. We also want to register our profound gratitude to the contributors for their patience and willingness to engage us in fruitful intellectual exchanges on the material discourses and practices of Black Atlantic rituals. This book is indeed a product of active collaboration among all the contributors, involving many levels of feedback and healthy debates by email and telephone. We even carried the discussion, over the years, to other conference venues where the flush of holy water and libations often lubricated our engagement with ritual.

Many people have contributed time, effort, and suggestions to make our work on this book come to fruition. We particularly thank Walter C. Rucker and anonymous reviewers for their detailed and helpful comments, which tremendously improved the overall project. Arlen Nydam, with sharp wits, read parts of the manuscript and offered clinically precise comments. Our friends and colleagues at Indiana University Press, including Robert Sloan, Dee Mortensen, Sarah Jacobi, Darja Malcolm-Clarke, and Margaret Hogan, among others, gave us unparalleled attention as they guided the manuscript through many production levels with ease and a high level of professionalism. We are grateful.

In addition, Paula Saunders would like to thank her colleagues and mentors, especially Samuel Wilson, Carol McDavid, and Peter Schmidt, among others, for their advice; as well as her family and friends, who provided unconditional support.

Akin Ogundiran is grateful to Danielle Boaz, Oweeta Shands, Shontea Smith, and Miranda Stephens, who cheerfully completed many tasks related to the preparation of the book manuscript. He also thanks Babatunde Agbaje-Williams, Kofi Agorsah, Toyin Falola, Chap Kusimba, Dee Mortensen, and Peter Schmidt for important interventions that kept the project on track. Lea (aka Mama'beji), Oyebanji, and Oluremi, who always make it possible for him to simultaneously work and play, with lots of laughter, have done it again. This "Ogundiran triumvirate" wondered many times when the "ritual book" will be completed. This is it! Thank you.

Akinwumi Ogundiran, *Charlotte, 2013*
Paula Saunders, *New York, 2013*

MATERIALITIES OF RITUAL IN THE BLACK ATLANTIC

CHAPTER 1

On the Materiality of Black Atlantic Rituals

Akinwumi Ogundiran and Paula Saunders

Ritual has been at the core of Black Atlantic studies since the pioneering works by W. E. B. Du Bois ([1903] 1982), Melville Herskovits ([1941] 1990), Fernando Ortiz (1906), Jean Price-Mars ([1928] 1983), and Arthur Ramos (1934, 1939), among others, appeared in the first half of the twentieth century. The term "Black Atlantic," coined by Robert Farris Thompson (1983), was not in vogue at that time to characterize the overlapping, racialized, and cultural geography populated by peoples of African descent on both sides of the Atlantic. The broad concerns of the pioneering scholars, however, were not far removed from those of many of their recent successors, who have made this term the centerpiece of their conceptual project: to account for the cultural formation of Africana peoples in the modern world. Stimulated by those foundational studies, a number of publications in different disciplines have appeared in the past fifteen years, focusing on Black Atlantic religion in order to explore questions of identity, sociopolitical negotiations, and the historical processes of African cultural formation in the Atlantic world (see, e.g., Brandon 1997; Heywood 2002; Matory 2005; Murphy and Sanford 2001; Olupona and Rey 2009; Thompson 1993; Tishken et al. 2009). Of course, there is even a far larger corpus of studies that is geographically circumscribed in particular regions or nation-states of the Black Atlantic world. Many of these studies deal with issues of the impacts of Atlantic modernities on Africana religious traditions, belief systems, and their role in social and political spheres (see, e.g., Baum 1999; Palmié 2002; Raboteau 2004; Rucker 2007; Shaw 2002).

Scholars of material culture, especially archaeologists and art historians, have also produced important studies that demonstrate Black Atlantic ritual and religion as important sites for understanding the African and African Diaspora experiences (see, e.g., Blier 1995a; D. H. Brown 2003; Cooksey et al. 2013; Fennell 2007a, 2007b; Ferguson 1992; Leone and Fry 1999; Lindsay 1996; Orser 1994; Ruppel et al. 2003; Thompson 1983, 1993; Wilkie 1997). The archaeological components of these studies are preoccupied with identifying the African or creolized African authorship of ritual signs in identity formation, cultural production, and social contestations in the Americas. On the other hand, the archaeologists of Atlantic Africa have stepped up efforts to relate the evidence of ritual actions in archaeological contexts to the broad cultural and social transformations that the region underwent from the sixteenth through the early nineteenth centuries (see, e.g., DeCorse 2001; Norman 2009b; Ogundiran 2002b; Stahl 2008).

This book builds on these previous studies in two primary ways. First, it makes use of the theoretical, conceptual, and empirical insights of material practices to inform how the entanglement of African-descended peoples in Atlantic encounters—commerce, commodification, slavery, Middle Passage, colonialism, and post-emancipation—shaped the forms, contents, and meanings of ritual practices in the Black Atlantic. In other words, it offers transregional and transoceanic understandings of the materiality of ritual practices in Africa and the African Diaspora by asking questions that interrogate the consciousness of modernity in Black Atlantic rituals, and the impacts of early modernity on ritual production. Second, this collection of essays asks what the materiality of ritual practices reveals about the processes and consequences of cultural formation, social negotiation, spirituality, and knowledge production in the Atlantic world in specific places and temporalities. By privileging materiality as a conceptual and empirical starting point for investigating ritual practice in the Africana world, the efforts of contributors cohere in answering the following questions:

1. How are rituals enabled and enacted through materials—objects, places, and landscapes—in Atlantic African and African Diaspora experience; and what can these tell us about the historical processes of cultural formation?
2. How do objects, places, and landscapes fulfill their communicative, symbolic, and semiotic roles in ritual practice?

3. How do seemingly ordinary objects become ritualized, assume agentive essence, and become coparticipants in the construction and transformation of reality?
4. How do objects, places, and landscapes become implicated in the rituals of memory, commemoration, identity, and self-realization?
5. In what ways do different planes of temporality as well as experimental and experiential moments shape and transform material and ritual practices?

These questions explore the use of the material world in symbolic expressions as well as their agentive action on ritual practice, and how those expressions help to uncover the very intimate but potent spaces in which rituals were invented and mobilized in the making of modern black subjectivities from the era of the transatlantic slave trade to the present. In their various answers to these questions, the contributors direct our attention to two primary purposes of ritual: for enacting or contesting social control and for meaningful active engagement with the world (a world that includes humans and nonhumans) in the process of being and becoming.

The everyday rituals, especially those associated with birth, death, healing, protection, self-realization, and other transformative stages and processes of life, are the central focus of this volume. Our goal is to account for those persistent and enriching spheres of social action where African and African Diaspora communities in the Atlantic world created and negotiated their values, ideas, beliefs, spirituality, and sociopolitical/ideological interests as knowledge and "knowable communities," to borrow a term from Raymond Williams (1973). Approaching the study of ritual practices through the materials with which these practices are constituted allows us to understand ritual as an action through which thought is realized, and a thoughtful process through which action is constituted and made meaningful. The materiality of rituals that deal with quotidian lives then take us out of the synchronic and structural boundaries of meanings to the open field of meaningfulness where we are able to investigate the roles of history and context in the process of becoming as well as in the negotiation of social relationships.

In the effort to understand what materiality of rituals did and meant, and how it worked in the Black Atlantic cultural formations since the sixteenth century, the contributors have benefited from two theoretical streams: practice and symbolic approaches. Catherine Bell's (1992, 1997) instrumentalist/performative understanding of ritual as a construction of power and social relationship and Charles Peirce's (1998) semiosis with his emphasis on the social construction of meaning have offered important insights for the volume. These operational frameworks, however, are interlaced in many chapters with the symbolic theoretical approaches that emphasize how human subjects meaningfully (re)produce culture as "an historically transmitted pattern of meanings . . . to communicate, perpetuate, and develop their knowledge about and their attitudes toward life" (Geertz 1973: 89), and how these meanings instigate social action and transformations (Turner 1969, 1982). With this theoretical collage, we hope the volume will overcome the conundrum of the rigid dichotomies between the objectivity of structure and subjectivity of agency in ritual and material studies.

This eclecticism also recognizes the weakening of the theoretical premise of *culture* as a holistic, persistent, orderly, and static entity (see Marcus and Fischer 1999; Ulin 2001). It helps shift the focus away, to some extent, from what ritual means to what ritual does in everyday lives, especially in the shaping of consciousness, forging of social relations, and historical process of culture formation (see, e.g., De Coppet 1992; Kreinath et al. 2006; Kyriakidis 2007a; Stahl 2008). To this end, we have placed emphasis on the *contingency* of *culture making* rather than on the *stability* of *culture made*. In fact, one revealing aspect of the materiality approach is that it gives an acute sense of the world as "unstable and shifting" (Hicks and Beaudry 2010: 7). Therefore, we conceptualize ritual practice as a sociohistorical process as well as a determined part of cultural formation and social relations in which individuals and aggregated social units—families, residential units, corporate groups, and so on—act out their everyday choices, desires, anxieties, fears, and aspirations. For the most part, we have emphasized those ritual actions mediated by the material and historical conditions of Atlantic exchanges, as well as their consequences. Our interest is to demonstrate the historical and contingent dimensions of ritual as opposed to invoking the view of ritual as a changeless and opaque tradition.

Of Ritual and Its Materiality

This book conjoins two complicated concepts—"materiality" and "ritual." Ritual is one of the most situated, embodied, and multivalent practices that constitute the social and cultural existence of individuals and communities. Unlike most other types of social action, though, ritual is not only about interactions among humans but also between humans and the nonhuman world—plants, geology, animals, and spirits that are within and beyond material elements, both natural and manmade. This starting point, as we will elaborate below, brings us closer to the realization of the elasticity of ritual and its intersections with other fields of social practice such as power, authority, citizenship, identity, consumption, deposition, behavior, self-realization, class, art and aesthetic, intellectual traditions, practices of knowledge, and religion, among others.

The study of ritual has been dominated by three perspectives in cultural anthropology. The first and most influential perspective since the publication of Émile Durkheim's *The Elementary Forms of the Religious Life* ([1912] 1961) couples ritual with religion, or makes the two indistinguishable so that ritual is seen as the form of action in which religion is realized. This approach is preoccupied with the symbolic aspects of ritual as a way of disclosing the structural elements of religion (Fogelin 2007: 56). The second perspective positions ritual as synonymous with public ceremony, performance, adaptive interaction, and play in both mundane and sacred spaces (see, e.g., Drewal 1992; Lewis 1980; Rappaport 1999). Hence, Roy Rappaport's declaration, "Unless there is a performance there is no ritual" (37), can be correlated with the insistence by David Parkin that ritual is "a formulaic spatiality . . . [and] can only be described . . . as movements between points and places and as positionings" (1992: 18). The third approach emphasizes the instrumentality of ritual as a set of practices in the negotiation of social relationships including power and authority in both spiritual and secular realms (see, e.g., Bell 1992, 1997).

Most studies have framed ritual as synonymous with religion and public ceremony (often associated with power and authority), in part because such projects have focused on communal events and politically sponsored ritual actions in elite or centrally/communally controlled venues (see, e.g., Steadman 2009; Wesler 2012). Timothy Insoll's all-encompassing definition of religion as a way of life and worldview that provide organizing principles for all other aspects of social life is particularly influential in this regard (2004, 2012). With this definition, Insoll equates religion with culture and makes ritual a practice of religion. The conflation of ritual with religion or ritual with public ceremony, however, mitigates against a broader understanding of what ritual is, means, and does for diverse contexts that are private, personal, and decentralized as well as public and centrally controlled (see, e.g., Bradley 2005; Kyriakidis 2007a). The chapters in this volume demonstrate that ritual is indeed an integral part of the worldviews, the ways of being, and the ways of life, but ritual transcends religion. In addition, given its experimental and contingent character, we would argue that ritual exists prior to and in spite of religion if the latter is understood as a system of beliefs with a constellation, or hierarchy, of supernatural forces whose relationships with the humans are mediated by priests and/or those with the authority to act on behalf of others. Religion, however, cannot exist without ritual because all the major constituents of religion—"the sacred, the numinous, the occult, and the divine, and their integration into the Holy" (Rappaport 1999: 3)—are all the creation of ritual. Whereas religion needs rituals, not all ritual actions are in the domain of religion (Renfrew 2007: 120). To say this much does not mean that it is easy to extricate ritual from religion and vice versa, because both are always part of the culture-specific philosophy, worldview, and existential reflections. Indeed, there will always be a fuzzy boundary between ritual and religion, and each exists in a continuum relationship with the other (see, e.g., Insoll 2012). Thus, whereas Timothy Insoll and Benjamin Kankpeyeng (chapter 2), Neil Norman (chapter 3), Candice Goucher (chapter 6), and Helen Blouet (chapter 15) discuss rituals within explicit religious traditions, most of the other chapters engage rituals within broad social interaction systems.

The material studies of rituals were originally implicated in the structuralist and interpretive theoretical approaches pioneered by Claude Lévi-Strauss ([1949] 1971) and Clifford Geertz (1973). They respectively seek to uncover the deep meanings and logic of culture that shape human behaviors, cognition, and social interactions. The goals of these approaches are also to account for the processes by which meanings are created and negotiated in various social actions, especially in myth, ritual, and other performances. Some of the signature archaeological and ethnographic works that articulate these approaches have been conducted in Africa (Schmidt 1978, 1996; Turner 1969). Not only do these studies demonstrate the indispensability of material to ritual action, but they also show the permeating quality of rituals in everyday material existence, from production and consumption to technology, social relations, sociopolitical hierarchies, power politics, worldviews, and thought (see also Boivin 2008; Insoll 2009b).

The silence of interpretive anthropology and structuralism on the role of human actors in social change, and in the historical constitution of social structure, however, led to the intervention of practice theory in the 1980s (Ortner 1984). One of the primary goals of practice theory is to account for the role of history and human agency in the making of social and cultural phenomena. Although an unwieldy label that encompasses a wide variety of perspectives in the social sciences (Rouse 2007), practice theory has opened up new perspectives that allow us to see ritual as a dynamic process of human actions, an historically shaped performance, and a critical site for negotiating power, identity, and other material aspects of the everyday life (see also Kelly and Kaplan 1990). The surging interest in the agentive qualities of objects or things stems from the advances in practice theory as a site for contemplating and interpreting cultural formation and social reproduction in the ever-unfolding history of experience.

The interest in materiality as an operational theory of practice has come to define the sets of relationships between human and material agents in the making of social lives. In this regard, the material practices—objects and landscapes—by which social lives and cultures are made lie at the center of the interest in materiality (see Hicks and Beaudry 2010; Hodder 2012; Meskell 2005). Since ritual is one form of social life intrinsically linked to material practices (Boivin 2009; Insoll 2009b), this book accounts for how objects, landscapes, and places illuminate the constitution of ritual as a dynamic social life in Atlantic West Africa and among the African Diaspora populations in the Americas. Yet, the distinction that is often erected between the structuralist/interpretive and practice theoretical frameworks in the study of ritual and its materiality is overdrawn. After all, Catherine Bell, whose work has been widely referenced as the epitome of practice approaches to ritual, drew heavily from the terminological constructs of structuralism in what she considers the major (though nonexhaustive) characteristics of ritual: formalism, traditionalism, invariance, rule-governance, sacral symbolism, and performance. As we shall see later, the contributors in this volume move easily between these two theoretical frameworks in their attempts to explain what materiality discloses on the meaning of ritual, what ritual does, how it is constituted, and how it is constitutive of the social world.

Two types of ritual are broadly identified in this volume. The first type is ritual that works on the manipulation and combination of the physical and chemical properties of organic and inorganic forms—rock, plant, animal, water, manufactured objects, and so on—in order to cause transformative results, such as healing, longevity, or protection. The second category refers to rites of passage that are performed as parts of processes of transition, transformation, self-discovery, and commemoration, such as in burial rituals and periodic communal renewal, as well as in retracing ancestral journeys (e.g., the Middle Passage) and restoring ancestral spirits for the purpose of full self-realization. Either category may or may not involve the invocation of any religious tradition. These two categories of ritual transcend the profane and sacred dichotomies often found in the scholarly conceptualization of ritual. And, as we will show throughout, such divisions or classifications are in fact alien to the experiences of the ritual practitioners and communities examined in this book.

Ritual is dense with material practices because of its metaphysical character. In the Africana world, as in many other societies, communities and individuals are recognized as part of the physical laws of nature whereby rocks, trees, rivers, and even animals have their own spirits, essences, or forces that are critical to the well-being of human subjects and vice versa (Idowu [1962] 1994; Mbiti [1969] 1990; Thompson 1993; for a few comparative perspectives, see Brown and Walker 2008; Descola 2009; Ingold 1988; Viveiros de Castro 2012). This is one reason why the elements of nature—animate and inanimate—are intrinsic to the ritual process. We are therefore better served, conceptually, to recognize ritual as the form of material relations that appeals to, appropriates, and manipulates the energies of forces within and beyond physical laws. Hence, materiality of ritual can be understood as the constellations of material, verbal, intellectual, and performative actions and processes by which ritual is experienced and enacted for transformational purposes. In all of these instances, the social values, meanings, and metaphysical powers with which an object is imbued are culturally determined and depend on an infinite number of factors, including the origins of the object, its luster and color, and even the onomatopoeic sound of the object's name in relation to the specific form or purpose of ritual in question (Bradley 2000; Jones and MacGregor 2002; Kopytoff 1986).

This elasticity of material resources by which ritual practices are constituted, performed, and deposited is discussed throughout the book, especially regarding why and how otherwise mundane objects such as dolls, horseshoes, bottles, or clay colanders become sacralized (see, e.g., Boaz, Fennell, Gundaker, Leone et al., Norman, Ogundiran, Reeves, and Saunders, all in this volume). By the same token, technical knowledge and processes such as iron production, a rational and scientific procedure, is not merely a secular activity but also a sacred process (Goucher, this volume; see also Herbert 1993; McNaughton 1993; Schmidt 1996, 1997, 2009). Our attention to the materiality of ritual facilitates the understanding that the contexts and materials of social distinction, consumption, enslavement, industrial capitalism, intercontinental trade, and technology have also served as ritual fields charged with supernatural powers and spiritual essence. For the same reason, places such as New York's African Burial Ground and European slave-trading forts in Ghana, as well as African American cemeteries in Georgia and the gravesites in St. John's in the U.S. Virgin Islands, are loci for negotiating power, identity, community renewal, and self-realization.

In the desire to escape restrictive anthropocentric thinking in the study of materiality of social actions, students of materiality have been attracted to Bruno Latour's (1993, 1999, 2005) and Alfred Gell's (1998) refrains that call for the recognition of objects as co-equivalent to human agents, whereby both are capable of acting on one another (see, e.g., Gosden 2005; Ingold 2007; Küchler 2005; Walker 2008). Latour's call for a "practical metaphysics" that recognizes the reality claimed by an actor on its own terms without subsuming it into the familiar categories of the scholar, has the potential to bridge the gaps that often exist between the anthropologist's interpretation and the subject's self-understanding of ritual action/process (see also Descola 2009; Viveiros de Castro 2012). This disposition seeks to account for the "ontological weight" and "complex metaphysics" of all social actors as intellectual projects with diverse but valid realities (Latour 2005: 51–52; see also J. W. Brown 2004; Mali 2003). This is no doubt compatible with the metaphysical interiority and outlook of the Africana subjects on material life in which perforated pots or colanders (chapter 3), assemblages of cowrie shells (chapter 4), buried horseshoes at the doorway (chapter 9), concretized bundles of metal objects and fabric (chapter 11), figurative hand-motif pendants (chapter 12), and material figurations in house yards (chapter 13), among others, have the agentive power to act on and transform not only people's agency but also what we may call the physical processes/actions of nature.

Yet, we would argue, in as much as human agency cannot act independently of the material or vice versa, objects do not have intrinsic primordial agency that precedes the human subject (see Hodder 2012). Neither is human agency autonomous of the material and other nonhuman worlds. We are aware that this tension complicates the entanglement of the material and nonhuman worlds with the human, but our goal is to draw attention to this codependency of the human and the material (and nonhuman) worlds, not to resolve the ramifications and complications that emerge between the two. We do, however, explore how the ramifications of the human-material codependency may shed light on how objects are meaningful as a result of the agencies accorded them by human cosubjects in the very process of forging social relations among people, the unseen occult forces, and the forces of nature (Ingold 2007). The empirical issues brought to life by many contributors in this volume demonstrate that as the genealogies of material agencies accumulate over time, and as the sources of valuation of the object, place, and class of objects (or the ideas about those objects and places) multiply, the agentive actions of the material become more embodied and potent in shaping the intentionality of their human subjects. Many contributors to this volume, then, make important efforts to figure out how an object, place, or idea came to have agentive qualities at any given time, and how those qualities changed over time as part of the historically determined agencies of their human subjects.

We also recognize that Africanist art historians have anticipated and put in practice some of the Gellian and Latourian approaches that have fascinated recent scholars (e.g., Hicks and Beaudry 2010; Mills and Walker 2008). Three generations of Africanist art historians have used direct-historical ethnographic approaches to study African and African Diaspora material and ritual lives. These approaches allow contemporary and recent historical information to be used as analogies and homologies for reconstructing the historical processes of materialities of ritual in their cultural and social contexts. These endeavors not only allow ritual practices to be unfolded, but they have been useful for disclosing the ideas and knowledge systems that produced these practices (e.g., Bascom 1973; Ben-Amos 1999; Blier 1995a; Cooksey et al. 2013; Doris 2011; Drewal 2008; Drewal and Mason 1998; Lawal 1996; MacGaffey 1991; Manuel 1998; McNaughton 1993; Pemberton 2000; Poynor et al. 1995; Rush 1997; Sieber and Walker 1987; Thompson 1983, 1993; Thompson and Cornet 1981). Those studies, for their emphasis on materiality of ritual as communicative systems, as meaningfully constituted, and as active purveyors of ideas in the negotiation of self-realization, power, and authority, have been important reference points not only for the anthropology of the African Diaspora but also for the archaeology of Atlantic Africa (see Fennell, Norman, and Ogundiran, all in this volume).

These Africanist interventions in visual and art studies have also broken down the schism between material and ideas (see, e.g., Doris 2011; Thompson 1993). Likewise, they have collapsed the social and material worlds through the consideration that human subjects are constituted within and through the material world. And they have shown the fluidity, creativity, and dynamism by which communities and societies have created themselves in the material world as part of their experience of time. Hence, the advances in Africana art history have taken place parallel with, and sometimes preceding, the issues raised in ritual and material culture studies within anthropology. It is therefore not surprising that the situated approaches of Africana material studies (e.g., Hardin and Arnoldi 1996), especially within the field of anthropological art history, have inspired the contextual approaches that various contributors pursue in this volume (especially Fennell, Goucher, Gundaker, Leone et al., and Ogundiran). We use the rest of this introductory chapter to address five major issues raised in the chapters that populate this book. These themes examine the implications of materiality of ritual for context and transmutability of objects, contestation of power and autonomy, innovations and communicative interactions, genealogies of cultural practice, and the making of memory and commemoration. This discussion not only highlights the overlapping contributions of the chapters but also points toward some of the directions that the study of ritual and its materiality can take in reframing the Black Atlantic cultural formation and transformations.

Context, Contextuality, and Transmutability

Archaeologists document, collect, and study material culture in order to make inferences about human behavior, values, and ideas in the past. Archaeology is object-dependent but without careful attention to the details of contexts and depositional practices in which objects are embedded (in textual, archaeological, and ethnographic sources), the rituality of most of the materials discussed in this volume would not have been recognizable. The discourses on materiality as a form and process of practice in which social action and ideas are intertwined have accentuated the need to pay attention to the depositional practices of objects in archaeological contexts. These practices are useful for disclosing the meanings, ontologies, purposes, characters, and strategies of ritual (e.g., Insoll 2004; Kyriakidis 2007c; Meskell et al. 2008; Orser 1994). As Pollard (2001) and Pauketat and Alt (2004), among others, have demonstrated for the British Neolithic and Ancient Cahokia respectively, the aesthetics and spatial compositional arrangements of deposition are the building blocks by which objects are ritualized and converted into statements about specific values, negotiation, and social process (see also Joyce and Pollard 2010; Mills and Walker 2008).

The idea that ritual actions are crystallized, repetitive, invariant, and formal symbolic processes (see Bell 1997) once encouraged the expectation that ritual actions should be as easily identifiable in the archaeological context as any other type of social action. Yet, we know that this is not always the case since these ritualized objects and motifs are the very same ones utilized in everyday living (Kyriakidis 2007b: 20). For example, one of the hotly debated topics in African American archaeology focuses on whether the cross signs inscribed on colonoware are cosmograms or potters' marks (see, e.g., Agha and Isenbarger 2011; Espenshade 2007; Fennell 2007a, 2007b, 2011; Ferguson 1992, 1999, 2007, 2011; Gundaker 2011; Joseph 2007, 2011; Mouer et al., 1999; Steen 2011). These debates have emphasized the need to develop rigorous, context-driven approaches that help relate artifacts and features, as closely as possible, to their depositional, behavioral, and cultural processes (see Schiffer 1987). This attentiveness to contextuality is *sine qua non* to understanding how artifacts and related materials are meaningfully constituted in particular spaces for ritual purposes (see chapters 2–4, 9–11), or how ritual actions meaningfully transform places and objects (chapters 5, 14–17).

Closely related to the issue of archaeological contexts and depositional practices is the elucidation of the power of location, place, and spatiality in the materiality of ritual processes (e.g., Thompson 1993). A majority of the chapters in this volume address and showcase the importance of positionality in the materiality of ritual. Whereas movements and large-scale directionality are far more relevant in burial grounds, cemeteries, commemorative sites, and public rituals (chapters 14–17), personal and small-scale rituals with interiority focus also have other kinds of spatiality that are repetitive, invariant, and potent. Objects buried under the house floor or entrance, placed along the thoroughfare, hung on the lintel of a house entrance, or strategically placed in the yard (chapters 3, 4, 8–12) complement the well- and the less well-known ritual spaces in the Africana world, such as the crossroads (Leone et al., this volume) and middens (Ogundiran, this volume) respectively. Communal sacred groves, initiation sites, and shrines at the edges of or beyond settlements are among the spaces where the ritual landscape is demarcated, a practice that is still alive in the Black Atlantic world (see chapters 2, 3, and 15). Victor Turner (1970, 1982), following Arnold van Gennep ([1909] 1960), describes these positionalities as liminal spaces, "betwixt and between" spaces of ambiguity, limbo, separation, transition, and reincorporation. Such locations serve as axial loci prescribing and enriching the bodily and sensory movements, imaginings, and actions for anyone in the community or household who shares in the value, knowledge, and communicative interactions of the ritualized and sacred location.

The integrity of context is necessary for the pursuit of meaning and symbolic interpretations, and the recognition of historical contingency in cultural, social, and assemblage formations (Hodder 1982, 1987). Context as a methodology of recovery and documentation, as well as the contextual approach of interpretation, allow one to grapple with the shifting processes of use, purpose, and meaning in the life course of an object. In this regard, Grey Gundaker, Pablo Gómez, Neil Norman, Akinwumi Ogundiran, Matthew Reeves, and Paula Saunders (all in this volume) show the transmutability of everyday objects in Black Atlantic ritual life. Saunders (chapter 9), for example, relates the occurrence of horseshoes buried under house entrances to beliefs about *duppies* (spirits of the dead) who could be manipulated by neighbors to cause harm. The horseshoes, she argues, served as the personal or individual way in which people within the dwelling protected themselves against potential harm caused by *duppies* and other malevolent forces. And, using the concept of self-realization, Ogundiran (chapter 4) explores the aesthetic and antiaesthetic patterns of deposition to examine how cowrie shells came to meaningfully constitute aspects of Yoruba culture and behavioral practices in the seventeenth and eighteenth centuries, and how the objects were also meaningfully constituted by both the structural and historically contingent processes of social valuation.

Animal bones and skins, plant materials, glass bottles, earthenwares, metal objects—nails, horseshoes, knives, slag—as well as glass beads and cowries, all have potent forces in the context of African spiritual lives and belief systems. Thus, the dichotomy between the mundane and the spiritual/sacred is collapsed in almost all the cases in this volume, consistent with many of the recent studies on the conceptualization of ritual (Bradley 2005; Brück 1999; Mills and Walker 2008). A persistent challenge faced by archaeologists and other scholars of material life in the Black Atlantic is how to retrieve the sacred and the spiritual meanings from quotidian objects (Fennell 2011: 35). Reeves (chapter 10) confronts the challenges that context has posed for recovering accurate information about the African Diaspora presence and rituals. He juxtaposes archaeological contexts in the Caribbean (Jamaica) and the United States (Montpelier, Virginia) to illustrate alternative interpretations of intentionally placed glass bottles. Reeves's use of narrative reflexivity to disclose the unfolding of his ideas about the ritual significance of glass bottles in archaeological contexts reveals the problems that a strictly materialist approach to Black Atlantic ritual might face (Schmidt 1983). Those challenges can be overcome, however, when engagement with the descendant community and ethnohistorical sources are brought into play to develop a more holistic approach to context. This involves foregrounding the authorities of the subject and the descendant communities so that, in research design, the ways of knowing of the latter may critically inform the theorization and interpretation of Black Atlantic rituals (see Goucher, Gundaker, Insoll and Kankpeyeng, LaRoche, Norman, Ogundiran, Reeves, and Saunders, all in this volume).

The transatlantic slave trade and industrial capitalism of the nineteenth century accentuated the process of global homogeneity in everyday material life and made it increasingly difficult to use objects to delineate "Africanism." Not unlike the challenges faced by Reeves, Christopher Fennell (chapter 12) seeks to uncover the meanings and material practices of a single class of artifacts—*figa* (figures with a hand motif)—from nineteenth-century African American sites. These objects, however, were not peculiar to those sites. They have also been found in European-American contexts. According to Fennell, they "present evidence of both parallel and intersecting facets of European and African belief systems." He then explores the currents of ideas and cultural traditions to which hand-motif figures belonged in the pre-Atlantic Christian, Islamic, and African worlds, and how these currents might have influenced the construction of African American relationships with these mass-produced artifacts of the Industrial Age. Dealing with the same subject of transmutability of objects, Gundaker (chapter 13) privileges the knowledge implicated in situated practices to shed new light on how postindustrial goods have been used in African American yard designs in the southern United States. Her insightful and richly layered ethnography demonstrates the importance of figural compositions from quotidian objects of industrial society and consumer culture for understanding the materialization of African American rituals of aesthetics, memory, self-realization, and community building.

Empowerment, Autonomy, and Contestation

The study of how changing sociopolitical, political-economic, and economic structures of Atlantic Africa impacted the organization, innovations, ideas, and practices of rituals between 1600 and 1800 has been unfolding incrementally but steadily over the past thirty years (see, e.g., Baum 1999; Belasco 1980; Shaw 2002). In Western and Central Africa, the seventeenth and eighteenth centuries were generally a period of increased political centralization and dramatic expansion in regional interactions. New states were created, sometimes at the expense of older ones, and in some cases, old city-states assumed the status of supra-kingdoms (for examples for Atlantic West Africa, see Monroe and Ogundiran 2012). As the networks of social, political, and economic relationships became diffused and itinerant contacts intensified, the directionalities and definitions of group identities also pluralized. The moral authorities that had constrained and enabled men and women of ritual power—healers, diviners, priests, and so on—in small social units often had to be renegotiated, frequently in favor of the larger political units within which smaller communities were being incorporated.

In that mix, individuals whose ritual power might have been perceived as threatening to the authority of the state or the power of the merchant-ritual-political class were often sold into slavery, among other punishments. As James Sweet (2011) has shown (see also Gómez in this volume), the Sakpata (Vodun of the earth) priests of Mahi, whose influence threatened the authority of the Dahomean king Agaja, were captured and sold into Atlantic slavery. This was a deliberate state policy by Agaja to neutralize the power of the antagonistic ritual specialists in his nascent, expansionist kingdom. Thus, priestly knowledge and skills in Atlantic Africa served as sources of empowerment for different purposes—for the state: to establish new political legitimacy; for the vanquished to resist (or sometimes collaborate with) that legitimacy and pursue self-determination or to regain autonomy.

Not unlike in Atlantic Africa, ritual specialists occupied salient positions throughout the Americas. The importance of ritual specialists, according to W. E. B. Du Bois ([1903] 1982: 216), as "the healer of the sick, the interpreter of the Unknown, the comforter of the sorrowing, the supernatural avenger of the wrong," gave the enslaved conjurer more control over the other enslaved than the master had in many instances (Blassingame 1972: 110). Their ubiquitous roles in many slave rebellions in colonial America has led Walter Rucker (2001: 86) to characterize conjurers as a revolutionary vanguard in the Americas (see also Agorsah, this volume; Suttles 1971; Thylefors 2009). Ritual specialists were also associated with less volatile but important everyday resistance against punishment and abuse. Although feared and respected for their occult and healing powers, conjurers were sometimes disdained for these same reasons by the black and white populations. Ritual specialists, therefore, often occupied a liminal social space (see Boaz and Gómez, both in this volume).

In the Americas, where social roles were poorly differentiated and group identity was amorphous among African Diaspora populations under the various slave regimes and in the post-emancipation years (Ogundiran and Falola 2007: 31), individuals with ritual power sometimes assumed the status of egocentric ritual entrepreneurs, with a heightened exaltation of self (Meyer and Smith 1994: 6). This is not unlike the patterns that we also have noted in Atlantic Africa during periods of social disruption, which were accompanied by the weakening of sociopolitical authority (Baum 1999; Okpoko and Obi-Ani 2005). Yet, the ubiquity of African ritual practices throughout the Americas, as part of the everyday lives, made them a cultural bridge not only among different African cultural/ethnic groups but also between them and Europeans and Native Americans (Rucker 2001: 91). After all, the Catholic priests in and beyond Recife, for example, made use of African instruments of ritual as much as the African priests appropriated the Native American and Catholic healing practices (Sweet 2011: 61, 62).

Thus, the perspectives offered by several contributors in this volume emphasize that we need to supplant the concept of resistance with broader notions of accumulation, empowerment, and contestation. Ultimately, ritual is about harnessing power for the betterment of human condition. Yet, the ontology of power in the Black Atlantic means that the very act of healing for one agent could mean sickness or even death for another (Harms 1981; Isichei 2002). Although empowerment is the goal of ritual as a social action, the social process of enacting, creating, or performing rituals was often dominated by contestation. For example, African healing practices via spiritual invocations and herbal medicine were central to the well-being and health of the enslaved and even of the European populations in colonial Latin America (Gómez, this volume). Yet, these practices—as a source of power for free and enslaved African healers—could also be a source of tension between a master and slave or a colonial authority and the healer. In fact, it was the belief in the efficacy of African rituals to harm colonial institutions, slavery, and authority that aggravated the persecution of African religious and ritual practices throughout the seventeenth and eighteenth centuries. This ritual power was not just about the knowledge to heal but also to contain and neutralize death, and even to harm and cause death in the process of healing. As one would expect, this was too much power to cede to an enslaved population or members of African descent, or to anyone, for that matter, in the totalitarian regimes of colonial society. The face-off between the colonial instruments of control—law and state—and the African ritual specialists constrained and also enabled African Diaspora cultural formations in unpredictable ways (see Boaz, Gómez, both in this volume).

What Danielle Boaz calls "implements of Obeah" were at the center of the contests between colonial institutions and African Diaspora ritual specialists. These objects were transformed into meaningful signs targeted by colonial governments in the Spanish- and Anglo-Caribbean in order to discredit a system of beliefs that they deemed threatening to their project of colonization and slavery. The institutional attitude of the colonial government and its plantocracy toward African beliefs and knowledge system is a reminder that the African Diaspora spiritual and religious traditions, as with citizenship, are products of struggles against the power of the colonial empire and the postcolonial racialized state. The African continuities in this case, in whatever form, are not products of "passive survival" (D. H. Brown 2003: 6). Seen through this prism, Obeah and other forms of African Diaspora ritual ceased to appear as mere retentions of African culture in the Americas, just as African cultures at points of origin were also never static, pristine formations from which retentions simply flowed westward across the Atlantic.

Innovations, Formality, and Communicative Interaction

The chapters that follow also demonstrate that the epistemology and ontology of Africana ritual expressions forcefully privilege dynamism over dogma. Whereas dogma presupposes closure and thrives on fundamentalism, dynamism offers open-endedness, innovation, creativity, intercultural communication, adaptability, and invention of new traditions—practices, beliefs, worldviews, and philosophy (Yai 1999: 34–35). In fact, one quality of Black Atlantic ritual traditions, as seen in some of their classical manifestations—the Igbo, Kongo, Yoruba, Fon, Akan, Mande, and others—is their flexibility (to paraphrase Dana Rush [1997: 2]) to perpetually adapt, invent, reinvent, and modify themselves, providing endless sources to re-form and extend the consciousness of their people, so that their transformation is forever unfinished. In these circumstances where dogma is undeveloped, canons of ritual can exist only in fragmented forms. For example, the accumulative aesthetic of the pan-Kwa rituals during the Atlantic period (e.g., Drewal 2008)—whether it is the Vodun rituals in Ouidah (chapter 3); the Asafo shrines in Kormantse, Gold Coast (chapter 5); or the cowrie-based ritual infrastructures in Yoruba region (chapter 4)—illustrate African-Atlantic cultural innovation and adaptation that also have clear manifestations in the Americas (Yai 1993). These innovations both preceded and paralleled the African Diaspora experience. They offer us insights about why cowries, silk, beads, gin, and other assortment of imported commodities were frequently used in votive, sacrificial, and other ritual contexts alongside African manufactures by the intellectuals of Atlantic Africa—priests, kings, queens, and clan and family leaders from the sixteenth century onward. These men and women presided over open societies by creating and cultivating new, efficient deities, as well as new materials to communicate with and have a better understanding of the various forces shaping their lives (Bosman 1705: 369; see also Drewal and Mason 1998; Thompson 1977a). This perspective should be at the center of our understanding of what Black Atlantic rituals are, what they do, what they mean, and what the process of their becoming is. We need to factor these into the theorization of Africana rituals as a phenomenon integrally associated with material and spiritual needs as well as with the contestation of social control, forging of social relationships, and reinventing knowledge and ontologies at different historical junctures (Allman and Parker 2005; Shaw 2002).

The materiality of Black Atlantic ritual therefore provides us with the intellectual space to account for how the material world was complicit in altering and sustaining the fluid structures of Atlantic African and African Diaspora beliefs. The selective integration of the external material goods into the ritual life reveals the processes of experimentation, improvisation, innovation, and pragmatism (D. H. Brown 2003: 10–11). Thus, we can recognize Black Atlantic rituals as a cultural critique, and African agents as cultural critics who sought to use genealogy, familiarity, traditions, innovations, and inventions to forge new existences—practices and meanings—within the new places and during the changing times covered in this volume.

The materiality of rituals in the Black Atlantic reminds us that tradition is not a static repetition of the past but a fluid, dynamic, innovative practice that looks back to the past but also to the future (Ogundiran 2013a). This quality of Black Atlantic ritual as a force of intercultural and intertemporal communication, for example, makes the ritual bundle in early colonial Annapolis, Maryland, untraceable to a particular ethnic group in Africa (see, e.g., Leone et al., this volume). This is not surprising since such straight-jacket ethnicization of ritual-making did not exist anywhere in Atlantic Africa. Moreover, Mark Leone, Jocelyn Knauf, and Amanda Tang (chapter 11) argue that in the early period of contact and interaction between Africans and Europeans in colonial Annapolis, there were commonly held beliefs in supernatural and paranormal activities, and, in the face of weak colonial institutions, both populations likely enacted ritual practices in public spaces (overtly and covertly) as instruments of social control. The American Revolution and the birth of the republican state, however, strengthened racialized dichotomies between white and black. Public institutions curtailed certain beliefs in supernatural forces in the everyday life, and African-descended rituals became more interior—rather than exterior—focused. This historical context helps bracket the interpretations of a mid-eighteenth century ritual bundle excavated by Leone and his colleagues in Annapolis.

The attention given to the materiality of ritual in this volume not only helps us uncover the historically situated practices of ritual but also exposes the misguided, formulaic submissions that have led many scholars to lapse into making mechanical opposites: Africanism versus creolism or *bricolage*. This volume demonstrates that the Black Atlantic is not made up of any of these absolutes. Without denying the fact of cultural exchanges as the groundwork for cultural formations in the Atlantic World, a number of chapters challenge us to explain and demonstrate the specificities of what such encounters as the African-European or African–Native American interactions actually produced. They also call on us to account for the constraints of such interactions rather than merely assuming such encounters in African Diaspora cultural formations.

In this regard, Hugh Matternes and Staci Richey (chapter 14) shed important light on the communicative quality of a ritualized landscape by focusing on an informal, Reconstruction-era African American cemetery in central Georgia. Lacking any overseeing and regulating authority, a cemetery like this offers the opportunity to examine the experimental processes that shaped the materialization of African Diaspora ideas about death, afterlife, and community-building in post-emancipation America. Matternes and Richey accomplish two goals in their chapter. First, they establish many lines of evidence to showcase the ancestral genealogies of ritual practices that spoke to both Christian and African worldviews, as well as to the material conditions of African Americans as aspiring citizens in the rural southern United States. Second, the authors discuss the performative processes associated with the rituals of death and burial. They emphasize the communicative interactions among the mourners, onlookers, and officiating individuals in relation to burial processes.

Genealogy of Practice

Practices, as actions and ideas, take place in the matrices of history, memory, antecedents, heritage, innovations, and experimentation. Therefore, to effectively understand any practice, ritual in this case, its genealogies must be reconstructed. The explanatory power of a genealogy of practice is invoked throughout this book, not simply to account for the biography of objects, places, and ideas within ritual moment(s) but also to even out the patchworks of experiential moments that constitute social and cultural practices. Two forms of genealogy of practice are underscored. The first is about understanding how particular objects were implicated in ritual practices, which we have already discussed above. The other refers to the social memories of practices, places, experiences, and events that are implicated in ritual processes, identity formation, and social organization (e.g., Agorsah, Blouet, Goucher, LaRoche, Osei-Tutu, all in this volume). The former emphasizes the social life and biographical approaches in material culture studies (e.g., Appadurai 1986; Kopytoff 1986), while detecting the visibility of ritual in archaeological contexts. The latter is closer to the idea of Pauketat and Alt's (2005) memory practices, as a process by which new identities, ritual forms, and societies are created through material, performance, and verbal citations (e.g., oral history/tradition) that extend back to one or many points of origin. Helen Blouet (chapter 15), for example, demonstrates the significance of burial sites, commemorative mortuary, and genealogies of place and practices in the dynamic processes of community-building and marking of racial boundaries in the U.S. Virgin Islands (St. John). Social memory could be noticeable in objects and cited on the landscape of a new society, such as the Saramaka of the Republic of Suriname (see chapter 5). It could also be located in the stories shared by members of descendant communities. These references, according to Mills and Walker, "are ways in which genealogies of practice are built, forming bridges between people across large expanses of time and space, and these can be expressed at different social scales ranging from the individual to larger social fields or collectives" (2008: 18).

The idea of genealogies of practice that manifests in this volume is a dialogic memory process which does not merely recall the past but invokes, imagines, and invents it in order to create a more meaningful present and future. In the Kromantin case-study that Kofi Agorsah discusses in chapter 5, ideas about identity and origins were negotiated and contested between the enslaved and their masters, and appropriated many times by different members of each group, until Kromantin as an idea was codified into an identity of power, fear, anxiety, and/or respect that is synonymous with bravery and freedom. Literally and metaphorically, Agorsah maps the topographies of Kromantin memory work in Africa and the New World, from the Gold Coast (modern Ghana) to Suriname, French Guiana, and Jamaica, and on to the United States, especially New York. He shows how Kromantin as a powerful idea elicited different responses from different segments of society—enslaved and free, black and white—and affected how various individuals acted on the world, whether in resistance against slavery or fighting to preserve a slave economy.

Digging through the archival records, Pablo Gómez (chapter 7) shows a different kind of dialogic memory and genealogy of practice. It is one based on the movement, identity, and self-authentication of an itinerant healer, Mateo Arará, in the New Kingdom of Granada (modern Colombia). Arará claimed that his "healing gifts had been transmitted to him through the womb of his mother" as well as by learning from his maternal uncle. The possession and display of heirlooms that linked Arará's free African past to his enslaved present in the New Kingdom of Granada reveal his agility in effective boundary crossing between different cultural environments and political, social, and economic regimes. Arará also demonstrated his creativity in using the Old and the New World resources to master his new space. He, like all the Africana subjects whose material lives we examine in this book, therefore, shows the compatibility of genealogies of practice with innovations and improvisation.

Many of the African classical traditions—for example, Kongo, Yoruba, Fon-Ewe-Aja, Igbo, Mande, Akan—that appeared in the New World from the sixteenth century onward boast over a thousand years of growth and maturation (McIntosh and McIntosh 1981; Ogundiran 2003; Shaw 1977; Vansina 1990). Each cultural complex constitutes a civilization of epistemologies and ontologies. Despite their distinct characters, they are also similar to one another because of their deep-time common origins and interactions (Ehret 2002; Thompson 1993). The evidence is overwhelming that their appearances as points of cultural or ethnic reference in the Americas demonstrate how embedded these civilizations are in the cognitive reference of the African Diaspora communities.

This volume engages those genealogies without being stuck in the morass of unidirectional origins or the de-Africanization and dehistoricization of the African Diaspora and Atlantic Africa's cultural formations. Genealogies allow us to locate the analytical framework of culture in their proper historical moments and geographies. Anthropology has done much in recent years to demonstrate the agentive act of individuals as the primary basis for meaningful living and culture formation, and to recognize the importance of memory and genealogy in the agentive process. It is rather odd that these qualities are sometimes suspended in ambivalence and unbelievability when conceptualizing the Africanity of the African Diaspora (e.g., Palmié 2013; Price and Price 2000). A temporal approach, such as the one adopted in this volume, cannot eschew questions of origins and genealogies of practice, because, "as agents, people act, and perhaps can only act, in terms of meanings they or their ancestors have conceived" (Mills and Walker 2008: 14; see also Falola and Childs 2004; Gomez 2006; Heywood 2002; Lovejoy 1997; Sweet 2011; Thornton 1993).

The attentiveness to genealogies of practice, therefore, opens up new perspectives, for example, on the transfer of African technologies to the Americas as an embedded, sociocultural process (see, e.g., Carney 2001). These perspectives move beyond abstract survivalism and creolism (especially the latter's ahistorical permutations). As Candice Goucher outlines in chapter 6, the genealogical approach engages the process of cultural formation in a more holistic way that is cognizant of the fact that technology and ritual are intertwined in African sensibilities. Focusing on the rituals associated with iron smelting and blacksmithing, Goucher's chapter is simultaneously about the ethnography, ethnoarchaeology, and archaeology of ironworking on both sides of the Atlantic, especially in Togo, Jamaica, and Trinidad. She demonstrates that the understanding of iron technology in the Black Atlantic can only be understood in the matrix of embodied ritual (that is, knowledge) practices. These practices provide the genealogies of memory and intellectual traditions that not only made the technology of iron production possible and continuous in West Africa but also ensured the continuity of African metallurgical practices, in social and technological terms, in the New World.

Rituals of Memory and Commemoration

Materiality of rituals, as performance, ideas, and social action, involves bodily movement—both axially and spatially—something that is difficult to capture in any archaeological context that is devoid of ethnography, spoken words, or written sources. As Timothy Insoll and Benjamin Kankpeyeng demonstrate in chapter 2, some archaeological contexts indeed lend themselves to understanding the axial and spatial bodily movements in ritual practices, especially with the aid of a comparative ethnographic-historical approach, and the realization that the past ritual behaviors are still part of living traditions. Taking this approach, the authors are able to identify the meanings of ritual postures represented in the clay figurines excavated in Koma and the dynamics of spatial movements in the Talensi Nyoo shrines. All of these are helpful in demonstrating the bodily movements and social actions that produced the ritual configurations in northern Ghana as well as the meanings of these materialities of ritual in Koma and Talensi cosmogonies. This is one of the very few cases of public and communal-based rituals explored in this volume (for others, see the chapters by Goucher, LaRoche, Matternes and Richey, and Osei-Tutu). Their emphasis on the performativity of ritual is a corrective to the tendency in archaeology to represent ritual in static terms.

What happens when archaeological or historical sites become spiritual sites for the descendant communities? How do the relationships that exist between those sites and members of the African descendant populations affect the processes, methods, and theories of archaeological science? These are the questions that Cheryl LaRoche and Brempong Osei-Tutu answer in their respective chapters. LaRoche's chapter in particular is an effort to bridge the gaps between archaeology of African American rituals as a scientific process, and the affective, spiritual, and politically charged qualities of contemporary commemorative rituals (chapter 16). She invokes her own experiential moments in ancestral commemorative rituals to inform the dynamics of relationships between the position of a scientist and that of a descendant member of the African Diaspora. In the case of the African Burial Ground in New York City and the President's House in Philadelphia, LaRoche demonstrates how the unprecedented archaeological discoveries at these sites not only created a new body of anthropological and historical knowledge but also elicited African American ritual expressions to honor the rich legacies of the ancestral past, restore memory, and make contemporary existence meaningfully rooted in history.

Laroche, Osei-Tutu, and Gundaker vividly show that it is through rituals of memory and commemoration that we become whole (see also Turner et al. 1992). In these rituals, disrupted memories are restored, broken genealogies are repaired, and the links between the past, present, and future are strengthened. Yet the processes of commemoration are informed by politics of identity and charged by political actions. All of these shape how the rituals of commemoration are (re)enacted at particular moments and which material symbols are appropriated for these enactments. Underscoring the tension and contestation between the concerns of racialized African American heritage and the nationalist postcolonial Ghanaian's interests in tourism, Osei-Tutu (chapter 17) illustrates how a European fort in Cape Coast, Ghana, has become a critical site for staging rituals of pan-African identity that at once commemorate the horrors of slavery and its abolition, and at the same time promote Black Atlantic unity.

Summing Up: Organization of the Book

This introduction is followed by sixteen chapters, many of which are transcontinental in their empirical and conceptual scope (map 1.1). Although the majority of the chapters are centered on archaeological field methods, studies that privilege archival and ethnographic sources are also represented. The conceptual and interpretational approaches are also eclectic. These are based on the nature of the questions posed for each chapter, but most draw from practice and symbol theories. The journey for this volume begins in West Africa with Insoll and Kanpeyeng's discussion of the ritual bodily postures and movements in archaeological contexts in northern Ghana during the late first through mid-second millennia CE (chapter 2). They offer conceptual and empirical analysis of how to retrieve ritual actions, performances, movements, and gestures, and their cultural meaningfulness, from archaeological patterns. Chapters 3 and 4 use the aesthetics and antiaesthetics of deposition to make sense of the ritualization of the everyday objects in the Bight of Benin and its hinterlands during the era of the Atlantic slave trade. They lay out the intersections of political economy and the rituals of everyday life, and show that these rituals are not simply embedded in cultural traditions but are also transformative of those traditions.

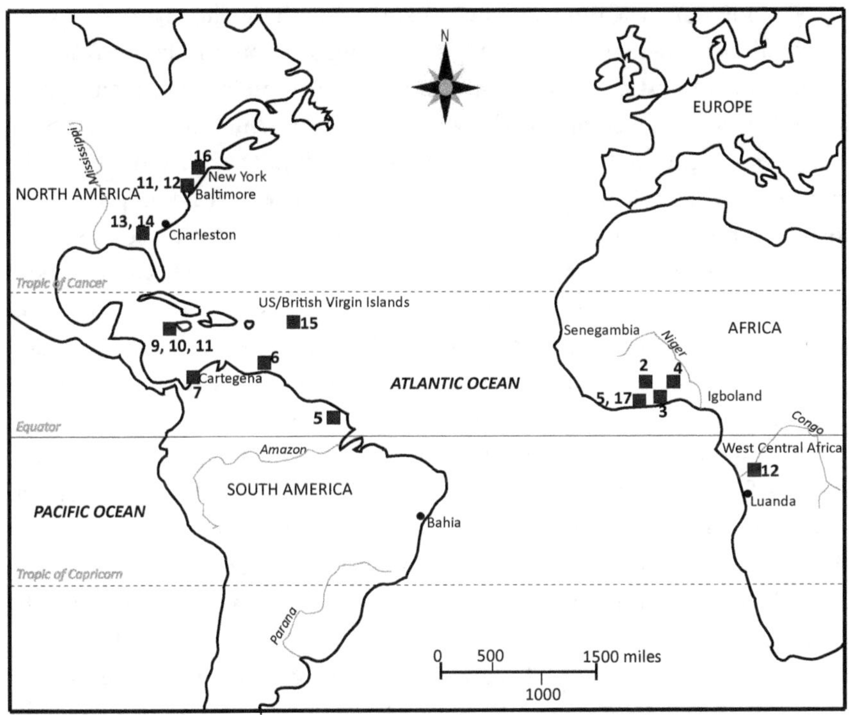

MAP 1.1. Location of places and regions mentioned in the chapters. *Courtesy of Akinwumi Ogundiran.*

Chapters 5 and 6 are two of the chapters that serve as bridges for Atlantic Africa and the African Diaspora case studies. Here, Agorsah and Goucher continue with the performance-based perspectives of the preceding chapters to offer transoceanic analyses of how objects, landscape, and technology have been mobilized to construct African Diaspora identities. Their empirical studies demonstrate how genealogies of ritual practice (action, thought, and ideas) were created and the purposes they have served in the performance of identity in West Africa and the Caribbean. In chapter 7, Gómez builds on Agorsah's and Goucher's emphasis on community and cultural identity in the Americas by using the Spanish Inquisition records to delineate how an itinerant healer of likely Bight of Benin origins, Mateo Arará, defined his genealogies and personhood through the agentive acts of his ritual paraphernalia as he navigated his way through the colonial society of the New Kingdom of Granada. Chapter 8 is also based on legal records, and it complements Gómez's essay by examining the agentive power of what Boaz calls "implements of Obeah" in the negotiation and contestation of social control and cultural identity in colonial Jamaica. Thus, chapters 7 and 8 give us rich insights into how materialites of ritual worked their ways into the institutional practices of colonial society. They give us the social context in which, as discussed in chapters 9 and 10, the rituals of protection, healing, and self-realization took place in domestic plantation contexts and as alternative power dynamics in the everyday lives of the African Diaspora peoples in the Caribbean. In chapter 9, Saunders discusses the use of horseshoes as a protective charm on a Jamaican plantation, while Reeves (chapter 10) examines the importance of context in deciphering the ritualization of bottles in plantation contexts in Jamaica and Virginia.

Chapters 11–14 take us through different material processes in the making of African American ritual experience. Leone et al. (chapter 11) remind us that the interiority of the African Diaspora rituals and the contestation of the legitimacy of their practices were preceded by other scenarios. They use the well-publicized ritual bundle dated to colonial Annapolis to illustrate the cohabitation of African ritual practices in public space as part of the eclectic and juxtaposed efforts of Africans and Europeans to make sense of their everyday lives at a time when the colonial city lacked strong institutions for security and stability. In chapter 12, Fennell shows how African Americans used hand-motif objects for communicative interactions and the forging of race-based social solidarity during the nineteenth century. This chapter recalls the themes of genealogies of practice as well as the improvisation and transmutability of rituals and their material essence discussed in other chapters. Gundaker's (chapter 13) ethnography and performance-based study of the ritualization of consumer culture goods in the design of African American house yards in the southern United States further demonstrates, though for the twentieth century, the processes for constituting materiality of ritual and how they may be transformed as a sign of culture and social life.

From yards to the broader landscape, chapters 14 and 15 direct our attention to the rituals of death as an integral part of the rituals of living in the southern United States and the U.S. Virgin Islands. The authors take us through the practices that drew gravesites and cemeteries into communicative interactions not only between the dead and the living but also among different modalities and hierarchies of power structures. The forms and iconographies of objects involved in these communicative processes, and the strategic implications of these burial sites for land property claims, forging group solidarity, and negotiating citizenship rights preoccupy chapters 14 and 15. The last two chapters conjoin genealogies of ritual practices and rituals of memory and commemoration to explore the ritualization of historical and archaeological sites in contemporary Black Atlantic, especially in the aftermath of colonial rule in Africa and the civil rights movement in the United States. Here, LaRoche and Osei-Tutu bring together some of the issues raised in chapters 2, 5, 13, 14, and 15 by focusing on the rituals of memory and commemoration. As places where the trade in African captives, enslavement, racism, and other manifestations of modernity were staged, New York's African Burial Ground and the Cape Coast Castle, among others, were implicated in rituals for psychological healing from the past trauma of slavery and racism, and the legacies of poverty, ignorance, and continuous criminalization of African Diaspora subjective existence in many parts of the Western Hemisphere.

As a contribution to the literature on materiality, the volume emphasizes that people create a world of practice, meaning, and ideas with objects and places. The contributors shed different rays of light on ritual as a dynamic, communicative interaction, a site of contemplation of abstract and existential value, a mode of knowledge production, a source and practice of empowerment, and fundamentally a process of meaningful living. Each chapter accounts, in unique and also converging ways, for how ritual gives us an appreciation of the historical contingencies through which the self—individual or community—was constituted in the Black Atlantic at the very onset of capitalism, colonialism, and racialization of the Africana subjects. In this melding of processes and patterns, the contributors demonstrate how Africana ritual expressions privilege dynamism over dogma, openness over closure, and creativity over conservativeness in the unfolding of history.

Note

Babatunde Agbaje-Williams, Christopher Fennell, Grey Gundaker, Timothy Insoll, Walter C. Rucker, and two anonymous reviewers read earlier drafts of this chapter and offered helpful suggestions to improve and clarify many strands of ideas. We are grateful to them and to the editorial team at the Indiana University Press for giving their time and ideas so generously.

CHAPTER 2

Reconstructing the Archaeology of Movement in Northern Ghana

INSIGHTS INTO PAST RITUAL POSTURE AND PERFORMANCE

Timothy Insoll and Benjamin W. Kankpeyeng

Catherine Bell (1992: 109–110) has indicated how movement can form a key element of ritual, and how movement is, in turn, related to time, memory, and space in the overall process of ritual action. Interconnected with this is also the concept of "performance," which, as its etymology and definition indicate, is complimentary with "ritual" (see, e.g., Lewis 1980: 33–35; Parkin 1992: 17; Schechner 2002). Unfortunately, the static is often given prominence in archaeological interpretation and conceptualization in relation to ritual and religion (Renfrew 1994; Brück 1999; Insoll 2004, 2009b). This is perhaps a correlation, albeit inadvertent, whereby encountering static material is taken to infer a static ritual (Insoll 2009a). Instead, it can be posited that the structures of archaeological materials were often products of much more dynamic, fluid, and active ritual behaviors (cf. Pauketat and Alt 2005; Pollard 2001; Gillespie 2008).

The frequent neglect of the potentially fluid, dynamic, and active elements of ritual in archaeological contexts are also a correlate of the weakness of the available interpretive tools. Ethnographic analogy can be limited for building inferences across contexts separated by time and geographical space (e.g., Parker Pearson and Ramilsonina 1998; Barrett and Fewster 1998; Oestigaard 2000). Greater potential might be offered in some instances through "broadening interpretive horizons rather than seeking direct resemblances" via ethnographic data (Insoll 2006: 223). In northern Ghana and potentially other areas of West Africa, insights gained from contemporary ritual actions, postures, movements, and gestures can assist interpretation of "ritual" archaeological materials and contexts. This idea will be explored with reference to two archaeological case studies from northern Ghana: the ritual postures possibly adopted in relation to the Koma Land clay figurines and what might be reconstructed of ritual movement through the archaeology of the Nyoo shrine in the Tong Hills, an area currently inhabited by the Talensi ethnolinguistic group.

Although geographical location across time is obviously similar between past and present, thus strengthening that aspect of analogy, ritual continuity cannot be assumed, and empirical weaknesses exist. For example, the absence of written historical sources in northern Ghana prior to the early twentieth century (Allman and Parker 2005), allied with the decline in effectiveness of oral historical sources beyond a putative five or six generations (Fortes 1945: xi; see also Vansina 1985), limits the available material that can be drawn upon. This weakness is slightly compensated for by the anthropological record for the region, but here references to ritual movements, postures, gestures, and actions are largely incidental rather than intentional records of research (Baduel-Mathon 1971). Indeed, though ritual has been a major focus of anthropological attention in northern Ghana, data on posture are often neglected, a significant omission that limits the interpretation of ritual processes and actions.

What is significant is the historical depth of the anthropological record—not as a correlate of the historical information it contains, which is minimal, but rather because northern Ghana was one of the key incubators of largely British structural functionalist anthropology (Rowlands 2007: 66; Allman and Parker 2005). Hence, there exists a body of ethnographic data, albeit in some instances unpublished (Insoll 2010a), that can allow comparisons of ritual actions and movement, in the case of the Talensi, over nearly an eighty-year period. This historical anthropological approach is utilized to explore the potential continuity in ritual performance, movement, and bodily practice in the Talensi Nyoo shrine.

Yet, such comparisons for reconstructing and interpreting the archaeology of ritual movement should not lead to the assumption of ritual stability over time. For even over comparatively short periods of time, ritual practices and the deposition events by which they are materialized archaeologically could have been subject to considerable trajectories of change (Insoll 2009a: 293). This notion of ritual change and flexibility needs acknowledging. Part of the problem as to why it is frequently not, and ritual stability suggested instead, could lie in how indigenous or so-called traditional religions have become "textualised," which can stand at variance with their truer "oral" character. Roland Hallgren (1995) considers this through the Yoruba concept of àse, or "life force" in southwestern Nigeria. He describes how the "process towards an orthodoxy" has taken place allied with the creation of what almost could be regarded as "canonical texts" by scholars of Yoruba religion, both African and European (83). This textual process has had profound implications where "alternative interpretations or research results run the risk of losing reliability or being rejected as 'heretical' in the light of the dominant view" (ibid.). These processes can lead to a certain "freezing" of time and tradition, and the notion of change in relation to ritual processes could become suppressed. In failing to recognize or consider the potential for exploring movement in "ritual" contexts, this static image could be projected onto archaeological interpretations.

In making these points, however, it is not the intention to deny the existence of an underlying core of stability in belief and practice with regard to ritual. This can and does exist, in religious beliefs, in bodily understandings in relation to the use of space, and in the symbolic and metaphorical qualities ascribed to objects and materials utilized in rituals (e.g., Baduel-Mathon 1971; Nooter Roberts 2000: 75–78; Argenti 2006: 49–50, 62). Additionally, movement can form part of these strata of stability, for stability does not equal "static" (e.g., Fowler and Fowler 1986: 885, 891). The potential net result of this could be the creation of the seemingly contradictory position whereby both "constructionist" and "primordialist" elements are evident in the overall ritual structure (Lentz and Nugent 2000: 4). Within such a construct there is then, conceivably, the fusion of, to adapt Lentz and Nugent's definitions, "primordial ties" that are "deeply rooted in the past," as well as "manipulated" elements reflecting the "strategic character" of ritual (ibid.). It is the interplay of these that is perhaps amenable, sometimes, to archaeological investigation where ritual movement and action are the focus of interpretation.

Archaeology of Koma Land

The archaeological region of Koma Land covers an area approximately 100 × 100 km within the basins of the Kulpawn and Sisili rivers in the northern region of Ghana (map 2.1; Kankpeyeng and Nkumbaan 2009: 195). It is famed for the anthropomorphic and zoomorphic figurines first recovered by James Anquandah in the mid-1980s (1987, 1998). Renewed research has been undertaken in Koma Land since 2006, directed by Benjamin Kankpeyeng, and

Timothy Insoll has participated in two seasons of the project in January 2010 and 2011 with an emphasis on interpreting figurine function. A key cluster of predominantly mound sites is located around the village of Yikpabongo. These were initially interpreted as burial mounds (Anquandah 1987) but are possibly the remains of shrines (Kankpeyeng and Nkumbaan 2009: 201), perhaps functioning in the context of healing (Kankpeyeng et al. 2011). In addition to figurines, copious quantities of locally produced ceramics, iron bracelets, utilitarian artifacts, grinding stones, and small numbers of glass beads and cowrie shells have been recovered (Anquandah 1998; Kankpeyeng and Nkumbaan 2008, 2009).

Interpreting the archaeology of ritual movement with reference to the Koma figurines can be approached in two ways: first, by studying the forms of the figurines and what they depict, and second, via the context of the figurines and what this implies about the actions and movements completed in relation to them and their deposition. The latter is similar to the approach of Lynn Meskell et al. (2008) to the figurines from the Neolithic Anatolian site of Çatalhöyük. The materials considered here are from excavations at one of the mounds in Yikpabongo, YK10-3. This is a mound of approximately 18 m east-west and 15 m north-south and was excavated using an inverted L-shaped grid of 10 m × 5 m × 10 m × 5 m. YK10-3 has been radiocarbon dated to Cal CE 1010 to 1170 (970+/−40 BP) (YK10-3-N-10-L2—Beta-274104). This concurs with the four TL and one other C14 date obtained from elsewhere in Yikpabongo that range between the sixth and early fourteenth centuries CE (Kankpeyeng et al. 2011). The highpoint of Koma Land occupation that generated the ritual mounds and associated settlement areas was between the sixth to twelfth centuries CE based on the dates from Tando-Fagusa and Yikpabongo (Kankpeyeng and Nkumbaan 2009: 200).

FIGURINES OF YIKPABONGO

Ninety-two fragments of figurines were recovered during the excavations of mound YK10-3, and only selected examples are chosen here to discuss the diversity encountered in the assemblage (table 2.1). The depiction of human features could generally be described as solemn. This is achieved through facial stance and posture, but primarily by the depiction of the eyes staring uniformly straight ahead. The majority of the anthropomorphic figurines from YK10-3 lack expression or emotion, and are framed in a static position, in standing or seating postures. Where complete human bodies are represented, prominence is often accorded the representation and posture of the

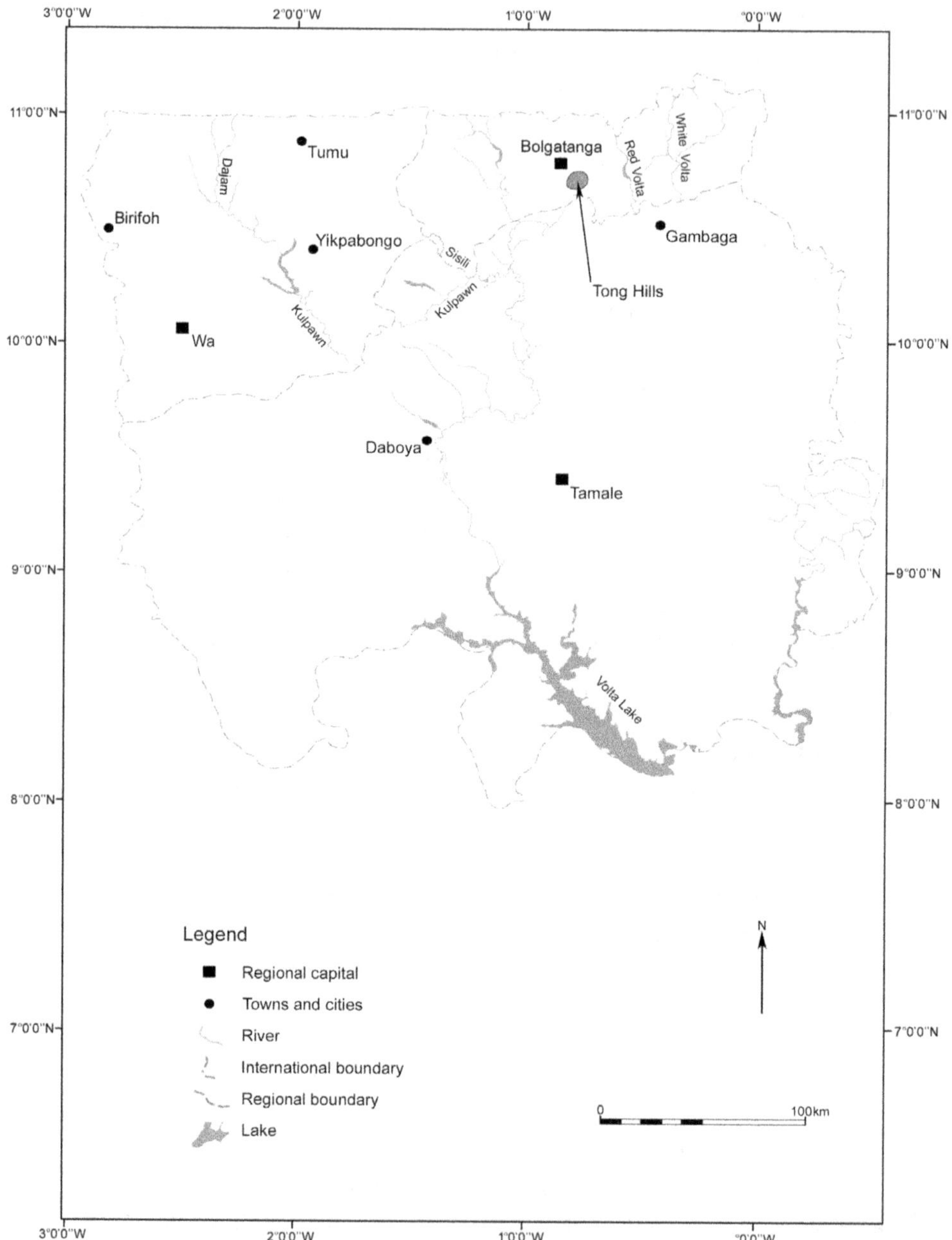

MAP 2.1. Location of Yikpabongo and the Tong Hills.

Table 2.1. Dimensions of the figurine and vessel examples discussed from the Yikpabongo (YK10–3) mound.

Context Number	Figurine Description	Maximum Dimensions (cm)
YK10-3-N11 (1)	Seated male figurine staring ahead. Mouth closed but prominent and downturned. Ears deeply incised. Hands placed to front of legs. Incised libations hole on top.	18 height (H) × 7.5 width (W) at shoulders
YK10-3-N11 (2)	Male standing figurine lacking its head. Hands placed to front of legs.	15.5 H × 9 W × 5.5 depth (D)
YK10-3-N11 (3)	Part of a small clay vessel modeled on a gourd or seed.	7.5 H × 7 W × 4.2 D
YK10-3-P13 (1)	Androgynous head with open mouth.	8 L (length) × 4.5 W
YK10-3-P13 (2)	Androgynous head with open mouth.	5 L × 3.3 W
YK10-3-N10 (1)	Androgynous head with incised libations hole on top and incised ear holes and nostrils.	6.3 L × 4.1 W
YK10-3-N10 (2)	Androgynous pointed figurine lacking part of its face and top of the head. Nostrils and ear holes incised.	11.5 L × 3.8 W
YK10-3-4-I15 (B)	Chameleon.	14 H × 4.5 W × 2.5 D
YK10-3-O11 (4)	Pointed male figurine with deeply incised head, ears, and nasal cavities.	16 H × 6 W × 4 D

hands. This is clearly evident, for instance, with four figurines illustrated by Kankpeyeng and Samuel Nkumbaan (2009: 200). These depict the arms pointing straight down and with the hands to the front of the body also pointing downward. (Baduel-Mathon [1971: 229] describes standing or kneeling figures with arms tensed as one of the postures of prayer among West African groups, especially the Agni, Akan, Yoruba, Bini, Malinke, Bambara, and Dogon.) Similar postures are indicated on two figurines illustrated by Kankpeyeng and Nkumbaan (2008: 98–99), and several illustrated by Anquandah (1998: 136–141).

The possible exception to an absence of expression or emotion is provided by one category of figurines with open mouths. Anquandah argues that the human figurines of Koma Land "are charged with vivid emotional expressions, whether they are depicted in an apparent state of wailing or shouting or chanting" (1998: 152). Presumably, this is in relation to the open mouths of a few figurines, but the majority could not be described as emotional. Anquandah draws precise ethnographic parallels with Bulsa or Buli eulogies, dirges, and war cries to explain the open mouths (ibid.: 164). Leaving aside the direct nature of these analogies, the depiction of open mouths on some figurines could also indicate terror or pain. They might also have functioned for the admission of libations or substances not now visible. This is suggested by the cavities sometimes pierced through the ears, mouths, noses, or tops of the heads. Although the location of the cavities can vary, the piercings on the tops of the heads are relatively frequent, surrounded by clay modeling possibly representing either cowrie shells or female genitals (ibid.: 160; Insoll et al. 2012). Experimental tomography scanning of a pointed anthropomorphic figurine, YK10-3-O11 (4), indicates that the cavities from the top of the head, ears, and nasal cavity were pierced deep into the body of the figurine. It is not yet known what substance or substances might have been used for libations, if any, but research is in progress to assess this (Van Dongen et al., under review). The nonhuman figurines seem to lack these cavities, and this was also confirmed by experimental tomography scanning of a chameleon figurine, example YK10-3-4-I15 (B).

It is not clear why emphasis was placed on piercing cavities on different parts of the human figurines. Comparative ethnographic analogies do not exist, but the material presented by René Devisch in relation to the Yaka of southwestern Congo is interesting. Among the Yaka, listening was perceived as "a horizontal movement from outer to inner" and smelling "the olfactory mediation between inner and outer" (1991: 295, 297). When surfaces—inner and outer—are deliberately pierced to access the inner core, as on some of the figurines, it is enticing to think of these deliberately produced cavities as more than an aesthetic or technical choice. Moreover, the addition of materials to the figurines might have served to activate the figurines' powerful essence.

THE CONTEXT OF THE FIGURINES

In order to understand the figurines, as well as interpret the associated ritual movements, it is also necessary to look at their context. Ritual has been defined as being concerned with "action in relation to material things" (Insoll 2004: 78). The contextual arrangements of the Yikpabongo figurines would seem to fit this definition as they show remarkable similarities in how objects are deposited and arranged (Kankpeyeng and Nkumbaan 2008: 99). This is exemplified in the recurrent patterning of spherical stone (quartz and granite) querns and ground circular pottery disks formed from potsherds overlying the layer containing figurines, and the figurines' being sometimes

FIGURE 2.1. Feature comprising vessel fragments (center), possible libations structure (bottom), and stone rubber or grinder on potsherds (center right).

"nested" within arrangements of potsherds and associated with what are possibly libation structures (see below). It also suggests that we are viewing the in-situ residue of ritual action, and that the majority of artifacts, including the figurines, are in their original positions as deposited. This is supported by the repeat patterning of deposition with layers of similar material culture in similar patterns "superimposed on each other" (Kankpeyeng and Nkumbaan 2009: 196). This pattern is evident in the stratigraphy in square YK10-3-I15 where a layer (YK10-3-I15-3) composed of an arrangement of potsherds was recorded. The sherds from a large vessel pierced at its base depicted in figure 2.1 (center) were associated with a clay structure, perhaps a libation hole (bottom) and a stone grinder set upon a bed of potsherds (center right). This deposit was over a layer containing two figurines, a chameleon, and a pointed, stylized anthropomorphic figure associated with pottery disks. Both figurines are recumbent.

Of the nineteen figurines and figurine fragments for which positional data are available, sixteen are recumbent and only three upright. This would not seem to be the result of postdepositional disturbance but indicative of how they were originally placed. From these contextual data, insights into movement and posture in relation to the figurines can potentially be

Table 2.2. Examples of seating/squatting ritual postures in Northern Ghana.

Ethno-Linguistic Group	Ritual	Posture	Source
Talensi	Sacrifice at Yiran House during Boardaam Festival, Bonchiog, Tong Hills	All seated on rocks except Yiran's son, who offers sacrifice to tall shrine	Insoll personal observation (10/29/2008)
Talensi	Libations offered at Boardaam Tamping, Boardaam Festival, Bonchiog, Tong Hills	All seated except for person filling calabashes with millet beer	Insoll personal observation (10/29/2008)
Talensi	Divination, Kpatar Section, Tong Hills	Seated on ground	Insoll personal observation (11/2/2008)
Talensi	Sacrifice to personal ancestor shrine, Bonchiog, Tong Hills	Seated on stool	Insoll personal observation (11/4/2008)
Talensi	Sacrifice and prayer	Squatting unless addressing a taller *bakologo* or diviner's shrine	Fortes (1987: 59; see also 1945: plate VIa and b, plate IIIb)
Talensi	Festivals—inauguration of the Golib dance (see figure 2.4)	"Squatting in the customary way"	Fortes (1987: 59)
Sisala	Divination	Seated on a cow skin	Mendonsa (1982: 120)
Sisala	Sacrifice at an ancestral shrine	Squatting	Mendonsa (1982: plate 3)
Bulsa	Addressing ancestors	Squatting	Kröger (1982: plate 1)
Bulsa	Sacrificing to ancestors	Squatting	Kröger (1982: plates 2, 3a, 3b)

gained. The low heights of the figurines and their associated arrangements would appear significant. They are not raised on mounds or discarded in heaps, but laid out in horizontal spreads rather than vertical clusters. The figurines themselves rarely exceed 15 cm in height (figure 2.2), and it is possible that squatting, crouching, kneeling, or sitting, rather than standing, were the original postures adopted in relation to these figurines. The recurrence of these ritual postures has been recorded ethnographically by Céline Baduel-Mathon (1971: 229–233) in her study of ritual gesture and posture in West Africa, and examples of their recent occurrence in Northern Ghana are given in table 2.2.

FIGURE 2.2. Figurine YK10-3-N10 (2).

Table 2.2 shows that squatting and sitting are dominant ritual postures in northern Ghana, and are associated with different types of ritual activities. The frequently low-roofed nature of shrines almost dictates such a posture. Ethnographic evidence indicates that these preferred ritual postures are fairly common among several ethnolinguistic groups in northern Ghana and are not peculiar to the Bulsa as Anquandah (1998) has implied. The ritual activities that were potentially associated with crouching or squatting positions could also vary. The possible importance of libation has already been noted, and squatting might have been adopted to offer libations to some of the figurines, especially the type referred to as A1 by Anquandah (ibid.: 129) and as "pointed" figurines here. Of the ninety-two fragments and figurines recovered, eighteen were broken points from the base of these types of figurines, indicating their ubiquity. Anquandah further suggests that the pointed figurines were manufactured in this way for hafting. It is more likely, however, that they were produced with a point or cone at the base so that they could be placed or inserted into the ground, hence some came to be at an angle or recumbent as they were not necessarily immediately buried following their being set into the ground. The recurrence of pierced holes on the tops of these figurines, as already described, could correlate with their being set in the ground via their points providing a maximum exposed length of approximately 8–10 cm. The seated and squatting positions of the figurines meant it would have been feasible to offer libations through the pierced cavities on them.

The recurrence of small clay vessels modeled on gourds or seeds, as well as small clay cups (Kankpeyeng and Nkumbaan 2009: 196), might represent the types of receptacle used for offering libations or for containing powerful substances as shown in figure 2.3. The frequency of libations as a ritual practice would also seem to be represented by clay bicones (e.g., YK10-3-P14), usually with pierced cavities (see Kankpeyeng and Nkumbaan 2008: 98). Anquandah (1998: 123) states that there is no evidence for usage of the figurines in their primary "domestic settlement context." Whether the figurines and associated material culture were utilized for ritual purposes elsewhere prior to their deposition in the mounds—contexts which Kankpeyeng and Nkumbaan (2009: 201) interpret as analogous to shrines—is unknown.

The Archaeology of the Nyoo Shrine

Whereas posture is the primary focus of study in the Koma figurines, the archaeology of movement will be the focus in this section on the Nyoo shrine,

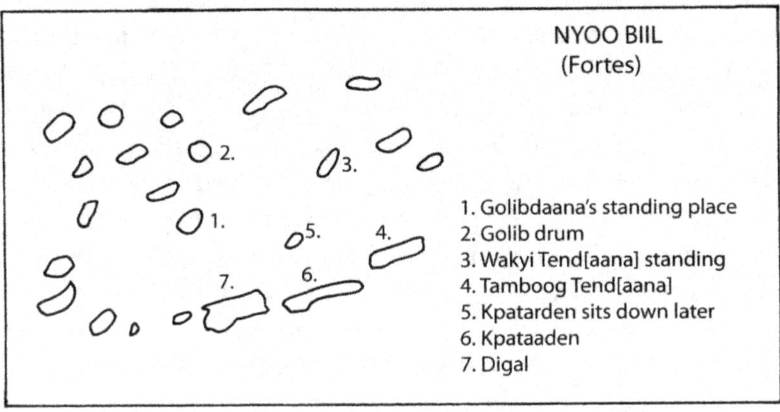

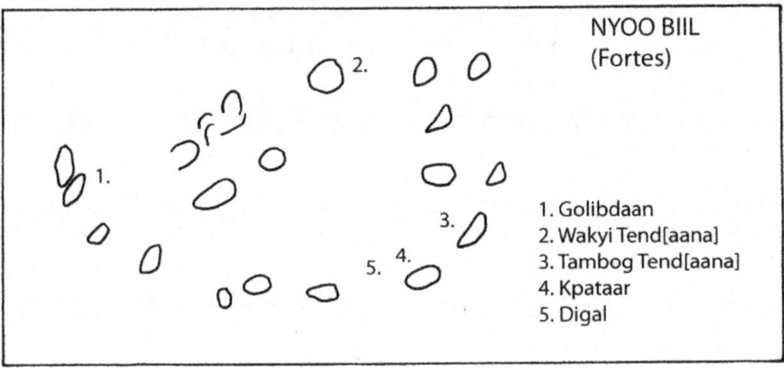

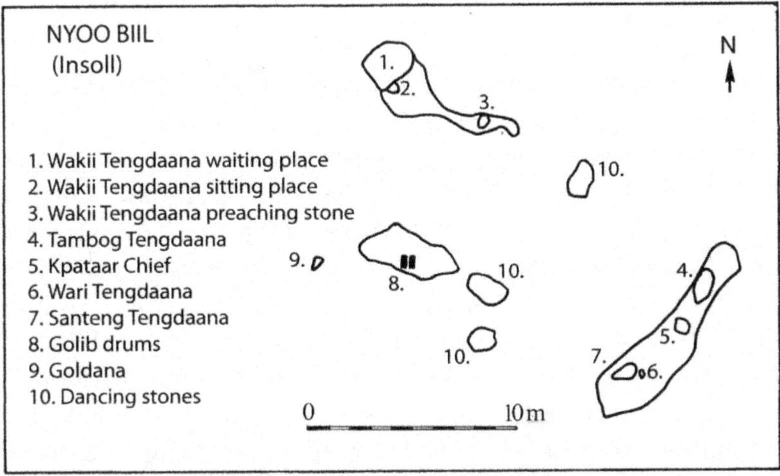

FIGURE 2.3. Seating plans in NyooBiil, top and middle (1 and 2) from March 1934 (Fortes 1934a); bottom from July 2006.

located on the Tong Hills (see map 2.1). The Nyoo shrine is an archaeological site and an active Talensi shrine as well as an arena for performance during the annual Gologo or Golib sowing festival. Three different zones exist in Nyoo: First is an area of stone arrangements and spreads of pottery that had been half-buried in the ground. Second, there is an area of standing stones produced from various rock types including Leocratic and Bongo granites and meta-chert (Baneong-Yakubu et al. 2006). These stand on average 60–80 cm above ground, of which 143 whole and fragmentary examples have been recorded. Third is an area lacking visible archaeological remains that serves as the contemporary place of sacrifice. Two units were excavated (Insoll et al. 2009). NYOO 06 (A) delimits seven stone arrangements that were formed largely of a single layer of stone in a trench 8 m × 4 m. A layer of potsherds of 15–20 cm deep surrounded and partially filled the stone arrangements. From this layer has come an optically stimulated luminescence (OSL) date (X2845) NYOO 06 [A] 5 [B5] of 951+/−101 (CE 955–1155) processed by the Oxford Research Laboratory for Archaeology and the History of Art. Within unit NYOO 06 (B), twelve clusters of either paired or single standing stones were recorded. These were associated with a range of material culture including complete pots, stone grinders, potsherds, iron bracelets, and points (ibid.). The two OSL dates from this context (X2864) NYOO 06 (B) 4 [D4] are 1234+/−121 (CE 650–895) and (X2847) NYOO 06 (B) 6–7, 1752+/−176 (CE 80–430) respectively.

RITUAL PERFORMANCE, MOVEMENT, AND BODILY PRACTICE IN THE CONTEXT OF THE NYOO SHRINE—THE GOLIB FESTIVAL

The stone arrangements of the Nyoo shrine are of significance in attempting to reconstruct an archaeology of movement for they provide insight into past spatial movements and an interpretive entry into performance and associated ritual action, if approached through the method of historical anthropology. The complementarity of ritual and performance has already been noted. This is evident in both the day-to-day rituals completed at major Talensi shrines such as Nyoo and Yaane, and in the great Talensi festivals such as Golib and Boardaam (Fortes 1987: 49). These festivals, and in particular the Golib—the "harvest festival"—are relevant for interpreting ritual movement and performance with reference to the stone arrangements at Nyoo. This is because the Nyoo shrine and the smaller NyooBiil shrine are the focus for the harvest festival's ritual activities. Golib is a festival held by the Hill Talis prior to the sowing of the early millet that takes place at the end of the dry season. It is composed of dances in various locations, for example at Yinduri, Wakii, and Tengzug, accompanied by other ritual activities including solemn congregations, as well as more esoteric rites (see Fortes 1987: 50–51, 54–61). Golib was recorded by Meyer Fortes in the mid-1930s and by these authors in 2006 and 2008.

Mapping the landscape of ritual movement is crucial to understanding Golib (Insoll 2009a), especially when considering the movement of ritual objects such as the two Golib drums and the dance staff, or sikpatuure; movement of individual bodies in dance; movement of different Talis communities in groups; and movement of ritual locations. Fortes indicates the centrality of movement to the whole festival when he states that "Golib is the name of the dance, signifying the meandering circular movement of the dancers at the climax of the festival" (1987: 53). It is necessary, however, to ask whether this observed image of ritual, movement, and performance has relevance to the archaeological context. Is it an ahistorical snapshot lacking the "primordialist" elements referred to in the introduction? Or is it representative of something more enduring and thus, potentially, of greater archaeological significance? Our own more recent ethnographic studies demonstrate that the rituals associated with the Golib contain some aspects that have remained stable or unchanged, and others that have altered in the seventy years between Fortes's study and our own observations of the festival. The dances, orations, locations, and structures of the rituals are comparable, in so far as the less-detailed records taken of the festival in March 2006 and 2008 permit comparison with Fortes's comprehensive accounts collected in the mid-1930s.

THE ARCHAEOLOGY OF PERFORMANCE AND MOVEMENT

It is important to note that landforms and cultural conventions could constrain the limits of innovations associated with ritual performance and movement. Likewise, bodily understandings of space, albeit sacred space, from a biological, physiological, or psychological perspective could stabilize over a long period of time (Insoll 2007: 49–50; Lewis 2002: 566). Hence, the continuity of ritual and performance is central to fostering particular forms of spatial understanding and material relations. The similarity in stone arrangements at Nyoo and NyooBiil is suggestive of ritual continuity between the two sites. The stones are used in NyooBiil as spatial markers for performance and movement, and it is possible that those in Nyoo served a similar purpose. People know their place in relation to natural features such as rocks and trees, and the manufactured ones such as seating places in shrines, as well as to ritual practitioners, elders, and other sections of Hill Talis. This locational knowledge leads to careful orchestration of the ritual performance.

There is continuity, for example, between the past spatial arrangement of the ritual site in NyooBiil and how the contemporary community remembers this practice. The first two plans in figure 2.3 (upper and middle) show the seating positions in NyooBiil as recorded in Fortes's unpublished field notebooks (1934a), and the lower illustration shows the seating arrangement as described by Eric Yin and Roger Naatoam in July 2006 (pers. comm.). Continuity is evident in the locations of the Tamboog Tendaana (Earth Priest), Kpataar elders, and Wakii Tendaana, Golib drums, and Golibdaana positions. Social memory is here seemingly "inscribed" (Connerton 1989: 73) in the layout of the shrine as evident over a seventy-plus-year period. Yet identifying continuity is not to imply that ritual activity is static. Stable foci might exist in the form of clusters of elders, chiefs, and Tendaanas in their customary places in the shrines, but these foci can be the focus of dynamic movement as is evident during Golib in NyooBiil. This movement is of a precise type (Insoll 2009a). The dancers process in single file, slowly shuffling along, moving the upper parts of their bodies in time to the songs, chants, and rhythm of the Golib drums but more so the rhythm generated by singing and the hard stamping of feet, especially the right one, which is accentuated by the iron dance bangles or nansahi attached to the dancers' ankles. Occasionally the dancers, individually, in groups in the line, or the whole line, become more animated, even ecstatic, wildly pounding their feet before dropping back to the slower movement, but always maintaining the same winding processional route in front of, and sometimes around, the chiefs, Tendaanas, and elders.

The description of the dance amalgamated from observations in NyooBiil in 2006 and 2008 is almost identical to a dance observed by Fortes seventy-four years before in March 1934 in an unstated location, possibly NyooBiil: "These appeared to be a synchronized rhythm of [unclear word] movements with the hand, shaking and thrusting movements of thorax and hips, exactly like those we saw at the funeral custom . . . and astonishingly suggestive of coitus, and a stamping of the inner foot, and a slow forward push of the outer foot, hardly lifting it." Similarly, Fortes refers to the dancers' staying broadly in the same place and, "thus they might have danced in what eventually amounted to a circle, a solid circloid body revolving on a fixed axis" (Fortes 1934b: 17, 18).

Both the description of the individual dance techniques and the group dance patterns are very similar. Fortes (ibid.: 28) recorded the latter in a sketch (figure 2.4); in the sinewy winding patterns illustrated, in particular numbers 1 and 2, they match those used by groups of dancers to move away from or into larger dance groups at recent Golib dances (numbers 1 and 3). The "solid circloid body" is mirrored in the main dance at Yinduri (number 1). Based upon this evidence, it can be suggested that the stone arrangements excavated in Nyoo might, possibly, be interpreted within similar frameworks. For rather than representing static markers, they too could, perhaps, have served to structure and direct movement, conceivably dance, of a similar type to that described ethnographically (Insoll 2009a). Paul Connerton's insightful statement to the effect that "relative sparseness" of ritual gestures such as attentive standing, kneeling, prostration, and dance, accords these actions their "performative power" is relevant here (1989: 59). In the Tong Hills, it is possible that dance of a certain type, or at least specific movement in relation to certain categories of spatial markers, would have functioned in a similar way to that described by Connerton (ibid.). Dance in ritual contexts among the Talensi is derived from a limited repertoire of ritual movements, and is therefore subjected to significant temporal continuity. In their prescribed formality, these movements convey meanings that make their ritual power effective.

Expanding the analysis of movement beyond the context of the Tong Hills is potentially helpful in assessing possible continuity of bodily understandings, movements, and practices. Some relevant comparative material from West Africa exists. Baduel-Mathon refers to group dance, and how it can qualify as "d'écriture corporelle" and be utilized to trace figurative paths on the earth, including the "ligne serptentine" (1971: 230). Walter van Beek, for example, refers to the dancers in the Dogon village of Anacana, Mali, marching "through the village in a snake like fashion, weaving in and out to the beat of the drums" (2001: 130). Similarly, Suzanne Blier describes the ceremonial paths that wind back and forth through Batammaliba villages of northern Togo, and that recall "the winding form of a python across village terrain" (1987: 104).

This material shows that a snaking, sinewy group dance movement is not unique to the Talensi, and, perhaps, we have the residues of similar movements locked in the archaeological record at Nyoo. This is as far as the suggested analogies can go, however, because it is both unwise and impossible to reconstruct either a specific dance or a complete Golib festival

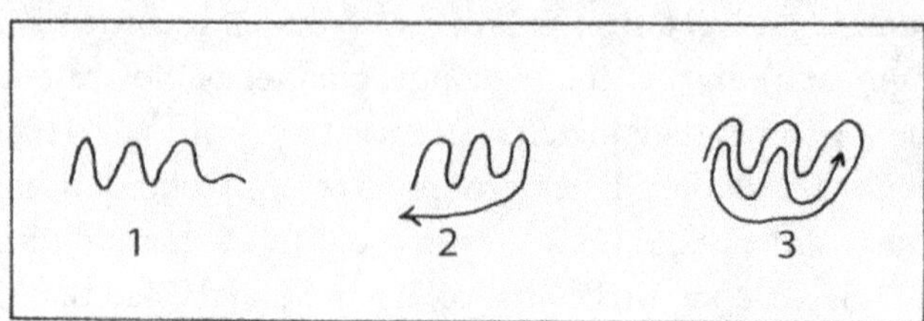

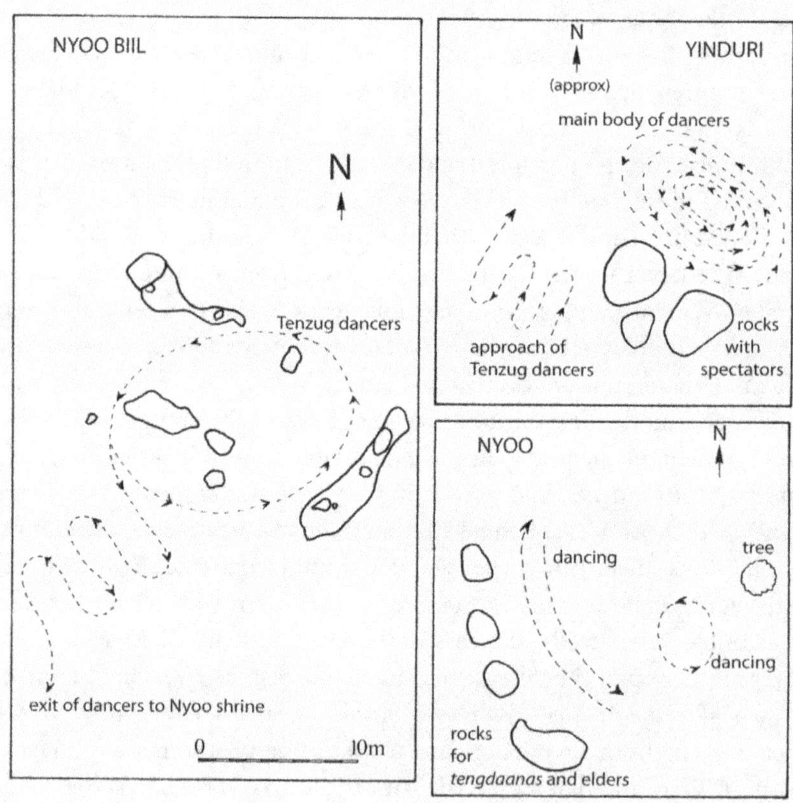

FIGURE 2.4. Dance patterns in the Golib festival. Top 1–3, recorded by Fortes (1934b: 28) at unspecified locations; bottom, locations as stated, March 2006.

for the beginning of the second millennium CE Profound differences with contemporary ritual practices exist. Nyoo is used for dances today, but the archaeological site is not used for this purpose anymore. There is also evidence for ritual acts that have no contemporary equivalence, as in the deposition of the potsherds previously described (Insoll 2010b). Interpretive limitations certainly need acknowledging, but it is also necessary to recognize the possible importance of how "embodied" memory (Connerton 1989; Hallam and Hockey 2001) could be locked into and materialized in Nyoo. This might be achieved through the stone arrangements enduring materially as ritual "aides memoires" (Ong [1982] 2002: 34). And in constructing memory with reference to places and material culture, the importance of the body as an agent in negotiating and/or understanding these through movement needs emphasis. This is especially so considering Jan Vansina's point that "studies of memory emphasize that remembering is action" (1985: 43). Likewise, Connerton describes how "memory is sedimented, or amassed, in the body" via "incorporating" and "inscribing" practices such as postures, and the "choreography of authority" (1989: 72, 74). These are unlikely to ever be reconstructed in their entirety, and this discussion has, to a large degree, focused on one element, movement, admittedly with an emphasis placed upon hypothesis. It is undeniable, however, that the archaeological record of the Nyoo shrine is the result of complex interrelationships among beliefs, ritual and performance, memory, and movement involving bodily understandings and practices.

In considering the archaeology of ritual in northern Ghana, and by implication in other contexts in West Africa, it is possible to question a static representation of ritual in archaeological literature. This has been achieved here with reference primarily to ritual posture and movement, but the possibilities for archaeological investigation extend into more complicated sequences of ritual actions/performance. Such new interpretations, however, will only be achieved if the evidence is interrogated with the archaeology of ritual movement, performance, and bodily understandings in relation to spatial use, placed as a primary research question.

The data from Koma Land and the Tong Hills indicates that great complexity was evident in ritual practices and performance in the late first through mid-second millennia. It cannot be categorized as indicative of "indigenous religion" in the singular, but rather in plural forms of indigenous beliefs and associated practices, significant parts of which remain irretrievable in the archaeological record. The implications for the broader Black Atlantic perhaps relate, first, to the longevity of ritual practices, postures and actions, performance and movement. These are themes often denied "indigenous" as opposed to textual "world" religions (Insoll 2004, 2009b). Second, the emphasis on relational materiality and substance that is evident archaeologically deserves comment. Clay is inserted in the earth in the form of figurines and layered in low mounds via potsherds in Koma Land. Libations are potentially offered deep into the figurines, perhaps in part as healing or medicinal practices (Kankpeyeng et al. 2011). In the Tong Hills, stone is significant as a possible marker of temporality and claims to ancestry and autochthony, but also potentially as a mnemonic device for movement as the analogies drawn between dance in NyooBiil and the Nyoo shrine suggest. Challenging the static nature of material residues and the archaeological record is not an easy undertaking, but is assisted in West Africa by the empirical wealth of this record, a database constantly expanding. The onus is now upon scholars to interpret this material and thus bring to life the rituals of the Black Atlantic world in all their complexity and potentially deep temporality.

Note

First, we would like to thank the communities and their leaders in the Tong Hills and Yikpabongo for allowing us to complete our research, and the Ghana Museums and Monuments Board for support and permission. We would like to thank Rachel MacLean for her critical comments on this chapter, though all shortcomings remain our own. Acknowledgment is also offered to Chris Martin of the Manchester Materials Science Centre for completing the tomography scans. Insoll would also like to thank the Wellcome Trust and the British Academy for funding the research in the Tong Hills and his participation in the 2010 and 2011 seasons in Yikpabongo. Kankpeyeng would like to thank Ghana Denmark Archaeological Co-operation and the Danish International Development Agency for funding the participation of the Ghanaian team in the Koma Land research project. Some of the material utilized in interpreting the Nyoo shrine has previously appeared in Insoll (2009a, 2009b).

CHAPTER 3

Sacred Vortices of the African Atlantic World

MATERIALITY OF THE ACCUMULATIVE AESTHETIC IN THE HUEDA KINGDOM, 1650–1727 CE

Neil L. Norman

Into the Material Vortices

Art historians researching the Bight of Benin region have convincingly argued that an amalgamative aesthetic underpins the ever-emerging character of modern Vodun (Drewal 1996; Rush 1999, 2001).[1] Paul Mercier (1960: 212) argues that below the surface of apparent conservatism in Vodun lies innovation and the need to accumulate and assimilate, even to the point of acquiring entire cosmologies. Suzanne Blier (1995a: 62) similarly characterizes the organizing principle or "primacy of assemblage" in Vodun arts where artisans, commissioned by initiated clients, bind together various base materials, surface additions, and textures to create objects and spaces representing a sacred mixed media. In his investigation of Mami Wata, Henry Drewal (1996: 308) records that initiates start with exotic *foreign* objects and interpret them according to indigenous precepts, invest them with new meanings, and then re-represent them in inventive ways to serve their own devotional and social needs.

In examining the intersection of Vodun aesthetics with the social role of sacred spaces and sacred objects, Dana Rush (1999: 61) argues that the accumulative artistic tradition of Vodun arts creates a "vortex" drawing material culture, symbolic structures, and even foreign pantheons into Vodun practices in coastal Benin, West Africa. This vortextual force of Vodun arts relates to an ongoing "unself-conscious accumulative sensibility" that brings together the "hottest" and newest inter-African, European, Indian, and more recently African American material culture and arts (Rush 1999: 75; 2001). In a similar fashion, Vodun initiates frequently incorporate the latest construction materials and architectural design techniques into the aesthetic mix of Vodun temples (Sinou 1994: 298). In historicizing this accumulative process during the precolonial period, Edna Bay (1998: 22) has shown how Dahomean kings, princes, and queens were always on the alert for "new" proven deities to welcome into their pantheons, just as they did conquered foes with specialized skills. In turn, Dahomean elites materialized elements of these new pantheons in, and on, *asen,* mostly metal memory shrines, used at the household and state levels.

This chapter builds on the project of historicizing the accumulative aesthetic underlying Vodun material culture through the investigation of archaeologically recovered material from seventeenth- and eighteenth-century ritual spaces surrounding the Huedan palace complex at Savi. It argues that similar processes were at play in societies with historic and ethnolinguistic ties to the Aja-Ewe speaking groups in the Dahomey Gap region (map 3.1). In tying the materiality of religious practice into the broader region and beyond, this chapter builds on the works cited above that have highlighted the cosmopolitanism of West and Central African cultural history during the Atlantic period. Moreover, the chapter endeavors to broaden the evidence available for generating transatlantic analogies with the Dahomey Gap region and related points in the African Diaspora, and, in turn, problematize regionally and ethnolinguistically bounded analogies that have been generated heretofore.

The primary case study presented in this chapter draws from archaeological, historic, and ethnographic evidence from the Hueda Kingdom. During the mid-Atlantic period (ca. 1650–1727), the Huedan palace complex at Savi served as a trading entrepôt and a primary point of transatlantic exchange between European and African traders, as well as a center for local social and political processes (Law 1991, 2004). During the mid-seventeenth to early eighteenth centuries, Huedan kings profited by controlling this local channel into the Atlantic world, while at the same time, internal divisions among regional community leaders worked to fracture the Huedan political coalition. European traders reported that twenty-three regional community leaders administered different zones of the kingdom. They further noted that nonelite people were densely settled around the house compounds of kings and regional leaders (see Law 1991 for a review). Following years of internal strife and marked profit taking, the kingdom of Hueda collapsed spectacu-

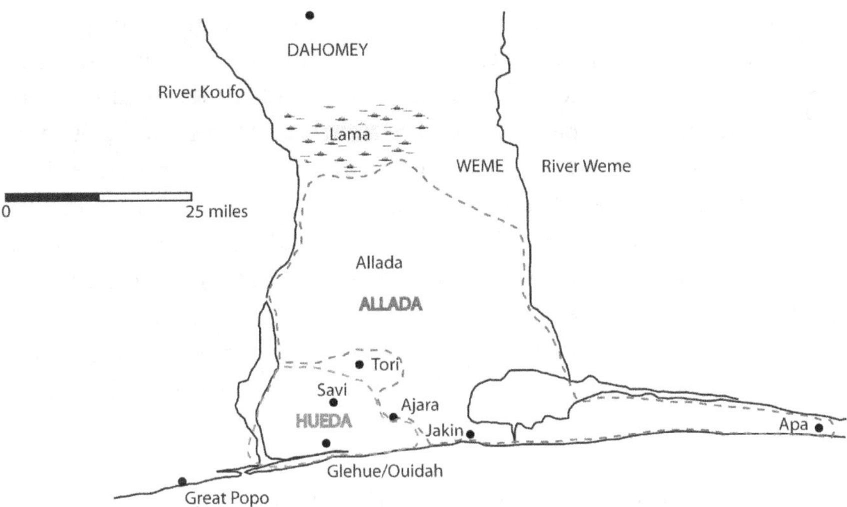

MAP 3.1. Aja-Ewe speaking groups in Dahomey Gap.

larly in March 1727 when the kingdom of Dahomey captured both Savi and the coastal Huedan trading town at Ouidah (Akinjogbin 1967; Law 1991). This campaign of conquest left a zone of burned and razed houses stretching up to 6 km from the center of the palace at Savi (Kelly 2001; Norman 2009b).

During its heyday, Europeans recorded vignettes of daily life in and around the palace at Savi. One European traveler, William Bosman (1705: 368), estimated that the Huedan pantheon contained 120,000 deities. Bosman gave few details on how he arrived at this figure, and it is most likely an exaggeration. It provides a glimpse, however, of an expansive pantheon that reflected the diverse population of Huedan towns of that time. Despite the vastness of the Huedan pantheon, European observers noted common patterns in the placement of religious objects, as well as the formal characteristics of the objects used in various Huedan houses. French merchant Jean Barbot visited the area around 1680 and recorded that the shrines of kings, much like those of the people, were large and constructed of wood and earth, often containing whitewash and anthropomorphic effigies (Hair et al. 1992: 638). In terms of the spatiality of these, another observer similarly noted that "I have often seen little figures of clay about their houses, with oil, rice, corn, and other offerings before them" (Phillips 1732: 224). These few written sketches, along with a small number of other accounts, represent the extent of our knowledge of the material dimension of seventeenth-century Huedan religious life; archaeological evidence from the burned and sealed houses surrounding Savi, however, offers another window into the Huedan past.

Although the holistic archaeological contexts of Huedan Vodun rituals are discussed in this chapter, I focus more on the role of hand-built, low-fired earthenware to interpret the early Huedan Vodun rituals. I achieve this by contextualizing a series of archaeological contexts, features, and finds with spoken accounts, ethnographic observations, and documentary sources. These archaeological data and their contexts are drawn from the towns, rural villages, and outlying palace centers surrounding Savi between the mid-seventeenth century and March 1727, when troops from the nearby polity of Dahomey defeated Hueda and burned many of the sites (Kelly 2001; Law 1991; Norman 2009a, 2009b).

Vodun Vessels in the Context of Ritual Earthenware in West Africa

In terms of the archaeology of Vodun, hand-built, locally produced earthenware vessels are the most diagnostic features for identifying and understanding ritual spaces. This is fortunate in that ethnoarchaeological analogies may be drawn between modern practices associated with Vodun and those in the deeper archaeological past. Practitioners use the vessels to serve as a backdrop for ceremonies, designate religious spaces, and contain or confine offerings. Ethnoarchaeological research among Vodun practitioners in the Bight of Benin region indicates that discrete collections of ceramics can serve as signal referents relating a shrine to a particular deity (Kelly and Norman 2004; Norman 2009a).

My research in the region documented Vodun practitioners who engage ritual specialists, ceramic artisans, and ceramic vendors to create sacred spaces for the purpose of cosmological intervention (see also Blier 1995b). Often, ritual specialists prescribe what ceramics and other items are needed for a given shrine, ritual, sacrifice, or ceremony, and their clients then acquire the necessary items from the market. Ritual specialists charge the sacred spaces with cosmological significance by conducting ceremonies that are considered transformative events which activate the inert collection of ceramics and other items into charged sacred spaces and objects (Cudjoe 1971: 190). The act of transformation involves role-inversions where ceramic objects used in the most mundane aspects of daily life are made to underpin the most sacred spaces in the Vodun world (Bay 2008). Accordingly, Claude Savary (1970: 48) is correct to point out that context of use rather than formal morphological characteristics should be considered the defining qualities of ritual ceramics.

Shrines with consecrated and dedicated collections of ceramics are found throughout modern house compounds in southern Benin. Roof overhangs shield shrines from torrential seasonal rain. Also under the house eaves and near to the doorway are found shrines with bridged twin vessels dedicated to the twin deity Hoho. Inverted pots are used to cover shrines to the family deity, or Aiza, which is centrally located within the house compound. At the feet of baobab trees and in freestanding shrines just beyond the house compound, shrines can be found containing *danzen*[2] or *dangbezen* ceramics with small applied snakes that indicate an affiliation with the serpent deity Dan. At times, initiates use ceramic vessels from these shrines as receptacles for offerings used in socially binding ceremonies that mark, sanction, and guarantee economic transactions, family relations, and other promises to be kept (Hazoumé 1956). Vessels for holding sacrifices to Legba, the deity of the crossroads, who initiates believe controls communication between the earthly and spiritual realms and aids in the protection of the dwelling, are arranged near points of access and egress in house compounds (Argyle 1966: 188). Legba shrines have ceramic offerings and, at times, human burials positioned underneath their aboveground, mounded, unfired clay avatars (Cudjoe 1971). *Adjalalazen,* perforated ceramics jars,[3] are found in numerous modern shrines variously associated with ancestral deities and other cosmological actors (Herskovits and Herskovits 1933: 69–74).

There are some general trends among the formal characteristics of modern ritual ceramics in southern Benin that can be synthesized with the broader patterns and processes from the Atlantic-Congo language speakers in West Africa to interpret the archaeological contexts in the Savi countryside. Modern ritual ceramics are very expediently constructed and low-fired, barely having made the transition from clay to ceramic. Also, they often exhibit thick and uneven rims and shoulders. These findings point to the fact that ritual ceramics are created specifically for use in shrines, and are placed in a zone of the house compound where the objects are not subjected to intense daily use (Norman 2009b). Modern ritual ceramics are rarely decorated with rouletting, incisions, and/or burnishing common on utilitarian wares (David 1983: 169). Exceptions in southern Benin, however, include *awogbãn* and *lebezen* vessels, which have burnished "X" patterns in their interiors. Throughout the Bight of Benin region, anthropomorphic or zoomorphic appliqués and decorations are diagnostic features of modern and past ritual ceramics. There are numerous studies of past ceramics (thirteenth–eighteenth centuries) in Yorubaland, especially in Ile-Ife, Ilare, Owo, and Benin, that demonstrate the use of appliqués on ritual ceramics (Connah 1975; Garlake 1977; Ogundiran 2001). It is important to note, though, that, when constructing shrines, ritual specialists often place vessels otherwise used for cooking or storage alongside the single-use ritual ceramics described above.

Several studies in the region have shown that the use of hand-built earthenware ceramics in ritual settings has a history that predates the emergence of transatlantic exchange (Eyo 1974; Garlake 1977; Ogundiran 2001). The challenge thus emerges to carefully work backward from the wealth of documentary, spoken, and material sources outlined above to the more opaque—in evidentiary terms at least—archaeological past (Stahl 2001). Fortunately, however, it appears that modern ceramic vessels for sale in the ritual market at Ouidah seem to relate in a direct way to a series of ceramics used in sacred settings dating to at least the nineteenth century. An illustration from *Les Missions Catholique* in 1875 (reprinted in Blier 1995a: 119) portrays a vodun shrine containing a vaselike *gozen* vessel in the background of the image. The foreground shows a representation of a *lisazen* vessel consisting of two parts: a plain dishlike base and a lid with an undulating central appliqué ridge and white stripes. Locally produced ceramic vessels apparently played an important religious role during the Huedan era, ca. 1650–1727, as well. Dutch geographer Olfert Dapper (1686: 307) noted after his trip to Allada in the mid-seventeenth century that principal family shrines there were covered with a "pot percé" or perforated vessel similar to the modern *adjalalazen* described above. Dapper reports that Alladan families conducted ceremonies at six-month intervals during which a hired ritual specialist offered beer, food, and other gifts to a shrine. Thereafter, the ritual specialist on behalf of the family made requests and inquiries of the shrine. This account is supported by seventeenth-century Capuchin missionaries who recorded shrines at Allada containing ceramic vessels with blood, feathers, and roots, thus materializing offerings, prayers, requests, and devotion (Labouret and Rivet 1929).

In a similar fashion, an anonymous European traveler who visited Savi around 1714 noted that the "somewhat higher-ranking" Huedans

> each have in their home their own God, not including the general one, these are pieces of iron in the form of bells on which there are different relief fig-

> ures, these bells fit on branches of iron that they stick in the ground; some clay pots and other similar things, it's on these iron fetishes that have a bit of iron or a stone inside to make noise and on these pots that they pour the blood of animals that they sacrifice in their houses. (Bay 2008: 43–4; Law 1991: 107)

What emerges from this brief review of the historical literature of the region is a clear affinity between modes of Vodun worship and locally produced ceramics. Fortunately for archaeological study, such ceramics are numerous in the archaeological record of the region (Kelly 1995: 139–61). Indeed, locally produced ceramics are the most durable material legacy of the international trading entrepôt that was Savi. Yet, the challenge remains to discern in the archaeological record the utilitarian ceramics from the religious ones, and the quotidian spaces from the sacred ones. The two following sections present archaeological material from recent field research in the region surrounding Savi. The discussion starts with a description of the largest and most elaborate structures and features interpreted as religious spaces; it then proceeds to use spatial and formal qualities of those areas to interpret more ephemeral ones. Each of the archaeological contexts described below exhibited evidence of catastrophic burning in the early eighteenth century, most likely related to a raid by the nearby polity of Abomey in March 1727. Datable Dutch trade pipes and the *terminus ante quem* of the burning lens indicate that the primary occupational range of the sites was between ca. 1650 and 1727 (Norman 2008: 2010).

Archaeological Shrines, Sacrifice, and Theaters of Social Action

Here, the term "shrine" is used to describe a place of worship and supplication that, at the time of its use, exhibited an above-ground edifice or facade. Shrines were points in and around the house compound where family members would have worshiped in private or as part of semipublic ceremonies, often led by heads of families and purposefully hired ritual specialists (cf. Bay 2008: 15–41). Such shrines are mentioned in historical accounts of the palace at Savi. After his visit around 1680 to Hueda, French trader Jean Barbot noted that "the prince [King Agbangla?] is very superstitious and a slave of his fetishes, of which the palace is full" (Hair et al. 1992: 638). Given the political tension in the region as well as within the polity of Hueda, it is not surprising that the Huedan king was earnestly communing with cosmological actors who were believed to bring both wealth and balance (Law 1991: 109–110). Beyond framing subjective acts of individual worship, the historical record suggests that these locales were theaters of social action for broader household and community rites. It is equally clear, as is shown below, that those supplicants who worshiped at shrines in the late seventeenth to early eighteenth centuries provided offerings and sacrifices.

In a sense, the structure of the ceremony resembled acts of feasting, used widely in other spheres of Huedan political negotiation (Norman 2009b). In these ceremonies, officiants and ritual specialists installed offerings of food and blood in the shrine in a manner that rendered it impossible to use otherwise. Historical sources indicate that a portion of the sacrifice was reserved for the ritual specialist performing the ceremony and the host family (Dapper 1686: 307). Thus, acts of immolation, consumption, and contribution were shared by the various participants of the ceremony. In examining contemporary practices, Michael Dietler argues that such feasts serve as "theater[s] of political relations" where people create, maintain, and contest positions of power and authority within a structured system in pursuit of their conflicting interests and at times transforming the systems themselves (2001: 66). As outlined above, public and royal shrines had a deep political dimension in Hueda. There can be little doubt of the close relationship between organizing ceremonies aimed at attracting the attention of cosmological actors, restricting precious items from networks of circulation, and the successful exercise of political authority. If modern political processes can serve as a guide, however, it is probable that practitioners used personal shrines for ceremonies of consolidation and incorporation (Bay 2008). Nonetheless, private house shrines are often thrust into the public sphere when family members achieve political notoriety, and, under those circumstances, various people make claims on what was once a point of private veneration between family members and ancestors (Apter 1992; Norman 2009a).

Within the Hueda social world, the feasting lavished on cosmological actors involved not only organic foodstuff but also hard currency, imported trade items, and durable local domestic goods (Norman 2009a). At a site (Locus 2) interpreted as an outlying settlement center approximately 2 km south of Savi (figure 3.1), excavators conducted a test unit to sample the highest concentration of Hueda-era local ceramics recorded during an archaeological survey of the region. The unit explored the central portion

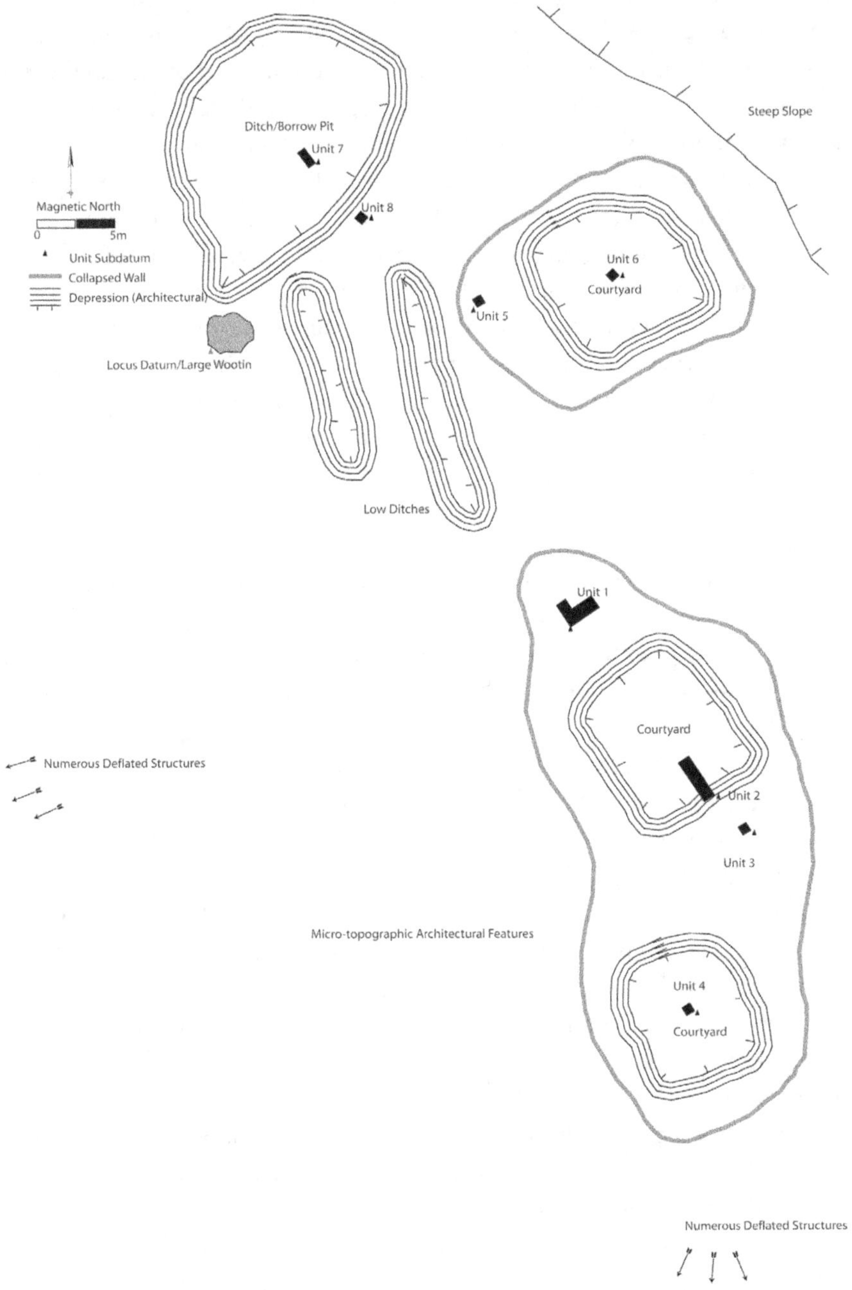

FIGURE 3.1. Excavation of Unit 1, Locus 2.

of a collapsed structure approximately 3 m in diameter, located adjacent to the main wing of a collapsed house compound. Spatially, this small, free-standing structure was constructed between a boundary ditch/borrow pit and the interior of the house compound. The form of the structure and its spatial placement vis-à-vis the other elements of the house compound is similar to a Dahomean "spirit house" or *djeho,* literally translated as a "bead house" (Blier 1991: 45). The opening layer of the unit revealed Hueda-era local ceramics and contemporary imported items including a yellow-and-black striped trade bead, iron fasteners, fragments of imported pipes, and perforated local ceramic vessel *adjalalazen* fragments.[4] Extrapolating from larger sherds, these perforated vessels were globular in shape, and the potters who created them used a circular reed or other organic stylus to pierce the base, shoulder, and body of the vessels. A majority of the perforated vessel sherds exhibited sharp edges on the interior of their perforations, indicative of vessels not used in daily cooking or food processing activities.

Early on in the excavation of Unit 1 (Locus 2, figure 3.1), excavators recovered a round vessel similar in construction and form to a ritual vessel, or *golizen*—used today to store offerings (Norman 2009a)—along the southern edge of the unit within a wall matrix. Apparently this offering vessel was cached in the wall at the time of its construction. At approximately the same depth (60 cm below the opening level of the unit), excavators noted the edge of a shallow bowl in the northern wall of the unit. After expanding the unit to uncover this bowl, the excavation team discovered that the vessel contained a fragmentary human cranium. In addition, nearby the excavation team recorded another fragmentary cranium with mandible. Both crania were disarticulated from postcranial material prior to deposition and located in primary context: the cranium and mandible were recovered encased within local ceramic storage jar fragments, and the other fragmentary cranium was recovered on the aforementioned shallow bowl. Apparently, both vessels were placed on rammed earth surfaces/floors as were the associated imported and local offering items (figure 3.2).

From historical accounts of the region, shrines containing skulls normally relate to two, not necessarily mutually exclusive commemorative events: the memorialization of patriarchal or matriarchal figures and the celebration of military victory (Law 1989). In the first, it was common to remove the skull of a prominent family member, often after months or a few years of internment, and install it in a place of religious prominence for veneration.[5] In the second case, European visitors to the kingdom of Hueda

FIGURE 3.2. Buried vessel with human cranium.

noted that in the eighteenth century, captives taken by Huedan soldiers belonged to them as did heads collected after battle, which were then placed in their households, and the successful combatant was "careful to put them in his home in a prominent place to make his bravery known to his posterity" (ibid.: 406).

As for the archaeological vessels containing the skulls at Savi, the interior of the base of the shallow bowl has an incised decorative pattern. The sharp edges of the incised lines suggest that the vessel was not used in grinding or other abrading activities. The form of the interior decoration is an incised quatrefoil "X" pattern highlighted as it stands in negative relief within a cross-hatched or lozenge incised field. The entire "X" pattern is enclosed within an incised circle (figure 3.3). The rim of the vessel was slipped with red slurry evocative of the blood offerings probably presented to the shrine. Taken together, the symbolic composite is similar to the Dahomean cosmographic marker or *weke* applied to thrones, drums, and bas reliefs in the Abomey area. The *weke* represents the four directions and the four main vodun associated with them (Blier 1991: 49).[6] Similar ritual vessel forms—shallow bowls—with a burnished and encircled "X" can still be purchased in the contemporary ritual markets of Ouidah and Abomey.

At another site (Locus 4) in the Savi countryside interpreted as a settlement center approximately 1.5 km north of the palace, excavators recorded a

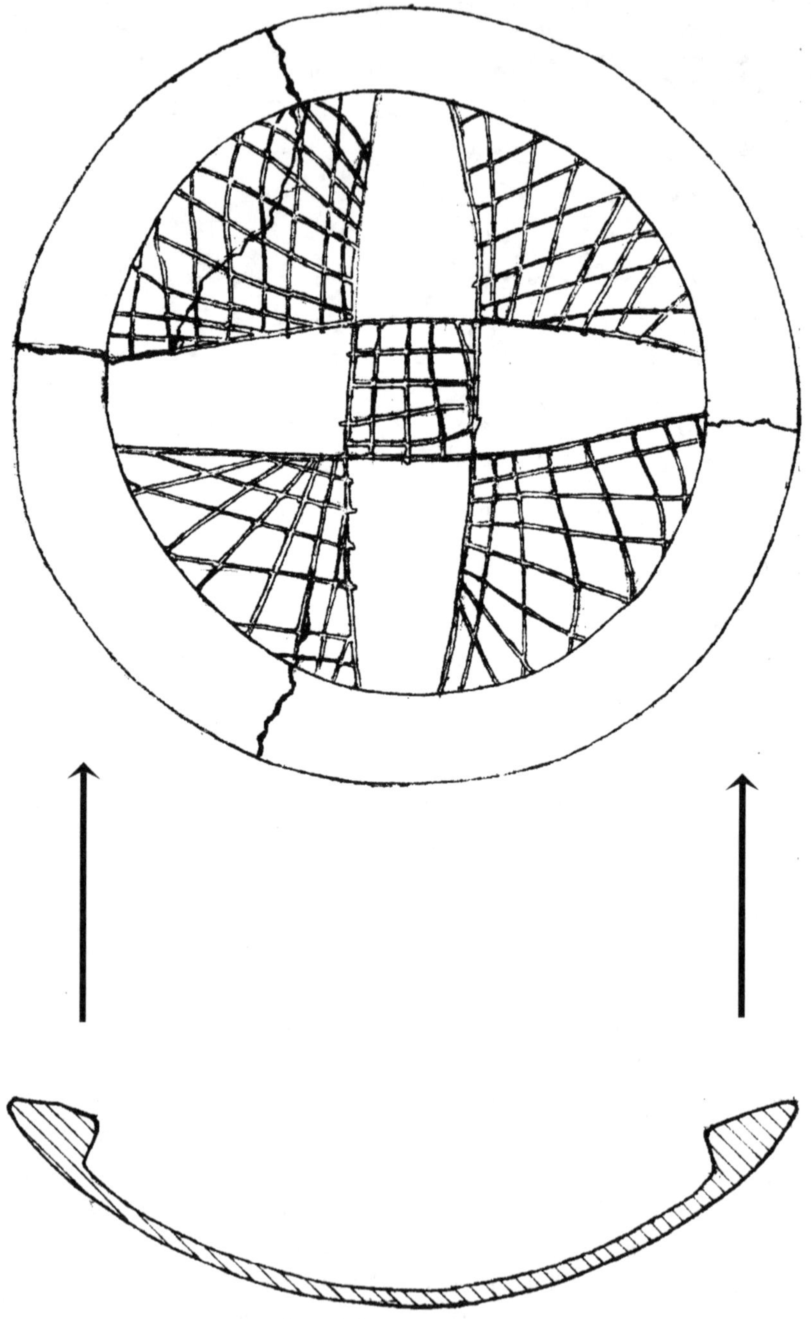

FIGURE 3.3. "X" pattern enclosed within an incised circle.

possible temple or ritual complex: a structure with a central courtyard where several of the surrounding rooms, the courtyard, and outlying buildings each contained shrines and offering spaces. At this site, excavators placed a test excavation (Unit 5), which was centered on a collapsed wing of the complex. The unit itself sampled a burned interior room that had been sealed by a collapsed wall. The unit contained a cache (n = 12) of faceted, colorless trade beads alongside fragments of a large, nonutilitarian vessel known in modern times as *gozin* (Norman 2000: 80–82). Excavators also recorded carbonized oil palm nuts and six knapped siliceous mudstone flakes, all of which apparently originated from the matrix of the *gozin* fragments. This vessel was unique in the archaeological assemblage in that it exhibited horizontal applied cordons, or ribs—diagnostic features of modern *gozin* vessels—along the neck and shoulder, and multiple openings with individual rolled rims along the body of the vessel. Modern Vodun practitioners use *gozin,* though without the secondary openings along the neck and shoulder, to mark shrines associated with patriarchal or matriarchal figures, or as offering vessels for sacred water, such as the annual ceremony to water the pythons in Ouidah (Akindele and Renaud 1953; David 1983: 153).

In the Savi countryside, our recovery of *gozin* vessel fragments alongside imported offering items indicates a ritual context, as does the recovery in the nearby Unit 6 of a highly friable ceramic anthropomorphic figurine along with river-smoothed cobbles. In southern Benin today, postmenopausal women offer quartz stones to family shrines. The stones are considered to represent the power and potency of water, as well as deities associated with water. Sample excavation of 1 × 4 m was conducted in a small, freestanding structure located between the interior of the structure and the steep slope of a nearby ditch segment. This structure appears to be another freestanding shrine similar to the one at Locus 2. The ceramic figurine is slightly cone-shaped with a flat base and applied, stylized breasts. It appears that the figurine's head was broken prior to deposition; it is unknown whether or not the figurine was purposefully destroyed. Extrapolating from similar statuary recovered nearby in contemporary deposits by Kenneth Kelly (1995: 157–161), it is probable that the head would have exhibited elongated facial features, including eyes, a nose, and a mouth.

It is unclear whether these figurines relate to a class of more personal deities represented by *bo* and *bocio* figures (Blier 1995a), anthropomorphic ceramic effigies used in modern times to represent more corporate deities (e.g., Mawu, Dan), or other forms of religious expression, such as the little-known terra-cotta figurines paraded by the Huedan kings' wives as part of the processions to the temple of the python (Labat 1730: 62). A myriad of interpretations are possible for this figure; however, based on its depositional context and form, it is likely that Huedans used these figurines, as well as the archaeologically recovered ones, in a manner similar to the empowerment figures of *bo* and *bocio.* Blier argues that these figurines are central to religious rites aimed at establishing calm, shaping the future, and communing with ancestors. One of the deepest and most complete historical accounts of such items is the *Agoye* or "God of Councils" recorded in the seventeenth-century town surrounding Savi. Regarding these sculptures, Blier writes, the *Agoye* statue of "black Earth, or clay" shares with *bocio* "not only markedly expressive features which are defined by the massing of diverse materials on the surface, but also a concern with averting danger from the community and those living in it" (1995a: 8).[7]

Excavations in the Savi countryside at Locus 4, Unit 9, revealed a collapsed room in the same complex that contained the *gozin* and nearby to the structure containing the figurine. In this unit, excavators recovered case gin bottles and Hueda-era wine bottle fragments. From the Hueda-era deposits, this unit revealed fragments of several imported pipes and two fragmentary human molars. These teeth were not deciduous and were most likely related to a highly fragmentary skull, or skulls, around which the imported offerings were arranged. Unit 4 sampled another room in the same complex and revealed a dense concentration of Hueda-era local ceramics, as well as fragments of imported pipes and a metal object similar in form to an *asen,* a metal object used from the nineteenth century to the present to commemorate ancestral figures (Bay 2008). Excavated levels approximately 50 cm below the metal object revealed a living surface, and subsequent excavations revealed a subfloor pit feature containing a collection of ceramic jars.

The finding of a prepared pit below a collection of ritual items matched descriptions of shrine construction in the early (Herskovits and Herskovits 1933: 36–38) and late twentieth century (Cudjoe 1971: 190–191; Norman 2009b; Savary 1970: 43). Generally, ritual specialists construct shrines by preparing pits in or around house compounds. A mixture of consecrated water, hard alcohol, leaves, and herbs are placed inside small *golizen* vessels, which are in turn covered by a larger cooking vessel. Depending on the ancestor being commemorated or deity venerated, myriad permutations of other objects (e.g., animal skulls, small metal representations of tools, seawater, beads) can be included in the pit, but almost without exception some form of locally produced ceramic is a part of the ritual mix. Only after the pit is filled and tamped down, or prepared into a low mound, are the visible outer collection of objects put into place. While the religious spaces described above were above ground and at least semivisible, the offerings in the archaeological context described below were more private, hidden from prying eyes, and arguably related to more personal acts of supplication and protection.

Vodun and the House

As practiced today, Vodun ceremonies often take place in intense secrecy. Although Ouidah contains an impressive array of large temples, they often serve a largely symbolic function to their associated adepts and lay congregations (Sinou 1994: 292). Similarly, around the house compound, larger family shrines are often the location for annual ceremonial rites to negotiate extraordinary events such as births, deaths, and so on. Yet, it is the smaller points of worship where daily cosmological dialogues take place (Bay 2008: 14–41 *passim*). Given the archaeological findings from the Savi countryside assemblage, it is probable that Huedans living in the seventeenth- and eighteenth-century communities surrounding Savi used a range of both public and private religious spaces as well.

At one outlying settlement center (Locus 2) near the freestanding shrine with skulls described above, excavators encountered an exterior wall of a wing of the house compound in Unit 5 at 84 cm below the opening level. After excavating through several levels of extremely compact and culturally sterile clay wall fill, excavators encountered a small, low-fired *golizen* earthenware jar at a depth of 237 cm. It seems likely that the jar was placed on a prepared clay surface before the wall was constructed on top of this offering. The context is similar to offerings in modern Vodun practices, where low-fired vessels are often placed within the wall matrices or under the walls of structures while construction is underway (Norman 2009b; Kelly and Norman 2004). Noting a similar phenomenon in the Abomey region, Paul Hazoumé (1956: 24) recorded that the Dahomean court official, or Agbadjigbeto, was charged with creating offerings in foundations and holes in and around the palace to keep enemies at bay and with preventing symbolic and direct attacks on the palace's inhabitants.

In the Savi countryside, ceramics were similarly used at various scales of the settlement system. At the settlement center (Locus 4) containing the ritual compound, Unit 8, we sampled the interior of a room overlooking a nearby ditch. Excavations revealed grinding-stone fragments, local pipe fragments, a knapped quartz cobble, and human molars that were recovered at 65 cm below the opening level of the unit. This archaeological context relates to offerings cached inside a pit or other prepared surface just below a living surface. At another secondary palace complex (Locus 7) approximately 3 km northwest of Savi, excavators sampled the interior of another collapsed structure within Unit 2. In this unit, excavators recovered European gunflint fragment, lead "dust" shot, colorless faceted trade beads, and numerous local and imported pipe fragments, all near an almost complete large jar located at 100 cm below the opening level of the unit. This jar and related offerings were recorded beneath the main living surface in a prepared pit. When the solidified contents of the jar were subjected to flotation, the process revealed fragments that represented a shallow bowl (the same form as the one containing the cranium at Locus 2), along with numerous human skull fragments including eleven large crania or cranium fragments (8 g), eight molars, and four premolar and incisor fragments.[8] Most likely, this jar represented a burial similar to ones reported by Jean Barbot where Huedans "bury their dead with many signs of mourning, but after the funeral they keep open house for five or six weeks. The dead are usually interred in the hut where they died, because they have no cemeteries" (Hair et al. 1992: 640). Barbot noted that the residential graves were marked with a large pot of water, located alongside offerings prepared from a black bird.

In today's context, the honor of being interred within or around one's house, usually under one's sleeping chamber, is reserved for illustrious family members, usually patriarchal or matriarchal figures. These cemetery rooms serve as points where deified members of the family are installed, taking up permanent residence in the structure. The set of rooms where members of the family line are buried often surround courtyards where family-wide ceremonies are held. Alain Sinou notes that families in Ouidah "pool their resources to maintain the sacred sites, that is, the worship rooms and cemetery rooms, and generally take little interest in the dwelling areas," which are often left unoccupied (1994: 294). Frequently the dead "occupants" of these house compounds, therefore, outnumber the living, and the structures may appear abandoned, except for the few times during the year when family members converge at the house to perform ceremonies to reaffirm the family line. Apparently, and not surprisingly, the dead during the Hueda era occupied prominent and proximate, though at times out of sight, positions in both the spaces where ceremonies took place and the social fields, which made these ceremonies possible. Given the role public and private shrines played in tethering Huedans to their ancestral past, celebrating economic gains and regional prominence, shaping the future, and mitigating the intrigues ever-present in early eighteenth-century Hueda, the violent dislocation of Huedans in 1727 should be viewed not only as a political and geographical displacement but also as the removal of Huedans from the physical places where cosmological actors were rooted to the landscape.

Conclusion

Some reoccurring artifactual and, more importantly, contextual themes can be outlined from a synthesis of archaeological, documentary, and oral data discussed above. Seventeenth- and eighteenth-century Hueda-era house compounds contained several levels, or stages, of sacred spaces. Huedans constructed the first and largest freestanding shrines between interior house compounds and exterior barrier structures, such as ditches. With modern practices as a guide, we can surmise that residents of house compounds placed offerings at shrines to cosmologically charge barriers, protecting the socialized space within the house compound from the more liminal space found outside. Both the shrines in the house compound and those located near the ditches were within the flurry of daily life as it unfolded in the interior of the house compound. In the Hueda social world, these shrines worked to connect the respective families with their pasts, secure stability in the present, and shape negotiation with cosmological actors over the nature of the future. Such cosmological dialogues also took place within the interior structures where small offerings placed inside walls provided protection against physical or cosmological threats. Enclosed room spaces within house compounds served as locales for subfloor interments, most likely the *living* abode of ancestral figures, as ancestors are rarely described as being *at rest.* If so, Huedan houses were built quite literally on the ancestors, who played an active role in the lives of those living above ground.

In terms of material culture, these sacred spaces attracted, and by extension cosmological actors demanded, regional finery: locally produced smoking pipes, ceramic vessels, oil palm nuts, various stones, and offerings of food. Shrines also pooled items from throughout the Atlantic world: imported smoking pipes, trade beads, wine bottles, and collections of iron nails. The few cowries recovered in and around these sacred spaces speak to many more that did not survive the acidic soils that predominate in the project area (Ogundiran 2002b). Moreover, the few recovered cowries raise the possibility that other delicate items (e.g., cloth, metal, faunal) were once included in this sacred mixed media but are now archaeologically invisible due to disintegration. The total artifact assemblage from excavations (i.e., 50 units sampling 7 sites, for a total of 268 m^3 of material excavated) contained striking regularity in the spatial arrangement of imported artifacts. Excavators recorded fourteen of the twenty-four recovered imported nails/spikes from units that also contained ritual ceramics. Today, such collections of metal fasteners often indicate an offering to the deity *Gu*, deity of iron and war (see Goucher, this volume).

Likewise, excavators recovered a fragmentary English or Dutch "Onion" wine bottle (ca. 1680–1715; see Noël Hume 1970: 60–71) from a unit also containing ritual vessel fragments. Similarly, sixteen of the thirty-four archaeologically recovered trade beads were unearthed from archaeological contexts that also contained ritual ceramics. The concentration of costly trade items near religious spaces in the Savi countryside suggests that Huedans, who profited directly or indirectly from the transatlantic trade in war captives, lavished a portion of these gains on vodun and ancestral members, who for this period were described as keeping the flows of Atlantic affluence possible by sanctioning, monitoring, and encouraging exchanges (Law 1991: 109–110). Despite these connections and continuities, much work remains both to chart the trajectory of vodun entering and presumably exiting the Huedan pantheon, as well as the exploring active social role that material culture and architectural features played in the history of the polity (Stahl 2008). One preliminary finding from the present project that might aid in the future exploration of this issue is the increased number of dedicated ritual ceramics available in the markets of Ouidah, especially when compared to the relatively few types currently identified in the archaeological record (Norman 2000). Many of these modern vessels represent relatively new deities (e.g., Mami Wata, Dan). Quite probably, the apparent increase in the ceramic representations of the relatively new entrants into the Huedan pantheon relates in a direct fashion to the ever-growing accumulation of vodun in and around Ouidah.[9] As Dana Rush succinctly states, "Vodun is a testament to the strength and flexibility of a belief system that perpetually adapts, invents, re-invents, and modifies itself. Within the religious system of Vodun, there exists endless sources which ultimately form, re-form, and transform Vodun arts and religious consciousness. As long as Vodun is on the move, its transformation is forever unfinished" (1997: 2). The vodun's accumulative and emergent structure apparently have been on the move since at least the mid-seventeenth century.

The archaeological material interpreted as part of the Huedan ritual assemblage includes ceramic empowerment figurines; quatrefoil "X"-incised ritual ceramics; and collections of nails, trade beads, smoking pipes, and river cobbles. As demonstrated above, similar material repertoires and symbolic/decorative motifs are recorded in archaeological contexts, as well as in historical accounts, of large-scale polities in the coastal and forest zone regions found in modern Benin, Togo, Ghana, and Nigeria. Most notably, there appears to be strong material similarities between ritual items used throughout the Bight of Benin. A greater understanding of the fluid currents linking regions of Atlantic Africa is a critical step before moving on to broader scales and doing the difficult work of confirming and calibrating the material signatures and social processes that characterize Huedan Vodun as it might have existed in the wider Diaspora.

In terms of the archaeology of the African Diaspora, such a finding should give pause to researchers investigating sites in the Americas who would assign ethnic, cultural, or regional affiliation based solely on formal characteristics of artifacts. To paraphrase Leland Ferguson (1999) and build on his work, *the cross is a magic sign* on at least some vessels recovered from riverine settings in the Lowcountry of South Carolina, as well as a sign used to mark ritual spaces across a broad region of West and Central Africa (Eglash 1999). Accordingly, we conclude with a plea for researchers in the Americas to deeply explore the dynamic human landscapes of Atlantic Africa (Ogundiran and Falola 2007). Specifically, archaeologists of the African Diaspora need to steep their interpretations of diasporic spaces with an understanding that the practice of incorporating seemingly quotidian objects in sanctified spaces alongside freely borrowing encountered deities, practices, and ritual objects did *not* begin in the New World. Furthermore, as is hopefully clear from the discussion above, depositional context of artifacts trumps their formal and decorative characteristics as an indicator of religious significance (see Ogundiran, Saunders, and Reeves, all in this volume). Yet with notable recent published exceptions (e.g., Ferguson 1992; Ruppel et al. 2003; Samford 2007), context has received little attention when compared to the ever-growing body of research on decorative elements as they relate to regions of Africa. This critique deserves a cautionary qualification as diverse groups in the southern Dahomey Gap region generated spatial similarity when creating spaces of worship and protection. In terms of materiality, perhaps it is exactly this flexible, fractal, regional, and accumulative dimension of the Huedan Vodun[10] that researchers should consider when interpreting influences from Bight of Benin groups on the ceramics, cosmographic markings, and subfloor spaces found in diasporic contexts.

Notes

I wish to thank Adria LaViolette, Kenneth Kelly, J. Cameron Monroe, Jeffrey Hantman, Jerome Handler, and Joseph C. Miller for comments on earlier versions of this chapter. This chapter was strengthened by detailed suggestions by Akin Ogundiran. Alexis Adandé served as the local coordinator of my project and offered his considerable knowledge of the archaeology of southern Benin. Joseph Adandé, Obaré Bagodo, Souayibou Varissou, Bienvenue Olory, Didier N'dah, and Elisée Soumoni deserve special thanks for their kind encouragement and local logistical assistance. Early field efforts in 2003–2004 were supported by the Explorers Club Washington Group; the Graduate School of Arts and Science, University of Virginia (UVa); the Department of Anthropology, UVa; and the Center for Academic Excellence, UVa. The longer field campaign in 2005–2006 was funded by a National Science Foundation Dissertation Improvement Grant (#0432893), a Fulbright-Hays Doctoral Dissertation Research Abroad Fellowship (#P022A0500), and a special grant by the Embassy of the Netherlands to Cotonou.

1. See Blier (1995a, 1995b), Deschamps (1960), Herskovits (1932), Herskovits and Herskovits (1933), Maupoil (1943), Médiohouan (1993), and Verger (1957) for broader issues in the study of Vodun. I use "vodun" to describe the generic term for deity or spirit, and "Vodun" to describe the religious tradition.

2. In the Gbe language cluster, the suffix *-zen* indicates ceramics (cf. Savary 1970: 36). Thus, *danzen* translates literally as ceramic for/of the serpent deity Dan.

3. David (1983: 170) suggests that perforations on *adjalalazen* represent the pocked scars of smallpox. These vessels are common in modern shrines to *Sakapata,* the deity of smallpox (Norman 2000). In the nineteenth century, Richard Burton noted a "perforated pot" in the same shrine that contained a "Bo-doll" (Burton [1864] 1966: 178–179).

4. Earlier in this paper, I argued that in the modern religious practices of the region, there appears to be a regionally reoccurring preference for perforated ceramic vessels in ritual settings. It appears from excavations at Aseye rock shelter, Iffe-Ijumu (Allsworth-Jones 1996: 320) and Old Oyo (Willet 1961: 76) both in southwest Nigeria; and at Begho in Ghana (Crossland and Posnansky 1978) that perforated ceramics were common in archaeological assemblages. In both the Ghananian and Nigerian examples, the authors used modern rites to interpret the archaeological material as having ritual significance.

5. David (1983: 174) notes that large ceramic cooking vessels are used by the Gunin in southern Benin to contain the skulls of family members.

6. I thank Suzanne Blier for sharing with me her thoughts on the incised decoration of this vessel and for bringing to my attention her work on the Dahomean *weke*.

7. Phillips (1732: 224) claimed to have shot a "wooden" figure, presumably the *Agoye,* after waiting several hours for it to speak and give a pronouncement. Based on archaeological research at the house compounds of Huedan elites containing ceramic figures similar in depositional context and form to modern wooden *bo* or *bocio* figures, it appears the Dahomey Gap zone used such figures in religious rites.

8. See Akinwumi Ogundiran's (2002a: 46–47) description of a thirteenth-century burial at Iloyi of a decapitated skeleton with a grinding stone, quartz stones, jar and bowl fragments, possible food offerings, the skull of a sheep or goat, and a land snail shell.

9. Georgina Beier (1980) suggests that in Nigeria certain types of ritual pottery have died out including ritual pots and relief sculpture made for the shrines of Orișa, in particular for Sango and Erinle. Beier argues that this decline relates to the rise in popularity of modern mass-manufactured ceramics in a sinusoidal relationship with the declining popularity of the locally produced ceramic ones.

10. See Sidney Mintz and Richard Price's (1992) discussion of "cognitive orientations" or dispositions transcending specific West African cultures, and Andrew Apter's (2002) discussion of the broad Dahomean-Yoruba complex in terms of regional ritual process.

CHAPTER 4

Cowries and Rituals of Self-Realization in the Yoruba Region, ca. 1600–1860

Akinwumi Ogundiran

Billions of cowrie shells were imported into the Bight of Benin between 1600 and 1860 by European merchant ships, mostly as payment for the human cargo in the transatlantic slave trade. These cowries, in turn, served as local currency in the Bight of Benin and its far hinterlands (map 4.1). This chapter takes on a project of hermeneutic anthropology to examine how cowries became central to the everyday rituals of self-realization in the Yoruba region, and the preeminent resource for accessing power, harnessing authority, and engaging in social reproduction during the era of the Atlantic slave trade. This approach privileges the meaningfulness of social action and how it is constitutive of social life in historical and cultural dimensions (Gadamer 1976; Ricoeur 1976). To this end, I examine the depositional patterns of cowries in the archaeological and historical contexts, focusing on the implications for their uses in ritual practices. I then use these contexts of ritualization of cowries to explore the fields of "practical consciousness" and "vernacular knowledge" (see Apter 1992: 4) that defined the Yoruba experience of the Atlantic encounters.

The central questions that I ask here are: how were cowrie shells deployed in the everyday rituals in Yorubaland during the Atlantic slave trade, and what were the meanings of these deployments. The rituals of everyday life are instrumental and personal, guided by improvisation toward the single end of self-realization. This improvisation, however, means that individual actors are able to contribute to the process of culture-making (innovations) while at the same time being located in cultural tradition, what

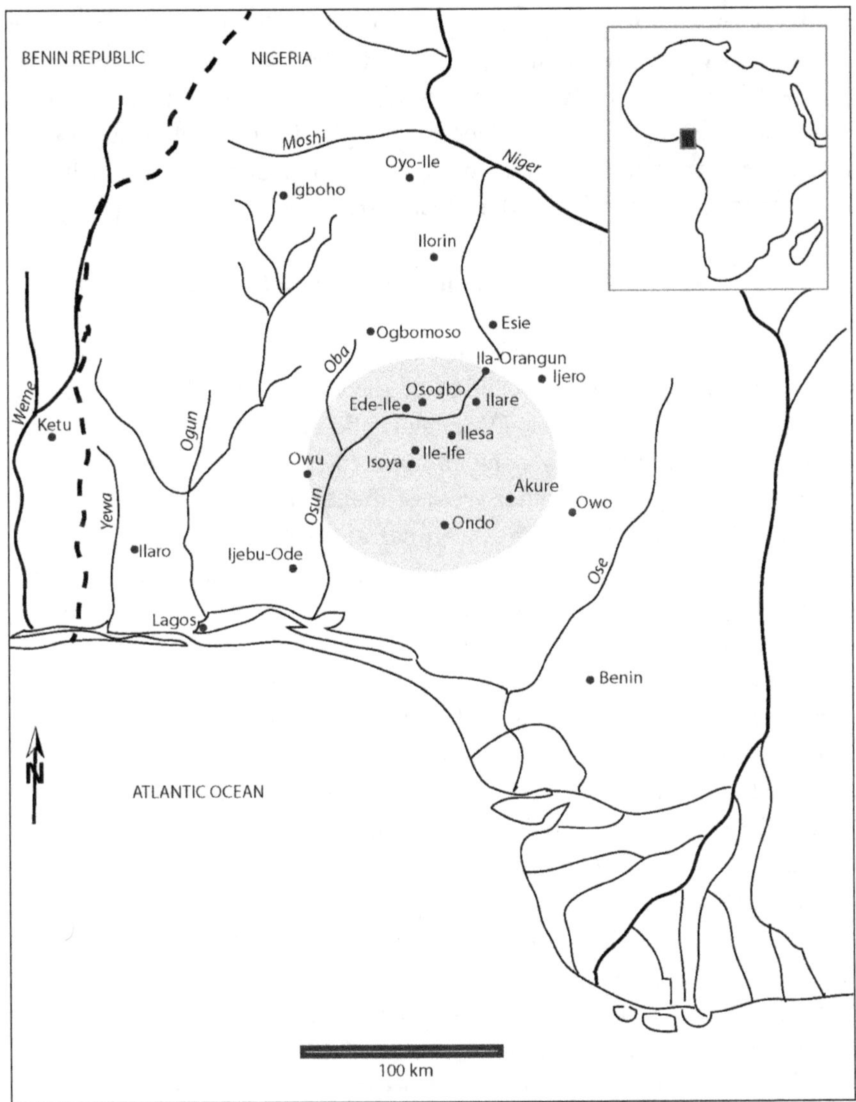

MAP 4.1. Yoruba region, West Africa. *Courtesy of Akinwumi Ogundiran.*

anthropologists refer to as core or dominant symbols (Turner 1973; see also Fennell 2007a and chapter 12, this volume). I intend to use some of the patterns of deposition of cowries in specific archaeological contexts to explore the meaningfulness of rituals of self-realization in the Yoruba world during the seventeenth and eighteenth centuries. Hence, rather than talking in general terms about what cowries mean symbolically, a goal that has been accomplished in earlier writings (e.g., Ogundiran 2002b), this chapter examines the specific contexts and places where cowries were situated—refuse mounds, houses, and burials. These spaces give insights into the episodes and processes of self-realization and social reproduction that were mediated by cowries in the era of the Atlantic slave trade and its aftermath.

Cowries in Yorubaland: A Historical Synthesis

Cowries, originating from the Indian Ocean via trans-Saharan trade, were already reaching the western Sudan by the early first millennium CE, as evident at Kissi, Burkina Faso (Magnavita and Pelzer 2000). It is likely that before the fifteenth century, some of these cowries trickled down to parts of the Yoruba region and other areas of the rainforest belt that were connected to the trans-Saharan trade (Ogundiran 2013b). Cowries did not, however, assume any cultural or economic importance in the Yoruba region until the sixteenth century, when the importation of cowries into the Bight of Benin began via the Atlantic trade.

The first major imports of cowrie shells—the moneta species[1]—into the region arrived in the Benin Kingdom from the Indian Ocean via Lisbon in 1515 (Hogendorn and Johnson 1986: 19), and it is from the kingdom that we have the first documentary evidence of monetization of cowries in the Bight of Benin. From there, cowrie currency spread westward, following the path of the expansion of African/European trading ports on the coast. Thomas Phillips, an English trader in Whydah, gives us the sense that domestic economy in the Bight of Benin was almost entirely monetized by the seventeenth century, when he noted that "when they go to market [in Whydah] to buy anything they bargain for so many cowries . . . and without these shalls [*sic*] they can purchase nothing" (Phillips 1732: 228). The rising demand for cowries to support the expanded and integrated domestic market in the subregion made it worthwhile for the coastal entrepreneurs to seek cowries as the preferred form of payment for enslaved captives and exports in goods—especially ivory, dyestuff, pepper, food supplies, and cotton products.

The impetus for the pan-regional adoption of cowrie currency was, however, due to the political expansion of the Oyo, Benin, and Dahomey states during the seventeenth and eighteenth centuries, as well as the expansion in the domestic economy across the region (Ogundiran 2007). Each state, taking advantage of the new economic and market forces unleashed by the Atlantic commerce, was responsible for the monetization of cowries in the Bight of Benin and the Yoruba hinterlands (see, e.g., Hogendorn and Johnson 1986; Law 1995). With the governments of the dominant states in the region levying taxes and toll payments in cowries, entrepreneurs were assured of the political security of cowries. Confidence in cowries as the medium for calculating prices and transacting business soared throughout the seventeenth and eighteenth centuries. This process of monetization took place in the context of the pre-Atlantic rarity and sacredness of moneta (and later annulus) cowrie. The monetization yielded four accomplishments: (1) it standardized the regional economic exchange system; (2) it allowed for a more efficient control of the terms of external trade, especially with the Europeans; (3) it allowed for a more efficient management of the "ever increasing volume and variety of trade goods" (Belasco 1980: 82); and (4) it allowed the different states to appropriate wealth more effectively through a single value register that could not be counterfeited. By promoting and facilitating the conduct of economic and social exchanges in cowries, the states also ensured that cowries, by their bulky nature, would be difficult to conceal and therefore make the evasion of levies and taxes difficult (Law 1995: 65).

Cowries accounted for approximately 44 percent of the value of all European imports into the Bight in exchange for human captives between 1662 and 1703 (Eltis 2000: 169). The eighteenth century marked the peak of the Atlantic slave trade (Richardson 1989), and also the peak in the importation of cowries into the Bight of Benin. It has been estimated that the Dutch and English traders who together dominated cowrie exports and the slave trade during the century brought slightly over 10 billion single shells to the Bight, about a 60–70 percent increase over the imports in the preceding century (Hogendorn and Johnson 1986: 43–46, 58).[2] The Bight of Benin and its Yoruba hinterlands were therefore integrated into the Atlantic world not so much through the Atlantic Age commodity production but through the cowrie-slave exchange. From the coast, cowries traveled inland serving as the currency that oiled the engine of the increased commercialization of local and regional economies. As this currency zone expanded, cowries accrued rich social meanings that are well preserved in the oral traditions, myths, folklore, divination literary texts, and panegyrics of the ancestors and deities of the era. There was perhaps no other category of objects in the Yoruba material world of the seventeenth through the early nineteenth centuries that was as evocative of thoughts, philosophies, and symbols about personhood and self-realization as cowries (Barber 1995; Falola and Adebayo 2000). Although much of its symbolic power derived from its use as money, it was the conversion of cowries into cultural capital that transformed it into the most elaborate repertoire of both symbol-making and spiritual expression. It is therefore not possible to separate cowries as money from cowries as cultural capital. The two are intertwined. It is, however, not the intrinsic worth of the cowrie as an object that defined its role as cultural capital, but rather what it represented in cultural production during this time. It was this latter quality of the cowrie—as cultural capital—that was deployed in forging new ideas about the world. As we will see below, cowries came to embody the material-intellectual infrastructures through which the Atlantic experience in the Bight of Benin, and the place of the individual and community in that entanglement, were conceptualized and translated into familiar theories and a worldview. From this condition, cowries became a critical medium through which the meanings, purposes, anxieties, and aspirations of human condition during the Atlantic Age were articulated and contemplated. In mobilizing its cultural capital, the cowrie became central to the rituals of self-realization in Yorubaland.

Self-Realization, Cowries, and Rituals of Everyday Life

I have borrowed and adapted the term "self-realization" from Jane Guyer (1993) and Karin Barber (1995). In the original usage, in the context of Equatorial Africa's culture of commoditization, commodity exchange system, and social valuation, Guyer explores the values that accrue to and are created by the singularity of individuals' work, skills, talents, and creativity in the production, exchange, and consumption or alienation of goods and services. She is especially interested in how different careers and their products are valued in currency terms, which are in turn based on a continuum of different value registers that serve to endorse particular types of personhood. Jane Guyer drives home the fact that the different configurations of linearity and/or circularity of production, exchange, skills, and social valuation constitute the processes for achieving certain types of elevated personhood. These processes were not only linked to the accumulation of capital in material form but also to the ability to immobilize or alienate the material basis of wealth (e.g., the currencies on the value register), control the knowledge and elasticity (both contraction and expansion) of the value register itself, and convert the material capital into human capital—"wealth-in-people"—and vice versa (see also Guyer and Belinga 1995). The ultimate goal of self-realization in Equatorial Africa, Guyer argues, is to harness resources—human and material—and to control the fates of others. Barber borrowed and adapted this Guyerian concept of self-realization to analyze the historicity of the social valuation of money among the Yoruba in the nineteenth century (see also Falola and Adebayo 2000, for twentieth-century historiographical extensions).

I find the concept of self-realization useful for understanding the historicity of culture-formation among the Yoruba even in the earlier centuries. Unlike Guyer's and Barber's preoccupation with self-realization in the matrix of the cultural economy of transactions, monetary systems, and the materialism of social valuation (Guyer 2004), however, I am interested in the convertibility of material life into rituals, spirituality, and signs of self-realization. The "self," in this case, is more than the atomistic individual but includes the family, community, and any other corporate group, though the interests and aspirations of the group may be vested in and represented by an individual. Moreover, I see the individual as one bookend in a spectrum of self-realization, with different social scales and types of communities at different positions on the spectrum. In this case the individual may belong to multiple communities on the spectrum. In this continuum of relationships, the individual and his communities use the complex and multiple meanings of cowries as resources for seeking, accessing, harnessing, engaging, accumulating, and expending empowerment, authority, and social reproduction in a matrix of divine interventions, uncertainty, as well as calculated social actions.

The access enjoyed by almost everyone in Yorubaland during the Atlantic Age to cowries made it a veritable object for revealing the "elements of intersubjective experience in everyday life" and a powerful tool of social communication (Arno 2005: 56). It is in fact from the intersubjective experiences and communicative power of everyday life that cowries derived their meanings. Cowries then formed a constellation of interrelated meanings in everyday life between habitual actions (use of cowrie currency in political, economic, and social transactions) on one extreme, and signs of culture (symbolic and iconic) exemplified by ritual on the other end. As I elaborate below, the cowrie moved back and forth between habit and ritual. It is this transmutability of cowries and their pervasiveness in everyday life as money, and as symbolic/iconic objects, that give them cultural luster as objects intimately involved in "the performance of . . . formal (and structured) acts and utterances," and at the same time, locked them into the habits of everyday existence (Rappaport 1999: 268).

There are numerous sociocultural fields of ritual in which cowries found relevance in Yoruba cultural history. Ethnography informs us that cowries participated in rituals for protection and good health of the individual and the community, for protection against mortal enemies and the malevolent forces—the *ajogun* (Abimbola 2006)[3]—and for cultivating favorable social relations with benevolent forces including ordinary people, "the mothers" (often mistranslated as "witches"; see Washington 2005), and various deities. Cowries were also implicated in rituals for transitioning the dead to the otherworld, for provisioning for the afterlife, and for the reproduction of the family/corporate group. Cowries were utilized in divination, ancestral veneration, and worship, and they frequently adorn or embody the votaries and votive arts of the various deities.

The cultural recontextualization of cowries as the essence of money and wealth, and their use in the reproduction and transformation of unequal social relations, played significant roles in shaping the local construction of the self and the economic objectification of human bodies and labor, in monetary and material terms (Sharp 2000: 293). Cowries as money meant three types of conversion: slaves/cowries, labor/cowries, and goods/cowries. The first refers to the exchangeability of human bodies and personhood for cowries. The second defines the partial monetization of labor as merchants and the political elite (and in the nineteenth century, warlords) employed servants, dependents, pawns, and free service providers as potters, dyers, weavers, and farm laborers, among others, in the production of goods and services. And the third—goods/cowries conversion—refers to the standardization of cowries as the means of payment for goods and commodities. These three forms of conversion centered on cowries as the most significant value register for measuring the adult individual's self-realization during the period of transatlantic commerce. Central to this process of self-realization in Yorubaland was the propitiation of Ori, the deity of fate and destiny, a force that resides in an individual's inner head. According to a nineteenth-century description of the rituals of the inner head by Samuel Johnson, "The Ori . . . is the universal household deity worshipped by both sexes as the god of fate. It is believed that good or ill fortune attends one, according to the will or decree of . . . [Ori]; and hence it is propitiated in order that good luck might be the share of its votary" (1921: 27).

Adults, both men and women, used cowries to make the altars for their Ori, the spiritual inner head and protector of one's fortune and destiny. The shrine consists of two parts—*ibori* (shrine of the head) and *ile-ori* (house of the shrine). The *ibori* is conical in shape with a projection on the top. It is made of "everything essential to a person's life" including "various ingredients associated with one's ancestors, gods, and the . . . taboos one must abide by" (Drewal et al. 1989: 32). All of these are tightly sealed in leather and cloth, and covered with cowries. The *ibori* is then placed inside a container, the *ile-ori* (house of the head), also made of cowries, which are set on a frame of fibers and fabric, and activated by the agency of powerful medicine (figure 4.1). *Ile-ori* is the power that conceals the inner/spiritual head, keeps *ibori* from the public gaze, protects its privacy, and prevents it from damage by "evil eyes." This two-piece shrine "conveys one's commitment to respect oneself and, by extension, all the forces shaping one's journey in life" (Drewal and Mason 1998: 199).

At the peak of the supply of cowries to the Yoruba region in the late eighteenth and early nineteenth centuries, as many as twelve thousand cowries were utilized to make a shrine of Ori, and the ritual specialist/artist of the piece would receive the same number of cowries as his wages (Johnson 1921: 27). Although the worship of Ori and its conceptualization as a deity possibly began before the advent of the Atlantic trade, the centrality of cowries to the making of *ibori* and *ile-ori* after the sixteenth century was a product of the Atlantic experience. The invincibility of Ori and its centrality to the individual self-realization possibly received a broader cultural interpretation with the advent of cowries as the most important index of self-realization. As cultural capital, the cowrie-based shrine of the head emphasized the individual over corporate accumulation, and accentuated the shift in the rendition of the image of Ori from the stylized human terra-cotta heads of the pre-Atlantic era to the impersonal and symbolic forms in conical and circular box shapes made of stiff calico and other potent ingredients covered with cowries, a reflection of the less personal dynamics in the flow, acquisition, and use of cowries as currency and cultural capital.

Late-nineteenth-century observers convey the sense that Ori was the most universal and, next to Ifa (the deity of divination and knowledge), the most portable of all the Yoruba deities (Peel 2002: 150). The point in time when Ori became so important a deity is difficult to clearly fathom from the oral traditions, but it is significant that in the Yoruba orature, Ori is identified as a late bloomer in the pantheon of the divinities. A genderless

FIGURE 4.1. Ile-ori—Shrine of individuality and self-realization. *Courtesy of the Fowler Museum at the University of California at Los Angeles, photograph by Don Cole. Reproduced by permission.*

force, Ori originally had junior status in the comity of the deities, and was involved in a protracted struggle for recognition as the preeminent member of the pantheon. Ori eventually triumphed, becoming the controller of the destiny of each of the other deities. Ori then proceeded to transform the destiny of all the deities, by assigning to them "their different functions" for which "they are revered today" (Abiodun 1994: 77). The foregoing narrative is a commentary on the new society that was created in the Yoruba region and outlying areas by the Atlantic trade, especially the transformative impacts of cowries in bringing individual and market-based accumulation to serve as the focal point in societal reorganization. The society was not only restructured economically as a result of the integration of the hinterland into the coastal economy, but the political system and social organization were also reordered, and this restructuring influenced the creation of a new belief system, myths, and ideologies. The spirit of individuality that is represented by Ori demonstrates that even the powerful, pre-Atlantic divinities and their corporate hierarchies were overwhelmed by the new economic order. As the circulation of cowries was changing the social relationships among individuals, spouses, families, and people of different statuses, these processes became codified in the religious system as the victory of Ori over all the other divinities.[4]

Given the expenses involved in making the Ori shrine, only the well-to-do members of the society could afford to construct these elaborate, cowrie-studded shrines dedicated to their individuality and the celebration of their self-realization. The shrines are discursively entreaties by the individual to his or her Ori so that "the endlessly slippery, circulating medium" of cowries could "stay with him, not to desert him for a rival" (Barber 1995: 217). It is significant to note that the immobile cowries were not employed as part of the repertoire of "ancestral veneration" after an individual had died. Rather, upon the death of the owner of the shrine, both the *ibori* and *ile-ori* would be destroyed and the cowries returned to circulation by distributing them to the deceased's survivors, who could spend the money as they wished. This process, from the construction of the Ori shrine to its destruction and the disbursement of the cowries, seems to testify to the Yoruba understanding that the wealth and values derived from Atlantic commerce, especially the flow of cowries, were unpredictable. Neither the state nor succeeding generations had control over the supply and direction of flow. Its accumulation depended on the individual, and the greatness and respectability that it accorded those who had it in abundance were not guaranteed to their descendants. Hence the popular Yoruba saying *owo ko ni ran*—"money has no relatives, natal affiliation, and family identity."

This meaningfulness of cowries discloses a new contemplation of individuality in social life, especially in seventeenth- and eighteenth-century Yorubaland. Evidence abounds that the individual as a source of social transformation was an integral part of the Yoruba practice before the Atlantic period (Drewal and Schildkrout 2009: 134–135). The naming practices, arts, historical narratives, and other aspects of cultural history going back to at least the eleventh century demonstrate the primary agency accorded the individual in Yoruba existential thought (Drewal et al. 1989: 61; see also Ogundiran 2003). Moreover, both naturalistic ancestral figures as well as stylized figurines that seem to represent deities of the inner head (individuality) have been found in a single shrine deposit at the Obalara site in Ile-Ife (Garlake 1974), showing the integration of heritage, ancestors, and individuality in one context. The new economic imperatives and political dispensations after the fifteenth century, however, expanded the framing of individuality in the Yoruba world. This was a period when the "traditional" process of labor allocation was challenged by the needs of the Atlantic trade, and when the gender division of labor increased the activity of women in the textile and dyestuff production sector and gave them an upper hand in the domination of the region's retail, crafts, and itinerant economy (Clapperton 1829: 21; Clarke 1972; Hallett 1984: 71). This was also the period when young men and women moved to major and newly founded market towns, and to the coastal region to pursue mercantile interests (Law 1977: 232). It was also an era during which several towns developed along the numerous traveling routes to service the provisional needs of caravan traders, porters, and state administrators who linked various kingdoms and market centers to one another (Ogundiran 2007). The point being made here (and an important clarification to earlier works on this subject) is that the integration of cowries into the material life of the region did not by itself create new meanings of individuality and personhood in cultural practice (Ogundiran 2009). Rather, cowries offered the most versatile intellectual resource (compared to other materials) to articulate, contemplate, and interpret the new experiences of individuality and personhood in multiple cultural domains—economic, political, and social (see also Ben-Amos 1999 for similar experiences in Benin).

As the embodiment and signifier of wealth and all the fortunes of life (since cowrie money could be used to buy good health, followers/clients, power, and status), moneta cowries came to occupy all three spaces that, according to Charles Peirce (1998), constitute signs of culture: iconic, indexical, and symbolic (see also Preucel 2006). The iconic sign refers to the use of cowries as currency—a standard means of exchange after the fifteenth century. As an indexical sign, cowries became associated with foreign contacts, the Atlantic trade, the ocean, and the external relations dominated by Europeans. After all, it was the transportation and use of cowries by the Europeans for payments that made the shells become plentiful. And, as symbolic objects, they were the value-register of ideas, knowledge, and social relations not directly related to the immediacy of production, consumption, and accumulation, and for which cowries were only referential and need not have been physically present. In this third instance, cowries became the materials for thinking about and giving meaning to the ideas of self-realization, success, authority, power, and even destiny. It is, however, in the domain of ritual—as cultural practice—that these three signs interface and become communicative and integrated, each sign disclosing how the other signs work and what they mean in social life. As the glue linking and binding these three signs together, the rituals of self-realization make cowries an elastic sign of culture. But this elasticity contracted and expanded according to the dictates of historical moments, shaping and being shaped by the constitution of the society. The materiality, then, of cowries in Yoruba cultural practice—as action and idea—helps make sense of the underlying premise of Peirce's theory of semiosis: that the meaning and meaningfulness of a sign are always shifting as they are continuously shaped by different temporal and contextual modalities of practice.

It is this elasticity that explains why the shells of Indian Ocean origins became an important component of grave goods after the sixteenth century, a phenomenon not seen in the archaeological contexts of the previous centuries. In mortuary contexts, cowries represent the material evidence of interaction between the deceased and their survivors. The eighteenth-century burials at Isoya town (14 km south of Ile-Ife) excavated by Omotoso Eluyemi (1977) offer some insights into the multifaceted meanings of these interactions (and conversations). Twenty percent of the cowries recorded in the excavations at Isoya were from burials, and eight out of the ten burials excavated contained cowrie artifacts (table 4.1). The number of cowries associated with each of the burials ranges from 2 to 202. The sample size, nine male and one female, is not large enough to understand whether the number of cowries varied according to sex and age, and the archaeologist did not tell us about the spatial pattern in the distribution of the cowries. Nevertheless, we know that cowries were found in-between the femurs of five of the remains. As grave goods, cowries could serve as a social and symbolic replacement of the personal belongings of the deceased, based on the idea that cowries were the essence of wealth accumulation and self-realization. The

Table 4.1. Distribution of cowrie according to sex and age in burials, Site I (Isoya).

Burial Units	Sex	Age Group	Number of Cowries
SK1	M	Adult	45
SK2	M	Old	39
SK3	M	Old	42
SK4	M	Old	15
SK5	M	Adult	180
SK6	F	Adult	0
SK7	M	Old	202
SK8	M (?)	Old	2
SK9	M	Adult	32
SK10	M	Adult	0

Source: Adapted from Eluyemi (1977: 107).

number of cowries included in each of the graves might indicate the level of wealth or social status, or might reference the age and sex of the deceased. Some of the cowries interred with the deceased could also be objects of supplications by the survivors to the deceased, so that the living descendants could receive the benevolence of the family member now venerated in death. As grave goods, the cowries also gave the deceased the expendable resources to help ease the transitional journey to the other world. After all, just as travelers had to pay tolls to enter a kingdom or city, the deceased had to pay tolls at the several gates on the path to the other world.

The presence of cowries around the pelvic bones of five of the human remains, however, raises a number of questions: Was this pattern of mortuary disposal of cowries meant to serve as assets to be expended by the deceased in his or her journey to the afterlife? By placing the cowries near the reproductive organs of the deceased, were the cowries expected to multiply so that the deceased would not be wanting of the provisions needed for his or her journey? Or do these cowries *signify* the complex Yoruba beliefs about fertility and rebirth of ancestor (Renee 2003)? Moreover, since the cowries were grave goods directly supplied by the mourners and survivors, in what ways did the cowries connect the deceased with the living? These are questions that we cannot answer in any specific way without knowing the details of the burial processes and the motives of the participants. We can only at this stage develop explanatory approximations: that multiple motives and intentions shaped the ritual placement of the cowries. Since

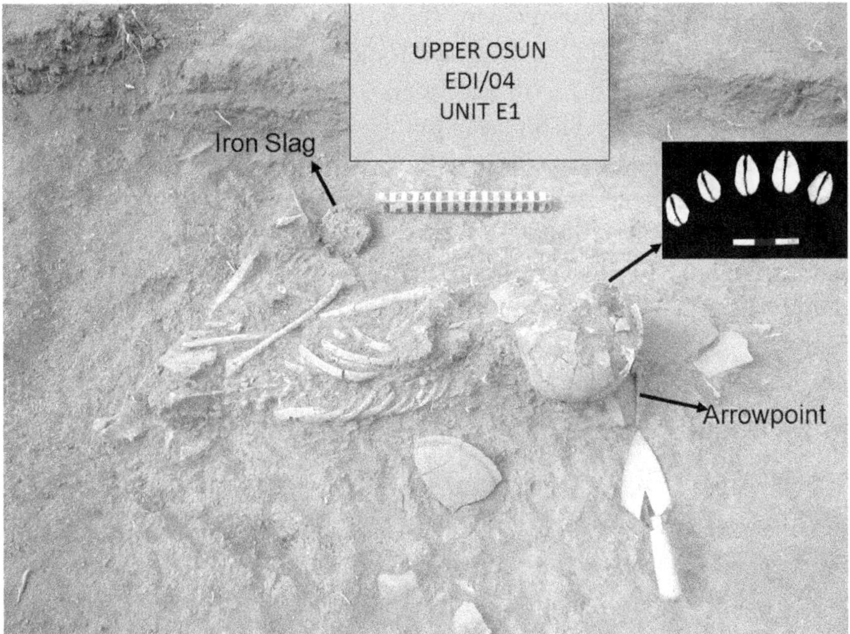

FIGURE 4.2. Human burial, Ede-Ile, ca. 1600–1830.
Courtesy of Akinwumi Ogundiran.

cowries, like beads, were tied to the notion of fertility and abundance, cowries as grave goods were supplications to ancestors and the dead for good fortune—money, children, long life, and good health.

A human burial that I excavated in the blacksmithing quarter of Ede-Ile town (ca. 1600–1830) sheds a different light on the ritualization of cowrie shells. The individual was in a crouching position, lying on the right side, and facing north. On top of the individual's skull were five cowries (figure 4.2). There were also one arrow and a serving bowl fragment below the head of the individual, and an iron slag was placed on the femur bones. Two meters from the burial was an ironsmith forge, a bowl furnace containing four pieces of iron slag, and numerous specks and fragments of charcoal. All of the mortuary goods—the bowl, the arrow, the iron slag, and the cowries—and their placement certainly had a purpose. The presence of cowries is what interests me here. The cowries could have been strung together with a fiber and used as a headband for the deceased. Or they may simply have been a mortuary good deposited by a relative of the deceased as a supplication to the spirit of the deceased during the burial. The five cowries might also be symbolic money that the deceased would use to "pay" for his entry into the land of the dead and of his ancestors. And yet, it is possible that the five cowries were meant to call on the individual's Ori to help him or her achieve a better life in, and easy passage to, the otherworld. After all, "the fortune and fate of a person is symbolized by Ori" (Awolalu 1973: 84).

The use of cowries for ritual signification and embodiment was profoundly elaborated in other contexts. The occurrence of cowries as ritual objects studded in the platforms and floors of residential and religious buildings has been documented in archaeological and ethnographic contexts in Yorubaland. At Isoya, for example, fifty-one cowries were found on a raised earthen platform above the house floor, "arranged in such a way that three shells in the center are surrounded by two rings of cowries, one containing 25 and the other 23 shells" (Eluyemi 1977: 109). Oral information indicates that the concentric pattern of these cowries symbolized good luck, and that the three shells at the center were meant to ward off misfortunes from the residence and its occupants.[5] Similarly, three moneta cowries were found inserted into the entrance floor of one of the rooms that I excavated in a courtyard house occupied ca. 1600–1750 in Okun settlement (Ogundiran 2002a: 66; figure 4.1). The continuity of this practice as a regional phenomenon is demonstrated in an ethnographic context in Ondo, described by Jacob Olupona in his late-1970s fieldwork (1991: 39). In the temple of the ancestral house of Sora, the priest of Oramfe deity in Ondo town, were "three cowries stuck into the floor." This is similar to the example from Okun settlement mentioned above. The potency of using *three* cowries as a ritual signification for warding off evil eyes and misfortune in Yoruba belief is rooted in the sociolinguistic meaning of the signifying verb *ta* meaning "to forcefully repel" or "to throw off." Hence, three (*eta*) cowries form the core of ritual signification that we see in both the archaeological and ethnographic records for repelling destructive agencies away from one's domain.

The excavated middens/refuse mounds in Yorubaland, especially in post-sixteenth-century contexts, have also revealed a fair number of cowries, as evident at Ede-Ile, a seventeenth- and eighteenth-century site (Ogundiran 2009, 2012). Previous finds of cowries in refuse mounds have been interpreted as items discarded in the same way as domestic trash (e.g., Ogundiran 2002a). The cowries found in these middens, however, are generally in good condition, and they sometimes occur in numbers large enough to negate the possibility that they were all lost by unwary or careless visitors to the refuse mounds. The midden, among the Yoruba, is not just a place where unwanted objects are discarded. It is also the site of frequent visits by the *ajogun* (malevolent forces).[6] These forces persistently threaten the peace of the world, the stability of communities, and the aspirations of individuals. In fact, they tend to be blamed for the afflictions faced by individuals and corporate groups, be they illness, death, loss, or any other kind of misfortune. These powerful *ajogun,* therefore, have to be appeased so they will be well-disposed toward individuals and their communities.

The sacrifices to appease these forces often end up in locations like market places, sacred groves, crossroads, riverbanks, and middens.[7] These are all liminal spaces also frequented by Esu, the heraldic deity and sole carrier of all sacrifices to the other Yoruba deities, the ancestors, and the malevolent forces. The sacrifices found in these spaces generally belong to purification rites, and they serve to exchange the affliction of the individual for a better condition. We have learned from ethnographic settings that cowries could be used, when assembled with other ritual ingredients, to cleanse a person of disease, death, poverty, joblessness, and other afflictions.[8] The cowries used for such purification and healing rites would then be thrown in the bush, crossroads, marketplace, or refuse mound. These sacrificial objects were recognized when found in these locations, and no sane person would pick them up because, by so doing, the person would be transferring the supplicant's affliction onto him- or herself.

In one of the refuse mounds (B1 site) excavated in Ede-Ile (see Ogundiran 2012), sixty-one cowries were found in two 2 × 1 m excavated units that were dug through a 260-cm-deep refuse mound. It seems that some of the cowries were deliberately thrown into the midden. They were most likely deposited in a process of spiritual cleansing or healing of an ailment, or rituals dedicated to certain life cycle improvements. Fifteen of these cowries were in fact found in an ash lense about 100 cm below the ground surface, a strong indication that the cowries were deliberately deposited in the refuse mound. By considering the refuse mound as, in part, a site of sacrificial rites, and some (if not all) of the cowries found on these mounds as sacrificial objects, it is implied that the other artifacts and remains that we have so far passively or actively regarded as discards—pottery, animal remains, and beads, among others—may not all be unwanted trash objects. Instead, some of these artifacts were ritually deposited in the liminal space of the refuse mound where humans, deities, and other forces were likely to encounter one another. Esu, the carrier of sacrifices to the other deities, is believed in Yoruba worldview to visit such liminal spaces regularly. The B1 refuse mound in Ede-Ile would have been an ideal place, therefore, to deposit ritual goods in order to achieve effective and immediate solution to the supplicant's problems.

Conclusions

The above case studies demonstrate the transformative power of cowries as ritualized objects mobilized and expended for procuring the welfare and well-being of individuals and communities. The examples illustrate the ways by which cowries-as-currency transitioned into cowries-as-ritual-objects, and vice versa. Both the cowries-as-currency and cowries-as-ritual-objects were linked to the process of self-realization. I would argue here that the Yoruba did not differentiate between these two domains of self-realization because the domains were permeable, complementary, and interwoven. As a Lukumi (Cuba's Yoruba-derived religion) and a West African Yoruba adage goes, "Without the market and money, there is no blessing of the deities." This means that the ability of the individual to propitiate the deities and receive their blessings depends on his or her ability to "nourish" the deities with appropriate goods which can be bought with money—cowries, in this case. The cowrie's function in the fragile and unpredictable but essential world of the market, "where the unexpected can occur and fortunes can be reversed" (Pemberton 1975: 25), is not unlike the ambiguous refuse mound, usually a liminal space in typically compact Yoruba villages, towns, and cities.

This chapter has been limited to the archaeological deposition practices as well as the few ethnographic assemblages in which the moneta (and later annulus) cowrie shells feature in different rituals of self-realization. Cowries permeate the Yoruba ritual practices today as they did in the seventeenth through nineteenth centuries. In all of these instances, the presence of cowrie shells demystifies ritual as a special symbolic activity or presence that requires anomalous and special equipment (e.g., Renfrew 1994). Instead, these artifacts and their contexts allow us to explore rituals in everyday life (e.g., Gazin-Schwartz 2001). The presence of cowries as part of the actions connected to the burial of a blacksmith or the purification of a household, for example, bridges the gap between the special moments of disjuncture represented by ritual actions and the processes of mundane everyday life, or between symbol and habit. The elasticity of cowrie for multiple signs and meanings reflects the complexity of its cultural biography and complex genealogy as a social capital (Kopytoff 1986) in many interacting fields that unite the secular and the spiritual spheres—exchange, transaction, and payment, among others.

The archaeology of cowrie shells especially yields new lines of evidence for exploring "the attitudes of ordinary people toward everyday life" at a particular historical era (Hutton 1981: 238). The hermeneutics of cowrie shells in specific archaeological and ethnographic contexts tell us about the symbols, images, and anxieties associated with the entanglement of the region in the Atlantic economy, and the sociopolitical and cultural ramifications at the local level. These hermeneutics also reveal the new consciousness and social practices that derived from the Atlantic encounters. Here, cowries constitute an exception to Richard Parmentier's semantic but dichotomous treatment of objects as "signs of history" and "signs in history" (1987: 11–12). Cowries not only evoke and comment on the historical moments (change and continuity) of the Atlantic Age and how the political, economic, and social characters of that age are embedded in cowries—sign of history. They are also actively involved as coparticipants in (and cofabricators of) the social lives that the historical moments created.

The rituals of self-realization in which cowries were implicated were not simply associated with life cycles and accumulation of material wealth. These rituals were also about the specific instances of everyday experience dealing with different aspects of human conditions—illness and healing as well as life and death. The analysis of the deposition patterns of cowries in archaeological contexts is helpful to understanding the communicative action of cowries in everyday lives. In as much as cowries came to represent the most versatile type of object for thinking about the wider world, and for making sense of the newness or radical changes of the seventeenth and eighteenth centuries, they are amenable to understanding the mental horizons of the Atlantic Age. In the shifting terrains of social, economic, and political relations of the period, cowries became central to the everyday institutions and practices necessary for forming "attitudes toward the self and the society at large" (Hutton 1981: 245), and for contemplating and articulating a consciousness of the world in the specific context of Africa's Atlantic Age.

Notes

This chapter continues my exploration in the fascinating world of cowrie shells. I am grateful to JIO for inadvertently calling my attention to this intriguing class of objects many years ago; and to all my informants in Ile-Ife, Ipole-Ijesa, Ilare-Ijesa, Ede, Osogbo, and Ibadan for generously sharing their knowledge with me over the years. This paper is based on the findings from the Eka Osun Archaeological Research Project (1992–2000), funded in part by the Boston Humanities Foundation (1997); and from the ongoing Upper Osun Archaeological and Historical Research Project funded by the Wenner-Gren Foundation for Anthropological Research (Grant Number 7099), the National Endowment for the Humanities Faculty Research Grant (HR-50114-04), Dumbarton Oaks, and the Office of the Dean, College of Liberal Arts and Sciences, at UNC Charlotte. I am grateful to the sponsors of the two projects. Finally, my appreciation goes to Ann Stahl who encouraged me to consider Peircean semiotics in relation to my interests in Yoruba hermeneutics, and to the anonymous reviewers who read earlier drafts of the chapter and offered helpful feedback. None of these scholars should be blamed for any errors in this chapter. I am solely responsible for the interpretation and final product.

1. *C. moneta* shells are native to the Maldive Islands in the Indian Ocean. They have angular outlines because of the four to six nodules on their upper surfaces, and their length varies from 1.3 to 1.9 cm. See Eluyemi (1977: 109).

2. Estimates of cowrie imports to West Africa from the records of the East India Company and Royal African Company (both English) and the Dutch VOC for some of the years between 1650 and 1699 indicate that possibly three to four billion cowrie shells entered the Bight of Benin and adjacent markets in the seventeenth century (based on estimates in Hogendorn and Johnson 1986: 43–46).

3. *Ajogun* refers to malevolent spiritual warriors. Kola Abimbola (2006) has identified the principal eight of these warriors in the Yoruba worldview as *iku* (death), *arun* (disease), *ofo* (loss), *egba* (paralysis), *oran* (big trouble), *epe* (curse), *ewon* (imprisonment), and *ese* (affliction).

4. It is therefore not surprising that during a Christian evangelism session in Ibadan in 1868, a female participant opined that the adoption of Christianity would not make them abandon their loyalty to Ori, “their god and maker” (Allen 1868).

5. According to Chief James Awosope, the former Araba of Ife (chief priest of the Ifa Oracle), interviewed by Omotoso Eluyemi (1977: 110), and independently corroborated by Kasali Akangbe Ogun, Osogbo (Nigeria), oral interview, 9 July 2011.

6. Safiriyu Atanda, oral interview, Ede, Nigeria, 2 April 2004.

7. Priestess Ibilola Omileye (chief priestess of Osun-Osogbo), personal communication, Osun Temple, Palace Compound, Osogbo, Nigeria, 7 August 2003; Safiriyu Atanda, oral interview, Ede, Nigeria, 14 March 2004; Priest Olalekan Orisadare (Aworo Osun), oral interviews, Osun Grove, Osogbo, Nigeria, 5 April, 2004.

8. Chief J. Aje, Loye of Ilare-Ijesa, oral interview, Ilare, Nigeria, 21 June 1997; Priestess Ibilola Omileye, oral interviews, Osun Temple, Palace Compound, Osogbo, Nigeria, 7 August 2003; Priestess Osunfunke Lakokan, oral interviews, Osun Lakokan Temple, Osogbo, Nigeria, 4 August 2011.

CHAPTER 5

Spiritual Vibrations of Historic Kormantse and the Search for African Diaspora Identity and Freedom

E. Kofi Agorsah

This chapter is about the archaeology of memory and spiritual genealogies. It is an attempt to explain the formation of a spiritual identity by enslaved Africans in the Americas, and the possible relationship of that identity—including its oral, artistic, written, and performed religious expressions—to an historical community in Atlantic Africa. It examines how the "Cromanti/ Kromantin" communities in the Caribbean and South America used the memory of Kormantse in present-day Ghana to generate discourses and practices of resistance against slavery and fight for freedom, as well as to create an autonomous African identity in the Americas. Historic Kormantse, a small village in modern-day Ghana, West Africa (figure 5.1), bears many historical and cultural markers, as well as archaeological indicators, that are useful for understanding the formation of identities among the peoples of the African Diaspora who are variously referred to as Kromantin and Cromanti, among others. Differences in orthography are the reason for the many and varied forms of the spelling of the word "Kormantse." The spelling adopted in this chapter appears to be the most appropriate one based on the way it is used among members of this community in modern Ghana, though other spellings will be referred to depending on the source material. The terms "Cromanti" or "Kromantin" are variations or adaptations of "Kormantse" in the Americas by descendants of those whose ancestors had direct experience and/or memory of the location. Yet, many African Diaspora communities in the Americas refer to this historic Kormantse site as "home."

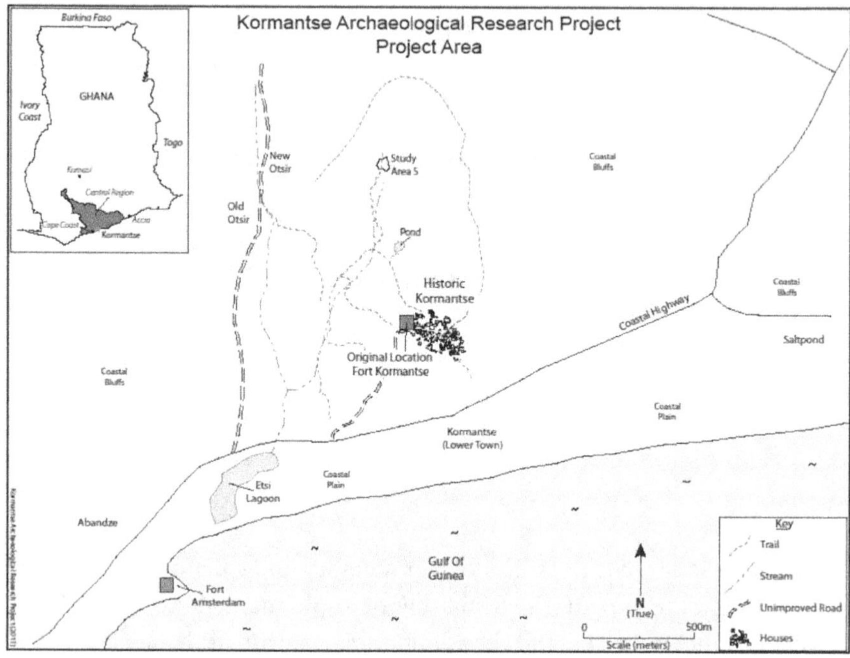

FIGURE 5.1. Historic Kormantse and surroundings.

My goal is to examine the historical and cultural connotations that link Kormantse in Ghana to the "Cromantin/Kromantin" identities in the Americas. Although much has been written on these American identities, almost nothing is known about the role of Historic Kormantse in them. I will use archaeological and ethnographic indicators to assess how the spiritual and ritual notoriety of historic Kormantse might have influenced the formation of identities among the peoples of the African Diaspora. I argue that the existing religious sites in Kormantse empowered enslaved Africans, especially those in Suriname and Jamaica, who passed through Kormantse on their way to the Middle Passage. These forced émigrés used the Kormantse's ritual potency to develop new discourses of power, justice, and values in their struggle for freedom, while celebrating their achievements and successes as freedom fighters. This chapter also explores the various ways by which Kormantse as a geographical or cultural entity impacted the African Diaspora's consciousness of their homeland, community and identity formation, self-determination, and beliefs. Resistance history, particularly marronage, in many parts of the Americas suggests that certain religious and spiritual connections to a Kormantse heritage empowered the enslaved, as they fought to define their power relations, as well as restore justice and their traditional values. Today, the mere mention of the word "Kormantse" would often simultaneously spark fear, pride, and empowerment among certain groups such as the Maroons of Jamaica and Suriname, that is, the descendants of escaped slaves. John Thornton rightly explains the impact of the use of the term: "As a means for social organization, it allowed Africans to remain a part of a larger community that was neither restricted to a single estate nor under the control of the masters. It was at the same time a religious organization, where principles brought from Africa could inform life and worship as much as the local environment would allow" (2000: 183).

Thornton is correct in recognizing the African identity of what he calls the "Coromantee," but the "Coromantee" were certainly not a "nation" nor an "organization," and definitely not an ethnic group as he implies. Of course, reconstructing Kormantse in the Diaspora assumes certain linguistic and cultural elements commonly observable among known Akan speakers of West Africa (Alleyne 1988; Bilby 1994; Harris 1994), but some of these elements cut across many other African cultural groups. Thornton refers to the kind of bonding that provided shared or common cultural experiences, which may have sparked the prestige, honor, bravery, and thirst for freedom and self-determination identified with aspirations and achievements of "Cromantis or Coromantee," as "social glue and religious institution" (Thornton 2000: 27). Douglas Chambers, however, describes the designations as "imposed European semantic categories or stereotypes, rather than historical African [or neo-African] realities . . . emergent identity groups (ethnies) . . . affinity groups or intentional communities with a shared proper name, language, cultural identity, links to a homeland, collective memories and, as significantly, 'shared amnesias'" (2001: 27). Such constructs fit well into the idea of "Diaspora Kormantse," imaginary but potent, versus the "Kormantse of the Gold Coast," the historical site that provides the inspiration for the African Diaspora's "Cromantis" identity. Modern Kormantse people are Akan, but they would not be culturally considered to represent all that is "Akan" because the range of differentiation among the Akan generally is very wide. The notion of "Coromanti nation" discussed by Thornton (2000) clearly should be considered as a sociohistorical construct that gives the impression of a homogeneous group in the Americas in both colonial and modern times. There is no doubt, however, that the notion of a nation created a psychological bonding, security, and a sense of pride, energy, and fearlessness among the Diaspora groups. Regardless of whether Kormantse was or is a geographical location, a culture, or a people, the spiritual or imaginary connection alone has been important for identity formation in the Diaspora. Although "Cromantin" in the Diaspora does not physically and culturally equate Kormantse in the Gold Coast, the discussion below shows that certain spiritual and religious factors associated with Kormantse played a role in the perpetuation of memories of an African ancestral homeland, as well as caused the name to remain a significant element of identity and freedom in the African Diaspora.

Kormantse in Africa and "Cromantin" in the African Diaspora: Roots and Routes of Connections

"Kormantse," as its people call it, is still a small fishing settlement located on a hill approximately 1 km northeast of Fort Amsterdam at Abandze on the Accra-Cape Coast main road in Ghana (figure 5.1). The settlement, which is said to have been founded by the Etsi and later joined by the Fante, constituted a landmark in the transatlantic English and Dutch slave trade. Kormantse was drawn into the transatlantic slave trade circuit in the 1630s, when the English attempted to build a permanent trading fort in the fishing village (now known as Historic Kormantse). The people of the fishing village of Kormantse, however, rejected the English presence, especially the slave trade that accompanied it. The agitation of the community prevented the English from establishing a trading post at the original site of their first lodge in the 1630s, and consequently forced the English to move to the Abandze location where they built a trading post they called Fort Kormantse. The Dutch conquered the fort in 1665 and renamed it Fort Amsterdam (Agorsah and Butler 2008; Schaffer and Agorsah 2010). The antislavery stance of Kormantse gave the settlement a notoriety and symbol of power, although the aversion of the Kormantse people toward slavery was limited to protecting themselves, not members of other sociopolitical affiliations, from enslavement. Enslaved captives from the interior and adjoining areas, along with their drivers, passed through Kormantse, and some of these people were lodged there temporarily before undertaking the final leg to the waiting vessels on the coast. The people of Kormantse, therefore, deployed weapons of the weak to protect their members from the vagaries of attack, abduction, and enslavement. They built defense walls, attacked and sabotaged European slavers on their territory, and summoned spiritual forces for protection. As shown in other parts of West Africa (Armah 1979; Diouf 2003), such resistance activities indicate that Africans on their own soil would not tolerate the new form of slavery that had been introduced with the coming of Europeans.

The local communities were certainly not docile. Kormantse did not live an isolated condition, however, nor were its people monolithic in their thoughts and actions. In oral traditions, the Etsi and Fante, the two ethnic groups at Kormantse, confirm their ancestors' active interaction and participation in the transatlantic exchanges, especially due to Kormantse's serving as a major transit between the coast and the hinterlands. As a settlement on the highway of trade and human traffic, Kormantse grew in the seventeenth through nineteenth centuries as it attracted both displaced and fortune-seeking migrants from a wide range of ethnic groups in the region. From the seventeenth century, the name "Kormantse" also become intertwined with the identity and traditions of groups of people who came from its surrounding areas or other distant areas in West Africa and passed through that location en route to the Middle Passage. Each family unit and individual immigrant brought its religious traditions to Kormantse, and soon the settlement became famous for its multiple deities drawn from across the Gold Coast and its hinterlands.

Thus, the history of the migration to Kormantse is often tied to the founding of Kormantse's deities and their contributions to the survival of the historic Kormantse settlement and people. Despite the waning observation of indigenous religious practices in Historic Kormantse today, due to aggressive Christian activities in the area, almost every compound in the town has at least a family or clan shrine. Many of them claim to be as ancient as the historic settlement. In spite of the historical ruptures that the region has experienced, from Atlantic slavery to the Asante military expansion and British colonial rule, the location of Kormantse remains the same. Likewise, its settler population appears to have been relatively stable and, therefore, can recollect the several generations of families who preceded them. The inhabitants of the settlement are Etsi- and Fante-speaking Akan, like much of the adjoining areas, today.

Kormantse/Cromantin/Kromantin in the African Diaspora Consciousness, Resistance, Culture, and Spirituality

References to Kormantse in the Americas consist of cultural definitions that cut across ethnicity, art and artistic expressions, stereotypical behaviors, and religious, political, military and other forms of identities, many of which have been central to recent scholarly discussions (Chambers 2001; Eltis and Richardson 1997; Lovejoy 1997; Morgan 1998; Northrup 2002; Thornton 1998b, 2000). Numerous references to the historical Kormantse site and its recognized, central role in the search for African identities in the diaspora demonstrate the need to explain its historical importance. This is accomplished by the use of both tangible and intangible evidence, examining shrines among African communities, as well as reviewing their impact on power relations, community identities, and inspirational values. Given the history of the struggle for autonomy and self-determination among the Historic Kormantse populations, it is important to investigate the impact of such an inspiration on the rebellions led and staged by the "Kormantyn slaves" on plantations in such places as St. Mary, Jamaica, in the 1760s (Hart 1985a, 1985b).

One popular reference describing the strong belief in the power of "Kormantse" in Jamaica and much of the Caribbean comes from Carey Robinson, a Jamaican journalist, who writes that

> Many of the captives came from war-like tribes which were called "Coromantins" by Europeans. They were described as fierce, bold, proud and courageous; possessing "an elevation of soul, which prompts them to enterprises of difficulty and danger, and enables them to meet death, in its most horrid shape, without flinching"; despite their dangerous reputation, the British planters preferred Coromantins because of their strength and ability to work hard. (1994: 89)

Similarly, oral historians such as Colonel C. L. G. Harris, a former chief of the Moore Town Maroons of Jamaica, refer to their original language as "Kramanti," said to be spoken freely among them until about the 1930s. According to Harris, an extremely specialized ritual ceremony, "Kramanti as my ancestors knew it to be called, is regarded as a hybrid having Twi, the Ashanti language of the Gold Coast as the more vigorous of its parents"; he further provides many examples of phrases and words of the language (1994: 39). Similarly, Kenneth Bilby, an ethnomusicologist who has done substantial research on the Maroons in Jamaica and Suriname, refers to "an esoteric language of the Maroons known as Kromanti to which several of African languages have contributed . . . now functions only as a liturgical language . . . repertoire of Kromanti songs" (1994: 77). The linguistic fascination is also exemplified by Charles Johnson and Patricia Smith, who noted that the main captives "were Fulani, Malinke, and Wolof, members of tribes with names like ringing bells. . . . They were the Whydahs, Asante, Fanti, Coromantees, pride filling their faces" (1998: 62). Likewise, Wim Hoogbergen, a prominent Dutch historian, lists eighteenth-century locations and rivers in Suriname, South America, that bear names such as Cromotibo and Kromoti-Kodjogron, names attributed to Kormantse (1990). Richard Hart (1985a, 1985b), a prominent Jamaican historian, has listed some of the expressions employed by the group, with varied spellings such as "Kromantine, Kormantine, Cromantee, Coromantee, Coromantyn, Coromantis, Kromatis, Kormantse," the last being the preferred (see Agorsah and Butler 2008; Bisnauth 1996; Chambers 2001; Harris 1994; Lovejoy 1997; Morgan 1998; Thornton 1998b, 2000).

In addition to the linguistic interest, there has also been fascination with Kormantse beliefs and associated material manifestations. In their detailed exposition of the religion and culture of Maroons in French Guiana, Thoden van Velzen and Wilhelmina van Wetering describe "Kumanti deity or spirits associated with the sky . . . Kumanti medicine men said to have formed the backbone of resistance against planters—among the Aluku-Kumanti spiritual medium" (1988: 21). The impact of the Kormantse, whether hypothetical or real, is well demonstrated by the examples of the religious practices, particularly those related to funerals among the Maroon societies in French Guiana. Beverley Carey, a notable Jamaican-born Maroon writer and authority on Moore Town Maroons, also talks about Koromanti or Karamanti drum and language and refers to Kramanti songs said to be derived from "Twi tongue" (1997: 184–185). Like Carey, many writers in the Diaspora have even gone as far as referring to a Koromantyn nation, carrying forward the notion and reference far beyond its role in our understanding of the formation of the populations of the African Diaspora.

Many enslaved Africans coming from the Gold Coast point of embarkation to the Americas were referred to as "Coromantin slaves" (Agorsah 1994), leaving unclear their specific cultural affiliations or identities. Kormantse was one of the major ports of departure of the enslaved, who could have originated individually or in groups from hundreds of ethnic groups in the West and Central African regions. The demographics also confirm that these groups were mixed and did not come from any specific ethnic group or groups (Eltis and Richardson 1997: 18–19). We should therefore expect that "Cromantin," as an identity label in the Caribbean or South America, refers to people embarking from the Gold Coast and adjoining regions in general, and that members of other African groups, such as the Igbo and Efik of the

Bight of Biafra as well as Yoruba, Baule, Agni, Fon, Mosi, Brong, and many others would have also assumed this identity in the Americas.

Historical evidence likewise confirms that many of the Akan trade brokers were located in and around the Kormantse area (Kea 1982). In the circumstances of African-European cultural interaction on the Gold Coast, it is logical to assume Akan predominance thereby leading European brokers to lump all who passed through Kormantse, Elmina, and Cape Coast as "Kormantse people." Massed into one group in European merchant records, Kormantse later evolved into an umbrella term—variously Cormantine, Koromantin, Kumanti, Kormantin, and so on. In specific European colonial enclaves in the Americas, especially in Jamaica, French Guiana, and Suriname, the Kormantse identity developed from a myriad of African cultural and ethnic groups. The term erroneously implied a homogenous origin, which, in turn generated a cultural search for a Cormantine African ancestral home.

Undoubtedly, the Gold Coast experience led the name "Kormantin" to begin to be associated with the lexicon for resistance and self-determination in the African Atlantic world. This makes sense since, as Johannes Postma has indicated, approximately 20 percent of the enslaved Africans arriving in the English Caribbean during the seventeenth and eighteenth centuries came from the Gold Coast (1992: 115). Hence, just as the captives leaving the Gold Coast ports came to be labeled Kormantin, the enslaved African rebellions taking place on the English plantations and colonies in the New World came to assume the different versions of the ethnonym of Kormantin.

CULTURAL LEGACIES OF KORMANTSE IN THE DIASPORA

The Kormantse legacy can be found among African Diaspora societies in festivals and festivities, often called "play." A description of a grand festival celebrated in colonial and modern Grenadines on the island of Carriacou introduces an example of one of the most significant impacts of the Kormantse or African connections:

> At the Nation dance festival . . . the head nation to be greeted and pacified is the Cromanti people. . . . During the Nation Dance opening ceremony at which all Kromanti ancestors are invited, the circle of devotees is opened and two towels are laid crossed on the ground—an opening is left in the circle so that the old people [ancestors] may enter as the music is played. This music is made by a single drum, a used weeding iron hoe struck like a bell. It is said that those who have second sight can see the old warrior ancestors as they enter the free ring. This ceremony is repeated at midnight and is called Cromanti cut neck. (Elder 1988: 33)

These so-called Cromanti ancestor-worshipers in the situation described here built no shrines nor possessed any established hierarchy; neither did they have any physical identity, though they were often thought to relate directly to the powerful Asante of the Gold Coast. Such ritual events have also been documented among the Moore Town Maroons of Jamaica and on Carriacou, a dependent island of Grenada (ibid.: 34). Oral traditions collected by Douglas Frimpong-Nnuroh during the 2009–2010 Kormantse Archaeological Research Project (KARP) in Ghana claim that in the settlement's early years:

> Every Friday the hours between 13:00 and 18:00 was devoted to communal worship where the whole community would play drums and dance at the communal shrines. On this auspicious day, priests and priestesses also dance and give cultic attention to the gods by making offerings. The whole community was cleansed and blessed with long life and prosperity. These ceremonies occurred at regular times as a requirement for the prosperity of the Kormantse communities. Although the traditions appear to be waning, its significance in the African Diaspora appears to indicate its new growth and revival of the historic past.[1]

It is easy to see parallels between this description and the Carriacou example. Similarly, there are parallels between Grenadian examples and "play" ceremonies among the Maroons of Jamaica described by C. L. G Harris: "Play is a ritual ceremony. . . . The drummers are seated but most of other participants must stand. The drums (Kramanti drums) are made from hollow portions of tree trunks covered at one end with a tightly drawn goat skin . . . and the songs (Kramanti songs) are sung to the music of the drums and the dance (Kramanti dance) is done by top-rated performers" (Harris 1994: 49).

According to Harris, spirit possession by a departed Kramanti ancestor helps performers to reveal matters of the past and connect them to current social issues. Harris explains that "play is a ritual ceremony held at a booth made after the pattern of that in which table setting was conducted" (ibid.). This special ritual has been researched and very well described by Bilby (1994). There are no indications that "play" takes place at shrine houses in Jamaica, but libation, an important aspect of religious ceremonies in much of West Africa, forms a major part of the ritual and is considered as a renewal of empowerment that helped the Maroons fight for their freedom. "Play" has been one of the most potent tools for both physical and spiritual healing among the Jamaican Maroons, even in the midst of fast-spreading Christian values. The Kramanti dancer is considered to be performing a serious dance that enables him or her "to glide from purely physical plane on to the metaphysical" (Harris 1994: 59). Again, like the Grenadian example, there is no evidence of shrines and temples for the performance of "play." The Kramanti dance is inspirational and spiritual, bringing within it a reminder of the Kormantse ancestry of the Gold Coast. The term "play" is used among the Moore Town Maroons to mean "ritual or spiritual healing performance" and in such ceremonies, the Kramanti language, now only ceremonial, is used.

Bilby further points out that "the Maroons seldom reveal to outsiders the meaning of more than a word or two of their secret African-derived language, called Kromanti" (1995: 170). The modern Akan-speaking Ghanaian performer, particularly the possessed priest of a shrine accompanied by drummers, performs a series of dances that follow patterns of jerky and erratic movements characterized by sudden leaps and spins alternating with calm movements. It is believed that they channel the tutelary spirits and thus can reveal unknown secrets, offer counseling relating to social or political situations in the society, and suggest ways to resolve problems including those of health and diseases. It is through these worshipers or performers that the historical connections with Kormantse continue to be established in the African Diaspora even in contemporary religious practices and ideologies of survival. The social and political identities of these African Diaspora groups are articulated in terms of their ancestral Kormantse heritage. These examples suggest that even without being a homogenous group, descendants of Africans living in bondage have continued their search for self-definition in relation to their ancestral past and places of origin. The contemporary citations of Kormantse identity in the African Diaspora rituals and cultures in the Caribbean and South America are the legacies of how their enslaved ancestors used intercultural communications to overshadow their cultural differences and backgrounds. Kormantse, as an idea and practice, was the rallying point for creating a unified African identity in a new land where Africanity was reduced to chattel slavery. Hence, the "Kormantse" mentioned in European historical documents refers to the invention of new identities and heritages, which make the imagined and real memory of Africa thinkable and relevant to material and spiritual needs.

Edward Long, for all his racist views about Africans, openly considered or credited the Kormantse with intelligence, stamina, and bodily perfection and agility; he suggested that "their dances serve to keep alive that military spirit, for which they are so distinguished" ([1774] 1970: 3:474). In the case of the Maroons of Jamaica and the Nation dancers of Grenadines described above, the power of Kormantse could also be felt in both physical and spiritual healing. With the conviction of their powers, the "Koromantins," according to Charles Dallas, led the first major slave uprising in 1690 in Jamaica and instigated the subsequent ones in 1760 and 1765–1766, which resulted in the Jamaica Assembly's imposition of heavy taxes on the "Coromantins," making it difficult for planters to purchase them. Dallas calls them "a people inured to war on the coast of Africa" (1803: 29–30).

KORMANTSE SPIRITUALITY IN SLAVE REVOLTS

Would it be right to assume that the strength of the remembered cultural connection with Kormantse, as a point of departure from the Gold Coast, became stronger than those related to other ports of embarkation on the West African coast such as Elmina, Cape Coast, Whydah, Calabar, Ketu, Anomabo, Badagri, Apam, and Port Novo (see Eltis and Richardson 1997: 23–25)? The Kormantse impact appears to have come with a political ideology and organizational ideals typical of what is often related to the past of the Akan people of Ghana. Why, then, did these other ports, which shared the same source of enslaved Africans, not carry with them the same or similar nomenclature identity as Kormantse, despite the fact that many of these ports saw much greater volume of the trade than Kormantse? It would appear that, confronted by new realities, enslaved Africans were able to invoke a common reference identity in order to establish potent connections with their physical and metaphysical past and present. Such bonding together under a single reference point or name would either disregard geographical and other divides or allow for individual relationships to totally slip out of generational memories. In addition, the dynamic nature of African religious thought and practice allows for the invention of new deities and religious relations, as the people of Kormantse did during their first settlement. In the Diaspora, Kormantse assumes a larger reference far beyond that of a small fishing village, blending with and labeling the whole as if it had harbored more popularly known ethnic groups originating from within and around the entire West African region. Ritual manifestation of Kormantse bonding and identity, especially in the spiritual realm, does not seem to have required elaborate infrastructures or institutions in either Africa or the Diaspora, although charismatic leadership seems to have been crucial to support and give this identity direction. According to Thornton, "the ideology and organizational ideals of Coromantee . . . did draw on Akan political ideology and even fairly specific modes of organization drawn from the immediate past of Akan slave in the Americas" (2000: 183), and we now know that that past is larger than the world of the Akan.

War oaths are known to have been popular among the Kormantse in the Diaspora, and proved inspirational. These included an oath of allegiance of a leader to his or her people, an oath of friendship, an oath of solidarity, an oath of trust (truth), and a cursing oath. For the enslaved individual or freedom fighter, oaths of solidarity and secrecy were crucial. Peter Linebaugh and Marcus Rediker have noted the use of such oaths by rebels in Antigua and by Nanny, the Queen and leader of the Jamaican Maroons in the 1730s, to spiritually establish continuity with and solidarity, power, and support from their Kormantse past:

> The most frequent of these involved swearing by thunder and lightning. . . . Many of the slaves swore by this oath to support the revolt and never to reveal the common secret. Military oaths invoking the primal powers of thunder and lightning were in use in the Gold Coast of Africa in the middle of the eighteenth century, suggesting both the origin and efficacy of the practice. . . . These oaths, like African traditions of resistance more generally, were not new . . . for they had been used generations earlier in 1712 in one of the bloodiest revolts ever to hit the North American mainland when a coalition of slaves of Coromantee and Papa background set fire to a building and then killed white people who came to extinguish the fire. (2000: 185–186)

Using the context of the 1994 state visit of the Queen of England to Jamaica, Kenneth Bilby (1995) demonstrates how seriously the Maroons continue to acknowledge the importance of the 1739 oath taken by Maroons and representatives of the British crown as part of a peace treaty signed that year between these two parties to end the wars between them. Bilby refers to Barbara Kopytoff's observation made during her anthropological research in Jamaica in 1979 that the treaties were "sacred charters—i.e. hallowed covenants that underpin and assure their very existence as separate peoples within the larger society of Jamaica" (ibid.: 657). The treaties are considered as "blood treaties" by the Maroons of Jamaica because both the Maroon and British signatories had to shed blood as ink for signing the peace treaty: "The African-derived concepts of sacred bonding that underlie the Maroons' views of their treaties have serious implications . . . until today" (ibid.: 658).

Bilby's analysis of Maroon oaths, the most comprehensive available so far, clearly explains the religious significance attached to the most crucial aspects of Maroon survival: the end of war and the search for peace. Kormantse tradition in the Americas might be considered the importation of the experience of rebellion, from the Kormantse tradition, which recalls the resistance of the Kormantse people to the building of an English trading lodge at Historic Kormantse. This forced the English to seek a new location, which eventually led to the development of the Abandze township around what later became known as Fort Amsterdam. The process of signing the peace treaty also brings back memories of the sacred oaths the Maroons had sworn on behalf of their African ancestors. Although the British took the signing lightly, as they disingenuously tried many times to break the spirit of the oath, the Maroons after more than two centuries still consider the "blood treaty" sealed forever. Oath-swearing continues to be a common and serious cultural practice among many African and African Diaspora communities.

AFRICAN DIASPORA RELIGIOUS LANDSCAPE IN CONTEMPORARY SURINAME

Different versions of the historical evolution of Kormantse along the coast of Ghana exist but they all have a common feature in the special role of deities and their related shrines. It is a difficult task to reconstruct the evolutionary transfer of shrines and other religious structures and their related locations in the African Diaspora. Although shrines have not been historically or archaeologically documented or observed in contemporary Jamaica, Carriacou, or other areas of the Caribbean, they have survived in Suriname and French Guiana in South America. The six Maroon groups of Suriname, for example, have shrine structures in their villages that they identify with their Kormantse religious heritage. Such shrines are located at entry points to the modern Saramaka village of Semoesi and Daume in the Suriname River basin. These community and individual shrines and monuments continue to invoke the memory of Kormantse. "Kromanti" herbal and spiritual healing processes (Van Velzen and Van Wetering 1988), including their continued use of traditional names of plants such as *Kromantikankan (Spigelia anthelmia), Kromantiwiwiri (Struchium sparganophorum),* and *Kwasibita (Quassia amara)* (Green 1978), are common and stand out as some of the most potent in healing (May 1982: 37–39). These "Kromanti" connections among South American Maroon groups emphasize the healing power and effectiveness (both physical and spiritual) of herbal medicine made from these plants (Green 1978). In the minds of healers, priests, and priestesses, their survival depended on the Kormantse spiritual legacy that enabled them to win freedom from slavery in the first place.

When a group of Saramaka Maroons of Suriname visited the Republic of Togo in the 1970s, it was reported that prayers were said by the Maroons in their "Kormante language, a sacred language . . . in which the Almighty God, Nana Kediapon, is invoked. This caused great emotions (in both the Togolese hosts and the Surinamese visitors), for the same Supreme Ruler is invoked in Ghana" (De Groot [1973] 1996: 392). Hermes Libretto (1990) confirms the significance of the visit, and the relief and healing it brought to the Surinamese. During that visit, the gift of an Asante stool was presented to the leader of the Surinamese group with the explanation that it was a symbol of the chief's authority, "a symbol that expressed their entire cultural heritage as well as the power of their ancestors" (De Groot [1973] 1996: 392). This incident further shows that the African Diaspora reference to Kormantse goes far beyond a geographical location and even a particular ethnic group. For the Surinamese Maroons, the important issue was the return to the assumed land of their ancestors, as Kormantse people.

The founding or establishment of certain settlements, now potential archaeological sites, by the Maroons in Suriname has often been attributed to the "Kromanti" people. Some of these include sites in the northeastern areas of Suriname between the Cottica and Marowijne rivers, such as Cromotibo and its creek, Kromoti Kiiki; Komanti-Kojogron; Kwamigron; Kosay; Kofi-hay; Quassigron; Coematibo River; and Tesisi (Hoogbergen 1990). The historical claims by the Maroons of Suriname to these sites seem to be strong, given the tenacity and success with which the Maroons defended those settlements during colonial times. They attribute that success to "Cromantee" powers.

It is among the Suriname communities that we see shrines, temples, and other paraphernalia that are linked to the practices of Kormantse spirituality. Indeed, of all the Kormantse manifestations in the Americas, Suriname offers rare opportunities to examine the material culture and landscape of Kormantse spirituality and beliefs in the Americas. Although archaeological excavations at Maroon sites in Jamaica (Agorsah 1994) broke new grounds in Maroon heritage studies, evidence of houses and structural features was lacking. Questions about the internal physical plan and organization of Maroon settlements and their spatial relationships, mortuary practices, and inferences about foodways, therefore, remain undetermined. While the Maroon sites in Jamaica did not permit the acquisition of material

FIGURE 5.2. Azampaau—a protective entry post to a Saramakan Maroon settlement, Suriname.

needed to address these and other related issues, comparative sites in Suriname appear to have the potential for evidence that could be used to address unanswered questions and explore new directions. Extensive ethnographic data on the Maroons of Suriname provide comparative data on settlement development, especially at Kumako, Tuido, Bakakum, and Sentea (Agorsah 2007; Agorsah and Childs 2005), which span the earliest, middle and later colonial periods respectively.

In many modern and historical Saramaka Maroon settlements in Suriname, shrines are built as the community's spiritual homes, where community affairs are deliberated and leaders perform their spiritual obligations—offerings, prayers, blessings, promises, and dedications. Most prominent among the structural features are those representing the community. A popular feature associated with the Suriname Maroon religion is the *Azampaau*, usually two standing posts with a crossbar holding palm fronds and other leaves, situated at the entrance of a settlement and serving as a reminder that one is entering a traditional village that is guarded by one of the protective spirits (figure 5.2). Among the Saramaka, no one carrying the Bible, or who is a Christian missionary or preacher, was allowed to enter such a village since the Bible was a colonial instrument through which their ancestors were enslaved, only to be saved by their ancestral African spirit. The Maroons argue that coming into contact with the Bible would weaken the potency of their ancestral spiritual powers. These perceptions are changing as more and more Maroons accept Christianity.

Similarly, community shrines among the Saramaka of Suriname are often found in the open, either at the entrance or the center of a settlement. One such shrine in the settlement of Semoesi on the Suriname River, the *Gaa-Gadu wosu* (house of the Great God), is a block enclosure that houses a standing libation platform with remains of previous offerings such as food, drinking glasses, cloth-covered bowls and pans, empty rum bottles, hoe blades, dry bones of previously sacrificed animals, and certain herbal plants in and around the wall. During their libation sessions, Maroons make mention several times of the Kormantse ancestors.

Alternatively, personal shrines are located in individual homes and certain rooms in the homes that are only accessible to certain people within the family. These personal/family shrines take many forms, some with a forked pole holding a bowl or pot containing herbal materials, similar to the *nyame dua* (God's tree) known to many African communities in present-day Ghana, Nigeria, Benin, Cote d'Ivoire, and Togo. Ritual bath and cleansing, for healing purposes, using herbal mixtures continue to be undertaken in order to rid individuals of evil spirits, sicknesses, curses, or other mishaps. Shrine ceremonial drums among Saramaka Maroon, when beaten or played, are supposed to commandeer the Kormantse spiritual forces that made it possible for the Maroons to win their wars of freedom resulting in the signing of peace treaties in the 1760s. Although far away from Kormantse, both geographically and temporally, the Saramaka of Semoesi continue to celebrate the spiritual legacy of the toughness, fearlessness, and defiance of their "ancestral" Kormantse.

Historic Kormantse Shrines and Archaeology

What is it about Kormantse that created these religious or spiritual references to a fishing village, and ostensibly a small corner of the Gold Coast, both in the past and present? The continuous reference to the rebellions led by "Coromantees" appears to have established their popularity as brave and defiant fighters during early encounters with colonial forces. The leadership of the Coromantees over the African populations in Suriname is also frequently mentioned (Hartsinck 1770). Archaeological exploration of the original site of Kormantse appears to be pointing to possible experiences that provided many of the enslaved people who came from or passed through Kormantse with the spiritual strength that helped them through the ordeal of the Middle Passage, as well as during their enslavement.

Evidence from Historic Kormantse in Ghana indicates that shrines formed the most common and visible structural features of the settlement, as well as in the surrounding areas. In modern times, while community shrines remain in open areas, personal shrines continue to be located inside compounds or in rooms. Among most coastal communities in Ghana, particularly in the western half of the area, community, clan, or Asafo shrines are very common. The Asafo are paramilitary groups whose primary function is defense of the community or polity although they also exercise considerable political influence in their areas. Their shrines are civic shrines. The Asafo system claims to predate European arrival on the Gold Coast (Datta and Porter 1971). The system is identified by a public shrine representing the ideals, religious convictions, and values of the particular clan, while celebrating the glories of the past. According to Kormantse tradition, the earlier Asafo shrines originally consisted of simple mounds in cane fences, usually with trees planted over them to provide shade. These shrines, however, have evolved into elaborate structures that incorporate Western symbols and material culture—such as cowboys, Adam and Eve, cannons, machine guns, muskets and rifles, glass bottles, airplanes, ships, and clocks—as can be seen in many towns around Kormantse and along the coast today (figure 5.3).

Community shrines other than the Asafo are those that have specific goals to protect the community, and these too tend to be located in public spaces. The Tigaare shrine that the Bentsir community of Historic Kormantse acquired from the north of Ghana for catching witches, for example, was kept strategically at the outskirts of the town ostensibly to ward off the machinations of evil people as they approached the community. Equally, evil-minded people who had committed wicked acts and were about to flee from the community could also be apprehended whenever they passed the altar of the deity, Tigaare. Communal shrines that were meant for protection of the inhabitants were sometimes located in the middle of the town. In the minds of the populations of Historic Kormantse, some of the principal deities, like deities in other parts of the world, are believed to continue to reside in natural bodies such as streams, lagoons, trees, rocks, and ravines. Notwithstanding all of these, there were also communal shrines that were constructed by the elders of Kormantse as abodes for their deities. When-

FIGURE 5.3. Asafo posuban (paramilitary post) and community shrine, Historic Kormantse.

ever the elders acquired a new deity and brought it to the community, they kept it in a safe-house or in a secure part of their rooms, usually in the rafters of their ceiling until they had prepared a suitable or permanent place to keep it. In the past, mud brick was used for the construction of the structure that housed the communal deities, but today cement and other building materials are used to provide dwelling places for the gods. These shrines were not made in any particular shape; rather, they were crafted to manifest the essential essence of the deity.

In addition to the community shrines, there are many other shrines that are personal or family-based (see Agorsah 2010: 32). In the 1.6 × 0.8 km Historic Kormantse settlement in Ghana, these include earthen mound shrines with ritual objects and substances, simple piles of iron slag and ore, or single slabs of rock and clay as platforms. These shrines are usually located in the middle of houses, in the back or front corners, near rooms' entrances, or on platforms. While the communal shrines continue to be owned by the entire community of Kormantse, the family and other shrines are individually managed. Therefore, they are often placed at locations that make them easily accessible to all those who directly have need to seek assistance from the shrines. With more than fifty shrines in various locations throughout Historic Kormantse, some considered to have been created from the earliest time of settlement, the significance of the religious factor in settlement during the Atlantic era (ca. 1500–1800s) is fairly certain, especially as the shrines have retained the names used in reference to the deities (Agorsah and Butler 2008). Although not unique to Historic Kormantse, the large number of shrines also suggests that the formation of the settlement would have been the result of incremental migration of many different groups or families, each arriving with its own deity. It may therefore be reasonable to speculate that the proliferation of shrines in Kormantse, relative to its size, and typical of the smaller coastal trading posts, may have been due to the fact that several settlers in Kormantse originated from diverse backgrounds from the region and brought with them their individual family's religious practices. It may also be due to the continuous acquisition of new deities to meet growing social, community, and family needs (Baum 1999; Stahl 2008).

The proliferation of shrines in such a small but important settlement over several hundred years could have been an important source of empowerment for the enslaved from that region of the Gold Coast. Clearly, Kormantse was more than a physical port of departure. Rather, it was also a major source of spiritual strength offering strong spiritual memories that appear to have traveled with the first generation of enslaved Africans from that coastal region and that were reinforced by new and fresh arrivals. As the first though aborted choice of the English traders in the Gold Coast for a trading post, Kormantse entered the English lexicon very early as a generic reference to the Gold Coast region. Its name was enlarged in the Americas because of the memory of ritual potency that the settlement embodied, as well as its symbol as an anti–slave trade and anti-English settlement. Thus, it is reasonable to assume that the family shrines would not be unique to this port village but would be found in the villages and households in regions far and near Kormantse from which captives originated. Rather than making the case that the enslaved merely received spiritual strength and hope by passing through Historic Kormantse, it is more plausible that their source of strength came from their own family and community experiences, not unlike the ones found in Kormantse.

When the English left their original site of Kormantse to build Fort Kormantse at Abandze, the Historic Kormantse which they left continued as a major contact point in the coastal trade activities that occurred between the three major coastal kingdoms of Eguafo, Asebu, and Efutu, as well as the chiefdoms in the immediate interior (Agorsah 1975). Following the growth of the coastal and caravan trade in the seventeenth century, broker organizations were established along the Gold Coast and at ports such as Kormantse, as well as areas to the north, each with merchant brokers who had high status in their areas of operation.

Although very important in the reconstruction of cultural identities in the African Diaspora, direct and distinct Kormantse connections are still unclear or difficult to define. Material culture obtained through future archaeological exploration should help to define and identify the embryonic stages of the formation of this African Diaspora identity. That memories of the traditional religions associated with real or imaginary Kormantse were of great significance is undeniable, as expressed in oral histories. Those who passed through Kormantse and those who originally came from Kormantse and adjoining areas together appear to have chosen to maintain their traditional beliefs as one unified people, as their colonial masters described them. Even in bondage, they succeeded in following most of the precepts of their religion and, with remarkable determination, maintained an intellectual life. The common circumstances of enslavement and the need for a united front and identity, especially in the common struggle for freedom and survival, reaffirmed that common name. This made Kormantse a dominant point of reference and a newly derived "ethnicity" in the Americas, but with cultural integrity from Africa. Some of the groups built traditions of resistance and revolt through hard work and communality, while others maintained traditional cohesiveness by focusing on one source of inspiration—the spiritual connection with Kormantse.

Kormantse's fame is tied to the fact that it was the first location where the English attempted to establish a trading post for the shipment of captive Africans out of the region. It also provided a staging ground for the labor supply to the fort that was subsequently established at Abandze by the English but later captured by the Dutch and renamed Fort Amsterdam. Its popularity was also linked to the fact that it became an important outlet for the enslaved that fed the Elmina and Cape Coast castles. Although it was not well known during the Atlantic era, except as one of the ports along the West African coast, it appears that the mental image and experiences at that last stop may have established an everlasting reference in the African Diaspora. While we are yet to establish the entire process of the Kormantse connection, there is no doubt that the Kormantse past was and continues to be a galvanizing force and catalyst for revolt against slavery and colonialism, and for the promotion of eventual freedom and survival of the African Diaspora.

Notes

The material for this paper derived from the Kormantse Archaeological Research Project funded by the National Science Foundation and the Fulbright USA Senior Scholar Grant. I wish to acknowledge, with thanks, the support of Thomas Butler Portland, archaeologist, and William Schaffer, University of Arizona, Tempe; the University of Cape Coast, Ghana, particularly Dr. Kwadwo Opoku-Agyemang, director of the Office of International Education; the Ghana Museums and Monuments Board, the Cape Coast Castle Historical Museum, particularly Mr. Nicolas Ivor, director, and Mr. Harry Monney, associate director, for permission and local support for the project. Support and collaboration with of all the chiefs and community leaders continue to be paramount in the success of the Kormantse Archaeological Research Project.

1. Field interviews conducted in 2009 as part of the NSF grant #0910457, Kormantse Archaeological Research Project. The oral history/tradition interviews were conducted by Dr. Douglas Frimpong-Nnuroh of the University of Cape Coast, Ghana.

CHAPTER 6

Rituals of Iron in the Black Atlantic World

Candice Goucher

For the African blacksmith and iron-smelter, technology was not distinct from ritual practice. Handling and hammering hot iron was not only dangerous but also afforded ironworkers access to economic and political power through their critical control of the supply of weapons and tools that ensured the continuity of life itself. Ritual in this context also became the voice of collective memory. Making iron was far more than abstract chemical or physical processes. No furnace was built nor smithy constructed without seeking and acknowledging the assistance of ancestors and spirits through specific ritual acts. Sometimes the ancestral references were as concrete as they were direct. Iron smelting required control over the natural elements of clay, ores, fuels, temperature, and airflow, as well as the metaphysical forces of unseen realms. The ritual embodiment of technological practice not only facilitated African technology transfer to the Americas; it also shaped the meaning and memory of iron in the Black Atlantic.

This chapter explores the mobility of African technological expertise during the Atlantic era. It argues that ironworking knowledge transferred material and spiritual advantages to those who possessed it. Importantly, the memory of technique and process resides in the structure, network, and practice of ritual. Ironworking technology provided the actual tools from which African-derived daily life was constructed, including the hoe, machete, cannonball, cooking pot, and knife. Equally significant was iron technology's conceptual framework for elements of African cultural resistance, extending its role in empowerment far beyond the workspace sphere of either blacksmith or smelter. This framework situated the contradictory aspects of violence and creativity in the meaning of iron, and the ability of its deities to transcend boundaries. Evidence for specific rituals associated with making and using iron includes archaeological remains, ethnographic observation, and archival records. Case studies from West Africa (Yoruba, Bassari, and Akan) and the Caribbean (Jamaica and Trinidad) reveal that Atlantic rituals of iron were essential components of technological practice and intellectual process, as well as the building blocks of community identity and emancipation in the Diaspora. Finally, in the transatlantic crossings are found the quintessential characteristics of Ogun. This pan-Atlantic deity of iron became a fundamental warrior for the persistence of memory and meaning.

Ironworking in the African Atlantic

Many scholars have noted how the social construction of landscape served as a primary mechanism for expressing and reinforcing social values while perpetuating cultural memory and claims to power (Mills and Walker 2008; Van Dyke and Alcock 2003). The African Iron Age, a culturally defined technological era that spanned more than two millennia in some parts of sub-Saharan Africa, also wrought important transformations of the physical landscape, furthering deforestation through the reliance on charcoal fuel; littering industrial regions with slag heaps, mining shafts, and discarded furnaces; and distributing significant pollution as the fallout of heavy metal ash and debris from large-scale combustion. Elite claims to the proprietary knowledge of iron smelting and to ritual command over transformative practices of iron production played a part in the legendary rise and legitimization of warrior roles linked to kingship. Small states and larger polities (Mande, Ife, Oyo, Benin, Hausa, Dahomey, Bassari, and Asante) exerted control over iron production and trade, using the complex interplay of ironworking's memory and meaning to successfully forge statecraft before and during the Atlantic era (e.g., de Barros 1986; Goucher 1993; Holl 2000; Stahl 1999).

Next to textiles, metal goods formed the second largest group of trade items received by African elites and merchants in exchange for enslaved captives (Eltis 2000: 300). Iron bars were imported from many parts of Europe and the Americas in various lengths and weights (with the average bar iron weighing about 30 pounds), but imported iron competed with high-quality local products during the Atlantic era (Sundstrom 1974). Imported iron greatly increased the availability of ferrous technology, tools, and weapons. Imported iron was used to manufacture a full range of utilitarian and ritual iron objects, including bullets, hoes, swords, knives, cutlasses, bells, staffs, and many other smaller items. Yet even the earliest European descriptions of coastal ironworking make it clear that iron technology was indigenous. Around 1561, the English merchant William Towerson described his admiration for "handsome darts and various instruments of iron" in Guinea (Williams 1974: 72). In the seventeenth century, Wilhelm Johann Müller observed on the Akan coast that "the blacksmiths in the Fetu country work in a different way from those in Europe. The anvil does not stand firmly on a piece of wood, but lies on the ground and is simply a large piece of iron" (DeCorse 2001: 125). Elsewhere, African smiths worked on either stone or iron anvils or both. They used stone and iron hammers for forging and maintained small finery forges operated by hand bellows made from goatskin.

IRON TECHNOLOGY AND RITUAL: BANJELI, TOGO

Few iron-producing African communities survived the transatlantic trade era into colonial times. Smelting in the Bassari region of Togo struggled against the shortage of fuel and competition from imported metals during and after the nineteenth century, when German entrepreneurs attempted to mine iron ores and transport them to the coast by railway. Finally, French colonial authorities, eager to exploit local ores, issued ordinances after the First World War prohibiting Africans from engaging in mining enterprises. By the 1920s, local smelting had all but ceased, and two generations later, only a few older members of villages remembered the technology they had witnessed as youth. Ritual was an essential component in retrieving the memory of iron. In the 1985 reconstruction of smelting at Banjeli, Togo, the genealogy of the furnace and its technicians was first established as a foundation for establishing the bodily practice of iron production (Goucher et al. 1986). First, the site selected for the construction of the iron furnace was inherited from earlier smelters. Second, libations were poured from a small calabash in the place that would become the furnace base in order to obtain the support of the ancestors. Third, pieces of the old furnace belonging to an ancestor of the current smelter were incorporated into the smelter's newly constructed one. In the rituals and prayers leading up to the smelting processes, the smelter acknowledged this past member of his lineage and all the other ancestors he may have forgotten, since ancestral agency would be a critical partner in the successful smelting ahead.

The new smelting furnace was believed to become a living and breathing essence through the rituals performed at the site. From this perspective, the furnace was related to the smelter as "family." The smelter would become the furnace's symbolic husband. Before the construction of the furnace commenced, the site and participants were cleansed and blessed, with workers and observers subject to sexual prohibitions during the smelt. Libations were poured as the master smelter beseeched the ancestors to "come and build this furnace. We [humans] are not the ones who build it." Medicines were used in the building of the tall furnace structure, and they would later be a critical factor in the smelting process. In the mud walls of the furnace, and visible only during construction, the smelter placed pieces of hippopotamus hide, unidentified leaves gathered from the mountainside, and stones to ensure the furnace's fertility and the success of the smelt.

As it was built, the furnace became a shrine through the intercession of spirits and ancestors. Upon completion, a celebratory meal of mudfish and pounded yam (*fufu*) was brought to the site. The mudfish is a symbol of the ability to transcend different realms since the fish is believed to swim in the water and walk on land, as it is observed moving from one puddle to the next at the end of the rainy season. They are widely used among the Kwa-speaking peoples of West Africa (including the Basari) as symbols of regeneration, rebirth, transformation, and protection. The smelter set the calabash of food in front of the furnace's mouth. "Give birth to good iron, give birth to good iron," he invoked. The workers painted an ash circle around the belly of the furnace and placed a leafy sprig in the center of a loop above the furnace's mouth. Then the furnace was fed with the sacred meal of *fufu* and mudfish.

Finally, a small child was led to the furnace and flogged. His cries were believed to mimic the cries of a newborn child and signal the breath of life when respiration begins. Thus, the furnace was fully a woman. She became a mother, who would give birth to good iron through the exercise of rituals. Through the smelter's intervention, the ore became gestating iron in the womb of the furnace. Iron blooms and eventually its products were the offspring of the ancestors and "spirits, whose assistance is deemed indispensable to all major enterprises." In this way, "the smelter thus usurps the creative power of the woman, becomes in a sense and for a moment, a woman himself—directly through his ability to build a functioning furnace and vicariously through the furnace's ability to deliver workable bloom" (Herbert and Goucher 1987: 12).

As the newborn "child" of the furnace, the smelted iron bloom itself now belonged to the family. At numerous archaeological sites in the Bassari region, individual furnace remains were remembered in relation to their smelters/owners at least five generations removed. The smelting technologies also relied on invocations, sacrifices, and offerings to establish the critical links between smelter and ancestors or spirits. The smelter's technical knowledge was secret and proprietary. It was protectively embedded in ritual requirements, which included sacrifices, medicines, invocations, songs, dances, and various prescriptive behaviors (Herbert 1993; Schmidt 1996). The blacksmith's smithy or forge, like the site of a smelting furnace, was also a place of ritual because its activities relied on the control of spiritual forces. Ritual actions provided the cultural mnemonics for the strategic organization of technological activities. Ritual was essential in the remembering of technical process, and helped to perpetuate the specific steps in a complex technological performance. Particular memories of the sight and smell of combustion were aided by the predictability of practiced movements. For example, comparison of 1913 film footage collected by Hans Schomburgk with 1985 Banjeli footage more than seventy years later reveals remarkable similarities of manufacturing and movement in the actions of ironworkers (Goucher et al. 1986). Even beyond the realm of the furnace or forge, the ritual memories were situated and embodied. Bodily practice produced iron offspring and relied on the scaffolding of ritual for their safe delivery.

IRON TECHNOLOGY AND RITUAL: THE CARIBBEAN

The mobility of iron and ironworkers was characteristic of West and Central Africa, since smelters and smiths followed resource availability (hardwoods for charcoal and ores) in their pursuit of metallurgical performance. This mobility extended to other parts of the Black Atlantic world, where enslaved Africans provided the intellectual and technical components of iron technology that helped to frame resistance against slavery and exploitation as well as define community identity. The technical skills of African metallurgists were widely recognized in the foundries, smithies, and furnace sites of the Americas, but the knowledge also was situated in the fundamental rituals of African-derived religions.

At the eighteenth-century foundry site at Reeder's Pen, in Morant Bay, Jamaica, the foundry workers included Maroons (escaped slaves and their descendants), enslaved, and free Africans. The African expertise in iron metallurgy was legendary and a valuable asset to the English coppersmith

John Reeder (1785), who claimed their African skills to be "perfect in every branch of iron manufacture." Although permission to smelt iron using charcoal fuel locally was granted by the Jamaican assembly, no iron-smelting sites have been identified yet. The archaeological recovery of a bottle, human teeth, and a cutlass buried under the foundry hearth are suggestive of African-derived rituals at the site. When recovered, their appearance prompted a demand by the local Africa-descended community for Kumina rituals. Kumina is an Africa-derived religion in Jamaica that involves sacrifices, prayers, music, and dancing. Although many Central African influences (dating from an influx of indentured laborers in the 1850s and 1860s) can be identified in the Kumina religion, local practitioners also remember vocabulary from other (presumably earlier) West African languages, such as the Twi word for the ceremonial iron cutlass (*afena*), excavated at the Reeder foundry site in 1990 (Goucher 1993). The utterance of the Akan word—*afena*—was believed to have brought the excavated object into being.[1] In response to local demand for compensatory rituals, the archaeologists participated the next night in the slaughter of a goat and a feast with tables set for ancestral spirits, who were served clear liquids (white rum and clear soda). Libations were poured and a cutlass was danced in a circle accompanied by the drumming of a local Kumina band. Such artifacts as those excavated are typically incorporated into Kumina religious practices in the area. The Kumina practitioners believe that the buried iron objects embodied *duppies,* ancestral shadow spirits, who had watched over the site since the foundry ceased operations in 1782 (on *duppies,* see Boaz, Reeves, Saunders, all in this volume).

Elsewhere on the island of Jamaica, local blacksmiths also practiced the forging techniques of their African ancestors. Blacksmiths at the port of Bluefields Bay were active from the eighteenth century until the 1950s.[2] At the nineteenth-century village site of Abeokuta, a free Yoruba settlement in Westmoreland, the last blacksmith died long ago, but the traditional drumming remains a vibrant art. The last surviving Ginger Ridge blacksmith called his anvil the "mother" of his forge, recalling the anthropomorphizing rituals of earlier generations of West African smiths and smelters. In essence, this identification was an acknowledgment of the vital forces possessed by women, who gave birth to Black Atlantic civilization.

As in Africa and other parts of the world, women were systematically excluded from blacksmithing activities and occupations in the Black Atlantic. The power of iron was a decidedly male domain, expressing the masculinity and strength of warriors and hunters. Although women were excluded from the production processes on both sides of the Atlantic, they were present in the mental understanding of the technology. Female forces were mothers to the great creativity of these acts of transformation. Working malleable metal was, as the Ginger Ridge blacksmith suggested, under the control of the "mother." This conceptualization mirrors a nearly identical terminology among a number of African groups, including the Tuareg, for whom the anvil is the mother and the hammer is the father of the forge (Echard 1992). Ian Fowler has observed that once-common blacksmithing events in Cameroon today are devoid of ritual *except* those associated with the anvil (Fowler 1990: 187–188).

While no evidence of taboos linked to female sexuality in Caribbean smelting survive, menstruating women were excluded from other transformative acts, such as cooking in Trinidad and on other Caribbean islands. The Candomble priestess Mainha de Bahia affirms the presence of Ogun in rituals of the kitchen.[3] According to Mainha, prayers to Ogun are said by the female cooks prior to preparing ritual food, and even the manner in which an okra is sliced is particular to Ogun, suggesting that the vocabulary of food was also a form of inscribed ritual (Thompson 1993: 154). In Yoruba-derived rituals, in particular, the association of female imagery was linked to active ritual performance and mental manifestations of iron's power, as well as to their subordination or reversal (see also the discussion of Ogun below). In the Afro-Cuban religion of Santeria, the iron deity's vessel is the iron cooking pot containing seven iron tools, an anvil, and a stone (Brown 2003, 173). The sexualized forge in Jamaica and the persistence of exclusionary taboos can only hint at African-derived continuities in the interpretation of iron and gender.

Blacksmiths across the Black Atlantic world may have viewed the lineage of learning their technology through transmitted traditions another way, emphasizing both hand and head. Modern blacksmith-anthropologist Charles Keller has demonstrated that the blacksmith's knowledge (design and plan) "can never be sufficiently detailed, sufficiently precise to anticipate everything that can happen during production" (Keller and Keller 1996: 118). Because the tool was an extension of the human body, its manufacture and use relied on social context and was shaped by physical practice. Thus, as much as the ironworker might follow prescribed patterns, there always needed to be room for unpredictability in the conceptual framework and practice of metallurgy. This quality of mutability was characteristic of African iron production and an essential aspect of identity associated with ritual action in both the mental and material realms of the technology of the Black Atlantic world.

African Atlantic Deity of Iron and Civic Life: Metallurgy as Ritual Performance and Memory Practice

The transfer of African metallurgical systems to the Diaspora could not have occurred without the support of Ogun, patron deity of iron, whose essence epitomized reversal and unpredictability. Ogun represented the overthrow of conditions of enslavement (Drewal 1997). One needed only to touch any two pieces of iron together and Ogun would be present. Ogun was in the chains of slavery and in the cutlass of resistance. Since most of the trans-atlantic trade–era ships were heavily fitted with iron even prior to the age of ironclad vessels, blacksmiths were almost always on board. So, too, were their beliefs. A major pan–West African deity widespread in Nigeria and Benin, Ogun has been described as an itinerant hero who legitimized the founding of communities (Barnes 1997). In fact, the Yoruba proverb *Ogun lo sale f'Orisa do,* meaning "Ogun is the one who clears the place where a shrine for the gods is established" (Drewal 1997: 236) suggests the belief that Ogun creates the opportunity for worship. Because Ogun clears the path of obstacles on land and sea, he is associated with new settlements and the viability of community. His qualities are contradictory, helpful one moment and vengeful the next. Ogun's ability to reintegrate after disorder, rebal-ance after instability, and produce something totally new out of the heat of violence made him the ideal patron deity for conceptualizing the African Diaspora.

Little is known of Ogun's origins, which likely predate the fifteenth-century arrival of Europeans on the West African coast. The idea of the deity possibly spread with the inevitable diffusion of iron technology itself. Observed on the West African coast by the Dutch before the beginning of the seventeenth century, dog sacrifices were commonly a marker of the worship of Ogun among the Yoruba and neighbors, including the Bassari, Akan, and Fon (Blier 1995a: 117). Ogun eventually became more than an amalgamation of meanings related to iron, war, and resistance. Ogun pro-vided the conceptual framework through which enslaved Africans could filter the collective memory of the Atlantic world (Ortiz 1989). Central to iron's meanings were notions of malleability and transformation, linked by the acceptance of life's spectrum of violence and creativity in the construction of community. For this reason, iron is found on many Atlantic world shrines, not only on the formal Yoruba shrines to Ogun. In Haiti, an altar to Ogun might consist of a forged implement or a heap of scrap iron (Courlander 1960). In other places, the power of iron may be remembered in the form of miniature iron implements (Thompson 1993: 184). As W. J. T. Mitchell has asserted, "objects . . . are never merely material things" (2005: 125). They are inscribed with meanings that reflect a mental world of unseen considerations. These conceptualizations are manifested in ritual contexts.

The Ogun deity in Haitian Vodun has many faces, the names of which reflect specific communities from Senegal to the Kongo. For example, among the coastal Kormantse, an anvil shrine marks a sacred community focal point for the descendants of peoples who gained a reputation for resistance in the Diaspora (see Agorsah, this volume). The path-clearing function of iron is present in the Fante annual community ceremonies of the Asafo companies, who use iron cutlasses to communally clear shared neighborhood paths. In several Yoruba-Edo kingdoms (e.g., Ife, Ilesa, Ondo, Benin) and Dahomey, iron figured in kingship rituals from at least the eighteenth century. An Akan ceremonial sword collected on the Gold Coast in the early nineteenth century and now in the collections of the Merseyside Maritime Museum in Liverpool, England, bears the sheet metal marks of A. E. Fritt & Sons and the notes that the sword was used to "worship Ogun." The smithies of Akan ironworkers have been observed to contain dog skulls hanging from rafters, and amulets associated with iron's powers have held their value into the twentieth century throughout Atlantic Africa. Whether framed by the beliefs of Vodun (in Haiti) or Candomble (in Brazil), Santeria (in Cuba), the Orișa religion (in Trinidad), or Kumina (in Jamaica), Ogun's forceful traits were equally at home with those who worked with iron tools in the Americas (metallurgists, sailors, farmers, seamstresses, cooks, and barbers) and those who sought to escape their iron shackles—captives and enslaved alike.

Hammering metal on metal or stone (usually granite or quartzite) on metal and stone (since the Bassari and other smiths sometimes used stone tools) in the act of forging creates a remarkable ringing sound and calls the spirits to attend to the transformation at hand. According to one German observer, the sounds of hammers were unforgettable and could be heard though the night in Bassari industrial settings in the late nineteenth century (Von Doering 1895). The liminality of realms (day/night, human/spirit, and visible/unseen) was reinforced by the interchangeability of stone and metal. Just as stone becomes metal through the intercession of blacksmith and spirit world, the stone hammers or anvils that traditionally were used to create iron tools and weapons became as metal bells, voicing the awesome nature of metallurgical powers at work. Elsewhere in Africa, observers have frequently noted that the rhythm of the bellows and the hammering on stone and metal provided a complex polyphonic "music" (Herbert 1993). The sounds of the anvil are also remembered on the other side of the Atlantic world. In Trinidad, they are associated with the local "anvil bird," whose ominous calls sound like clashing metal and evoke African-derived beliefs in the fearsome power of blacksmiths as Obeah men and healers, as well as craftsmen (Boaz, this volume). Their musical sounds are contained in private ritual and dance associated with Africa-derived Sango religion and, as we see below, with the most public of celebrations during the days of Carnival of the circum-Caribbean.

SHRINES AS PLACES OF HISTORICAL MEMORY

Shrines and altars were places of worship, but they also functioned as sites of memory and history ("lieux de memoire") in the Atlantic world. They served as visual and spatial reminders of the shared relationships among individuals and spiritual forces acknowledged by groups. The Orișa tradition of Trinidad is historically related to the Yoruba religion and named after its inclusion of Yoruba Orișa, or deities. At the Kenny Cyrus Alkebulan Ile Ijebu Shrine dedicated to Ogun in Enterprise (Chaguanas, Trinidad), an authentic and deeply historical expression of Orișa worship is still found. Kenny David Cyrus (1875–1972), who was the grandson of a Yoruba slave and ironworker brought to Grenada, founded the shrine about 1897. During and after slavery, Orișa worship was outlawed and hidden under Spiritual Baptist practices. Drumming was forbidden until the early twentieth century. Most recently, a ban on drumming was again in effect in the 1950s. Yet drumming, candles, and possession commonly acknowledged the powers of Ogun and other African deities. Today, Ogun's red flag flies above the shrine compound, and a modest altar for Ogun is situated inside the inner walls, although the last local blacksmith practiced some forty years ago in Enterprise. This shrine contains raw earthen and manufactured iron elements; it receives regular attention and is visible from the chapelle (a small chapel in which the ritual objects are stored) and meeting space. While most of the 150 or so Orișa shrines in Trinidad worship Ogun, the Kenny Cyrus Shrine is *dedicated* to Ogun. The deity Ogun manifests regularly at the shrine, where the Orișa are fed through sacrifices and offerings at weekly ceremonies. Initiations and healings take place on occasion, and for some travelers, small protective packets of seeds and medicines tied in red cloth bundles are prepared for their departures by automobile and then airplane back to the United States or Canada.[4] Also known in the Fon language as *kpen* (meaning to solder or join), the bundles or packets embody the essential powers of Ogun, joining believer and shrine regardless of distance.

Another smaller shrine studied in some depth since the 1950s is the Antoine family's Rada compound in Belmont, Port of Spain. Robert Antoine (born ca. 1855) founded the Rada group. He was an enslaved Dahomean diviner and the grandfather of Antoine Sedley (b. 1918), who organizes annual ceremonial feasts dedicated to Rada. In December 2003, at Ogun's shrine, where a stepped, earthen mound has been built, cocks were killed and libations of rum were made to propitiate Ogun. Other offerings included dishes of parched corn, black-eye peas cooked with olive oil and red *adobo,* and fritters (*accras*), along with drinking vessels. An hour after the beating of iron, drumming, and call-and-response singing, Ogun appeared; having mounted a woman, Ogun was armed with a symbolic wooden sword and red colored scarf. He danced with the cutlass and an infant, the red scarf connoting the blood of continuity and the red energy of transfer that is a product of the blacksmith's red-hot forging fires. Not only iron but also the memory of iron could and did empower believers.

MEMORY IN MOTION: METALS IN CARIBBEAN FESTIVALS AND PROCESSIONS

The early Orișa presence in Port of Spain drumming may also explain the remnant Yoruba dance steps associated with Ogun that are still visible in the Fancy Sailor dances of Trinidad Carnival. While military masques date from at least the eighteenth century, the modern sailor bands originated in the Belmont neighborhood and in the hills above Port of Spain, where West India troops cleared the hillsides with machetes in the mid-nineteenth century. The Carnival in 1848 included a masquerader chained with a padlock to his leg and decidedly thought to be a representation of slavery. By the mid-twentieth century, masqueraders in fancy sailor costumes and those dressed in all white known as king sailors were followed by stokers or firemen dressed in sleeveless work shirts, blue denim pants, thick gloves, sailor hats, and goggles. The firemen carried long iron rods, sometimes the actual equipment from onboard ships. According to Dan Crowley, "The firemen also had a characteristic dance similar to the 'limbo,' with the body bent sharply backwards, knees projecting, and lower legs almost on the pavement. In this position, the firemen pushed their rods forward in mimicry of stoking a[n iron ship's] boiler, with a great deal of shoulder shaking and arm movement as they crept forward through the street" (1956: 61; figure 6.1). But, this was no limbo—the dance bore the recognizable dance steps of Ogun, still identifiable to the Orịṣa practitioners at Kenny Cyrus. According to Fido Blake, a local historian of the steel drum, "the [Africans] could do anything with inspiration. In the 1880s after the riots, drums were banned, but they got the same rhythms with different weights and sizes of objects. The deity Ogun was in power and manifested when the Orịṣa people were involved."[5]

Although goatskin drums once used in Orịṣa ceremonies were outlawed in 1884, the beat went on and the street bands survived through the use of substituted instruments such as the tamboo bamboo—hollow bamboo poles used as percussion instruments (idiophones). A wide range of metal objects such as glass bottles and spoons also accompanied these new drums. From about the turn of the twentieth century, sailor bands took advantage of the increasing number of metal containers being carried on ships. By the 1930s, the sailors played on paint cans, old biscuit drums, oil drums, dust-bins (metal garbage cans), and old pieces of automobile chassis when they headed for Marine Square on *Jour Ouvert* (literally "the opening day's") morning. From Diego Martin to Belmont, biscuit drums became the musical instrument of choice.[6] Passing crowds following the musicians were considered loud and raucous by the onlookers. The early innovators of the steel drum, a musical invention of the twentieth century, were also participants in sailor bands, and frequently they were Orịṣa men known for "beatin' iron in the pre-pan days" (Blake 1995).[7]

The pioneering steel drum musicians included Andrew Beddoe in the Laventille Hills and others from John John (also called Yaraba Village), who beat Orịṣa drums and biscuit pans in the bands. By the mid-1930s, further experimentation in steel was taking place. These early bands sang lusty songs, some with references to the powers of Ogun, as they moved along the streets to Ogun's rhythms. Local Trinidadian historian Fido Blake notes, "When Ogun manifested you had to bring iron to the street. Today, only a few of the Pan Tuners are in tune with Ogun. . . . The Desperadoes in New York City [still] have a religious connection with Ogun."[8] These connections may have been present in the nineteenth century or even earlier, but they went unnoticed by the island plantocracy (Liverpool 2001).

FIGURE 6.1. Fireman/stoker, Fancy Sailor Band, Trinidad Carnival, 1999.

Trinidad processions were only one manifestation of Ogun in the Black Atlantic. The African-associated masquerades were known as Jonkonnu (also variously as Junkanoo, John Canoe, or John Connu). They were widely elaborated processions that linked iron and performance. At the end of the eighteenth century, observers in Jamaica noted the large number of enslaved, "beating old canisters, or pieces of metal, singing 'ay, ay, John Canoe' in annual celebrations" (Abrahams and Szwed 1983: 233). The planter Edward Long observed that one of the John Connu masqueraders in Jamaica carried a wooden sword and bellowed "John Connu" ([1774] 1970: 2:424). Could these words have been recorded as a distortion of "Ogun o," literally "Hail Ogun," a praise song to Ogun, and remembered as far away as Trinidad (Warner-Lewis 2009)? In the early nineteenth century, groups of iron-wielding "butchers" with "steels and knife cases by their sides" accompanied John Canoe, whose costume had "tin or white iron frills, with loose pieces attached, which tinkled when he moved, and set off the dingy paws that were stuck through these strange manacles," and who was termed the "boatswain" of the party along the Kingston wharf (Scott 1829: 33). The movements from left to right mimic the balancing of the sailors onboard a lurching ship, but they also memorialize the vengeful Ogun, who kills on the left and on the right.

The maritime connection was resurrected in the Bahamas in the twentieth century, when local smith Donzel Huyler (1917–2005), the son of a blacksmith, forged not only iron bells for Bahamian Junkanoo processions but also the iron fittings for ships, including "dead-eyes," the iron that held riggings; "gergens," which held the rudder; "gambling irons," which held the bow splits; large iron sponge hooks; harpoons; spears; tongs; and chain links. Like the iron instruments played by sailors in Trinidad Carnival, the Bahamian rhythms called for social and community action, when the musicians "rushed" the street with their bells.[9] The late Joseph Townsend, blacksmith artisan of St. John's, Antigua, similarly found his training and inspiration in the naval dockyards of the island.

How these links between Ogun and the sailors were forged is not entirely clear, although the association between the warrior deity and the fighters/stokers of the sea seems to have resulted from their work with iron tools, charcoal fuel, and the red-hot, fiery furnaces in the engine rooms of ships that traveled on the Atlantic Ocean. Collective remembering and forgetting within the context of Carnival processions and ritual performances served the process of public history formation (Connerton 1989). Ambiguity was created in that what was remembered, what was spoken, and what they meant were divergent; some knowledge was sacred, and when fuller meanings were kept secret or proprietary, as were the essential parts of ironworking technology and their sacred meaning, that knowledge could become a powerful tool or weapon for political mobilization.

In the British colony of Guiana, ironworkers congregated in Winkle Village, Berbice, and their solidarity during a 1796 uprising helped usher in freedom prior to emancipation (Goucher 1993). T. J. Desch-Obi has demonstrated that the African traditions of stick-fighting/dancing in the Americas were adaptations from machete-wielding ceremonial war-dancing by Ogun followers in the Yoruba/Fon/Ewe/Aja religious traditions of Saint Domingue. The double-meaning of stick-fighting as a symbol for Ogun Feray and the sword-wielding Saint James may have had wide appeal for freedom fighters from Kongolese traditions, which developed from the intersections of Catholicism and Kongolese religion (Desch-Obi 2008). Maroons in Palmares, Brazil, and in Jamaica comprised other groups of warriors for whom iron and attendant rituals were used in oaths and daily survival (Goucher and Agorsah 2011).

Above all, the practical experience of actual craftsmen and practitioners tested the quality of materials in the Atlantic world. This helped to make the metallurgist, whether in Africa, Europe, or the Americas, the primary driver of innovation and industry. Most sailors, soldiers, and farmers during the Atlantic era could easily assess the quality of wrought iron offered for trade by physical examination of the metal's appearance and performance (Gordon 1996). Symbolic and physical processes of transformation remained embedded in the reverence afforded African blacksmiths, iron smelters, and foundry men. For much of the technology that traveled the Atlantic, the hidden histories of transformation became a source of empowerment trapped in performance, ritual, and artifact.

Forging iron makes an apt metaphor for understanding the African-Caribbean construction of community and civic life in the crucible of slavery, capitalism, and now globalization. The unyielding iron bar, rigid and inflexible, appears at first glance to be unchangeable. Yet in the hands of the ironworker, it is transformed. Its transformation requires belief and technique, knowledge and practice rooted in a cultural framework. This chapter has explored the work of the African blacksmith as a fusion of trained bodily movements and the expression of cultural cognition or ritual. The head and hand hybridity was fundamental to the African Atlantic world, which produced knowledge and goods as surely as it consumed vast resources and enslaved labor. This, then, was the central core of ambivalence in the conceptualization and ritualization of iron. The individual blacksmith was expert at hearing, seeing, touching, and tasting—his sensual knowledge was essentially bodily knowledge expressed individually in the fired moment of creativity and problem-solving and practiced imitation. The collaborative nature of artisanal production, however, has meant that the transfer of technology must be discerned also in the patterns of material use and the techniques of fabrication, as well as in the conceptualization of that practice. The situated nature of learning, remembering, and understanding appears most readily in networks of manufacturing, for which African metallurgists were essential nodes, and ships and dockyards critical sites in the thinking and acting of metallic performance (Lave and Wenger 1991). In the Black Atlantic world, the ways of making and the ways of knowing intersected in the work of African metallurgists—both embedded in the larger social framework.

Finally, memory of iron—as knowledge—also resides in objects. Both commodities and practices were displayed, translated, and performed. The ownership and meaning of goods and skills depended on the spaces where they were made and used. Further excavation and study of iron objects, when understood as active participants in the conceptualization of ritual and community building, can be used to discern the mechanisms by which Africans remembered iron and recreated the contexts for individual empowerment and collective survival in the Black Atlantic. Based on the remnants of archival, ethnographic, and archaeological evidence, the associated meanings of iron include the expression of cultural cognition or "ritual" that culminates in and is trapped by the object and "performed" by the larger community.

The act of working metal called forth the spiritual powers into the metallurgist's realm and made those powers available for the construction of civic identity. As technology was transferred with human and metallic cargoes across the Atlantic, slavery embraced remembered ritual. References to the past were embedded in metalworking practices on both sides of the Black Atlantic. Sometimes the references were direct; sometimes they were subtle. The enslaved African's continued embrace of ritual furthered the dual process of creating community and maintaining the group's distinct historical memory. In the Caribbean, iron as conceptual force and as technology gave birth to new lineages of memory and practice.

In summary, the act of making and forging iron in the Black Atlantic world conveys the historical ambiguity of contradictory forces at play. The great Atlantic system produced knowledge and goods, even as it consumed vast resources and enslaved people. African ironworkers, who welded and forged the shackles of captives, also wrought the implements of resistance and hammered the tools for their survival. No other material captures this terrible ambivalence as does iron, leading its metallurgy to be termed by the historian Cyril Stanley Smith a fully human experience (1975). The ritual embodiment of iron was an essential component of African technology transfer. The technological performance of iron involved empowering relationships between the collective past and individual agency. Its memory in the Atlantic resided on land and at sea, captured in static and unyielding iron objects, as well as in the performed dances that placed the emancipatory impulses of African-derived resistance into motion.

Notes

1. William Gordon, Morant Bay, Jamaica, pers. comm., 1990.
2. Stephan Blackwood, Bluefields, Jamaica, pers. comm., 6 January 2009.
3. Mainha da Bahia (Maria de Lourdes Silvestre dos Santos), Los Angeles, pers. comm., 2 October 2009.
4. Priestess Iya Makeda Joan Cyrus, Alkebulan Ijuba Shrine, Enterprise, Trinidad, pers. comm. 19–29 February 1995 and 18–19 February 1998.
5. Fido Blake, Port of Spain, pers. comm., 25 February 1998.
6. Carlos Kendall and Nell Kendall, pers. comm., 25 February 1991.
7. Fido Blake, Port of Spain, Trinidad, pers. comm., 25 February 1998.
8. Fido Blake, Port of Spain, Trinidad, pers. comm., 25 February 1998.
9. Donzel Huyler, Nassau, Bahamas, pers. comm., 25 July 1997.

CHAPTER 7

Transatlantic Meanings

AFRICAN RITUALS AND MATERIAL CULTURE IN THE EARLY MODERN SPANISH CARIBBEAN

Pablo F. Gómez

Mateo Arará's career as one of the most renowned healers of the early modern New Kingdom of Granada began with propitious events four thousand miles east of Cartagena de Indias. Sometime during the 1620s, Arará's maternal uncle Soo chose him as the heir of the family's most sacred tradition. Arará would become, as his uncle and many of his matrilineal ancestors had planned, the priest and healer at the king's house. Three decades later, African *ladino* (acculturated and Spanish-speaking) translators from the Jesuit College in Cartagena translated Arará's testimony. In front of Cartagena's Inquisition tribunal, where he found himself after having been accused of being a *sortilego* (a conjurer), Arará declared that his healing gifts had been transmitted to him through the womb of his mother (Archivo Histórico Nacional de España, Madrid, hereafter AHN, Inquisición 1021, fol. 340r–341r).

African-born ritual specialists like Arará served as effective mediators of the cultural exchange between Africa and the Americas during the early modern period. His is just one of several histories of African ritual practitioners located in Spanish and Colombian archives. These rich depositories hold unique Inquisition, government, ecclesiastic, personal, and medical records related to populations of African descent coming from early modern New Kingdom of Granada (modern-day Colombia; see map 7.1) and several other Caribbean spaces. This chapter highlights the richness of available evidence related to the material culture of populations of African descent in early modern Spanish Caribbean records, and its value for the study of ritual practices in the seventeenth century black Atlantic.

MAP 7.1. Caribbean and northern South America. *Courtesy of the author.*

Records coming from the highly legalistic and punctilious Spanish courts are rich sources for an examination of the uses of material culture and the ceremonies of which they formed an essential part. Ritual specialists of African descent appear in Inquisition records as defendants and sometimes witnesses. During the seventeenth century, the Spanish Inquisition was mainly concerned with the prosecution of Jews and Protestants, for religious and political reasons. Occasionally, and for different reasons, people of African origin found themselves at the center of Inquisitorial inquiries. Petty fights, professional jealousy, marital affairs, or plain zealotry of inquisitors or neighbors brought ritual specialists to the front of the Inquisition Palace during the seventeenth century.

For the most part, however, the Inquisition paid little attention to the abundance of unorthodox African religious and cultural practices taking place in Cartagena. For early modern Cartageneros, these were not the "uncivilized" superstitions that appear in so many Western narratives (see Boaz, this volume). Instead, African rituals and healing practices were accepted and understood on equivalent terms to European healing traditions by a majority of seventeenth-century Cartagena's population (Gómez 2013).

As Joyce Chaplin has correctly pointed out for early modern English accounts of Native Americans, European "ventriloquizing" accounts of the rites of people of African descent in the Caribbean have much to offer (2001: 27–28). Although Inquisition scribes sometimes shaped testimonies and accommodated them to the demonological narrative of European Inquisition courts or to the particularities of a specific case, Spanish processes still carry exceptionally rich accounts of African voices. West and West Central Africans provided Inquisition officials with accurate, and surprisingly candid, descriptions of rites and customs that, in most cases, did not fit within the Iberian's demonological repertoire yet were recorded faithfully. As was the case with Mateo Arará, translators were available in places like Cartagena for trials of Africans who did not speak Castilian and did not know, or follow, Iberian tenets. Hence, Spanish and Iberian sources provide detailed accounts and serve as important interpretative tools for African material culture in the early modern period. These sources have, however, been underutilized. The descriptions of Caribbean ritual specialists' ceremonies I examine in this chapter, for instance, represent some of the earliest written references to rites and material elements that were paramount to Africans and the creation of *Africanness* in the Atlantic world.

Ritual practitioners were essential cultural links between Africa and the Americas. Because of their high societal rank, most ritual specialists captured and sold into slavery had likely been taken by enemy troops during raids in their homelands. In Cartagena, African ritual specialists held societal positions similar to those of their counterparts in Africa. For West and West Central Africans, religious and political power went hand in hand. Ritual practitioners became central and vocal figures in shaping societies in the Americas. In colonial Spanish America, African ritual specialists formed essential parts of a rich and variegated health-care delivery system. Some of these healing practices are referred to in opaque and prejudicial ways, such as was the case with Mateo Arará. Africans were also accused of practicing *brujeria* (witchcraft) and *hechiceria* (sorcery), but we know that these African healers also served as *parteras* (midwifes) and that they worked in hospitals, cleaning, cooking, and using their knowledge to take care of diseased people. Similarly, they provided health care in the *lazaretto* (leprosarium) and assisted in preparing medicines in pharmacies.

Before delving into the analysis of material culture in Cartagena, it is important to remark on the artificiality of the labels imposed by Europeans on Africans in Iberian colonial documents. In Spanish and Portuguese America, traders and owners of captive Africans named enslaved Africans with European first names and their presumed regions of origin as their last names. These surnames, as we know too well, often do not accurately reflect the originating ethnic provenance of the captives. Whereas traders of captive Africans frequently named these newly enslaved people after the ports from which they were purchased, the captives sold in these ports could have come from captive raids or wars from a radius of hundreds of miles inland, as well as from along the coast. The accuracy and contentions of these labels and what they meant for enslaved Africans are still the subject of scholarly debate (see Agorsah, this volume; Chambers 1997; Gomez 1998; Hall 2005; Northrup 2000; Sweet 2009a). Yet, these ethnonyms are the best available written evidence from which to infer the regional origins of enslaved Africans in the Diaspora, including those reaching Cartagena's shores.

Cartagena de Indias

Established in 1533 on the Caribbean coast of the New Kingdom of Granada, Cartagena de Indias was a key military and commercial Spanish outpost in the region, and grew to become one of the most important commercial centers in the Americas (see map 7.1). The city was also the official port of entry for the transatlantic slave trade coming into South America during most of the seventeenth century, and consequently a propitious place for development of a prosperous merchant class. Europeans of all origins and denominations made up an important part of its population. By the seventeenth century, Cartagena de Indias had become a metropolis in its own right; it was larger than any place north of Mexico City, and most urban locales in Europe and the rest of the Americas. Cartagena had around twenty thousand inhabitants in 1607 (De Sandoval [1627] 1956: 347; Vázquez de Espinosa 1969: 219–222). This ever-increasing population during the late sixteenth and early seventeenth centuries was what prompted the Spanish Crown to establish an office of the Inquisition in the city in 1610, in an attempt to exert control over fast-growing Protestant and Jewish immigrant populations.

Being the main slave entrepôt in Spanish America, Cartagena had a large population of African descent. The same was true for the larger regional network of towns, mines, and plantations in northern New Kingdom of Granada, for which Cartagena served as the political and economic center. Contemporary sources estimated that the number of Africans and African descendants living at different points in seventeenth-century Cartagena were in the range of seven to twenty thousand. According to the province's governor, Garci Giron de Loaya, the city and its province contained more than twenty thousand people of African origins, enslaved and free, in 1622 (Archivo General de Indias, Seville, Spain, Santa Fé 38, fol. 176). During the seventeenth century, most Africans arriving in Cartagena came from West Central Africa. Slave traders, however, also brought thousands of captive Africans from Upper Guinea, the Gold Coast, the Bight of Benin, the Bight of Biafra, and even East Africa (Wheat 2011). Among them were enslaved people like Mateo Arará, who came from Adja in the Bight of Benin, which the Spanish sometimes referred to as Ardra or Arará.

Africans and their descendants who ended up in cities like Cartagena shared with Europeans a variety of social, cultural, and religious scenarios in ways not possible in contemporary British, French, or Dutch realms in the Americas. Unlike most other places in the New World, enslaved Africans in Iberian colonies could gain manumission and become *negros horros* (free blacks). The ability to access freedom and some measure of autonomy, as well as the expression and visibility of African culture in cities like Cartagena, stand in stark contrast to the characteristics of chattel slavery practiced elsewhere in the Americas (Elliott 2006). One of the arenas where this autonomy and expression of African culture can be readily seen is the diversity and visibility of African religious and ritual practices.

African Ritual Specialists in Cartagena de Indias

Mateo Arará's Inquisition trial record includes a description of his initiation rite to become a healing specialist. The ceremony took place on the banks of a river in Adja. During this rite of passage, Arará had to swear that he "would not do evil to the people." After taking the oath, "something like a mule" came out from the bottom of the river. Mateo said that the mule-like creature determined the righteousness of the oath taker. In his words, the mule "grabs the one making the oath and takes him to the middle of the river, which is very big, and if [the oath taker] swears false things he stays there, and if he swears the truth [the creature] returns [the oath taker] to the shore" (AHN, Inquisición 1021, fol. 341r).

After his initiation ceremony, Arará claimed that he traveled the kingdom with his uncle, who had many "things that he used to cure" and taught him the rituals and traditions as well as ritual implements and ingredients (AHN, Inquisición 1023, fol. 341r). Sometime during the 1640s, Arará was sold in the port of Ardra, most probably after warriors from a neighboring polity captured him. He was then sold to European slave traders, most likely Portuguese, who brought him to Cartagena de Indias (ibid., fol. 341v). Healers and other spiritual specialists like Arará underwent long training periods, and occupied a high, and commonly hereditary, echelon in West and West Central African societal ranks. According to Jean Barbot, a seventeenth-century French commercial agent, ritual specialists in the Gold Coast "are very serious people and lead a prudent life. They vow never to drink palm wine. This office is hereditary within families; there are some families which have held it since time immemorial, which gives them greater esteem among the blacks" (Hair et al. 1992: 580). Testimonies from individuals in Cartagena seem to confirm Barbot's observations. For example, Antonio Congo, a free African ritual specialist from West Central Africa, said in 1690 that "in his land his mother had taught him how to make the herbs and the *curaciones* [healings]" (AHN, Inquisición 1023, fol. 481r). Similarly, Catalina de Barros, a free *zaori* (or *zahorí,* a priest or ritual specialist) *mulata* from Jamaica, also declared around 1649 that she was "*mulata* de parte de sumadre" (*mulata* on the part of her African mother) and that her gifts had a divine origin and were transmitted to her through "her [the mother's] womb" (AHN, Inquisición 1021, fol. 343v). In West and Central Africa, this identification of hereditary spiritual knowledge and practices effectively contained political and social power usually associated with elite families.

Dutch compiler Olfert Dapper (1686: 226) wrote that in Adja, "all important people had their own *fetiseros* [ritual specialists] who are ready for their families when somebody in the house is ill. [They] call the *fetisero* who sacrifices cattle, sheep, chicken [and then] sprinkles with blood [the family's] *Fetisi.*" Barbot also said that, "like all the others in Guinea, the people living in the Kingdom of the Great Popo, in the Bight of Benin, defer blindly to the opinions of the priests . . . who are all dressed in long white robes, with a crooked stick in their right hand" (Hair et al. 1992: 630). Once in the New World, African ritual specialists articulated and reimagined societal and family structures. West and West Central Africans' material culture was an essential part of this process and of the building of communal spaces for the appropriation and shaping of spaces in Spanish-American society.

Such modeling happened not in isolation of mainstream Iberian culture but in the midst of the rich intermingling of African, European, and Native American cultures happening in Caribbean cities. Caribbean ritual specialists of African descent reimagined healing objects using the environmental resources of their new homes, adapting these objects to meet the social and cultural needs of the places to which they had been forcibly transported (Gómez 2013).

The Material Culture of African Ritual Specialists in Cartagena de Indias

Upon his arrival in the Americas as an enslaved person, *mohan* (master of sorcerers) Mateo Arará began to study native plants and make an *esterita* (a little mat). Like many other enslaved Africans, Arará would have spent a considerable amount of time roaming the streets and outskirts of the city. The enslaved in urban spaces like Cartagena enjoyed considerable autonomy. Some of them even lived in their own dwellings in the African neighborhood of Getsemani with free Africans. Enslaved Africans often worked on their own in different occupations. They made meager daily salaries, and at the end of the day, or week, paid their masters an accorded amount.

Arará, for instance, worked as a health specialist and described in detail the uses of two of his healing artifacts, a gourd and mat. The gourd, he said, "was from a pumpkin, and that it had inside powders from a plant called *ariajua,* which is cultivated at the Santa Catalina gate of this city" (AHN, Inquisición 1021, fol. 304v). The mat, which he had made "after arriving in this kingdom, from his wits," was crafted "out of palm leaves" that he "tied" to itself on each end. In its upper part, the little mat "was divided in two parts like arms." When the Inquisition's prosecutor asked Arará about how he used his *esterita,* he answered that to use it, "he had taken a chicken and opened its beak, and cut its throat with a knife and with the blood that came out of the chicken he sprinkled the *esterita.* After [the *esterita*] was soaked with blood he put on [the mat] powders of all types of *counter-herbs* [remedies]." These "counter-herbs" would be specific type of plants with properties to neutralize particular diseases. Most intriguingly, during his interrogation, Arará claimed that he had learned which herbs were beneficial in healing various health conditions by asking the *esterita.* If the herb was useful, the mat opened itself, and if it was ineffectual, it closed itself and moved from one side to the other (ibid., fol. 340r–340v). The mat and the gourd were central parts of Arará's rituals. This is evident from his recollection of rites he performed to cure a group of enslaved Africans in a place called Morocí.

After arriving in Morocí, seventy miles south of Cartagena and close to the city of Mompox, Arará, who had been summoned by the owner of a mine, congregated all the enslaved Africans around him. While "praying" in his language, Arará circled the enslaved Africans with his mat and gourd. At a certain point during the ritual, the little mat turned toward an enslaved African man named Ventura Anchico. After repeating the procedure three times, with similar results, Arará declared that Anchico was the witch causing the mine's plague. During the same trip, Arará also healed several other enslaved Africans and two Catholic priests using the bark of a tree called orejón, on which he tied a cross, then took the bark and mixed it with water and honey (ibid., fol. 340r–340v).

The record does not give notice of what happened to Anchico. As in West and West Central Africa, many "witches" like Anchico became social outcasts in the Americas. This, on the other hand, did not mean that their masters would punish them. While in some cases they would resort to physical chastisement, slave owners, many of whom unabashedly believed in the power of the rites performed by African practitioners, would rather sell their enslaved Africans when they suspected that *maleficios* (curses) were behind unexplainable deaths of animals and men, plagues, or failed harvests (Sweet 2011: 68–71). In other cases, owners would report African ritual specialists to the Inquisition, as was the situation when Francisco de Santiago denounced Guiomar Bran and Leonor Zaper, both from Upper Guinea, after Santiago became paralyzed from the waist down (AHN, Inquisición 1020, fol. 215r–215v).

The healing rites used by Arará in Morocí share important characteristics with ceremonies recorded by Europeans on the other side of the Atlantic. German Wilhelm Johann Müller, for example, described how in Fetu, a kingdom neighbor to Adja, ritual practitioners had to repeat divination procedures three times for them to be accurate, like Arará did ([1676] 1968: 62). In the Fon-Ewe languages, the number "three" is pronounced similarly to the Yoruba word *eta*. Akinwumi Ogundiran suggests that the phonetic root of *ta*, as in *eta*, also signifies "to shoot of," that is, to enact a counteraction that would expel or deflect a curse (2007: 86). Also, Christopher Fennell (this volume) discusses the role of phonemic and phonetic associations in ritual practices, material life, symbolism, and efficacy. In addition, and similarly to Arará, ritual practitioners from Fetu used ritual gourds filled with, among other things, the bark of trees and chickens' bones sprinkled with blood (Müller [1676] 1968: 53–54).

During his trial, Mateo Arará narrated other rites he performed. He testified that:

> While being in the Morocí mine, a little black boy was sick, and that, to cure him, he made a cross with some sticks which he put on the door of the hut [where he lived with his mother] . . . and then he made them bring a chicken, and [after] having "cleaned" the boy with the bird, and putting it [on the boys head] . . . he said that if the chicken died the boy would live, and that if [the chicken] lived, the boy would die. (AHN, Inquisición 1021, fol. 341r)

Other Cartagenero practitioners used chickens in healing rituals as well. For example, a Spanish woman giving evidence in 1670 during the trial of Francisco de Llanos, an enslaved African who originated from the "llanos de Guinea" in Upper Guinea, said that,

> Being sick of a mass on one side of her belly, she looked for the defendant in the farm where he lived. . . . [Francisco] told her that it was [a curse] sent by a man that had courted her, and that she had rejected. [The woman] then said that [Francisco] had cured her from the mass by using the *contra* [the counteracting substance] and sucking the wounds [he had made on her]. [She also said] that while doing this he threw through his mouth some bundles that seemed to be toads. He also took a chicken and told the witness to [cook the chicken] in a pot together with, in lieu of two *reales* [coins], two corn kernels. . . . She [then] cooked the chicken and was healed. (AHN, Inquisición 1023, fol. 235r)

Like De Llanos, Miguel Arará, newly arrived from the Bight of Benin, was said to "apply remedies for health problems with good results" (AHN, Inquisición 1023, fol. 228v). Testifying in his 1666 trial, Miguel Arará, who worked as a woodcutter in Cartagena, explained that in his land (likely in the Bight of Benin, as his name implies), when the healer wanted to differentiate between sorcery and poisoning, they "gave water to a black chicken and that when [the chicken] died it meant that the person had drunk poison" (ibid., fol. 228r). Another Arará, Francisco, also used chickens when curing. In 1685, two witnesses declared that he had "scrubbed the body [of a sick woman] with some living hens. [They also said that] he had then spat on one of the chicken in the beak and told the sick woman to do the same. After this, he did crosses with the chicken over the [sick woman's] belly three times" (ibid., fol. 313v). Chickens are well-known elements of West and West Central African ritual practices, and, as described elsewhere, their color had specific ritualistic connotations. They also, however, figure prominently in popular medical practices in early modern Europe, and their use in New World spaces suggests not only reproduction of African traditions but adaptation to local culture.

Besides birds, West and West Central African ritual practitioners also commonly used horns for divinatory and healing procedures during the seventeenth century (Hair et al. 1992: 86). In fact, they appear in contemporary European depictions of African ritual specialists (figure 7.1). Like his counterparts in Africa, Domingo López, like Mateo Arará, used a small horn in his healing practices. López, a free African resident in Cartagena, was forty years old when he appeared in front of the Inquisition tribunal in 1651. An imposing figure, he was tall, bearded, and filled a big body frame. When curing, López asked a *cuernezuelo* (small horn) "about what illness the sick person had, whether it was caused by herbs. To say no, the *cuernezuelo* moved from one side to the other, to say yes, it went up and down." The horn was about "a quarter of length [25 cm] in which [at the end] it had a hole and inside it a cord, and that he held one of the ends of such cord with his feet, and the other end with his hand, and that in this way he asked [the *cuernezuelo*] about what affliction the person had, and if it was caused or not by herbs." If the cause was by herbs, it indicated that the illness was caused by intentional human intervention to harm. When the interrogators asked him how the *cuernezuelo* moved, López answered that the *cuernezuelo* "moved by itself," and that, like Arará, the only thing he did was to talk to it in its "native tongue." López was also considered to be an expert in curing snakebites and poisoning, a gift he said was of "divine provenance" (AHN, Inquisición 1021, fol. 385r–385v). Ritual practitioners like López filled their medicinal horns with special herbs to conjure and empower them with life force and foundational energy, what the Yoruba call *ase* (Abiodun 1994), before using them to probe the etiology of illnesses, offer protection, or perform other types of rituals. For example, Juan de Salzedo, also known as "Juan the Englishman," used a horn that was "full of the root *Capitana*" as a cure against snake bites (AHN, Inquisición 1023, fol. 404r).

African healing practices are described in surprising detail in seventeenth-century Spanish documentary sources. This is evident in the case of slave healer Pedro Congo, who was captured when he was twenty years old in Congo (West Central Africa) and had been in "several places in *las*

FIGURE 7.1. Depiction of seventeenth-century West Central African ritual specialists from the printed version of Capuchin missionary Giovanni A. Cavazzi's diary (1690). Original at the John Carter Brown Library.

Indias" before ending up in Cartagena's province. Congo came from "the Nanboa nation" and worked as a farmer in Mompox, a town some 160 km south of Cartagena. He walked the streets of that town brandishing the fang of a leopard around his neck. Around 1678, one witness declared that Pedro had applied potions to several denizens of Mompox to prevent scorpion bite. He would rub the hand of the person with wine while he pronounced words that could not be understood (ibid., fol. 418v). More frighteningly, he was said to be able to transform himself into a tiger. He told the inquisitors that the sticks he had in his bag were used as cures against the bite of snakes and "ventosidad" (bloating). He was also believed to have cured ulcers with roots and leaves, and "belly obstruction" with water of roots and honey. For other abdominal ailments, he used the skin and stomach of a type of bird he called *cocolí* (ibid., fol. 419v–420r). For heart diseases, he said one could use "the nail of the right leg of a female hog [extracted] before she dies and clean it of earth. Then [the healer] should dry it, remove the bone, and put the nail in a narrow pot of water. [Finally] the pot should be left covered and the sick person should drink the potion for two or three weeks" (ibid., fol. 256r).

There has been very little archaeological work done in Cartagena and, to the best of my knowledge, none on African material culture from the sixteenth to eighteenth centuries, hence the value of the testimonies of Caribbean ritual specialists of African descent contained in inquisition records. African rituals and objects conveyed myriad cultural structures and traditions to the Americas. These documents describe in unparalleled detail for the time West and West Central African ritual material culture and the ceremonies in which they were used. These healing artifacts were essential pieces of highly elaborated rituals, like the ones examined above, and became effective only when practitioners used them under specific circumstances. These rites and their accompanying objects were shaped by various influences from all over the Atlantic world, making it necessary to consider the multiple origins of the artifacts used by Cartagenero ritual specialists.

Power-Objects and Their Spirits in the Early Modern Caribbean

Several Europeans described power-objects in seventeenth-century Africa. Father Capelle wrote in 1643 that in Congo, they consisted "of small rocks, little bones, feathers, herbs. . . . The moquisis are wrapped in the skins of certain small animals. They kept them on their person or suspend them in their homes . . . Others wear bracelets with which the fetishers transmit their magical forces" (Jadin 1966: 231). Olfert Dapper described similar objects in 1676 Kongo, though not without an air of prejudice: "The *moquisiecossi* is a small bag of shells and other nonsense they use for divination. The worship of this Moquisie is celebrated to the sound of wooden rattles" (1686: 337).

Yet, most Europeans around the Atlantic world often believed in the power of the very same "fetishes" they decried as "savage." Capelle, for instance, became convinced that ritual specialists were transmitting their forces through the objects themselves. These African ritual objects bear vivid resemblances to the ones used by Africans on the other side of the Atlantic in the Americas. The content of the bags described by Dapper and Capelle closely resembled the ones African ritual practitioners in seventeenth-century Cartagena, as many other blacks in the Atlantic world carried around their necks. Ritual objects, like those in Kongo or the Bight of Benin, had very real powers not only for Africans but also for Europeans and their descendants in the Americas. These objects arrived to destinations ranging from St. Augustine in Florida to Rio de Janeiro in Brazil.

For example, when captured by the Holy Office in Cartagena on charges of being a sorcerer, Antonio de Salinas possessed a bag similar to the ones depicted by Dapper and Capelle in Kongo, which were called in Luso-Atlantic spaces *bolsas de mandinga* (Sweet 2009b). Born in Cartagena some sixty years before his encounter with the inquisition, Salinas, in his words, descended from "blacks from Guinea" (AHN, Inquisición 1023, fol. 401r). After living in Nicaragua and Guatemala for more than a decade, Salinas returned to Cartagena and began working on healing practices. Many believed that his powers to inflict or prevent death were great. In 1689, for example, eleven witnesses, "seven white and four black," declared that through the use of "magic," he was able to survive the close range impact of a "cannon bullet" that hit him in his chest (ibid., fol. 400v–401r).

A free black fisherman, Salinas, faced the Inquisition tribunal in 1666 after Cartagena's civil authorities confiscated from him a bag in which he allegedly "had *ominas* herbs and sticks to kill" (ibid., fol. 401r). The inventory of these supposed "deadly objects" is extensive and unique. There is currently no other known, comparably detailed, written description of an African power-object bag in seventeenth-century Cartagena. The bag contained white powder, sticks, stamps of saints, and a piece of wood that appeared to be part of a cross. It also had fragments of white, blue, and red fabrics; a stick that was a *contra* (antidote) against snake bites; a corn kernel; ten splinters of a tree; leaves from another plant; a painted image of the Virgin Mary on a piece of paper; two pieces of Saint Nicolas bread (a supposedly miraculous type of bread associated with the Catholic saint Nicolas de Tolentino); and an old papal bulla, as well as two written prayers to save him from "ferocious animals" and from being drowned, and which were also "very beneficial for the body" (ibid., fol. 400r).

Salinas's bag contained elements clearly recognizable as related to African rituals. For instance, the prayers could have been American Catholic versions of the Koranic scriptures that Mandinga ritual practitioners packed in bags they used as power-objects. European narratives of West and West Central African rites commonly describe sticks and herbs as elements of ritual practices. The use of particular colors in the papers and fabrics suggests a West Central African influence. Anita Jacobson-Widding has studied extensively the significance of the triad of red, white, and black colors in West Central Africa. White is generally the color of the dead, black of the living, and red of the interstices between dead and alive; sometimes red was the color of dying (1979).

Apart from the African influence present in this rich bag, its contents also suggest both the literacy of Salinas, a second-generation enslaved African, and his familiarity with Christian religious practices and symbols, as evidenced by the images of the Virgin Mary and saints as well as the cross. We know that Salinas and many other Africans and their descendants in Cartagena learned how to read and write (Gómez 2013, 2010: 79). Their literacy, as well as their participation in Catholic rituals, gave them access to text-based practices, particularly in the use of Catholic themes and images, which they then incorporated into their ritual practices. Thus, it is not surprising that Salinas had packed papal bullas, together with Catholic prayers and a fragment of a crucifix, in his bag. Linda Heywood (2002) and Wyatt MacGaffey (1986) have shown that the incorporation of European material goods and ritual elements for use as power-objects themselves was not exclusively an American phenomenon. According to McGaffey, West Central Africans had long considered crucifixes to be powerful *minkisi* (power-objects). Crucifixes with protruding nails, and images of corpses and blood in red and white must have conjured up clear reminiscences of traditional African religious themes on both sides of the Atlantic. Indeed, they were considered by many Congolese to be highly effective power-objects (MacGaffey 2000b: 78–80).

Salinas, in all likelihood, manufactured his bag using materials of European and American origins. From the list of "ingredients" he used, it is evident that Salinas did not reproduce African power-objects following "African" rules, which never existed in the first place (Ogundiran 2008: 23). It is the transmutability of the material life in African rituals, their disposition to be substituted and yet empowered by the core African belief systems, as well as to draw energy from other rituals—European or American—that make them quintessentially African. This is no different from the way that imported cowries, glass bottles, beads, horseshoes, or iron, for instance, were deployed in ritual processes both in Africa and in parts of the Americas. Salinas, most probably, was following what is now recognized as the "accumulative sensibility" of indigenous African religions, belief systems, and ritual practices in which later and newer material elements are continuously incorporated into the paraphernalia and processes of rituals (Drewal 1996; Mercier 1960; see also Norman, Goucher, Ogundiran, Saunders, Reeves, Gundaker, all this volume). Robert Farris Thompson captures the reimagination of power-objects in the Diaspora by referring to these materials as "strategic objects" (1983: 117). Africans adapted such strategic objects and rituals to the natural and cultural resources of the American environment, both out of necessity and due to the accumulative, inventive, and dynamic characters of their African religious backgrounds and cultural origins.

Not all ritual objects used by Africans and African-descended peoples, however, were manufactured in or indigenous to the Americas or Europe. African ritual specialists brought few but highly relevant symbolic material elements from Africa to the Americas. The richest descriptions of material culture appearing in extant records from the Spanish Caribbean refer to those used by West Central Africans. For example, Domingo Congo, a famous healer and ritual practitioner living in Caracas during the first half of the seventeenth century, declared that in his cures, he used chickens, leaves, crosses, and some red powders called *barquisi*. An animated and talkative little black figure helped Congo find the herbs most appropriate for his rituals. The figure, which he claimed to have brought with him from Kongo some five decades earlier, was of "very dark color" and moved freely while instructing Congo on the appropriate roots for the treatment of specific ailments (AHN, Inquisición 1022, fol. 102v–103r).

Domingo Congo's story provides a very rare example of evidence demonstrating how, besides reinventing the material elements of their rituals, specialists were able to bring power-objects with them to the Americas. Power-objects were an essential part of rituals both in West and West Central Africa. In Kongo, it is believed that *mbumba* (very old ancestors) materialized in *minkisi*. In Upper Guinea, Africans from the "rios de Guinea" prayed to *corofines* who were "the idols which they adore and whom they revere like their god [in the form of] the statues of their ancestors and several other wood or mud figures" (De Sandovai [1627] 1956: 47). These objects, rather than being powerful by themselves, acquired their qualities after being inhabited by a particular spiritual force (see also Fennell, Norman, Ogundiran, Saunders, all this volume).

In seventeenth century Kongo, a *mbumba* revealed its intention of serving a particular individual by appearing in the form of oddly shaped objects like grains, stones, or sticks. The *minkisi* were not formal power-objects until infused with the power of the otherworld. Dapper reported how *baganga* (ritual specialists) in Kongo activated power-objects by burying them under trees (1686: 338). Similar observations were made in 1697 by Luca da Caltanisetta in Kongo (Caltanisetta and Bontinck 1970: 82). After activation through appropriate rituals, such objects contained the power of the spiritual entities (Brasio 1960: 86, 125; Jadin and Boxer 1961: 495, 546).

Power-objects, a black figurine in Congo's case and a bag for Salinas, were essential in the construction of relationships between the earthly and immaterial/spiritual realms. These items provided a sense of communal continuity between Africa and the Americas, and must have functioned as recognizable and formidable tools for the reinvention of African culture in the Spanish Caribbean colonies. Besides their obvious symbolic value, these ritual elements were instrumental in the channeling of specific African social and cultural norms and components.

The recorded stories of these Africans contributes to an admittedly broad interpretation of the symbolic uses of this type of artifacts in the early modern African Atlantic world. They served as mediums for the introduction of recognizable representations of the natural and supernatural worlds to groups of enslaved Africans, who observed and participated in the rituals of their homeland. The power of the material culture, which Africans brought with them or re-created in the Americas, as well as of the associated rites in which Africans used them, is evidenced by their efficacy. These artifacts and rites conveyed multiple meanings, a concept that Christopher Fennell has called "an array of metaphors, made polysemous by design" (Fennell 2007a: 201; see also Fennell, this volume). African power-objects, either brought from West and West Central Africa or made in the Caribbean from local materials, engulfed the incorporative nature of African religious practices. They became essential in the performance and recognition of West and West Central African healing practices, and in their incorporation into the cultural grammar of places like northern New Kingdom of Granada.

As this essay shows, African-derived ritual traditions, such as healing with herbs and ritual paraphernalia, were ubiquitous in the Spanish Caribbean. Precisely because of their ubiquity and the rich contact between ritual practitioners, however, African rituals and ideas around body and health did not remain "pristine" representations of "an archetypical Africa." Both in Africa and the Americas, Africans were involved in processes of cultural interchange for centuries. Even those initiated in ritual practices in Africa, like Mateo Arará, acquired new healing skills and modified their practices in the Americas. In fact, Pedro Congo, one of the most powerful and feared ritual specialists of the late seventeenth century in the province of Cartagena, declared that he had learned his trade in the Americas from other Africans (AHN, Inquisición 1023, fol. 419v).

The practices of African-born health ritual specialists came from regions all over the western African coast, from the mouth of the Cacheo River to the tropical forest of the Congo. As their forebears did in Africa, however, African-descended populations in the Americas not only used and reproduced practices from their particular cultures, but eagerly engaged in a rich exchange of ideas, objects, and rituals in places like Cartagena. Unlike other areas more familiar to scholars of Latin American history, like Mexico or Lima, Caribbean port cities like Havana and Cartagena were mainly populated by people of African descent. The Africanness of these places allowed enslaved Africans to spend lifetimes in Cartagena without having to learn the supposed *lingua franca* of the place, in this case Castilian. Still, that very same Africanness that allowed them to navigate society and culture using ideas and cultural tools learned in West and West Central Africa enabled them to appropriate new life experiences in the Americas. In Cartagena, Africans did not have to enact their practices in the shadows of a mainstream culture shaped by European ideas and practices. The various West and West Central African cultural practices were the norm in Cartagena. Because of their visibility and vitality, these practices transformed in ways that both maintained some traditions even as they adopted new ones in the Americas. In so doing, they had to reimagine ways to incorporate pragmatic strategies of living and healing, which were learned from the multiple cultures that arrived in the Iberian Caribbean.

Written historical accounts, like the ones presented here, further belie what by now are, hopefully, outdated concepts that portray enslaved or free Africans as dispossessed beings. The material conditions of slavery no doubt marginalized them, but they were able to use their cultural knowledge and rituals of healing rooted in African experiences, experimentations, practices, and belief systems to advance their living conditions in "the key to the Indies," as contemporary Europeans referred to Cartagena. To deal with the great many ailments experienced by all in seventeenth-century America, African ritual specialists not only reproduced or substituted materials but also adapted them to meet the social and cultural needs of the place to which they had been forcibly brought. Their stories carry with them prominent clues for the contextualization and interpretation of spiritual ideology derived from Africa, as well as their combining with American and European-American goods in the Diaspora. African specialists' rituals conveyed myriad cultural structures and traditions to the Americas. The incomplete but unique descriptions of black ritual specialists' practices coming from the early modern

Caribbean provide some of the earliest available written accounts of specific symbolic rites and associated materials developed by people of African descent in the Americas. These accounts are important for establishing solid bases for a richer interpretation of the material cultural grammar in the larger Atlantic African world. Finally, they constitute evidence of the pervasiveness of African cultural motifs, both as they might have been in Africa and as they existed in the Americas, where they transformed, adapted, and applied them in their everyday reimagination and reconstruction.

Note

The research for this chapter has been supported by grants and fellowships from the following institutions: American Council of Learned Societies; Department of History, Vanderbilt University; College of Arts and Sciences, Vanderbilt University; Center for the Study of Religion and Culture, Vanderbilt University; Center for the Americas, Vanderbilt University; and the Program for Cultural Cooperation between Spain and the United States, University of Minnesota. I want to thank Kathrin Seidl, as well as the anonymous reviewers, for their helpful suggestions.

CHAPTER 8

"Instruments of Obeah"

THE SIGNIFICANCE OF RITUAL OBJECTS IN THE JAMAICAN LEGAL SYSTEM, 1760 TO THE PRESENT

Danielle N. Boaz

Many scholars have sifted through colonial documents searching for the "subaltern" voice of enslaved and oppressed individuals in the Americas. These researchers, as shown in the preceding chapter, for example, have attempted to uncover the spiritual practices of African and African-descended populations through deep and critical readings of "outsider accounts," such as court records, legislative debates, statutes, journals, and newspapers. Unlike many of these studies seeking to reveal the rituals and beliefs of populations that did not document these practices for themselves, I utilize these official records to understand the objectives and strategies of the colonial government in describing and proscribing certain items and actions associated with African religion and ritual practices in the Caribbean. I believe that in order to analyze the origins and development of African culture in the Western Hemisphere, we must first understand the colonial definition, categorization, and suppression of these acts. I argue that the preservation, attenuation, and transformation of African Diaspora religious and ritual practices were shaped through interactions with the legal and media institutions of the colonial government. I focus in this chapter on the efforts of the state of Jamaica to suppress the practice of Obeah (a term used by the British to describe African-Caribbean medico-religious practices). I demonstrate that Obeah objects constituted the subject and focus of these suppression efforts, and the contestations that ensued between the state and Obeah practitioners.

Judges, constables, lawyers, and legislators had ample opportunity to debate the meaning and boundaries of Obeah, with well over one thousand cases reportedly prosecuted in Jamaica alone and at least fourteen revisions to Jamaican Obeah statutes between 1760 and 1903. This vast number of cases and laws, accompanied by detailed media reports of prosecutions, provided the colonial authorities with numerous occasions to also heavily influence the public's understanding of the meanings and practices of Obeah. In this chapter, I contend that the colonial government singled out certain ritual practices for prosecution because they believed that these acts posed the greatest threat to maintaining a stable plantation economy and subservient African labor force. As Jamaica transformed from a slave society to an economy dependent on wage labor and indentured servitude, tactics of resisting colonial oppression also changed. I argue that the laws and strategies for prosecuting African ritual practices in Jamaica changed a number of times in order to suppress new forms of resistance generated by the shift from a slave-based to wage labor–based economy. In order to illustrate these, I evaluate the rationale behind the use of "instruments of Obeah" to prosecute medico-religious practices in Jamaica, and the basis for the inclusion of the items specifically listed in early Jamaican statutes, as well as why and how the use of material objects in Obeah cases changed throughout the three overlapping chronological stages of Obeah prosecutions in Jamaican history: the eighteenth to mid-nineteenth century, the second half of the nineteenth century, and the twentieth century.

Obeah Prosecution before the Mid-Nineteenth Century

In the former British Caribbean, particularly in Jamaica, the prohibitions of Obeah in colonial laws and practices often targeted the material objects that possessed ritual and spiritual significance to slaves and free blacks. When the first law was enacted against Obeah in the Caribbean, possession of "blood, feathers, parrot's beaks, alligator's teeth, dog's teeth, broken bottles, grave dirt, rum and egg-shells" were specifically proscribed (Act 24 of 1760, 1771: 55). Mere discovery of these items in an enslaved person's residence or in their possession was considered conclusive proof of the practice of Obeah, which could result in a sentence of transportation from the island for life. In fact, because the medico-religious and ritual practices classified as Obeah were typically conducted secretly, objects, known under Caribbean laws as "instruments of Obeah," were often the primary or sole evidence for arrest and conviction in eighteenth- and early nineteenth-century Obeah cases.

The earliest statutes outlawing Obeah were broad, sweeping proscriptions against any form of "pretense of possessing supernatural powers" or having "communications with the devil" (Act 91 of 1781, 1786: 277). Although these imprecise statutes that left Obeah itself undefined make it difficult to ascertain what Obeah was and why it was prohibited, an examination of contemporary sources alongside these laws helps elucidate the threat it posed to plantation owners, overseers, and other colonial authorities. The easiest place to begin is the most notorious component of eighteenth-century Obeah rituals—the administration of blood oaths.

Many researchers have noted that the first known law on Obeah was passed after a rebellion led by an enslaved man named Tacky, who was believed to have employed the use of an Obeah practitioner to mix grave dirt, gunpowder, human blood, and rum to administer a sacred oath and provide ritual protections that made the insurgents believe they were immune to bullets from plantation owners and colonial authorities. Modern scholars have argued that this oath bound the participants to support the rebellion or suffer death for betraying the oath (Price 2009; Waters 1985). Indeed, the 1760 law prohibited possession of blood, grave dirt, or rum. Then in 1809, the legislature amended the statute to list the use of grave dirt, human blood, and rum for "administering unlawful oaths" as a separate offense in the Obeah statute punishable by death, while possession of other Obeah materials, such as pounded glass, parrots beaks, or dog's teeth, was only subject to a sentence of transportation off the island for life (Act of 1809, 1816: 125).

There was frequent mention of these types of oaths throughout the Americas during the period of slavery (see also Gómez, Saunders, both this volume). One of the earliest known Obeah oaths was reported in Antigua in 1736. According to court records, a group of enslaved people across the island allegedly made a pact with rum, grave dirt, and blood from a chicken. They promised to stand by one another to defeat and kill the whites and establish a new government (Gaspar 1993; Lazarus-Black 1994). While colonial officials were certainly concerned about these oaths, they were not often the basis for Obeah prosecutions. After Tacky's rebellion of 1760, there was only one well-known instance of the use of a sacred oath preceding an attempted rebellion in Jamaica. In 1824, in the parish of St. George, an enslaved man named Jack was reported as having prepared and administered an oath using a mixture of gunpowder, rum, and blood to a group of enslaved people who were believed to be involved in the planning of a revolt ("Trial of the Conspirators" 1824). Jack was also reported to have rubbed their faces with a bush that he said would make them immune to bullets. He was tried and convicted for practicing Obeah later that year (*King v. Jack and Prince* 1824).

The prosecution of Jack's alleged accomplice in the 1824 revolt reveals that judges narrowly interpreted this component of the statute targeting only the individual who administered the oath. A man named Prince was tried alongside Jack, both for participating in the rebellion and for Obeah (ibid.). Prince was convicted of all charges except practicing Obeah, because the evidence showed that although Prince assisted Jack, he did not actually prepare or administer the oath. Additionally, the other alleged conspirators were tried for their part in the rebellion but not for practicing Obeah, even though they participated in the meeting, drank the concoction that Jack mixed, and swore the oath to kill white people ("Trial of the Conspirators" 1824).

The fact that all of those enslaved Africans who took part in the oath-taking were not tried for Obeah reveals the point of view of the judges and lawmakers regarding what they perceived to be the structure of Obeah and who within that structure represented the greatest threat. Whereas colonial laws in Haiti (St. Domingue), for example, focused on prohibiting anyone from participating in "clandestine ceremonies" (Desmangles 1992) and outlawed possessing talismans that were designed to protect against bodily injury (Rigaud 1985), early Jamaican prosecutions focused on the Obeah practitioner himself and not his followers or the people who believed in his power. This is most likely because in other regions like Haiti, sacred oaths were believed to be a promise between the enslaved people and their deities that if they would participate in the rebellion, the gods would bring them victory. Therefore, if the participants failed to engage in the rebellion, they would have incurred the wrath of the spirits or deities. Unlike other places, colonial reports of sacred oaths in Jamaica and other parts of the British Caribbean did not describe them as agreements between the participants and deities. Instead, these pacts were between the Obeah practitioner and the people who partook of the mixture and swore the oath. Therefore, any punishment from breaking an oath made during an Obeah ritual was the wrath of the Obeah practitioner upon the offending individual, not a result of divine retribution.

In part, this may be explained by the fact that Obeah is generally understood in Jamaican society and its statutes as a system of beliefs and practices based on individual consultations between a client and an Obeah practitioner. The latter receives payment from the client to perform rituals to bring success in love and legal proceedings, health, and prosperity (Olmos and Paravisini-Gebert 1997; see also Reeves, this volume). Hence, Obeah has never been perceived as a religion involving group assembly to honor and worship a deity or deities. In other parts of the Western Hemisphere, where African-derived religions involved collective acts of worship, followers of African-Caribbean religions were considered to be complicit in the illegal act of "practicing" these religions, and were arrested at various times in the nineteenth century merely for attending or participating in religious ceremonies. In Jamaica, on the other hand, Obeah prosecutions regarded men like Jack who administered an oath as the perpetrator, while the other participants were viewed as the victims of both the Obeah practitioner and their own superstition. Thus, prohibiting the possession of blood, rum, and grave dirt was an attempt by the colonial government to target Obeah practitioners, specifically to curb their influence and prevent them from binding their followers, through the use of these "potent materials," to participate in revolts.

This perceived threat from the power of the Obeah practitioners, and their ability to use Obeah to "delude and impose on the minds of others" (Act 24 of 1760, 1771: 55), is also what motivated the inclusion of all the other items listed in the eighteenth- and early nineteenth-century Obeah laws. While the legislators expressed concern that enslaved Africans believed themselves to be invulnerable to harm if an Obeah practitioner was protecting them with oaths or charms, plantation owners were equally concerned with fear of the Obeah practitioners (see also Gómez, Saunders, both this volume), who they believed caused the deaths of numerous enslaved people. The most commonly expressed concern about Obeah during slavery was not that Obeah practitioners led rebellions, but rather that they brought about the death of many enslaved Africans through "imagined illnesses" caused by belief in the Obeah practitioner's power to inflict supernatural harm (Moseley 1800; Poole 1753). Thus, Obeah was perceived and believed to adversely interfere directly with the plantation economy in particular and the colonial economy in general. This concern for the potential loss of enslaved lives was so great that, as early as 1788, Jamaican representatives reported to the Privy Council that they "ascribed a very considerable portion of the annual mortality among the Negroes in that island to that fascinating mischief" (Wilberforce 1823). Additionally, some of the items prohibited in the 1760 Obeah Act, such as eggshells and glass bottles, were often described as components of Obeah charms that enslaved persons used to protect their provision patches. These charms were believed to cause wasting illnesses if someone stole from the owner of the charm (Burdett 1800: 20; Poole 1753). Furthermore, in 1787, a line was added to the Obeah statute that prevented the use of Obeah to "affect the health or lives of others" (*New Act of Assembly* 1788: 20).

In colonial Jamaica, legislators not only sought to prevent the "imagined illnesses" that they believed were brought on by the beliefs of African-descended populations in Obeah, but also to prevent Obeah practitioners from actually mixing poisons and giving them to owners and other enslaved people (Lewis 1861; Renny 1807). Therefore, the proscription of natural materials such as hair, teeth, and beaks of animals and certain types of plants was, to some extent, a result of the fear, belief, and concern of the planters that enslaved Africans had the potential to use their unique knowledge of local plants, roots, and animals to destabilize the political economy through the use of Obeah implements to cause slave revolt and inflict fatal injuries on both whites and blacks (Atwood 1791; Madden 1835; Moseley 1800). As a result, colonial officials sought to prohibit the administration of potions and treatments by Obeah practitioners in order to counter and neutralize their power and influence.

Although Obeah practitioners were often accused by their owners of causing the deaths of numerous enslaved Africans, either through the use of actual poisons or because the enslaved individuals wasted away from an "imagined" illness, according to plantation owners and colonial officials, it was difficult to get enslaved people to testify against them out of fear of retaliation (Renny 1807). Yet, once they were arrested or imprisoned, accusations against them flooded in, presumably because enslaved people believed that an Obeah practitioner could not harm them once they had been incarcerated (Kingsley 1887). Therefore, it appears that instruments of Obeah were particularly useful in arresting an Obeah practitioner where no other evidence could be secured (e.g., Lewis 1861). Technically, according to early Obeah laws, an enslaved individual had to be "detected in making use" of these materials in the practice of Obeah or witchcraft (Act 24 of 1760, 1771: 55; Act 91 of 1781, 1786: 277). Despite the wording of the statutes, however, numerous eighteenth- and nineteenth-century cases appear to have been prosecuted only on the basis of possession of "instruments of Obeah" (e.g., Madden 1835).

These cases and accounts show the importance of the discovery of animal and plant byproducts in early prosecutions of Obeah. Fear of being poisoned or harmed by supernatural means prevented many enslaved Africans from testifying against Obeah practitioners. Therefore, searching for "instruments of Obeah" allowed plantation owners to secure the necessary evidence to rid themselves of individuals who, they claimed, were causing the deaths of many enslaved Africans due to Obeah poisonings, real or imagined. Prohibition of items such as blood, grave dirt, and rum also allowed colonists to arrest those in possession of materials that could be used to administer the types of sacred oaths which threatened the security of the plantocracy and productivity of the island.

Mid- to Late Nineteenth-Century Prosecutions

The second stage of Obeah prosecutions began in the middle of the nineteenth century, when legislation prohibiting the practice of Obeah changed remarkably. This new stage began with the removal of the "instruments of Obeah" from the statutes in the 1820s. It continued in the 1840s and 1850s with a shift in the focus of Obeah prosecutions from alleged "harming" rituals like poisoning to prohibitions of healing rituals. Then, by the end of the nineteenth century, colonial officials changed their focus yet again, primarily prosecuting rituals to increase luck and prosperity, as well as fortune-telling and palmistry as acts of Obeah. During this period, "instruments of Obeah" became less important as evidence in court cases because, as fear of Obeah practitioners declined and practitioners were less frequently accused of poisoning people, witnesses came forward more regularly to participate in trials. Additionally, as the types of rituals that colonial officials categorized as Obeah shifted to healing and divination, instead of poisoning and sacred oaths, items used in the rituals that were prosecuted became more commonplace, the possession of which could no longer definitively identify an individual as an Obeah practitioner.

The first major changes to Obeah statutes and prosecutions began with Jamaica's "Act to Alter and Amend the Slave Laws of This Island," which removed the list of "instruments of Obeah" from the statute except for the possession or use of "poison, or poisonous, or noxious drug, pounded glass, or other deleterious matter" (1826: 90). A commentary to this statute asserts that other specific materials were not delineated because they were no longer commonly used in the practice of Obeah ("Commentary on the New Slave Law" 1827). Failure to incorporate items other than glass, drugs, and poisons also demonstrated a shift in colonial belief that these were the only objects that represented a legitimate threat of physical harm. Accordingly, possession or use of these substances was still punishable with death or transportation. By the late nineteenth century, however, cases of poisoning were increasingly prosecuted as separate offenses unrelated to Obeah (e.g., *Regina v. Aaron Mowry* 1865; *Regina v. Maria McKewzie* 1880). Poisons were most likely removed from the Obeah law because, by the middle of the nineteenth century, many individuals believed that while Obeah practitioners may have previously had special knowledge of alternative forms of poison, Obeah poisons had become more commonly known items such as rat poison or arsenic (Gardner 1878; Wilberforce 1823).

In addition to poisons and drugs, pounded (or ground) glass remained in the Obeah statute until the mid-nineteenth century, but there were debates at this time about its efficacy in actually producing harm (D.P.W. 1851; *Queen v. Cunningham et al.* 1876). It was ultimately removed from Obeah statutes in 1856, apparently because, like plants and animal matter, pounded glass was no longer believed to be an effective component of poisons. Further, if pounded glass was capable of causing harm, it was prohibited through statutes regarding the use of "destructive substances" ("Acts Causing or Tending to Cause Danger" [1864] 1889).

Another change to Obeah legislation and prosecutions in Jamaica was the addition of the word "Myalism" to the statute in 1856. Although a clear definition of the term has not yet been developed, modern scholars have largely distinguished Obeah and Myalism by describing the former as the practice of harming or administering poisons, and the latter as the practice of removing or counteracting supernatural afflictions that had been imposed by Obeah practitioners (Moore and Johnson 2004; Olmos and Paravisini-Gebert 1997). Without reaching into the realm of how these two practices were viewed by the people who performed them, Obeah and Myalism were treated as one entity under Jamaican law. Myalism was defined in an 1857 statute as "one in the same meaning" as Obeah ("An Act to Explain the Fourth Victoria" [1857] 1890). Additionally, nearly identical acts of healing were prosecuted alternately as Myalism or Obeah in the mid- to late nineteenth century without any explanation or distinguishing factors to clarify the use of one category or the other for each case.

At least as early as the 1820s, before Myalism was mentioned in Jamaican statutes, individuals who performed rituals to counteract Obeah curses or poisons had been prosecuted as Obeah practitioners (Murray 2007). They, however, were initially prosecuted alongside individuals who supposedly engaged in poisoning and administering oaths. Increasingly, over the course of the nineteenth century, as fewer Obeah practitioners were discovered with poisons, animal matter, and pounded glass, healers became the prime target of prosecutions under those statutes. In fact, out of twenty-six cases between 1850 and 1870 that are recorded in the trial books in the Jamaican archives, nineteen (73%) were for healing while only three (11%) were for harming or attempting to harm.

As other scholars have noted, Myalists became a major concern for Jamaican officials after their influence spread among a segment of the African-Jamaican population who organized not only against Obeah but also against forms of oppression such as hardships related to poor labor conditions. It became a prevalent concern after a year-long Myalist procession from 1841–1842 disrupted life and labor on more than twenty plantations in the parish of St. James. During this time, Myalists stormed onto plantations and even into houses to dig up Obeah that they believed had been buried on these properties. The police were called in to break up this procession, which consisted of preaching, public rituals, and work strikes (Schuler 1979).

In addition to the labor disruptions, Myalism was also a focal point of prosecutions during the middle of the nineteenth century because it impeded the progress of Western medicine. Disease was rampant in Jamaica in the middle of the nineteenth century. Tens of thousands of people died from outbreaks of cholera, smallpox, and measles (Bolland 2001; Schuler 1979). European travelers and officials lamented that black Jamaicans continued to attribute every illness to Obeah and sought supernatural healing for physical ailments (D.P.W. 1851: 150; Thornton 1904). The number of Western medical practitioners, however, was wholly inadequate to supply the population with medical care. There were only two hundred physicians on the island in 1833, and this number decreased to fifty by 1860 (De Barros 2007). In 1858, the *Medical Times and Gazette* published an article stating that a lack of licensed physicians on the island allowed Myalism to run rampant, and that the local population maintained the "absurd delusion" that Myal men could cure their illnesses. They urged the legislature to do something to encourage medical science and reduce "quackery" (1858: 527).

This focus on Myalism meant that, while prosecutions of harming practices involving pounded glass were no longer typically conducted under Obeah statutes, healing practices involving glass were. Particularly in the 1850s and 1860s, Jamaicans were tried for rituals called cupping, through which an Obeah or Myal practitioner would use their hands, mouths, or a calabash to pull or suck various items from a person's body. The belief was that through supernatural means, these items had been inserted into a person's body to make them ill, and the removal of the objects would cure the sickness (see also Gómez, this volume). In the 1850s, court records indicate that the most common substance found inside a person was pieces of glass, often accompanied by lead. Unlike the items used in prosecuting the allegedly harmful Obeah practices in the eighteenth century, however, those materials pulled from a person's body were not typically produced as evidence at trial during the mid-nineteenth century. Instead, the Obeah practitioner was convicted based on the testimony of a witness or even the patient. In fact, glass, lead, and other items were usually only briefly mentioned in court records when prosecuting Myalism or Obeah cases. It is possible that they were destroyed after their supposed extraction from diseased clients, particularly since they were believed to be part of illness-inducing Obeah magic and would likely need to be disposed of in a special way to prevent them from harming someone else.

Cupping is not the only healing process that was prosecuted as Myalism or Obeah. The African-descended populations in Jamaica also believed that Obeah practitioners had the power to capture the spirit of an individual and place it in a tree so that the individual would become ill and perhaps die. Both Myalists and Obeah practitioners were believed to have the ability to perform a ceremony to remove the person's spirit, also known as a *duppy*, from the tree in order to heal them (Stewart 1992). In the ritual to remove the person's spirit, a white fowl was sacrificed and its blood dripped on the tree. The Obeah practitioner sometimes threw rum on the tree or rubbed a mixture of chalk and rum on the hands of individuals involved in the ritual. Like Myal cupping cases, however, these mid- to late nineteenth-century prosecutions also appear to have been based almost entirely on witness testimony and not production of the carcass of the chicken, rum, or chalk as instruments of Obeah (e.g., *King v. Polydore* 1831).

Another major change to Obeah statutes in the mid-nineteenth century was that, instead of proscribing the use of poisons, the administration of blood oaths, and similar offenses, the Obeah statute prohibited "pretending, or professing to tell fortunes . . . palmistry, or any such like superstitious means, to deceive or impose on any of her majesty's subject" ("Act for the More Effectual Punishment" 1856: 512). Diane Paton (2009) argues that the shift in Obeah laws in Jamaica to focus on broader, more benign forms of "superstition" was a result of the implementation of vagrancy laws in Britain and a growing belief among the British that "witchcraft" was not real and should be treated as charlatanism. While Paton's observation about the correlation between Caribbean and British vagrancy legislation is correct, the focus on particular kinds of "charlatanism," such as palm reading and fortune-telling, was likely a result of changes in the ethnic composition of British Caribbean colonies.

Slavery ended in Jamaica in 1834 and was followed by a short period of apprenticeship, which forced formerly enslaved Africans to continue to work on plantations until 1838. Plantation owners were worried that, after the end of apprenticeship, they would face severe labor shortages that would threaten the productivity of their individual plantations and the economic stability of the island (Bolland 2001). They argued that blacks would desert the plantations if they were not forced to work, and owners lobbied for a law allowing indentured servants to be imported to ensure an adequate supply of labor and drive down wages through competition for jobs. Some colonists, however, opposed the immigration of indentured workers, arguing that "the introduction of a number of heathen and pagan foreigners with their religious superstitions, idolatry and wickedness, will act most injuriously on the morals of the inhabitants of the island and hinder very much the efforts that are now in operation for their moral and religious improvement" (House of Commons 1859: 211). Missionaries were often opponents to immigration, claiming that the influx of African indentured laborers had revived practices that had been suppressed in black Jamaicans through Christian education (e.g., Waddell 1863).

Africans were not the only immigrants viewed as impeding efforts to "civilize" Jamaican people. Indians were also brought into Jamaica and other parts of the Caribbean in the 1840s to work as wage laborers (Bolland 2001). Modern scholars have noted that Indians brought traditions of palm reading to the Caribbean (Campbell 1976: 2). Additionally, contemporary newspapers reported that Indians, or "coolies" as they were pejoratively called, had taken over Obeah practices, growing wealthy from their ability to play on the superstition of black Jamaicans ("Land We Live In" 1890). These individuals were prosecuted for violating Obeah statutes alongside African-Jamaicans. Between 1887 and 1892, two Indians were tried and convicted for "professing to sell fortunes," and each was sentenced to seven days' imprisonment with hard labor (Obeah and Myalism Law 1892). Other Indians were simply described and accused of "practicing Obeah" and sentenced to various terms of imprisonment of up to twelve months with hard labor ("Coolie Obeahman" 1899; "Charges of Theft" 1902; "Obeah in St. Elizabeth" 1891; "Severe Sentence Passed" 1932). As a result of the new immigrant involvement in supernatural rituals, the mid-nineteenth-century revisions to the Obeah statutes had to be vague enough to encompass Indian ritual practices too. The desire to prevent all non-Christian spiritual practices may, therefore, explain the general breadth of the 1850s revisions to the Obeah statutes, and specifically mid- to late nineteenth-century Obeah prosecutions to include palmistry and fortune-telling, which may primarily have targeted Indian indentured laborers in Jamaica.

Despite these drastic changes to acts prosecuted under the Obeah statutes and increasing reliance on witness testimony rather than the material evidence of Obeah practice, the law certainly did not ignore ritual objects as evidence. The 1857 statute banning Obeah gave any justice of the peace the power to issue a search warrant to a constable allowing him to enter any residence "by force if necessary" to conduct a thorough search for any "charms, characters, or other things" used in "occult" and "evil" practices, but did not list any examples of what types of items "instruments of Obeah" might be (An Act to Explain the Fourth Victoria [1857] 1890: 45). Possession of these vaguely described items would result in imprisonment and hard labor for up to sixty days.

Implements of Obeah remained an important part of Obeah cases through the end of the nineteenth century. The nature of these items, however, changed drastically, from animal and plant byproducts to more common household items. In the 1890s, Inspector Herbert Thomas from the Jamaican Constabulary created an exhibition of objects that had been seized during the arrest of various Obeah practitioners in his parish. The most common items were playing cards, unknown herbs, chalk, and calabashes. The calabashes may have been from individuals arrested doing healing rituals, as the only reference to a calabash in Obeah cases was their use in "cupping," as described above. The use of chalk in Obeah ceremonies increased in the nineteenth and twentieth centuries as it gained currency in the rituals to remove a person's spirit from a tree. It was also incorporated into other early twentieth-century healing rituals, frequently to make a cross on a person's forehead or above them on the sick bed ("Case under the Obeah Law" 1909; "Practiced Obeah" 1902). While chalk and calabashes were mentioned in early Obeah cases, playing cards were first identified in the late nineteenth century as a tool for divination ("Obeah Case" 1900; "St. Thomas Obeah Case" 1893).

Yet, what is most notable about Thomas's exhibition is not what was included but what was excluded. There was very little mention of animal byproducts. The only animal matter incorporated into the display was a piece of a cow's horn and an unknown substance that Thomas assumed was animal excrement (Thomas 1894). The types of items listed in his display reinforce the idea that the materials used in Obeah rituals had shifted from a variety of natural animal and plant byproducts to more commonplace objects like chalk, chickens, and calabashes for healing, or candles and cards for divination. Since these objects were not easily distinguishable "Obeah tools," witness testimony began to offer a viable alternative to reliance on discovery of instruments of Obeah.

Twentieth-Century Prosecutions

The laws prohibiting Obeah still exist in Jamaica today. The most recent Obeah Act, passed in 1898, represents the beginning of the last phase of Obeah prosecutions, which ran through the middle of the twentieth century, when Obeah cases became less common and the inclusion of instruments of Obeah in those cases further declined. The 1898 Obeah law continues to mention possession of "instruments of Obeah" as evidence of practicing Obeah, but not as a standalone offense. Additionally, throughout the twentieth century, judges attempted to further restrict the use of physical objects in the litigation of such cases. The Jamaican Court of Appeals and Supreme Court repeatedly had to address the collection of evidence in Obeah cases, holding that the prosecution must prove that the accused himself used the materials found in his possession in the practice of Obeah. A constable was not permitted to seize items from the accused person's residence, and was prevented from testifying that, in his experience, the items were typically used in Obeah rituals (*Rex v. Chambers* 1901). In addition, under the 1898 Obeah Act, the discovery of implements of Obeah is not sufficient to warrant a conviction because possession of these items is not a criminal offense. The statute only allows seizure of instruments of Obeah to be refutable evidence that an individual is practicing Obeah (*Rex v. Bulgin* 1919).

The waning acceptance of material objects as evidence in Obeah cases in Jamaica was a consequence of many factors. In part, it was the result of a shift in the legal definition of Obeah from poisoning and blood oaths to rituals involving healing, securing employment, bringing luck, and finding love. With this change in colonial perceptions of the threat of Obeah, officials no longer searched for items that could cause physical harm, such as pounded glass and poisons. Instead, late nineteenth- and early twentieth-century cases forced constables to prove that an accused had used objects to "pretend" to possess supernatural powers and "delude" others into believing that they could treat illnesses or remove supernatural afflictions (Law 5 of 1898, 1898).

It is clear that, as time progressed, fewer and fewer officials believed that Obeah practitioners had any unique knowledge of healing or harming practices. In fact, prosecutions for this kind of Obeah nearly ceased in the twentieth century, with only two or three dozen prosecutions for attempts to cure illness reported in the twentieth century and even fewer for attempts to poison or otherwise harm anyone. Hundreds of Obeah cases were prosecuted in the early twentieth century, but most of the practitioners arrested during this period were performing rituals to bring luck, particularly in matters of court cases and employment. The public's fear and estimation of Obeah practitioners declined alongside the number of prosecutions for harming practices. Whereas at one time the prosecution had been unable to find anyone willing to testify against an Obeah practitioner, by the end of the nineteenth century more and more Jamaicans were stepping into the witness box ("Is Obeahism Increasing" 1893). Thus, material objects were no longer the only, or even the primary, source of evidence for Obeah cases. Moreover, in the twentieth century, "instruments of Obeah" became even more commonplace items than those in the late nineteenth century, such as looking glasses (mirrors) and candles ("Alleged Obeahman" 1899; "Charge of Obeah" 1907; "Obeah Case in St. Andrew" 1900; "Allman Town" 1907).

The rationale for the changes in types of material objects that Obeah practitioners were believed to employ is outside the purview of this chapter. What is obvious is that "instruments of Obeah" no longer played an important role in twentieth-century prosecutions. Frustrated by increasing numbers of foiled attempts to secure convictions based on possession of candles and playing cards, constables turned to witness testimony as the primary vehicle for securing Obeah convictions. This shift is seen in the fact that at least around two-thirds of prosecutions after the 1898 statute relied on witnesses as evidence, and many of them began with the police employing a decoy to hire the Obeah practitioner and observe the ritual. Instruments of Obeah, on the other hand, were only reportedly used in less than 10 percent of cases.[1]

Since the 1960s, Obeah prosecutions have sharply declined. Only 33 individuals were prosecuted for Obeah during the three-year period from 1961 and 1964 (Annual Reports of the Police Department, 1962–1964, University of West Indies Library, Kingston, Jamaica), as opposed to 138 that were prosecuted from 1898 to 1901 ("Crusade against Obeah" 1901) or 181 that were prosecuted from 1913 to 1916 ("Report of the Inspector General" 1916). Today, though Obeah statutes remain in effect in Jamaica and several other countries such as Guiana, Antigua, Barbuda, and the Bahamas, Obeah prosecutions in the former British Caribbean have nearly ceased.

Obeah laws, however, have already left their mark on public and academic perceptions of the practice. Researchers rarely fail to refer to the items listed in the 1760 statute as common instruments of Obeah, despite the fact that these items only remained in the statute for the first sixty-six out of two hundred years of prosecutions and never represented an exhaustive list of objects used in Obeah rituals. The poisonings, oaths, and supernatural afflictions associated with these items have achieved the same level of infamy, although they represent far less than half of the prosecutions of Obeah in Jamaican history. Indeed, colonial assumptions about the ritual processes of Obeah, and the function and nature of the objects that Obeah practitioners employed, have shaped the definition of the term.

Herein I have argued that the economic interests of slave owners influenced legislators to prohibit ritual objects used in oaths that preceded revolts and items believed to be used by Obeah practitioner to poison both owners and enslaved Africans. Financial incentives also caused colonial definitions of Obeah to expand to encompass healing rituals, because healers known as Myalists were conducting labor strikes and otherwise disrupting plantation productivity. Obeah prohibitions, however, also became a method of policing the morality of the newly freed black population, "protecting" them from African and Indian immigrants who might introduce or revive what the colonial society labeled "superstitions." By the twentieth century, charlatanism had become virtually synonymous with the legal definition of Obeah, which includes any supernatural or spiritual rituals from fortune-telling to rituals for obtaining luck and love.

The heavy weight that has been given to colonial sources in determining the boundaries of Obeah necessitates a deeper inquiry into the perceptions of colonial officials and the extensive laws and prosecutions of Obeah in the Caribbean. While Obeah charms and rituals may have been instruments for black Jamaicans to resist slavery and oppressive post-emancipation conditions, Obeah was also a powerful target of the government toward the suppression of any African practice it found threatening to its authority. So while scholars search for the meaning that Obeah practitioners ascribed to ritual objects, they must also consider the importance that colonial officials assigned to those same items, as a reflection of those officials' own views on the practice itself. Only between the divergences and convergences of the two distinct realms of ritual and legal significance can the importance of material objects in Jamaican Obeah be fully understood.

Note

1. These statistics are based on a compilation by the author of approximately six hundred Obeah cases prosecuted between 1898 and 1991. Unfortunately, similar calculations are not available for mid-nineteenth-century cases because the types of evidence used in these cases were not recorded frequently enough to make an accurate statistical analysis.

CHAPTER 9

Charms and Spiritual Practitioners

NEGOTIATING POWER DYNAMICS IN AN ENSLAVED AFRICAN COMMUNITY IN JAMAICA

Paula Saunders

In recent times, the focus of African Diaspora archaeological research has moved to examine the spiritual-based practices of people of African descent throughout the Diaspora (see, e.g., K. L. Brown 1994, 2001, 2004; Fennell 2007b; Russell 1997; Stine et al. 1996; Wilkie 1997, on spirituality and ritual paraphernalia). The results of these studies often produce more questions than answers, and demonstrate the many complexities involved in examining such places of ritual activity, as well as the impossibility of creating standardized theories and methodologies to deal with such complex sites. As a result, archaeologists are still attempting to find ways to address the use of spirituality as one of the means whereby oppressed women, men, and children in the Diaspora negotiated power, resistance, and discourse inherent within the colonial state, as well as how these practices may be seen in the archaeological record.

This chapter presents some findings from the enslaved village at Orange Vale coffee plantation, located in Portland, Jamaica. This research applies an interdisciplinary approach by combining documentary, archaeological, and oral sources. In addition to information on daily living conditions and settlement patterns within the enslaved African village, additional findings include (1) the recognition of various levels of power negotiation, and (2) clues to the enslaved people's ritualized spiritual practices through their use of charms. Further, this research underscores the importance of including descendant communities throughout the archaeological process, as well as the need to engage oral traditions in the interpretation of past societies, particularly for marginalized groups excluded from "official"—that is, written—stories of the past.

The archaeology at Orange Vale reveals that enslaved Africans were in a constant state of negotiation within the various restraints placed on them, opting to make use of the available material culture for their physical, social, and spiritual needs. The archaeological recovery of several horseshoes, as well as evidence of the presence of Obeah practitioners at Orange Vale, generates some insights into the ideology of the members of the village community. This chapter explores how these materials were used within the constraints of plantation slavery, as well as the roles spiritual specialists played within the enslaved community at Orange Vale.

Here, I discuss the parallel power dynamics within the plantation context and the ways in which enslaved Africans mediated, sidestepped, and negotiated the forces they believed were potential threats on both the plantation and village levels. The investigation reveals that ritual practices within this one enslaved African village community in Jamaica simultaneously served as a means of personal protection, communal solidarity, and resistance, as well as the creation of parallel sources of power in the racially stratified colonial society. The initial goal of the research sought answers for a number of questions, such as, in what ways did autonomy by enslaved Africans create pathways of agency in the controlling world of their enslavers? How were these acts interpreted in the "official" historical record? What means did they use to deflect European-dominated power and negotiate authority within the inherently violent system of slavery? How was this agency manifested in the archaeological record they left behind?

It has been well established that African-descended peoples in the Americas have constantly negotiated or reconstructed their practices in response to changes in their sociopolitical realities. In this chapter, I use the archaeological evidence at Orange Vale coffee plantation to argue that enslaved Africans did not entirely conform to Eurocentric notions of power. Rather, the study serves as one example of the ways in which men and women of African descent demonstrated autonomy at both individual and communal levels. The enslaved people who lived in the plantation's village developed parallel authorities (here in spiritual healers and material objects) to deal with ailments, as well as with benevolent forces, reflecting deep relationships between living humans and spirits of the dead. These parallel power entities were based on a combination of traditional African and European beliefs, as well as African-derived medicinal knowledge. These identities in the Americas were reflective of the new, dynamic cultural systems that were created in unique contexts.

Both ideologies and medicinal knowledge were used to heal, as well as to elude and mediate, the many structures of control in colonial society (Payne-Jackson and Alleyne 2004: 62). One such method of mediating the violence or threat of violence that was inherent in enslavement was the use of a variety of primarily African-derived spiritual practices, collectively classified as "Obeah" in Jamaica (Cassidy and Le Page 2002: 264). For the people at Orange Vale and elsewhere in the Caribbean, these African-derived spiritual practices were an integral part of their everyday rituals. As a result, it is possible that the rituals related to these practices would manifest themselves in the archaeological record, if only we, the archaeologists, understand, recognize, and acknowledge these people's beliefs and associated practices. In order to conduct such an analysis of the materials we recover, we must be open to work in conjunction with descendant communities, as well as with those who are familiar with the cultural practices, who could shed significant light on the artifacts we recover.

The Material Culture of Orange Vale

Located on the hillside of Jamaica's Blue Mountain, Orange Vale was one of the largest coffee plantations from the late eighteenth to the mid-nineteenth centuries (map 9.1). It was a vast, self-contained entity wherein 260 enslaved African peoples provided forced labor in the production of coffee for consumption in European markets. Excavations at Orange Vale were conducted in two of three areas within the plantation's enslaved residential village. Based on the artifacts recovered, Village Area 1 appears to have an earlier occupation period, possibly as early as 1800, while Village Area 2 had a later and longer occupation period that extended well into the late 1800s. All of Village Areas 1 and 2 were excavated in 2 m × 2 m units, and the archaeology revealed a wealth of information on the innovative techniques and materials used in the building of homes, as well as domestic, kitchen-related, and work-related artifacts. Metal artifacts dominated the material culture recovered in excavations, most of which appear to have had primarily architectural and utilitarian functions. In addition, many of the metal objects appear to have served first in the plantation's coffee factory, and were then recycled and reused in a variety of ways within the enslaved African village.

All of the horseshoes recovered were found near the entrances, which were identified by the presence of rectangular-shaped sandstone steps and/

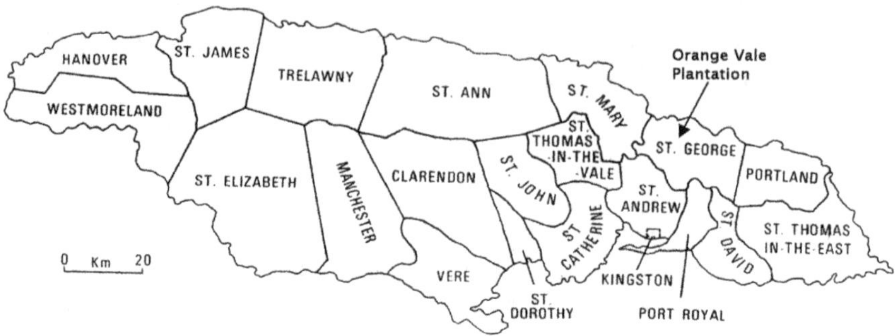

MAP 9.1. Nineteenth-century map of Jamaica, indicating the location of Orange Vale Plantation in St. George Parish.

or thresholds leading into the dwellings. Four of the horseshoes were intact; three were about half intact, broken at the toe or arch; and two were quarter fragments. All of them contained rectangular-shaped holes, indicating the locations where hand-wrought nails were used to secure the shoes in place on horses. Four of the fragments had horseshoe nails attached to the shoe itself.

While it is not possible to date the partial fragments with great certainty, it is possible to assess the relative manufacture date of the more complete horseshoes following Ivor Noël Hume's (1970) classification. According to Noël Hume, the two complete horseshoes recovered from Village Area 1 belong to his Type 6, with an average date of ca. 1800. Three horseshoes from Village Area 1 had nails attached and also resembled Type 6 (see, e.g., figure 9.1). A fourth horseshoe recovered in Village Area 2, along with a latch, had round nails and resembled Type 7, which were manufactured between 1800 and 1862 (ibid.). The dates of these horseshoes support the interpretation suggested by oral accounts (Saunders 2004) that Village Area 2 was occupied for a much longer and later period than Village Area 1.

In addition to these horseshoes, other artifacts were also found in the same context giving us a good picture of the meaningful practices that produced these assemblages. These items were mostly made of metal content, such as nails. The nails were building- or architecture-related and may have been used in the construction of the frames or doors of houses. In one instance, one horseshoe was found buried with a scissor handle, another with a spoon fragment, and yet another was found with a door latch. Additional

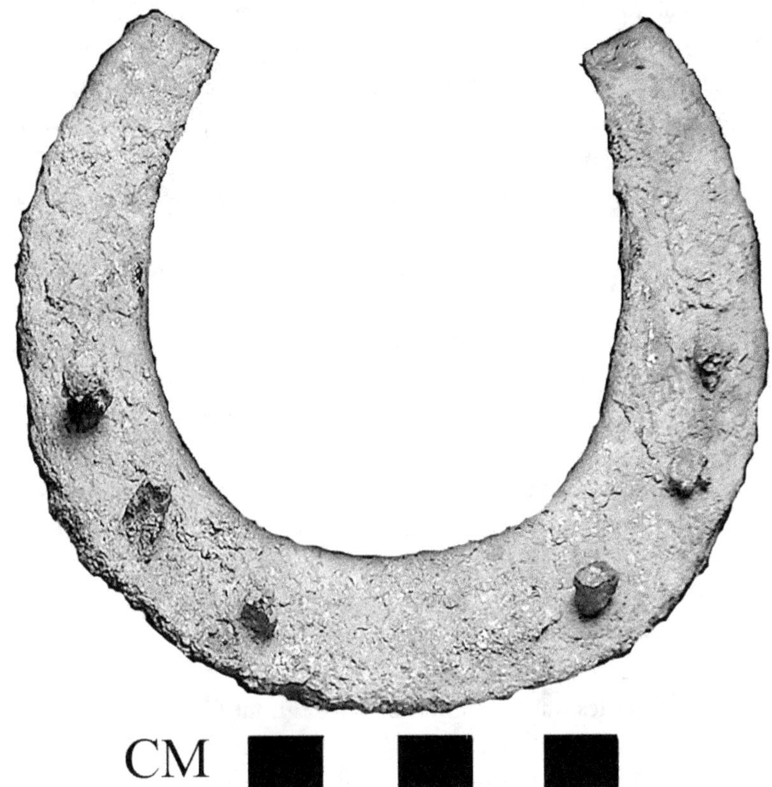

FIGURE 9.1. One of several horseshoes recovered from beneath a house entrance in the enslaved African village at Orange Vale Plantation.

metal objects recovered within the same contexts with these horseshoes were spikes and metal tool fragments, such as sharpening files.

Whether these associated items were used for their primary purposes as architectural- (nails, spikes, and latch) and task-related (scissor, spoon, and file) tools, or for some other secondary purpose, such as spiritual-based ritual, remains uncertain. Local field participants in the excavations, however, immediately identified these horseshoes as objects used to protect one's household from malevolent forces, especially to prohibit unsolicited visits from *duppies*, the Jamaican term to refer to spirits of the dead (Cassidy and Le Page 2002: 164). Human encounters with the spirit world, especially with *duppies*, were and continue to be commonplace experiences referenced in rural Jamaica, and reflect the very belief that the spirit of the dead can be manipulated to affect the living (Payne-Jackson and Alleyne 2004: 8). This common acceptance of the comingling of the spiritual and secular worlds is reflective of West and Central African traditional philosophy (Kamara 2000; Parrinder 1976).

If these horseshoes were, in fact, used to protect households from *duppies*, then these horseshoes represent an example of the materiality of rituals related to African-derived spiritual beliefs at Orange Vale. Most African societies believe that the spirits of the dead can affect the living in both positive and negative ways. In Jamaica, this belief in *duppies* and their potentially malevolent abilities toward the living dictated the ways in which the dead were treated. Historically, care was taken during burials to perform rituals in order to simultaneously respect the dead as ancestors and prevent the living from manipulating *duppies* to cause harm. According to these and other local accounts (Saunders 2004), the horseshoe served as one means to protect one's home from a potential visit from *duppies*.

The horseshoe's prevalence in the archaeological record suggests that it was a very important object for the residents of the households in the village. Documentary records for Orange Vale also indicate that there were only a few horses and mules on the plantation throughout the period of enslavement. With the exception of those who cared for the horses, most enslaved peoples who lived in the village did not come into contact with these horses or their horseshoes. Given the legal restrictions imposed on enslaved Africans and the limited access to horseshoes, it was clearly very important to maintain these objects, and the Africans must have made great efforts to acquire the shoes. Thus, the presence of such a large number of them within the village space is significant.

Folklore of Horseshoes

Why was it so important to have these horseshoes at entrances? The local interpretation that these horseshoes served as protective forces against malevolent forces steers us into a realm of the many lores of the people who populated Jamaica. The U-shaped piece of iron, nailed to a horse's hoof, has traditionally served as a shoe in protecting the hoof against rocks, pebbles, and hard, uneven surfaces. Horseshoes have also historically served spiritual functions, representing good luck in many cultures, especially in Europe and the Americas. Throughout the eighteenth and nineteenth centuries, people in those regions often nailed horseshoes to houses and used them as charms on jewelry.

The horseshoe, in particular, has a basic shape of either a crescent, an arch, or a cup, all of which were long considered "signs" of good luck or fortune (Lawrence 1898). The crescent is a moon symbol that was believed to have properties of prosperity in many cultures and religions in Africa and the Mediterranean. The shape has also been used as an important symbol in many religious and spiritual organizations. The typical number of nail holes in most horseshoes was seven, the symbolic number of good luck in most Afro-Asiatic–derived traditions. Similarly, in the British Isles, the cup-like, open end of the horseshoe is believed to gather luck (Aaronson and Kwan 2008; Lawrence 1898). Conversely, some thought the cup of the shoe itself was filled with luck and, thus, should be nailed on doors with the open ends pointing down so that good fortune could pour out on those entering the houses. Horseshoes have also become symbols of luck to African-descended peoples in the Atlantic world (Lawrence 1898).

Horseshoes in Archaeological Contexts

Horseshoes have served important functions within the African Diaspora ideology throughout the historical period, and have been recovered in a variety of ritual contexts in several archaeological sites. For example, at New York's African Burial Ground, a partial ox- or horseshoe was found in relation to a burial of a child or adolescent (Cheryl LaRoche, pers. comm., 2007; Perry and Woodruff 2006: 440). Although recovered within a disturbed context and near the right leg of the human remains, this shoe, archaeologists suggest, could have been a grave offering to the deceased. Horseshoes have also been found as part of grave decorations in other African Diaspora contexts of the nineteenth and twentieth centuries (see, e.g., Thompson 1983; Vlach 1990) and may have served similar spiritual functions in ritualized practices to honor the dead, bring good luck, and provide protection.

Based on oral traditions in Jamaica, the location of the recovered horseshoes near the entrances at Orange Vale suggests that they were spiritually significant. The rich oral "sayings" in Jamaica suggest that, in order for horseshoes to work as protective charms against *duppies,* they must either be buried at the entrances or hung on the interior of the doorway, on the door itself or above it. Several local informants have suggested that the location of the horseshoes recovered were likely buried at the entrances, rather

FIGURE 9.2. Sandstone steps at the entrance of a village house, near which horseshoes were recovered.

than hung on, above, or near the door (Abercrombie Thomas, pers. comm., 2003; Violet Grayson, pers. comm., 2003). All of the horseshoes at Orange Vale were recovered near doorways, which were evidenced by the presence of thresholds and shaped sandstone steps (figure 9.2). The locations of these horseshoes at entrances were consistent with and, most likely, reflected burials under the dirt floor in the interior of the entrance.

A few archaeological studies have suggested the intentional burial of spiritual-related items near entrances, steps, doorways, and pathways (Brown

2001; Davidson 2009; Gundaker 1993, 1998a; Reeves 1996 and this volume; Ruppel et al. 2003). Matthew Reeves's (this volume) excavations at Juan de Bolas plantation in Jamaica revealed two nearly intact bottles that were recovered upright and located next to the doorway of a dwelling belonging to an enslaved African. This bottle appeared to contain charcoal and a white residue, and Reeves's interpretation was that the bottle could have served some kind of spiritual and protective purpose. Kenneth Brown (2001) found an amulet at Jordon, while Timothy Ruppel and his colleagues (2003) also found a bottle buried near an entrance at the Brice House in Annapolis, Maryland, which was interpreted as a spiritual offering. Similarly, Grey Gundaker found that bottle trees served as a way to keep evil spirits from coming into the homes of African Americans (1993), a practice with Central African origins (Atwood 1791). Similarly, James Davidson's (2009) find of what he identified as a sacrificed chicken buried at the entrance of an enslaved dwelling at Kingsley Plantation in Florida also fits the pattern of the spiritual importance of entrances for people of African descent, as well as the associated material culture recovered at these locations.

The fact that these horseshoes were found near doorway entrances is significant for a variety of other reasons. First, burial under the floor on the interior of the doorway allowed for the private and secret use of the horseshoe as a charm of protection, away from view of enemies, including both the enslaved and enslavers. In addition, in many societies, the entrance doorway is symbolically viewed a transitional space because it is the location where residents first come into contact with the outside world, a space that is dangerous. Thus, neutralizing this space is a major theme in the oral accounts of many traditional societies (Essabal 1961: 266; Lawrence 1898). Similarly, in some African and African-descended communities, entrances and doorways are viewed as a kind of liminal space, filled with hazards, which require magical precautions to move through. In Jamaica, the entrance (i.e., doorway and threshold) is also the path through which *duppies* must pass to enter a dwelling. As a result, it is at the entrances that residents of the village performed rituals and "fixed" various means of protection in order to avoid unsolicited visits from the *duppies*, as well as to ensure the welfare and prosperity of those who resided in these dwellings.

Thus, the horseshoe, recovered near the entrances of the dwellings at Orange Vale, represent one way in which village residents sought to protect themselves in their most private spaces: their dwellings. Given the various laws in Jamaica that forbade activities interpreted as "superstitious" or related to spiritual practice (collectively referred to as "Obeah") on the part of enslaved peoples, the interiors of houses would have been the most logical locations for the placement of such charms because they remained hidden from plantation managers, who would have been obliged to enforce the laws. Spirituality, and ways to manipulate and manage it in the secular world, were endemic in the everyday lives of people of African descent in Jamaica. As a result, various laws in Jamaica attempted to curtail these practices by dictating how they should behave and what materials they should be allowed to access. For example, laws were passed that forbade the trade and use of metal objects by enslaved Africans, except for the tools necessary to perform their various work tasks (Acts of Jamaica 1774, 1799, 1802).

The general rationale that governed these laws suggested that enslaved peoples could manipulate metal and form them into tools for use in rebellions against the system that enslaved them. Although the enforcement varied depending on individual circumstances, the acquisition of any metal items—whether bought, traded, or stolen—would theoretically be considered illegal because these items were seen as threats to the hierarchy of power within the plantation system. Thus, the persistent presence of these horseshoes in enslaved contexts would have been considered illegal possession of metal. There would have been the need to keep such items hidden away from the view of enslavers. More importantly, the fact that possession of these items would have been considered illegal and carry severe penalties further demonstrates their importance.

The metal horseshoes seemed to have served powerful spiritual functions for the residents in the dwellings at Orange Vale. In fact, the oral traditions affiliated with the magical power of horseshoes have dictated that horseshoes with nails still intact bring extreme good luck (Lawrence 1898). Nails, in particular, were important because they served as binders in both the physical and spiritual worlds. According to oral tradition in Jamaica, one spiritual use of nails was to bind an individual to someone by driving nails into that person's footprints or depositing them in graves, forcing *duppies* to "stay put." Oral tradition suggests that enslaved Africans and their descendants believed in these traditional "sayings" and altered their behavior according to such beliefs.

Duppy and the "Obeahman"

The recovery of the horseshoes and their use as protection against *duppies* reflects an important aspect of Jamaican engagement with the spiritual world, especially the spirits of ancestors. As a result of the prevalence of *duppies* in Jamaican society, there is a rich oral tradition about them. There are not only stories and songs relating to *duppies* but also plants, fruits, trees, flowers, and places either named after or associated with them (Rashford 1986). Typical "*duppy* lores" were not simply stories told for the purpose of entertainment or to instill fear (Beckwith 1969; Dance 1985; Senior 2003; Salkey 1980; Tanna 1984). Rather, they presented the reality for Orange Vale's village residents, whereby their secular worlds were intertwined with spiritual beings. The residents lived with the knowledge that spirits existed all around them and had the potential to harm and protect the living. Thus, the beliefs associated with *duppies* need to be examined in order to have a better understanding of the spiritual purposes of horseshoes in Jamaican culture.

Most early writings demonstrate that *duppies* have historically been seen as "superstitious" and evil by Europeans, some "educated" people, those living in urban areas, and, especially, plantation managers (Long [1774] 1970; Robinson and Walhouse 1893). For enslaved Africans, however, most of whom lived on rural plantations, *duppies* were an important aspect of their cultural and spiritual reality, as well as part of their cultural geography. People of African descent in colonial Jamaica tended to believe misfortune and general bad luck occurred not by accident but by some kind of interference from the supernatural world.

In both the historical and contemporary Jamaica, *duppies* were believed to be the spirits of ancestors whom one must not offend because they have the power to influence the lives of the living in both negative and positive ways. As a result, they should be appeased in various ways. But these African-descended peoples also recognized that the spirits could be manipulated by the living to be vengeful if mistreated or disrespected. Knowing this very important concept is critical in understanding the African-descended people in Jamaica, both past and present.

The origin of the word *duppy* has been credited to several ethnolinguistic groups in Africa, including in Sierra Leone where it means either a child or a ghost ("Folklore of the Negroes" 1905; Cassidy and Le Page 2002: 264; Leach 1961: 207). Jamaicans believe that *duppies* are created after death and during the burial, if proper precautions are not taken. One version tells of the creation of a *duppy* three days after burial and represented by a cloud of smoke that rises out of the grave ("Folklore of the Negroes" 1904a: 90). This smoke becomes the *duppy*. They can appear in many forms, such as animals, an object, the human form of the body it once possessed, or simply a "presence" (ibid.; Leach 1961). The idea of a *duppy* or spirit existing alongside the living is very much an African-derived concept.

Enslaved Africans undertook a series of rituals during burial to prevent the creation of *duppies* and appease them (Hopwood 2006; Trowbridge 1896: 281), a practice that continues today in many parts of Jamaica. According to Jamaican oral tradition, several steps must be taken to guard against a *duppy* at various times after the death of an individual. It is believed that *duppies* can be stopped at the source and prevented by making sure that the dead body is "planted down" (Leach 1961: 211; Banbury 1894; Bates 1896). If these precautions are not taken, however, the *duppy* will continue to roam freely. There are also several steps that can be taken to prevent *duppies* from entering one's dwelling. One method suggests marking a circle on the front door, which will prevent them from entering ("Folklore of the Negroes" 1904b: 207). Another method includes "cutting ten [on a door]. . . . The duppy cannot count beyond nine and, confronted by ten, must start counting over again and so gives his victim opportunity to escape; . . . the magic of the sign of the cross stops them. Peas, rice, sand cast before a pursuing duppy will stop him, because he must halt to count the grains before he can continue" (Leach 1961: 212). If this is not done and a *duppy* enters a dwelling, it can be expelled by a series of steps. One method suggests burning cow dung mixed with pieces of hoof and horn, while another recommends burning rosemary bush, cow dung, and horn ("Folklore of the Negroes" 1904a: 90; "Folklore of the Negroes" 1904b: 207). Additional "rules" related to avoiding *duppies,* as collected by Jamaican students in 1896, include "sprinkle sand before your door at night" ("Folklore of the Negroes" 1904b: 208) and "do not spit or throw water through a window at night, for if you do, and happen to wet a duppy, it will box [slap] you" (ibid.: 209).

One of the most important beliefs identified was that nailing a horseshoe to the front door of one's dwelling will help prevent *duppies* from entering a house ("Folklore of the Negroes" 1904a: 90; Carvalho 1998: 7; Leach 1961). Clearly there is tension between the simultaneous recognition that *duppies* must be pacified but, at the same time, kept at bay, reflecting the understanding that *duppies* can cause both good and harmful outcomes. Thus, it becomes important for the living to control their contact with *duppies.*

This belief in the ability of the spirits of the dead to intervene in the lives of the living continues today among the descendants of Orange Vale and the surrounding areas. In fact, contemporary Jamaicans believe that some measures must also be employed to appease *duppies*. For example, while we conducted research at Orange Vale, local community members and field assistants insisted on numerous occasions that we acknowledge and pay homage to the *duppies* at the site, often through the pouring of alcoholic libations to appease them so that we could "work in peace." All events at the site that were perceived as bad luck were attributed to the *duppies'* intervention and the pouring of libations always followed. This ritual acknowledged the *duppies'* presence on the site.

In the past, if these preventative methods were not employed or did not work, a specialist—an Obeahman or Obeahwoman—must be consulted to "catch" the *duppy*, for a fee (Leach 1961: 212; Trowbridge 1896: 281). Believed to have derived from the Igbo word "ubio" (meaning a charm to cause sickness and death), Obeah is an African-derived syncretic religion, much like Vodun and Santeria, that uses charms, divination, herbal medicines, and manipulation of the cosmic order to gain a desired outcome (Carvalho 1998: 6; Olmos and Paravisini-Gebert 2003). During the period of the occupation at Orange Vale, Obeah specialists at the plantation were believed to understand and practice rituals that could cure ailments but also break or counteract the evil acts of *duppies*. These spiritual practitioners combined ideology with healing through herbs, roots, and other materials (Payne-Jackson and Alleyne 2004). Individuals who solicited Obeah were willing to pay the required fees for the "cure" because of the great fear they had of *duppies*, particularly those who might want to take revenge. During enslavement in Jamaica, the practice of, or the solicitation of, an Obeah practitioner was considered a crime and punishable by death or "transportation" (exile) from the island (Act 24 of 1760, 1771). The practices of Obeah were seen as a threat to the plantation system because of the power and influence Obeah specialists had in enslaved communities. Such activities, thus, involved a high level of secrecy.

While the use of horseshoes as charms to ward off *duppies* represented the individual ways in which people at Orange Vale protected themselves from malevolent forces, ethnohistorical evidence also indicates that they employed spiritual practitioners. These individuals would have served as healers, as well as providing protection and good luck. In the case of Orange Vale, it is likely that spiritual practitioners/healers would have been consulted in the preparation of, or even during, the ritual burying of the horseshoes at the entrances, thereby empowering the utilitarian object.

The historical records from Orange Vale document two African-born male individuals who practiced Obeah at Orange Vale (Return of Registration 1826, 1829). The 1826 Return of Registration of Slaves notes that one individual, "Henry Turner Burke," estimated to be around forty-three years old, was "transported" from the plantation and the island after having been "convicted of practicing Obeah" (87: 217b), as was the law in Jamaica. Individuals such as Burke were likely present at most, if not all, plantations, providing their services to their internal communities.

Throughout the Americas, Obeah practitioners and other spiritual specialists were either men or women who offered a wide range of spiritual and medical services to African-derived communities. They were grouped into three broad roles as "midwives, root-doctors, and conjurers" (Wilkie 1997: 84; see also Brown and Cooper 1990; Feng 2002). All three services were considered to be "magical" by the colonial authorities, and filled with negative connotations. Midwives were known for combining spiritual and physical techniques to assist with childbirth. Root doctors, often called "spiritual mother/father" in Jamaica, used plant and animal extracts to heal and prevent diseases. Conjurers, often referred to as "Obeahman/woman" in Jamaica or "hoodoo doctors" elsewhere, were in the business of providing a variety of services that involved influencing behavior and social outcomes through the use of ritual paraphernalia. Generally, most of these practitioners were skilled to various degrees in each of these tasks in Jamaica, where healing is believed to be necessary on both physical and spiritual levels. Thus, all three practitioners were commonly referred to as "Obeahman" or "Obeahwoman." In Jamaica, it was the Obeah practitioner who specialized in the treatment of "*duppy* sickness" or spirit sickness, as well as viewed as having the ability to influence the negative behavior of *duppies* on the living (Payne-Jackson and Alleyne 2004: 105).

In general, Obeah practitioners were seen by the African-descended peoples as possessing dual power to create both negative and positive outcomes in relation to spiritual forces like *duppies.* On the one hand, practitioners were thought to have the means to cause harm to the living through their manipulation of those spirits. Simultaneously, practitioners also theoretically had the formulas to protect against *duppies* and even the ability to "catch" *duppies,* remove them from possessed individuals, and prevent these spirits from roaming freely. According to informants and oral traditions in the region, Obeah specialists like Henry Turner Burke were likely consulted secretly on a variety of matters by enslaved Africans at Orange Vale. Within the enslaved village community, much like duppies themselves, Obeah practitioners were both revered and feared. Thus, the relationship between Obeah practitioners and village members was mitigated on appeasement, but also fear. In legal cases involving conviction of Obeah practice, historical records suggest that some practitioners were often convicted based on evidence given in court by fellow enslaved Africans (Return of Registration 1817–1832).

Numerous documentary and oral historical sources indicate that African-descended peoples in the Americas used magical techniques to protect against spirits, maintain family relationships, attract or dispel mates, gain material things, and harm their enemies or rivals (Hurston [1938] 1990; Powdermaker [1937] 1993; Wilkie 1997: 86). In addition, Obeah practitioners like Burke used techniques believed to provide justice and order, as evidenced in the common practice of determining who committed acts of theft (e.g., Reeves 1996).

Within the violent context of the plantation system, oral traditions suggest that enslaved Africans living on Orange Vale would have consulted Obeah specialists to provide a variety of services to mitigate or counter violence, especially within the village (Payne-Jackson and Alleyne 2004: 104–120). Burke might have performed a number of services and served in various important functions within the community, empowered by community members themselves. Although he was seemingly powerless when compared to the larger plantation society's laws and advanced weapons used to enforce laws, he and others like him served as localized power sources for those within the village. On the other hand, he also had the potential to be a threat to the enslaved population due to his power to connect with spirits. As such, he was both respected and feared. Whether or not individuals used his services personally, he would have been respected and served as a source of healing, protection, and good luck.

The presence of spiritual healers and practitioners at Orange Vale is indicative of the type of spiritual individuals who were present at the burial or hanging of the materials left behind in the archaeological record. A few archaeological studies of the African Diaspora in the Americas have also found evidence related to these traditional healers/magicians. For example, Kenneth Brown's excavations at Levi Jordan Plantation in Texas found an assemblage of artifacts that he interpreted as being a magician's kit possibly related to the Kongo-influenced *mniski* (Brown 2001; Brown and Cooper 1990: 16–17). Laurie Wilkie and George Shorter found a large number of medicinal bottles at a dwelling in Mobile, Alabama, which they conclude may have been used to treat ailments of young children and related to the practices of midwifery (Wilkie and Shorter 2001). Other scholars have found similar artifact caches that could have been used in similar ways.

While we do not know for sure that the horseshoes recovered at Orange Vale were necessarily associated with the spiritual practitioners on that plantation, it is possible that the practitioners would have been consulted in the preparations, or likely even performed the rituals, which "fixed" the horseshoes in place. Although hated by plantation managers, these spiritual practitioners/healers were respected, revered, and feared for their power to cure or curse. Thus, by employing these individuals for various needs and using metal items with strong spiritual connections, as evidenced in academic literature and oral histories, members of the village community at Orange Vale were creating a parallel power structure alongside that of the larger plantation scale.

Understanding the relationship between spiritual practices and their practitioners in enslaved communities like Orange Vale is a complex and daunting undertaking. Add to this the secret nature of the practices and the complexity deepens. The recovery of horseshoes and evidence of the presence of Obeah practitioners at Orange Vale provides some insight into the practices of the members of the village community. On a personal level, the use of objects such as horseshoes by individuals, households, and families served as one of the many ways in which they sought to alleviate the potentially malevolent forces within the constraints of plantation slavery.

In the continuous process of religious creolization, enslaved Africans at Orange Vale were innovative in creating various "mechanisms" by which they could assert their own authority, even within a confining plantation system, such as through the use of horseshoes and Obeah practitioners (Bisnauth 1996: 100). The ritual practices of African people throughout the Americas served important functions in the physical, spiritual, and psychological healing of many, both during slavery and up until today. At Orange Vale, the use of horseshoes represented the individual or private ways in which enslaved Africans protected themselves from what they considered to be harmful forces, especially *duppies*. These malevolent forces could extend to include the white plantocracy, as well as other African village members considered threats by a family or household. The use of a horseshoe represents a syncretic way in which enslaved Africans mediated the forces they considered to be possible threats to their bodies and well-being as dictated in their African-derived ideology by reinscribing a European object with an African-derived meaning.

Although horseshoes represent a type of good luck charm in many cultures, it takes on new meaning in this African-descended context, particularly given the fact that there were many restrictions on enslaved Africans' engagement with and access to horses and horseshoes. Given the limited numbers of horses at Orange Vale, as well as the law prohibiting enslaved Africans' contact with horses, and limits on their ability to possess metal, the prevalence of these many horseshoes indicates that these items were deemed important to the enslaved people living at Orange Vale. It was so important to them that they would have had to go out of their way to access them, risking severe punishment. Thus, enslaved Africans' use of the European-made horseshoe and its association with protection and good luck to mediate the possible threat of violence they believed could cause harm to them, gives new meaning to an old material form.

Regardless of the constraints, it is clear that these African-descended peoples found alternative sources of power to deliver physical, spiritual, and emotional healing; for protection; and for favorable outcomes. The horseshoes, and the practitioners who were consulted to "fix" them, served important spiritual-medical functions and wielded significant power within the village community. Enslaved Africans at Orange Vale demonstrated their autonomy by creating a parallel source of power. Despite having enslaved status, they managed effectively to establish ways in which they took charge of how they healed and protected themselves from forces they considered malevolent. These residents at Orange Vale's village figured out ways in which they could imbue objects with power, as well as to authorize power to the specialized individuals who administered spiritual practices.

Note

I am deeply grateful to the people of Charlestown, Portland, Jamaica, for their kind hospitality and support, and for sharing their vast knowledge with me. I would also like to thank Mr. Dorrick Gray and his very supportive staff at the Archaeology Division of the Jamaica National Heritage Trust. In addition, I wish to thank Samuel Wilson, Cheryl LaRoche, Peter Schmidt, Carol McDavid, and my family for their unwavering support. Finally, this research was funded with grants from the National Science Foundation, I. I. E. Fulbright, the Mellon Foundation, and the Wenner Gren Foundation.

CHAPTER 10

Mundane or Spiritual?

THE INTERPRETATION OF GLASS BOTTLE CONTAINERS FOUND ON TWO SITES OF THE AFRICAN DIASPORA

Matthew Reeves

Archaeologists of the African Diaspora have been drawn to the study of artifacts with potential spiritual use because of the many possibilities that these objects offer for a deep understanding of Black Atlantic cultural formation. The presence of such items on sites has been heralded as representing everything from African survival to resistance against hegemonic patriarchy (Leone 2005; Orser 1994; Stine et al. 1996; Vlach 1993; Wilkie 1997). Many of the scholars involved in this search have called for careful consideration of the archaeological contexts from which they were recovered (Wilkie 1997). In addition, researchers have also called for interdisciplinary examination of ethnohistorical texts to allow for interpretation (Leone and Fry 1999). In this chapter, I consider how the steps from observation to interpretation are enacted, specifically, how we take an otherwise commonly occurring artifact, such as glass bottles, to determine whether their placement at the site was intentional or a secondary result of disposal, and finally whether the intentional placement reflects their use as spiritual objects or simply for mundane purposes, such as storage. What makes bottle glass an interesting case study is its common occurrence on historic sites. Due to the multiple uses for bottles, their particular use and contents can be a bit enigmatic (Smith 2008: 22–28), but with proper study of context, it is possible to differentiate potential spiritual use of such bottles from those of more routine origins.

For this case study, I discuss glass bottles located in concealed contexts and determine their use as potential spiritual containers—otherwise known as Obeah, hoodoo, witching, or conjure bottles (King 2006: 294; Merrifield 1987). In this chapter, I describe bottles recovered from African-Jamaican and African American contexts. What ties both of these together is the presence of glass bottles that are buried in specific contexts, which were not meant to be seen by casual observers. Such placement of bottles is consistent with both Euro-American and African American traditions. Some of the best-defined contexts for the spiritual use of bottles are those "witching bottles" recovered in England—ranging from bottles found below hearths and thresholds, in houses at the bases of stairs, and even in yards (King 2006: 294; Merrifield 1987: 174). Such English examples have contained very specific object caches, such as bent straight pins bound into a cloth heart, iron nails, and brass tacks. Several bottles with spiritual potential have been recovered from both within the walls and below the floors of cabins of enslaved Africans in Virginia and Kentucky (Samford 1996). The contents of these bottles have included single buttons but some were simply empty bottles; as a result, determining the original contents of such bottles has remained elusive. Whatever the case regarding contents, for both the English and African, the common denominator was use of glass bottles to hold spells or charms, and the concealing of bottles in locations where their potency could be directed toward an intended target (Merrifield 1987; Wilkie 1997). Given the interplay of belief systems of African Americans, European Americans, and Native Americans, as well as the common use of these material goods among European and African Americans, there is little doubt that the physical manifestations of such conjure bottles were influenced by many sources, not just African (Fennell 2000; Wilkie 1997: 84). For sites in Jamaica, as discussed below, there is a well-established tradition of conjure bottles, known as "Obeah bottles," used for similar purposes and often placed in concealed locations. I examine the presence of such bottles at two early nineteenth-century sites: a buried bottle feature located beside a house in a Jamaican enslaved African village and three features located in the cellar of a Virginia plantation great house.

Beyond considering the specifics of spiritual traditions surrounding glass bottles, this chapter uses the example of this particular class of artifacts as an excellent counterpoint for examining the potential for spiritual use of objects at archaeological sites. Bottle glass is ubiquitous at historic sites with its presence normally representing disposal of broken vessels. Such vessels, most especially olive-green bottle glass and medicinal vials on both eighteenth- and nineteenth-century sites, are common across a range of socioeconomic groups, and often make up a substantial percentage of artifact and vessel components on these sites.

What this chapter attempts to determine is how to assign interpretive value to these objects when their presence at a site is suggestive of intentional placement. For the sites being discussed, I describe the stratigraphic contexts for these bottles in detail and use these contexts to determine the significance of the bottles as either intentionally placed objects with spiritual meanings or as mundane objects related, for example, to a broader category of actions such as trash disposal. In the following analysis, the Jamaican bottle feature turns out to have the highest potential for representing an intentionally placed spiritual object. In contrast, of the three features recovered from the Virginia context, only one has any potential of significance as an intentionally placed object. I use these two separate examples to relate my own personal experience in researching these sites and some of the inspirations and frustrations that stem from the interpretation of the features encountered.

Contextual Approaches to Archaeology of Ritual Objects in North America and the Caribbean

In understanding the intent of this chapter, it is important to provide background on the genesis of its topic. When I was invited to be part of a Society for Historical Archaeology session and present my findings from my excavations in Jamaica, I was initially very excited about presenting my findings not only from Juan de Bolas (the site where the potential Obeah bottle was found) but also from recent "concealed" bottle contexts located in the cellar of the eighteenth-century Montpelier mansion in Virginia. At the juncture of writing the abstract for the session, I made the uncritical assumption that all of the bottles found in the various subfloor pits in the cellar of the mansion had some particular significance, namely as intentionally placed objects for spiritual purposes. Following the initial excitement of writing the abstract, I got down to the task of critically examining the contexts for some of the bottles we had located. In particular, in reviewing other artifacts found in the same context, I began to doubt my initial interpretation of these as spiritual or even intentionally placed bottles. In two of the three contexts considered—a bottle base and neck placed in a wall; and the other two, bottle bases within a subfloor storage pit—the feature contained multiple vessel fragments that came from different bottles than the bases located in the features. As such, these unrelated bottle glass fragments were more suggestive of trash deposits than intentional placement. In addition, there were no additional materials found that would suggest the use of these bottles as vessels for holding specially prepared concoctions. This finding underscores the importance of critically examining the surrounding archaeological context as the basis for interpreting objects that may have been charged with ritual meanings and powers (see Ogundiran and Saunders, this volume). The pertinent question that arises is how to differentiate the more mundane uses of bottles from those that were more spiritual in nature (see Gundaker, this volume).

The answer to this question rests in how the bottles were deposited in the archaeological record. What informs this line of inquiry is the combined concepts of cultural formation processes and contextual analysis of the strata from which they were recovered. Cultural formation process, in its basic form as defined by Michael Schiffer and others, seeks to understand the activities responsible for the formation of deposits (Schiffer 1983, 1987; Stein 1987). Essential to this interpretive process is assessing how objects found in the deposits we excavate become part of the site. For the sake of this discussion, we are seeking to determine whether artifacts are intentionally placed or disposed of following breakage or the end of their usefulness (known as secondary deposit or de facto refuse). Making this determination is dependent upon a careful examination of the physical context in which the objects are set, including associated artifacts, context within the larger site, and physical relationships within the depositional matrix. Beyond stratigraphic context, understanding the broader cultural context is extremely important for defining intentional placement versus casual deposition.

To move away from the conundrum, I use intentionality of placement to define the special nature of an otherwise "mundane" artifact, such as bottle glass. To recognize the act of intentionality of placement, I rely upon what Joshua Pollard has called "depositional citation," in which the position of an artifact marks intent through repeated and contextualized patterns of material placement (Pollard 2008: 58). Carefully defining intent in the placement of a set of artifacts has the potential to allow archaeologists to begin to ascribe meaning to the otherwise ubiquitous material culture found at historic sites.

An interesting case study of polemics in ascribing significance to unique contexts comes from the finds of marked pots in tidewater rivers in South Carolina. As originally reported by Leland Ferguson, the discovery by divers of locally made pots with "X" marks was ascribed ritual significance as offerings made by enslaved African Americans within a riverine setting (1992). The fact that these pots were unbroken was an important factor in determining the intentional disposal of otherwise useful objects in rivers. A reassessment of these riverine pots, however, places them in the context of the market economy, with the alternative hypothesis that they originated from potters or merchants who accidentally capsized their canoes during transport to and from market (Joseph 2007). Such an alternative explanation moved this seemingly unique deposition of whole pots from an intentional context to accidental deposition.

The spiritual nature of everyday life is another area that deserves mention in this discussion of contextualizing everyday objects in the spiritual milieu. Mark Leone, in his work in Annapolis, has been one of the most prolific proponents of examining everyday items in primary and secondary deposits for spiritual significance. By interpreting finds of objects through the lens of ethnohistorical texts, he has devised a strategy to breathe meaning into everyday objects (Leone 2005; Leone and Fry 1999). In his analysis of spiritual contexts, Leone mirrors discussions by other archaeologists and scholars who have expressed concern that the prevalence of spiritual practices has been greatly underestimated not only for African American contexts but also for eighteenth- and nineteenth-century sites in general (Bilby and Handler 2004; Fennel 2000; Wilkie 1997). In other words, while we interpret such features as rare or unusual, for practitioners in the eighteenth and nineteenth centuries, these were part of the everyday cycle of life. Setting a pot for one's ancestors, giving libations at the beginning of a meal to pacify spirits, or lighting a fire to bring common ground between the living and dead were acts that served as part of the daily routine. As such, spiritual actions were part of daily activities much in the same manner as the mundane cycle of food preparation, consumption, and disposal of trash. Scholarship on ritual actions have attempted to move beyond such a dichotomy by explaining that ritual permeated the acts of everyday life (Bell 1992; Pollard 2008: 43), and difficulty exists in drawing out the spiritual from the mundane even when it comes to secondary trash deposits (Stahl 2008: 160; Edwards 1998: 260). Further, William Walker has even defined ritual meaning within the act of deposition and burial of strata in carefully defined contexts (2002: 162).

What I am proposing in this chapter is the careful consideration of context—in this case, the kind of context that archaeologists are particularly adept at establishing, that is, the spatio-temporal context of the archaeological record and the cultural context that guided the formation of these deposits. In the case of assessing the placement of glass bottles, it is first necessary to define the depositional context that provides clues to the substance and meaning behind the actions which resulted in their placement. By examining the surrounding deposits for related artifacts, evidence for postdepositional disturbance, and critical clues for substances contained within, we can begin to differentiate between intentional and secondary placement. Moving beyond placement, an important part of defining the broader context is the variety of sources we can consult—whether it be oral history, local traditions, ethnohistorical accounts, or examples drawn from contemporary sites. Such information is critical for defining spiritual use of everyday objects. The two case studies that I consider are the early nineteenth-century enslaved African contexts in Jamaica and the U.S.

Jamaican Nineteenth-Century Obeah Bottles

Of the two case studies discussed in this chapter, the one with the clearest defined context for spiritual use of bottles was found in my excavations of an early nineteenth-century community of enslaved workers in the interior portion of St. Catherine's Parish in Jamaica. This case study was part of a large analysis of household remains from slave settlements in the northern St. Catherine's district (Reeves 1997, 2011). The house area was part of a settlement for an early nineteenth-century coffee plantation known as Juan de Bolas, and was occupied by over 120 slaves from 1799 through full emancipation in 1838. Following emancipation, the absentee owner sold land lots to former enslaved Africans, whose descendants continue to own land in this district today. Most residents now work their own garden plots and market produce in the local internal market system. Due to the long-term family ties in the area, oral traditions and local knowledge of the history remain strong. In fact, this survival of local history made survey of the area incredibly efficient, with local informants simply taking me to where the enslaved African village settlements were located. In many cases, descendants remembered stories related to these communities, and individual owners reported finding broken ceramics, glass, and other items in the abandoned settlements, most of which are now active garden contexts. The village settlement, known as Slave Center in local oral traditions, was located below the coffee works (the water-powered mill used for crushing and washing coffee and large,

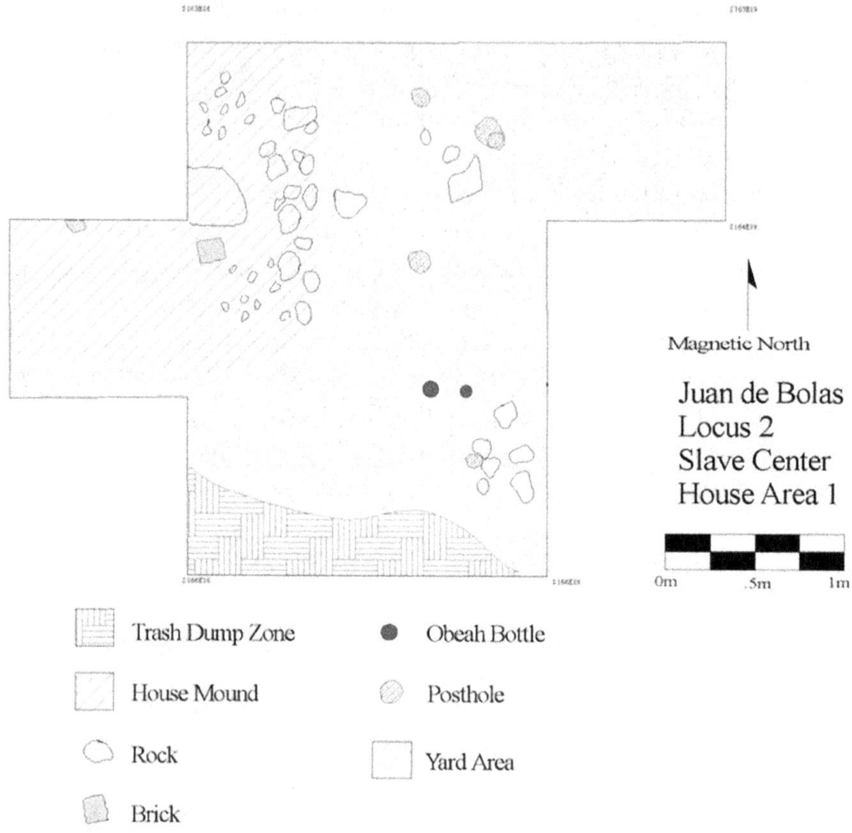

FIGURE 10.1. Plan of House Area 1, showing relationship of house mound to Obeah bottle feature.

leveled barbeques used for drying beans) and was one of two settlements associated with the plantation.

Excavations at Slave Center revealed several house areas, one of which was surprisingly well preserved, due to a series of wash deposits that accumulated over the site in the late nineteenth and early twentieth centuries. Surveys and excavations had uncovered the remains of a house mound—likely a decayed wattle-and-daub structure with a raised rubble and clay floor (typical construction found well into the mid-twentieth century for the district). An area of the structure suspected of being a porch extension into the yard was excavated (figure 10.1). In addition to several post holes that defined the extent of the porch, a barely discernible feature was uncovered

FIGURE 10.2. Obeah bottle bases in context, with insets of restored bottles.

immediately adjacent to the house and under the porch extension. When the fill for this feature was removed, two bottles were found sitting in an upright position. Excavations of the surrounding yard revealed that the structure associated with the bottle feature had been occupied between the 1810s and 1820s. The occupation period for this structure was determined by its stratigraphic relationship to surrounding deposits. Its yard surface and house features were located below a trash and wash deposit, which dates to the late 1820s–1830s. The yard surface was characterized by a scatter of smaller artifacts, which were rendered into the yard floor by foot traffic. Based on the site's stratigraphy, the feature that contained the bottles had been dug into this occupation surface and intruded into earlier yard deposits, which date to the 1810s. As is shown below, determining that this feature was located within a house yard and adjacent to the structure was of critical importance to interpreting the intent of these bottles' placement beyond their mundane forms.

For their part, the bottles were not complete; both were missing their necks with portions of the shoulders and sides shattered (figure 10.2). The most likely explanation for their disturbance comes from the area being worked as small garden plots for well over 150 years following emancipation.

Forking and hoeing of the soils resulted in the shattering of the necks and these portions being discarded as encountered during garden work. Unfortunately, excavation units placed to the east of the bottle feature revealed only a few additional fragments; the necks or finishes were not recovered. Both bottles contained fragments of charcoal as well as a lime residue in the bottom of the vessels.

What made this feature a spectacular find was not just their context, nor their relatively good state of preservation in an active yard and garden, but the individual who discovered them and his reaction. During my fieldwork in Jamaica from 2002 to 2004, a local resident, Linton Rhule, served as my main informant and assistant during excavations. Rhule traces his ancestry through enslaved Africans who lived and worked at Juan de Bolas Plantation during its operation as a coffee plantation. Following emancipation in 1838, Rhule's ancestors purchased several small plots on the plantation when the owner subdivided and sold the land to the former enslaved laborers (Reeves 1997). As a result, Rhule and others in the Juan de Bolas community can trace their ancestral and land ties back for over 160 years. This stability has allowed for an incredibly rich set of oral traditions to survive, as well as a highly specific set of spiritual beliefs, most of which revolve around the appeasement of *duppies*—spirits of the deceased (see Saunders, this volume).

It was the tie that these settlements held to Rhule's ancestry, combined with his interest in local history, that inspired him to work with us for eight months on the excavations we carried out at Juan de Bolas and at neighboring enslaved African villages. In addition to the interest in finding various items, there was a real and living connection between the local community and the ancestors who resided in the old settlements. During excavations at these former living spots, building a fire and making food and drink offerings to *duppies* was a part of the everyday field operations. The combination of direct ancestral ties to the settlement and persistence of local spiritual traditions came together in the discovery and interpretation of the bottle feature. To understand the combined significance of the bottle feature and its association with the descendant community, we must delve into Rhule's discovery of the feature, in terms of both its physical and spiritual essence.

The discovery follows an all-too-familiar recitation of last-minute finds at many archaeological sites. As a final wrap-up for the excavation, we decided to return to Slave Center and do some cleanup shots of a particularly well-preserved house area. The discovery of this intact yard area was an exciting prospect, as the past three months had been spent excavating in downslope middens and deposits disturbed from horticultural activities. We had spent the morning setting up for a school group to visit. I decided that we should spend the afternoon doing cleanup work on House Area 1 for final photos, and then open some additional units in a new area.

With the five units of House Area 21 scraped down and cleaned for final shots, something looked amiss against the eastern wall in one of the units. I decided to have Rhule excavate further down in this part of the unit, designating this as level 4. Just as I started to clear bush for an adjacent unit, Rhule called to me that I should come and see something. He was encountering large amounts of glass in a level that otherwise had been sterile. Upon seeing that Rhule was uncovering what appeared to be two intact wine bottles, I grabbed my camera to get some photographs of the excavations in progress (figure 10.2). I was not sure what Rhule had found, but it seemed interesting.

After Rhule had exposed the bottles, we started to muse as to their origin and use. Why would two intact bottles be discarded so close to the house and buried in an upright position? In pondering this curiosity Rhule suddenly declared, "These are those Obeah *duppy* bottles!" With a start, I realized that we had stumbled upon a truly personal and cogent connection with the past. These were more than simply bottles; rather, they were keyholes to a belief system that still has relevance in Jamaica today. What made the discovery of particular importance were the conversations that followed—centering on Rhule's knowledge of Obeah bottles. When I asked him about how an otherwise mundane set of bottles, especially in their broken state, could be Obeah objects, he simply stated that the meaning was a matter of where they were found. Finding such objects buried upright in a yard gave their placement meaning; if they were found in a dump with other broken crockery and glass, they would simply be trash. His insight into this spiritual milieu came from his early childhood experiences growing up in the Juan de Bolas district with his great uncle, whose home was built on the same barbeques on which his enslaved ancestors had dried coffee. Being raised in his great uncle's home, Rhule was exposed to the oral traditions related to both the early nineteenth-century history of Juan de Bolas and the spiritual traditions and uses of herbal medicine. Rhule's great uncle, Jasper Rhule, was born sometime in the late 1870s, and was himself the grandson of one of the enslaved drivers at Juan de Bolas Plantation.

In his youth, Linton Rhule remembered working the bush with his great uncle and coming across similar bottles near old living spots or house areas. Upon these encounters, Rhule's uncle explained these finds as bottles that were buried near gates, corners of houses, or in the middle of the yard. Such bottles contained powerful medicine and were meant either to hurt someone or for protection. Jasper Rhule explained to Linton that human hair was placed in the bottle for destruction, bush medicine for protection, and an individual's nail parings to bind the person's spirit to a certain place, usually a cotton tree. As such, Linton Rhule's great uncle was essentially identifying and explaining archaeological examples to Rhule through the lens of ethnohistorical traditions in the 1950s, some forty years before historical archaeologists began delving into the particulars of ritual features! Such bottles had a particularly close relationship for Rhule's great uncle through the role he served as a constable in the Juan de Bolas District in the 1910s and 1920s. His uncle's status and position as a law enforcer resulted in his frequent encounter of such bottles in his own yard—doubtless buried by constituents attempting to thwart his uncle's ability to intercede in their quasi-legal activities.

For Jamaica, there is a well-defined and specific history for African-based spiritual practices—Obeah—which involve a mixture of conjuring, herbal healing practices, and manipulating spirits. Chief among the physical forms of spells are Obeah bottles, which are mentioned in nineteenth-century accounts as serving various uses, such as deterring thieves, warding off malevolent spirits, appeasing the spirits of the dead, and inflicting collateral damage to perceived enemies, among others. Filled with powerful substances, these bottles were placed in conspicuous locations or hidden spots to induce spells (Bell 1889: 10; Kingsley 1887; Phillippo 1843: 247). The concept of Obeah is one that, while more prominently cited in Jamaica, is present throughout the Anglophone Caribbean. Kenneth Bilby and Jerome Handler (2004: 11) have postulated that the term "Obeah" comes from the corruption of the Igbo (present-day southeastern Nigerian) word *dibia,* which refers to doctor or healer. Some have also suggested that it may be derived from the Akan-Twi word *o-bayifo,* what anthropologists would call a witch, wizard, or sorcerer (see Saunders, this volume). Whatever the etymological origins of the word, the term is consistent with the medicinal, spiritual, and supernatural practices and beliefs found across West and West Central Africa. Historical sources, mainly Jamaican parliamentary accounts, recall that in the eighteenth and nineteenth centuries, Jamaicans, both Europeans and Africans, were aware of Obeahmen and -women (see Boaz, this volume). While Obeah practitioners were almost exclusively of African ancestry, their spiritual beliefs—exclusively non-Christian—were both feared and respected by Europeans and Africans. In many ways, Europeans feared Obeah for what it represented for people of African descent: gaining power not controlled by whites (Bilby and Handler 2004: 8). Legislation passed in Jamaica and other British Caribbean islands made the practice of Obeah illegal and punishable by either execution or transportation (ibid.: 16; see also Boaz, this volume). Later in the nineteenth century, missionaries pushed Jamaicans away from this practice by labeling it "black magic" and "witchcraft" (Bilby and Handler 2004: 9). As such, the ritual behind Obeah appears to be very much African-based, but recognized and feared by both European- and African-Jamaicans through the eighteenth, nineteenth, and twentieth centuries.

The above three contexts with reference to Obeah bottles—the feature encountered at the 1810s house area, Rhule's travels in the bush with his uncle and locating such bottles at old house areas, and his uncle's personal connection with such bottles in his daily life in the early twentieth century—all have one thing in common: the glass bottles were placed in similar spatial relationships. All three of these contexts took place within the same region and even involved the same set of descendants. In other words, the site where we found the bottles was inhabited by the ancestors of Linton Rhule, my main informant who identified them in the first place. For Rhule, the link was made physically tangible through the intergenerational connection of his great uncle to the names, characters, actions, and beliefs of his enslaved ancestors. In the end, the process of associating archaeological examples with specific spiritual practices was made possible by interpreting the bottle feature based on an existing set of oral traditions. Remarkably, these oral traditions can be traced back to the same site at which the archaeological feature was found in the first place. What brought about the identification of this feature, however, was the careful consideration of its context and placement within the archaeological deposits being excavated.

Bottles from an Early Nineteenth-Century Virginia Context

The second case study for interpreting the placement of bottles comes from excavations carried out at the eighteenth-century home of James Madison. The Montpelier mansion was built in the mid-1760s by the fourth president's parents, and it witnessed extensive renovations in the 1810s, just prior to James and Dolley Madison's retirement from the White House. During

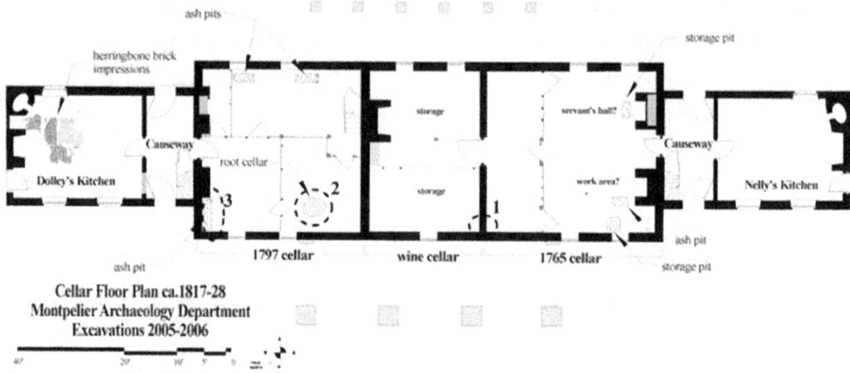

FIGURE 10.3. Plan for Montpelier mansion cellar showing various features encountered during archaeology carried out in this space. 1 = bottle cache under brick wall partition, 2 = root cellar with wine bottles, 3 = subfloor pit with medicine bottle.

the Madison occupation (1763–1844), the cellar spaces were primarily used by the Madisons' enslaved workers (figure 10.3). The cellars were spaces in which enslaved people performed some of their daily work for cooking and preparing foods and for long-term storage, as well as spaces in which they could socialize and rest in a location separate from the house's white occupants. In the dozens of visitor accounts that describe the Montpelier house and grounds, not a single one mentions or describes the cellars. Such omissions support the idea that the cellars were spaces quite separate from the formal ones of the house and grounds. Despite this separation, however, the actions of enslaved workers in the cellars were carefully supervised by the Madisons. Within the cellar, all actions were directed toward the daily activities needed to support the Madison family and their entertaining activities during their retirement years.

Prior to the excavation in the mansion being carried out, I was quite aware of the similar context shared between the cellar spaces of Montpelier and that encountered by Mark Leone in Annapolis. The use of cellars for a combination of storage, work, and cooking is widespread across the Chesapeake region. In all of these spaces, the cellars were chiefly inhabited by enslaved Africans. Leone's finds in Annapolis cellars emblematically fixed the potential of these spaces for ritual features (2005). In fact, while attending an archaeological conference in Deerfield, Massachusetts, on African American rituals in 2003, I discussed the upcoming cellar excavations with

Mark Leone, who was quite adamant about critically examining all of the spaces for evidence of intentionally placed objects. This charge was taken to heart in our examination of the cellar spaces at Montpelier.

What made these excavations particularly exciting and promising for finding potential secreted caches of objects was that the entire portion of the cellar floor (all five rooms) had a concrete floor poured over the area shortly after the duPont family purchased Montpelier in 1901. As a result, the nineteenth-century surfaces in these rooms were protected from twentieth-century disturbances, leaving them untouched and protected for another century. Starting in 2003, and continuing for almost two years, Montpelier archaeologists carefully removed the concrete with jackhammers and chisels, and then completely excavated the cellar floor spaces. This complete excavation was necessary due to structural repairs required for the mansion's failing framing and masonry foundations, as well as for the installation of underground utilities. In addition, part of the goals for the mansion repair was the complete restoration of the cellar spaces, and this made archaeology an invaluable tool for discovering room use and function. What archaeologists found during excavations is that the 1901 concrete floor preserved in place countless eighteenth- and early nineteenth-century features such as storage pits, wall partitions, evidence for flooring, and small items related to the daily activities that occurred in the cellar spaces (Tinkham and Reeves 2010).

While the excavations revealed many extraordinary features, what was particularly disappointing was not to have located any obvious features or caches such as those found in Annapolis—no caches of pins, bent nails, or crystals—just the normal detritus of work areas. The closest we came to any deposits outside of the expected objects was in the form of bottles—albeit broken—that appear to have been intentionally placed in discrete locations. Three such contexts were found: one within the brick wall of the mansion, another in a storage pit, and the third in a subfloor pit (see figure 10.2). Similar to the Obeah bottle feature located in the Juan de Bolas slave settlement and those described in ethnohistorical sources, these bottles would not be visible to the casual viewer in the cellar. The question that arises is whether such concealed bottles were intentionally placed or a product of secondary deposits.

One of the first features containing upright bottles was found in a storage pit in what is termed the 1797 portion of the cellar. The excavations of this pit revealed the feature to have originally been lined with a barrel and potentially used for the storage of vegetables to preserve them during the winter months. During the removal of fills from this pit, two bottle bases were located at the bottom of the depositional layers. Similar to the examples seen in Jamaica, these bottles were missing their necks and shoulders, and were sitting next to each other. Unlike the Jamaican examples, however, the bottle glass fragments found in the overlying fill were from other bottles (based on color gradation and oxidation), and one was upright while the other was bottom up. In addition, no residue was found within any of the bottle bases. Combining the context of additional debris (brick rubble, ceramics, and nails) being found in the fill deposit and multiple partial vessels being present in the context, these bottle bases were ruled as representing secondary deposits with no apparent evidence for intentional placement.

The second potential bottle feature was found within a brick partition wall near the exterior wall shared between the two rooms. When located by archaeologists, this feature was thought to be part of a rodent-disturbed area because much of the base for the brick wall had been undermined by rodent tunnels. Upon removing clay and brick rubble, however, the finish for a wine bottle was exposed that appeared to be stuck inside and under the brick partition wall. More excavation revealed that this bottle was placed in a niche created by the removal of several bricks from the base of the wall. The bottle itself was broken, and only the base and neck present (much of the body of the vessel was missing). The soil removed from this context, once water screened, was revealed to only contain a couple of shattered bone fragments and three egg shell fragments—all finds consistent with the low amount of domestic deposits in this corner of the cellar.

What was unusual about this bottle context was the fact that, to place the bottle, the bearer had to not only remove bricks to create the cavity that concealed the bottle but also excavate part of the clay floor to allow access to the bottom courses of the wall. While the cellar room was in the portion of the house built in 1765, this bottle appears to have been put in place after 1808, when a series of repairs were made to the exterior mansion wall (Tinkham and Reeves 2010). This feature is located in the north corner of the room and is in the direct corner formed by the exterior brick wall and the brick partition wall that separates this room from the secured storage cellar.

As to the position of the bottle within the wall, difficulty exists in ascribing an exact meaning to its position. That it was meant to be out of sight is certain. With its position below the level of the packed clay floor (the Madison-era surface in this area) and within the brick wall, it would have been all but invisible, except to the trowel of an archaeologist. Another possible explanation for its presence comes from this feature's relationship with the secure storage cellar room just on the other side of the wall. During the eighteenth and early nineteenth centuries, the secure storage space was the locale of all foodstuffs, wine, and other supplies bound for the Madisons' table. Only the most trusted slaves would have been provided the key to this room, and access would have been very limited. This secure storage area was located on the opposite side of the wall from where this bottle was located.

What initially presented itself as a concealed niche used for placing a bottle within a wall—a context found at other sites for secreting conjure bottles—provided much discussion as to the spiritual origins of this feature. The critical analysis of the archaeological context for this feature, however, began to provide more mundane, but just as intriguing, explanations. The relationship of this feature to the secure storage space—which included storage of wine bottles—made us re-examine the adjacent room for any features that might be related to this niche on the opposite side of the partition wall. A similar feature was found on the wall opposite, where brick had been removed below the floor level, and there was the presence of additional wine bottle fragments. This niche was directly linked to the concealed space on the opposite wall that contained a wine bottle neck and base. With these two spaces joined, it would have been possible to pass a wine bottle beneath the wall of the secure storage area into the adjacent workroom.

The connection between this feature and the storage room led to several alternative explanations to its origin and use beyond the spiritual realm. Possibly the space below the wall was used to stash bottles and other items for access at a later time from the opposite side of the wall. By quickly placing items in the niche within the secure storage space, workers could access them at a more discrete and opportune time from the inconspicuous vantage of the adjacent workroom. Another possible use was simply as a place to stash bottles accidentally broken during handling, which might explain why there were two partial bottles present within the space. The fragmentary nature of the bottles suggests the particular vessels were placed there after they were broken, rather than being broken in place, with the most prominent portions of the bottle (neck and base) stashed in the niche. While such use of this feature is highly conjectural, with the absence of any additional contextual artifacts (items that would have been contained in the bottle), the incomplete nature of the bottles, and subsequent rodent disturbance, it is difficult to draw strong conclusions toward any of the hypotheses. The use of this space to hide and conceal bottles for long-term purposes, however, is doubtful due to their fragmentary nature and presence of multiple bottles. Such ongoing concealment is a critical characteristic of conjure bottles but is missing from the excavated context.

The third and most intriguing bottle was an aqua-tinted medicinal bottle base recovered from a subfloor pit located in the north corner of the adjacent north cellar room. This pit was arranged between the north corner and the structural base for a chimney. This feature was similar to two other rectangular subfloor features located within the same room of the mansion cellar in that it contained layers of hearth ash and shattered remains of wine bottles. All of these pits shared common features of being less than a foot in depth and were likely situated between floor joists, a common aspect of shallow subfloor pits (Samford 2007: 110). Within these ash pits, there was a high amount of egg shells, animal bones, and small items (such as straight pins) that were discarded with the hearth ash and were indicative of hearth sweepings. Within hearth ash from eighteenth- and nineteenth-century domestic sites, it is common to find items that were either thrown or swept into the hearth. Hearths would be regularly cleaned of ash, and as such, they served as convenient repositories for items from the "dust bin." Based on ceramics found in this and two other ash pits located in the northern room of the cellar, these pits were used in the first quarter of the nineteenth century.

What was unusual about the bottle located in this pit was that it was placed upright in the northwest corner of the feature and filled with charred material. The material within this bottle made it visible at the top of the feature as a small circular patch of what appeared to be charred wood. Once the subfloor pit was completely excavated, the circular patch was revealed as an aqua-tinted medicinal vial whose neck and finish were missing. The possibility exists that the top portion of the bottle was sheared off by leveling activities following the removal of the wooden floor and prior to the pouring of the concrete floor in 1901. Given that there are no other charred wood concentrations found in the vicinity of the bottle, the charred material within this vial appears to have been intentionally placed there. In addition, the fact that the bottle was placed directly in the north corner of the pit (also the north corner of the cellar) suggests intentional placement, and its locale appears to have some significance for the bearer of the bottle. Similar placement of ritual objects in corners has been noted by Mark Leone in Annapolis (Leone 2005).

In addressing the intentional placement of this third bottle, difficulty exists in interpreting its exact function and that of the contents held within. What we likely will never know is whether the bottle was placed upright and filled with charred material for symbolic/spiritual purposes or placed simply on a whim. It is possible that the bottle was kept in the corner of the ash pit for safekeeping in a concealed location and was never intended to be used for supernatural purposes. In contrast to the Jamaican bottle feature and possibly the bottle niche located in the south cellar room of Montpelier, it is difficult to ascertain whether the placement of the medicinal vial was originally intended for storage rather than for secreting the bottle. The alternative use of this feature to hide the bottle doubtlessly relates to the charred wood contents of the bottle. That material within the bottle was completely pulverized and precluded exact identification of its original organic contents. I am not aware of any other ethnohistorical or archaeological examples of similar bottles being found, though close examination suggests its potential origins.

The closest examples for bottles within subfloor pits comes from those discussed by Patricia Samford in her review of subfloor pits in Chesapeake slave quarter sites (2007). In particular, she asserts that some subfloor pits were potentially used as shrines and notes the presence of bottles in these features. These pits also contained a wide array of carefully arranged material goods, such as animal bones, shells, and iron objects (ibid.). What defined these features as shrines was the context of a complete range of carefully arranged objects, precluding the pits' use for other, more mundane functions. The absence of other intact items in the pit containing the medicinal vial makes it more likely to have been a former storage pit relegated to an ash/debris pit.

The isolated nature and careful arrangement of this bottle in what otherwise would be a refuse pit suggests its intentional placement. In addition, considering that the vial contained pulverized charred wood suggests the vial's potency as opposed to its being placed for storage of a valued substance (which presumable pulverized charred wood would not be, unless endowed with some alternative function). The placement of the vial in the north corner of not just the pit but also the room further highlights its special circumstances. Samford has noted that in other pits used for spiritual purposes, objects were placed in corners (ibid.). Thus, the combination of its intentional placement, its being distinct from other trash and debris placed in this pit, and its position in the corner of the building suggests its meaning as potentially moving beyond the mundane.

In contrast to the bottles located in Juan de Bolas, the lack of ethnohistorical or oral testimony in regard to spiritual practices connected to the bottles at Montpelier makes interpretation beyond loose speculation very difficult. The use of bottles to store concoctions used for conjuring is documented in 1930s Works Progress Administration narratives of former slaves (Rawick 1972, vol. 3). The few narratives that discuss these bottles refer to them as being placed in concealed locations; however, being able to tie these occurrences to a specific region and cultural tradition is challenging.

Another factor to consider in interpreting the African spiritual milieu in North America is the ever-present surveillance and control of white owners. Chris Fennell has contrasted the rich ethnographic set of spiritual beliefs in the Caribbean with the more private, individualized symbolism of North America as stemming from the increased surveillance present in the latter area (Fennell 2007b: 92). Of particular interest at Montpelier is the early history of resistance on the plantation. Sentencing documents from the 1730s relate that enslaved Africans owned by James Madison's grandfather were convicted of poisoning him shortly after the Madisons' arrival in the Piedmont. Such a public spectacle might have hovered over the family as a "collective memory" and made the Madisons ever vigilant against individual-based spirituality and action (Chambers 2005). How this would affect the ability to identify individual expressions of conjuring and spirituality in the archaeological record is difficult to state. The open expression of African-based spiritual practices would, doubtlessly, have been frowned upon by an owner family with such a turbulent past, although this does not mean that such practices were absent within the enslaved community. Rather, if present, they would have been subjected to more secrecy. The potential need for secrecy among the enslaved residents at the Montpelier plantation places even more meaning on the careful placement of the medicinal vial in the corner of the 1797 cellar.

At Montpelier, while we lack a direct ethnohistorical context, we have thoroughly explored the archaeological context for the cellars. The excavation of all of the contexts in the cellar provides us with the comparative contexts to contrast the presence of objects such as glass bottle fragments, charred wood, and other items found in the features under archaeological investigation with features of known uses and origins in ethnographic and historical records. The arrangement of this archaeological feature recalls what Pollard calls "depositional citation" (2008: 58). He uses this concept to explain the structural compositional arrangement of artifacts in Neolithic southern Britain, which he sees as "a strategy in the negotiation of value" (Pollard 2001: 316). By being able to cross-mend and compare the bottles found across all cellar deposits, however, we were able to differentiate between bottles that were placed in secondary trash deposits and those intentionally placed in primary contexts. Such constructive use of depositional contexts allows us to call out those bottle features that appeared to have a unique signature for potential spiritual importance, such as the medicinal bottle in the ash pit.

Conclusion

When I started the analysis of the materials presented in this chapter, my assumptions about some of the bottle features I had located were very different from my final conclusions, resulting from a critical analysis of the features, their archaeological context, the associated artifacts found in the features, and surrounding environment. Initially, with the findings of the Jamaican bottle feature in mind, I had made the assumption for the Montpelier cellar study that I was dealing with three concealed bottle features of some significance outside of the discard of broken items. Through the process of re-evaluation involving insights from different contexts, I was able to better understand other possible explanations for these bottles.

What to make of all this? What I took away from this analysis is that the presence of spiritual caches and features is something that cannot be forced. We are all aware and inspired by examples that have been found at such sites as Annapolis, the Levi Jordon Plantation, and the Jackson Homesite in Maryland (Brown and Cooper 1990; Leone 2005; Schablitcky 2009). I submit that the bottle feature found at Juan de Bolas Plantation in Jamaica is another such example. These will usually come to us as a surprise and as a "eureka" moment, but need to be addressed for their particular context and even regional expression. Trying to make objects such as glass bottles found in unique or unusual contexts fit the bill for a universal expression of spirituality is to miss the mark and even distract us from finding new material expressions of spirituality and other cultural practices.

Taking a critical look at my haste in interpreting the bottles found in the Montpelier cellar made me realize that I was attempting to potentially shove a round peg (in this case, the bottles found in the cellar) into a square hole (the conjure or witching bottle interpretation), and miss the unique and truly valuable expression of alternative actions, such as a potential petite resistance. To assume the bottle(s) found in the wall in the Montpelier cellar represent another example of spiritual practice is to miss the opportunity of recognizing this context as evidence of the ability of the enslaved Africans to work around the restrictions placed on the secure storage room of the cellar and provide items for their own use. While a relatively mundane example of everyday life, such daily action is readily observable in the archaeological record. Thus, forcing such a context into a spiritual interpretation would have misrepresented the material expression of another form of accommodation that the enslaved community used in response to stress.

In the end, rigorous and critical analysis of the context in which spiritual features and objects are located needs to be employed to ensure the accuracy and robustness of our interpretations. While this chapter deals with the material phenomena of glass bottles, the methods and critical insights should be extended to other categories found and interpreted on historical sites, ranging from straight pins to buttons. As archaeologists, we deal with material culture whose presence in the archaeological record can be explained through myriad possibilities. Divining their origins and placements based on surrounding context is the first and crucial step in interpreting their significance. This is not to say that we should become skeptical of spiritual-based interpretations. Such features are undoubtedly more common since individualized spirituality was a pervasive aspect of most eighteenth- and nineteenth-century societies, and localized traditions made these beliefs and expressions even stronger. But we need to remain ever vigilant regarding our ability to assess the relationship of artifacts to their surrounding depositional contents, and be willing to consider and reconsider new interpretations with work from other disciplines. As many archaeologists have cautioned, in order to identify the physical manifestations of spiritual beliefs in the material culture we excavate, we need to examine their contexts with a critical eye for placement, depositional history, and assemblage composition. In the struggle to interpret finds from the archaeological record, we can only continue to seek out additional contexts that provide more evidence for the use of everyday items for spiritual purposes.

Note

I would like to give thanks to the many individuals and groups who have contributed to the data in this chapter. First, the excavations and information derived from my research in Jamaica would not be possible without my friendship with Linton Rhule. His guidance, advice, knowledge of the history of the Juan de Bolas community, and camaraderie have always served as an inspiration to me. I would also like to thank the dedicated staff with whom I have worked at Montpelier—their excellent excavation skills and keen sense of observation allowed for the discoveries discussed in this chapter. Combining the two very different sets of fieldwork on the Atlantic African Diaspora have resulted in the critical examination of the features discussed here. This chapter was drastically improved through the reviews and comments of Jerome Handler, Eric Schweickart, Erica D'Elia, and anonymous reviewers.

CHAPTER 11

Ritual Bundle in Colonial Annapolis

Mark P. Leone, Jocelyn E. Knauf, and Amanda Tang

The 2008 archaeological discovery of an eighteenth-century ritual bundle in Annapolis, Maryland, was widely reported in the press (Johnson 2008; Wilford 2008). The reports rightfully acknowledge the bundle as a product of African-descended culture, rituals, and beliefs. The likely African cultural provenience of the bundle has also been highlighted in those reports. We revisit this ritual bundle in this chapter as the basis for understanding the spiritual and otherworldly beliefs in Annapolis before the Age of Revolution and its status as a new capital of the colony of Maryland. We argue that the Annapolis of the Enlightenment, well known for lawyers, printers, and patriots, began as a town characterized by paranormal beliefs and eclectic ritual practices, especially at the time when the official Maryland government first moved there in 1695. These beliefs and practices—both European and African—were important parts of everyday lives in Annapolis until the 1750s, the dawn of the local Enlightenment and its political offshoot, the American Revolution. We not only want to show an Annapolis most historians neglect but also an Annapolis with some evidence of African or African American ritual practices.

The chapter has two objectives. The first is to examine the role of rituals and paranormal beliefs as a form of social control with emphasis on how African religious practices and European extra-Christian beliefs established social control in colonial Annapolis (Aberle 1966; Evans-Pritchard 1929; Malinowski 1948; Wilkie 2000: 182). The second purpose decenters the Enlightenment in the narratives regarding the origins of Annapolis. We want to describe a time and culture when Enlightenment rationality was not in place or not fully formed. We argue that Annapolis in its beginning phase had at least two cultural traditions of ritual and religion existing side by side. One was a European, Christian culture, a product of the Reformation that included Anglicans, Roman Catholics, and Puritans. The other was the African religious tradition originating from perhaps dozens of cultures in West and West Central Africa. These two traditions, however, shared strong beliefs in paranormal occurrences and practices such as the ones shown in appendix 1. The people who selected, read, and believed the stories excerpted from the *Maryland Gazette* in the appendix were Annapolis Christians. These notices of odd or paranormal events were within the Christian knowledge of Annapolis residents and other colonial Americans. And, as historical and ethnographic studies in Africa and the African Diasporas have shown, such beliefs are also familiar to the African cultural and religious traditions (Geschiere 1997; Isichei 2002; Sansi and Parés 2011).

During the late seventeenth and early eighteenth centuries, a strong government did not exist in Maryland. We argue that paranormal beliefs were common during the period and rituals that appealed to supernatural forces were used by some colonists for the type of social control that could not be enacted or enforced by governmental policies. These public practices then disappeared when they were no longer needed, due to the intellectual accession of the principles of Enlightenment rationality and the establishment of stronger government institutions. We posit that, given the belief in paranormal and supernatural forces in early colonial Annapolis, publicly displayed rituals were used by African practitioners to actively establish a sense of place and control over the landscape. In other words, we see both the public descriptions of European supernatural beliefs and the visible placement of West African ritual objects for managing spirits as coexisting traditions in early eighteenth-century Annapolis.

The work of Yvonne Chireau is relevant for understanding the spirit practices developed by African-descended populations in early colonial Annapolis. "Magic," Chireau argues, is a "particular approach or attitude by which humans interact with unseen powers or spiritual forces" (2003: 3). It is efficacious, private, and used for personal ends; operates mechanically; manifests in focused events; and lacks a developed theology. Within the African American religious traditions, hoodoo and conjure are examples of these "magical" practices. Although both are often used interchangeably to describe nineteenth-century African American religion, there are fine distinctions between them based on regional differences, the type of ritual being performed, the person performing the ritual, the type of medium employed, and the biases of scholars based on what they consider normative (ibid.: 3–5; Mitchem 2007). These vernacular traditions (otherwise labeled as "folk beliefs"; see Levine 2007) were, however, part of all established religions. They were as much a part of African religions—Vodun, Santeria, Candomble, and so on—as they were a part of Christianity in the early modern world (Thornton 1998a: 235–253; see also Breslaw 2000; Muir 2005).

Of specific interest to us is the African ritual practice in the context of colonial Annapolis before the codification of hoodoo or conjure as a quintessential African American tradition in the post–American Revolution era. The eighteenth-century ritual bundle found in Annapolis is a precursor to hoodoo or conjure practices, and it illustrates how an African-derived ritual might have enabled internal community regulation in the colonial period (Anderson 2008; Mitchem 2007).

The Annapolis Context: European/ Euro-American Supernatural Beliefs

Newspaper accounts about Europeans in Annapolis, when combined with information about African and African American ritual bundles, provide a way to see pre-Enlightenment Annapolis. European beliefs and rumors about supernatural occurrences were prevalent and openly discussed in the *Maryland Gazette,* the weekly public newspaper in Annapolis since 1727. Everyday events were especially prominent in the *Maryland Gazette* between 1728 and 1734, during which 364 issues were published by William Parks. Only fifty-six of these issues survive, but they contain important evidence of European beliefs in the supernatural (see appendix 1). These issues reveal that early eighteenth-century Annapolis was a world of fabulous events, miraculous natural occurrences, and wonders attributed to either the hand of God or the devil. Similar reports continued into the 1750s under its subsequent publisher, Jonas Green, but references to such paranormal beliefs and events began to diminish dramatically after 1758. Until then, such newspaper reports, detailing paranormal events both locally and from Europe, were common occurrences, though these *Maryland Gazette* stories were primarily based on rumors (for the potency of rumors in the construction of reality, see White 2000). There was one public trial for witchcraft discussed in the newspaper in 1728. There were also citations of multiheaded dogs, wondrous births of freak animals, and diabolical nighttime apparitions. The reports of the witchcraft trial discussed how suspected witches were subjected to several ordeals before they were eventually condemned to be burnt alive (*Maryland Gazette* 1728, 17–24 Dec.). A few weeks earlier, the paper also ran a story about a school-aged boy who, weeks after his death, "appeared in school in his usual place, and a coffin behind him," and then appeared again three days later in the field where his body was found. The article tied the haunting to the coroner's conclusion that he had been murdered by strangulation (*Maryland Gazette* 1728, 3–10 Dec.).

In later reports, especially after 1750, there began to be doubts about the supernatural, and there was an effort to gain control over aspects of life and nature through the use of different rules for thinking and behaving. Use of the phrase "supposed devil" began to appear by midcentury, when writers now attempted to stand apart from the paranormal events and ideas about which they were writing. There was also a shift away from naming individual community members who had experienced odd situations, and instead talking about "peasants" in other areas of the world who held those superstitions (*Maryland Gazette* 1750, 28 Feb.). By 1753, articles were still commenting on paranormal events but only as superstition. One article describes "country people . . . so full of ignorance and superstition, that they imagine there are several witches and wizards in the neighborhood," and were conducting witch hunts of their own by capturing, binding, and throwing suspected witches into the rivers (*Maryland Gazette* 1753, 2–7 Jan.).

A substantial change occurred in reporting the monstrous, fabulous, and supernatural around the middle of the eighteenth century. Although causes of events and experiences were still otherworldly, they were placed in nature, not in the supernatural realm. There were 12 illustrations of magical and paranormal events in the surviving 26 issues of the newspaper (out of 624 total issues) published between 1745 and 1757. Between 1758 and 1784, of the 52 issues examined (out of a total of 1,352 issues), there were only 10 examples of such references. The conceptual world that replaced the use of magic and the paranormal as causative factors has two characteristics: first, reliance upon human reason and uniformitarian views of nature, and, second, the Enlightenment's segmenting effect on life and the shift toward individual disciplines and etiquettes (Shackel 1993).

Our point is to establish that the early eighteenth-century Annapolis to which Africans were brought was one suffused with European beliefs in the supernatural, not unlike African beliefs. Those two broad traditions might have easily comingled as the basis for fashioning worldviews and seeking answers to existential concerns. This was the social and cultural context in which Europeans and Africans enacted and fabricated rituals and bundles, each group tapping into its own historical traditions but making use of materials and ideas available in the local environment. We argue that there were separate as well as comingled European and African traditional beliefs in the use of magic and rituals in early Annapolis. This is the backdrop for explaining African ritual actions and beliefs in the supernatural.

Archaeological Research

In 2007, Mayor Ellen Moyer of Annapolis commissioned an archaeological research project, Archaeology in Annapolis, to excavate in the middle of the city in preparation for extensive renovations to put utility lines below ground. The research goal of these excavations, which took place during the three hundredth anniversary of the city's charter, was to study the early history of the city and make the research findings available to the public. It should be noted that by 1694, Annapolis had replaced St. Mary's City as the center of the colonial government in Maryland. Annapolis was also a commercial and agricultural hub and a main entry port for enslaved Africans. In the late seventeenth century, enslaved Africans accounted for about one-sixth of the population of Annapolis, approximately 450 people (Reid 2006: 22–24).

There were many enslaved Africans living with their owners in the area of our excavations, yet it is difficult to establish exact ties among owners, enslaved, and addresses. Prominent Annapolitans often owned real estate and property throughout Maryland, and therefore easily moved enslaved individuals among properties in Annapolis and the countryside. For example, Robert Gordon owned the Ship Carpenter's Yard and many other properties around the City Dock, which were in our area of excavation. He also held public offices in Annapolis. At the time that he was first elected to the colonial assembly, he owned 5.5 acres on the strip of land along City Dock and had a seventy-six-year lease on a lot in Annapolis. In the 1720s and 1730s, he acquired additional land in Annapolis, a lot in Baltimore Town, and approximately 150 additional acres in Anne Arundel County. At the time of his death, nineteen enslaved people were listed among Gordon's personal property, and he retained the lease on one lot in Annapolis, as well as the 150 acres in Anne Arundel (Papenfuse 1979).

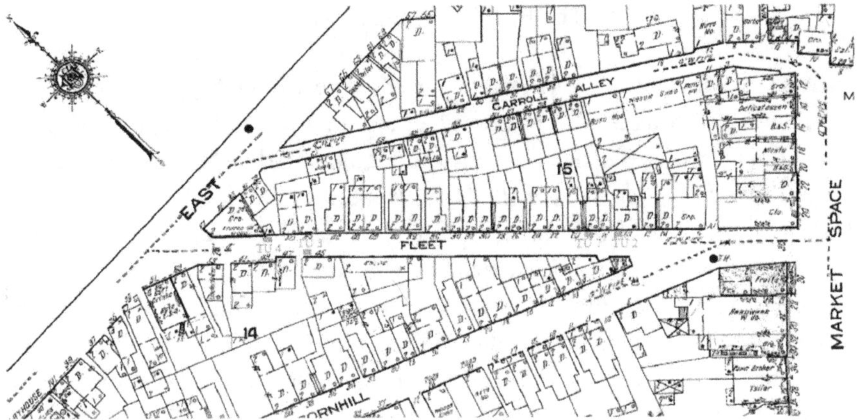

MAP 11.1. Four test units were excavated under the sidewalk spaces along Fleet Street. The bundle was found in Test Unit 4 (TU 4), and the log road was discovered in Test Unit 2 (TU 2) at the end of Fleet Street close to the City Dock of Annapolis.

In 1771, Charles Wallace, a local merchant, began to subdivide the land that we would later excavate for commercial and residential development (McWilliams and Papenfuse 1969). Few historical records documenting the use of these properties survive, underscoring the importance of archaeological investigations of the area as a way to understand their African histories. We placed ten excavation units under the sidewalks on Cornhill and Fleet streets, the heart of our study and excavation area, most abutting the curbstones. No excavations were conducted in the streets themselves. From previous experience in Annapolis, we knew that very little archaeological information remained stratigraphically intact underneath the actual streets.

Of the four units dug on Fleet Street, two are discussed in depth here (map 11.1). Fleet Street rises from the Annapolis harbor, now called City Dock, up to State Circle—the hill's top where the Maryland State House has stood since at least 1710. Historical records from the eighteenth and nineteenth centuries, including census records, document the presence of Africans (first generation) and African Americans (subsequent generations) in Annapolis, although surviving documents do not focus on what their experiences would have been like living in the city. Many of these documents report enslaved people as chattel. These records also indicate that enslaved African people were present in the project area, though they do not link any to specific addresses on Fleet Street.

The Bundle on Fleet Street

In April 2008, a bundle of materials we believe are related to African religious practices was discovered on Fleet Street. The bundle supplies a great deal of new knowledge of the environment of an early African-derived tradition. Two of the units excavated on Fleet Street provided the supporting information about this bundle. In a test unit at the lower, or harbor, end of Fleet Street, where it joins Cornhill Street, archaeologists found a well-preserved log road about three feet under the surface and below the water table. Based on evidence from datable ceramics, as well as historical references, the road may date to the 1680s. A town plan of Annapolis was drawn up in 1684, before Annapolis was officially recognized as a city. Although no map of this town plan survives, existing documentary sources suggest that Fleet Street corresponds to a road on that town plan (Jane McWilliams, pers. comm., 2008). The log road consisted of logs lined up side by side, covered with twigs and leaves to smooth out the surface, and held in place with wedges. Because the pine logs of the road were adzed flat, they could not be directly dated through dendrochronology. The road also could not be excavated fully because it was originally laid on the beach or marsh at the edge of the Annapolis harbor and so was underwater.

The log road was a spectacular local discovery because it has been the only element found archaeologically that dated to before 1695, when Annapolis was named the capital of Maryland. In order to determine whether the road continued further up the street, closer to State Circle, a test unit was excavated near the top of Fleet Street just before it enters East Street. The unit was excavated to approximately 1.2 m below the current sidewalk surface. At about 1.1 m down was the hard-packed surface of the seventeenth-century road that had continued from the log road about 60 m downhill. Appearing first and situated next to the road, however, were the top elements of a densely packed, amorphous clay object with a prehistoric stone axe head sticking out from it. This bundle is 45 cm high and about 30 cm long by about 25 cm wide, but the bundle has no shape in a Euclidean sense.

A central element to the discovery of this bundle was its location, in the gutter of the hard-packed road surface. The surface of the upper portion of the road ran into a gutter, most likely to carry water away and down the hill (figure 11.1). On the uphill side of the bundle were many micro-stratified levels of fine-grained silt, deposited by the water that ran down and around the bundle to the waterfront. This indicates that the bundle was not origi-

FIGURE 11.1. The bundle in situ during excavation. The stone axe is visible, coming up out of the bundle, near the top center of the excavation unit. *Courtesy of Matthew D. Cochran and Archaeology in Annapolis.*

nally buried, and was instead placed in the gutter. Therefore, the bundle was most likely exposed in plain view. African ethnographic correlates and the historical context of magical practices in the city at the time indicate that placing the bundle in view where water would run over it was not accidental. The context of the bundle's placement convinced us that it was deliberately positioned. This may have been a visible attempt to control this important space near the commercial port of Annapolis and to influence one or more episodes of activities associated with this location, or the space may have been meaningful for accomplishing a life experience for which the ritual bundle was made.

Interpretation of the Bundle

Nothing like this bundle has been found in continental European contexts and does not belong to the cultural logic of European rituals. In contrast, many African contexts have similarities to the material under discussion (see Insoll and Kankpeyeng, Normal, Ogundiran, all this volume). We concluded that this object was likely an African-derived feature related to rituals. We have discovered and interpreted many other African American archaeological features, and concluded that the object was likely of West or Central African origin in its shape and composition (Cochran 1999; Neuwirth and Cochran 2000). While materials related to African ritual practices have been found in contexts related to enslaved Africans or African Americans during the eighteenth and nineteenth centuries in Annapolis (Leone and Fry 1999) prior to the discovery of the bundle on Fleet Street, no other evidence of West African religious traditions in seventeenth-century Anglo-America had ever been found (Leone 2005).

The bundle on Fleet Street is also the first such ritual feature found in Annapolis that appears to have been intentionally left out in the open, which we argue is connected to the wider acceptance of eclectic ritual practices during this period. Comparative studies of African rituals and patterns of the transatlantic slave trade make it compelling for us to conclude that the bundle is a manifestation of open-air rituals common in West Africa, especially in public spaces and crossroads. We have found other bundles in Annapolis very close to Fleet Street at the Brice House, which date to the 1880s, as well as at the Charles Carroll House, the Slayton House, and the Adams Kilty House. These bundles date from 1790–1820, 1880–1920, and 1900, respectively, and were placed in specific buried locations, including thresholds, northeast corners, and hearths. These items were associated with the efforts to seek cures and fortune or to secure safety. Unlike the Fleet Street bundle, these features had been deliberately buried in kitchens, laundries, and pantries, spaces where the enslaved or freed Africans and African Americans on these properties would have worked and lived away from the public gaze (ibid.; Leone and Fry 1999).

In the 1990s, members of Archaeology in Annapolis surveyed the archaeological reports from sites associated with enslaved people in several southern states. This project was undertaken simultaneously with a survey of the information from the Works Progress Administration (WPA) Slave Narratives about the meanings associated with conjuring and spirit practices, in collaboration with folklorist Gladys-Marie Fry (Leone and Fry 1999). While the WPA narratives (e.g., Rawick 1972) are from the 1930s and focus on the period immediately prior to the Civil War, Leone and Fry (1999) observed that they contained valuable insights for spirit practices that were found archaeologically and dated to earlier periods. Analysis of the narratives provided a list of objects used in West African spirit practices

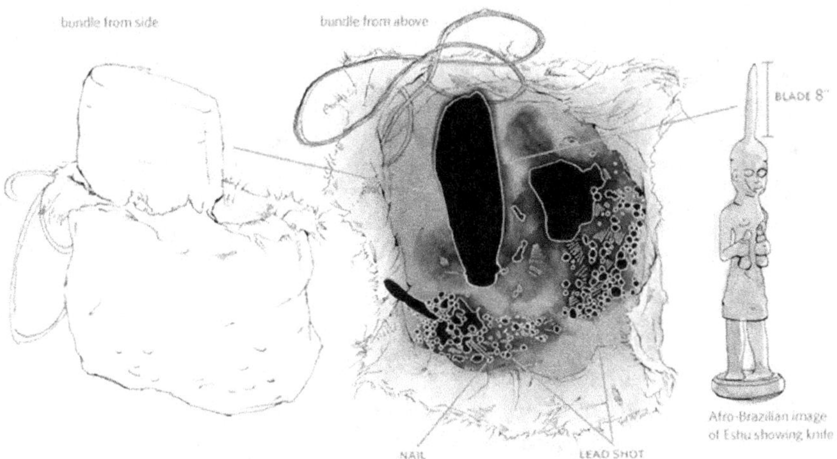

FIGURE 11.2. An artist's rendering of the possible appearance of the bundle when it was placed in the street gutter. *Courtesy of Brian G. Payne and the University of Maryland and Archaeology in Annapolis.*

and their functions according to the WPA interviewees (Leone, Fry and Ruppel 2001).

The WPA Slave Narratives are filled with details of how to make a bundle and what problems a bundle can address, including bringing luck, providing cures for illnesses, offering protection from whippings and from competing magic, and avoiding detection (Leone and Fry 1999; Leone et al. 2001). There are over one hundred items that WPA interviewees indicated could be used in a bundle, and these are found to be similar in form, purpose, and meaning to West African ritual practices (see also Boaz, Gómez, both this volume). The most common items include buttons, pebbles, pins, nails, glass or crystal objects, chalk, iron objects, items that reflect light, white objects, and red materials (Leone et al. 2001).

Within a few weeks of discovery, the bundle was X-rayed to determine its internal composition. The X-rays revealed the specific materials used to construct the bundle, providing evidence of connections to African practices and African Atlantic culture. The exterior of the bundle is rounded and pointed at the top. X-rays indicate that the interior materials were organized prior to being wrapped in a sack or pouch—made of cloth or leather—which was probably held together with a string or sash (figure 11.2). The X-rays further reveal that the inside was filled with metal pieces and sandy clay. At the

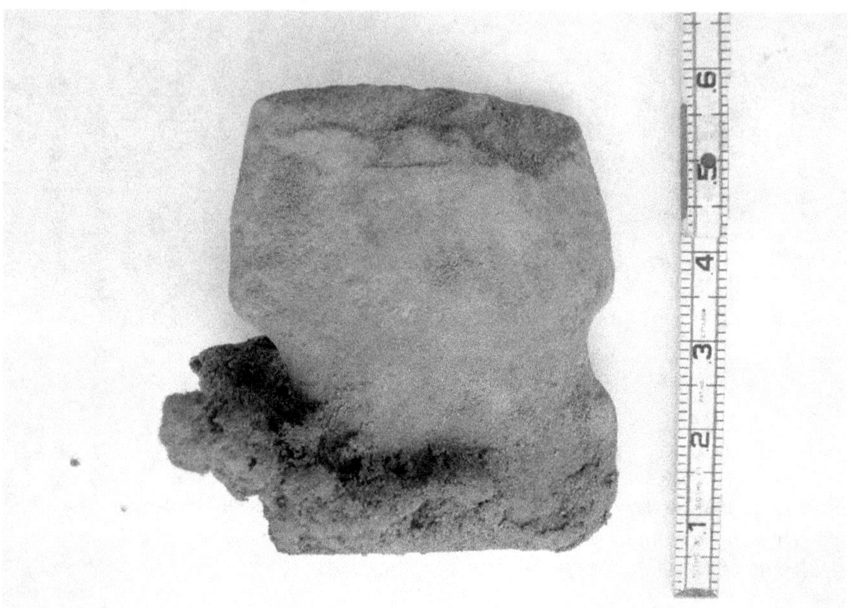

FIGURE 11.3. The prehistoric stone axe at the top of the bundle. *Courtesy of Matthew M. Palus and Archaeology in Annapolis.*

bottom, forming a kind of loose base, were over three hundred pieces of shot of varying diameters. This collection of small, round pieces of lead formed the base on which all the other associated materials rest. Approximately two dozen common pins, some of which were bent to form right angles, were also placed in the bundle above the lead shot pieces. Above the pins were about a dozen nails of different sizes, and the bundle also contained a rivet or an object that resembles a cuff link. In addition, it holds two round discs attached to either end of a short staff, which sits about halfway up the bundle. The bundle's outer pouch has disintegrated but it left the impressions of its wrinkles on the hardened mixture of sand and clay that encased its contents.

Moreover, wedged among the nails and pins was a prehistoric stone axe (figure 11.3), which was identified as a chipped stone axe from the Archaic Period, about 8,500 years ago. Like all of the other materials contained in the bundle, the axe could have been acquired in the Annapolis area or the nearby region. Curated Native American artifacts have been reported by historical archaeologists working in African American contexts in Louisiana

(Wilkie 2000), South Carolina (Orser 1985), and Texas (Brown and Cooper 1990). The stone axe may have been found during activities like digging or plowing, and then curated because it was believed to have spiritual importance. This is still a common practice in Western Africa, where the Yoruba, for example, refer to it as *edun aara* (thunderbolt). In fact, during an interview in the 1920s, a man from Mississippi described the beliefs of an elderly conjure doctor in Mississippi: "Indian arrowheads often found in the locality were not made by man at all, but were fashioned by God out of thunder and lightning" (Puckett [1926] 2003: 315; cf. Wilkie 2000: 189). Inside the pouch, the maker(s) of the bundle used a mixture of sand and clay to stratify the contents. The metallic properties of the pins and nails interacted with the clay and sand to create a solid mass of all the contents, so that by the time of its recovery, the bundle had formed into a solid mass. The mass is hard, and the iron objects have disintegrated into voids that are little more than impressions of their original forms, making it impossible to see the many individual pieces if the bundle were taken apart.[1]

Spiritual Significance of the Bundle and African American Correlates

By June 2008, we had a good sense of the physical and internal makeup of this complicated object but needed to understand its use at the site. It became obvious that the physical and internal construction had correlates with Niger-Congo ritual objects. Given the cultural area origins of the Africans in Annapolis during the seventeenth and eighteenth centuries, it became necessary for us to look for ethnographic and archaeological examples of such materials in West and Central Africa. This was done to determine the most proximate meanings that the bundle may have had for the person who placed it on Fleet Street.

We are aware that it is impossible to relate this bundle to a particular ethnic group in Atlantic Africa, but we believe it is important that the primary cultural system of this area, what Christopher Ehret (2002: 44) has called the Niger Congo Civilization, serves as the basis of our interpretations of what it represents. Since it is impractical to comb all the literature of this vast zone, from Senegambia to South and Eastern Africa, we have zeroed in on three representative cultural areas: the Mande, Yoruba, and Northern Congo. We particularly favor a West African connection because historical sources indicate that many of the enslaved people brought to Maryland in the eighteenth century arrived directly from West Africa. Through historical sources, Lorena Walsh (2001: 148) was able to identify the regional origins of 43 percent of the enslaved people brought to Maryland in the eighteenth century. Sixty-nine percent of these people came from Senegambia, Sierra Leone, and the Windward Coast or Gold Coast hinterland. Twenty-three percent came from West Central Africa, and 7 percent came from the Bight of Biafra. Although the origins of all the enslaved people brought to Maryland were not recorded, most of those whose origins were unknown probably came from Upper Guinea or the Gold Coast, where the London traders who brought them to Maryland concentrated their work (ibid.: 148). The enslaved individuals who would have lived and worked in Annapolis during the time that the bundle was placed were probably at most one generation removed from West Africa.

Most of the scholars consulted agreed that the bundle was associated with a West African–derived practice, citing the various classic cultural areas of the region where some of the physical correlates of the bundle have been found. As scholars of North America, these correlates are useful in order to make sense of the African cultural presence in the Americas. Hence, while some Africanist and African Diasporist scholars see the collection of nails and other metal objects as reminiscent of the Yoruba deity Ogun, others see them as strongly implying the *kongo nkisi* lore and contents. And yet others emphasized the meaningful implications of the public space where the bundle was found as indicative of the crossroads complex in West African religious traditions. Among the Yoruba, for example, the crossroads is "the juncture of the spiritual realm and the phenomenal world . . . a liminal space where sacrifices are often placed" (Drewal 1992: 205).

John Thornton has argued that the complexity of shared characteristics among many West and West Central African ethnic groups and cultural regions complicates identification of the bundle. Even with the extensive linguistic variation in West Africa, different groups of Africans were in constant interaction with one another through trade, war, migration, and religion (Thornton 1998a). The African antecedents to the bundle must therefore be understood in a more general sense. He writes, "These sorts of bags are of course ubiquitous in Africa because in that region (Lower Guinea and Gold Coast) . . . there was a lot of exchange of deities around the region and a lot of syncretism" (Thornton, pers. comm., 25 October 2008). Thus, while scholars are calling for more research of African contexts in order to better gain a transatlantic perspective on the African Diaspora (Games 2006; Gilroy 1993; Ogundiran and Falola 2007), it is generally understood that a comparison of African Diaspora sites with African examples is not enough. There must also be a theoretical apparatus in place that can account for changing historical contexts and power relations, as well as to examine cultural change and exchange (Singleton 2006). Understanding the African cultures that influenced practices within the African Diaspora is, however, a necessary foundation for this work.

While we can appreciate that these practices found in Annapolis have African antecedents, it is also important to think about how these beliefs may have functioned in a different context, namely colonial Annapolis, as well as the effects that interactions among different groups of Africans, African Americans, European Americans, and Native Americans may have had on the use and meanings of African spiritual practices. The ability to effectively share cultural knowledge, even with disparate regional locales of origin (see Norman, this volume), facilitated the creation of artifacts such as the bundle. While the bundle cannot be directly traced to any specific ethnic group, it was certainly rooted in African thought while simultaneously being made and used by an Annapolis resident.

Interpreting the Use of the Bundle in Eighteenth-Century Annapolis

This bundle would have served as a precursor to hoodoo and conjure bundles, which have been found archaeologically in later times in Annapolis (Leone 2005). We also, however, needed to figure out who likely used the bundle and why. The archaeological deposits from the site indicate that the bundle sat out in the gutter on a major thoroughfare for forty years, uncovered, because it continued to accrue silt deposits when water ran over it during this time period. It likely had water running up against it every time it rained, or may have had water poured over it deliberately.

The public quality of the bundle is important because hoodoo and conjure were all practiced out of view, in secret, at night, or in a household context. In these instances, the rituals were frequently disguised through the use of common objects so that they were unnoticeable except to the practiced eye (Leone and Fry 1999). Why would the bundle and any daily activity associated with it be tolerated by slaveholders or anyone in the English community who lived next door and all around? Although there were hardly a thousand European Americans in Annapolis in 1700 to 1740, they were mostly composed of Puritans, Anglicans, and a few Catholics. On the surface, this was not a tolerant time; there was a state church. Puritans had been banished from Virginia, while Catholics had been disfranchised in Maryland and could not worship in public. Yet, this bundle, a distinctive, African-derived spiritual object, was placed in plain view. We argue that this could occur because it was a time when the use of ritual power was an important supplement to rule by law for all people, and that ritual alternatives may have been more important than law on many occasions. In this context of early colonial Annapolis, public African ritual may have been a tactic used by its practitioners to actively establish a sense of place and control over the landscape in a new context where life was structured in a different way. The placing of this bundle in sight, on a street that led from State Circle to the main commercial spaces on the city's waterfront, may have altered the political geography of that street, publicly asserting the relevance and vitality of an African presence in early colonial America.

By the 1750s, the world of rituals and belief in paranormal activities had been altered and was disappearing from public sites, a change that corresponds to the increasing authority of state institutions. The world of Enlightenment rationality and cultural formalism noticeably increased in everyday practices. We can see this in the ways that tables were set and manners prescribed for eating, time was told, history was recorded and cited, and, more familiarly, when the rights, liberties, and obligations believed to belong to individuals were established. The modern era's systematization of the world became more evident in Annapolis over time through changes in the *Maryland Gazette,* in the archaeological remains of gardens and dishes, and even in how printer's type was used (Leone 2005; Little 1992; Shackel 1993).

When magic and paranormal activities were cited less and less in the *Maryland Gazette* by people of European descent, the use of protective supernatural caches or bundles by peoples of African descent became more restricted to secret settings and personal spaces, with ritual caches being placed in buried locations in houses and slave quarters. The bundle at the Charles Carroll House, for example, was dated to after 1790 by a pierced coin found in it (Leone 2005; Leone and Fry 1999). After 1750, hoodoo or conjure flourished among African-descended populations as a fusion of several Western and Central African worldviews and religions. This regularly included the burial of bundles at doorsteps, under hearths, and in northeast corners (Leone 2005).

We are arguing that the disappearance of such materiality of rituals in the public space coincides with the rise in the rule of law, and the more emphatic use of state institutions to regulate public and everyday lives. On the one hand, the most famous result of the rule of law is American independence, beginning with the declaration of rights and laws, and ending with the Constitution. On the other hand, this time period also brought an increased rigidity in American slavery as the number of European indentured servants decreased and the construction of racial difference intensified (Epperson 2001). Increasing eighteenth-century regulation of property and public spaces in the city of Annapolis necessitated that African-influenced practices be conducted secretly, away from the view of European Americans, an idea that is suggested in several slave narratives (Leone and Fry 1999).

In summary, we see two processes not described by historians of early Annapolis. First, Annapolis was a city whose residents, both African and European, were familiar with paranormal beliefs and rituals that interacted with the other world of powerful forces. We do not imply that everyone engaged in such ritual practices, but we do suggest that there was a widespread belief by many Annapolitans, African and European, in the efficacy of ritual actions that sought to manipulate supernatural forces. This was especially so in less predictable and contested spheres of everyday lives such as health, social relations, economic success, and so on. Second, the archaeological evidence supports the idea that supernatural rituals were openly practiced by Africans or African Americans, at least some of the time. In the early 1700s, these rituals were likely used as a form of social control in the absence of a powerful colonial government. Annapolis was a new capital with a weak royal government. The city was seeking its own charter, granted in 1708, so that it could run more independently. It was an unsettled time. The stability that the new republic offered to European-descended populations did not extend to African Americans because they were not incorporated as equals into the Euro-American legal system (Levine 2007; Raboteau 2004). As a result, African rituals became restricted to the private spaces of the African-descended populations. We see the Fleet Street sacred bundle as a part of the public commons in Annapolis and conclude that it presents a compelling, if fragmentary, commentary on the contributions of African beliefs to the forming of America.

Appendix: Excerpts from the *Maryland Gazette*

The scenarios in this appendix refer to European experiences of paranormal events. African rituals such as the bundle discussed in this essay were not connected to these paranormal everyday events. While there is no link established between these events and the bundle, it is important to show the broad contexts and everyday beliefs of the society in which the bundle functioned.[2]

> There is a cat 140 years old; several persons now living remember her above 60 years; and the owner, Mr. William Lloyd . . . can himself remember her for 50. The account given of her by him and his family is that she was reared by his grandmother when a child about five years old, who was born on the 35th year of Queen Elizabeth. (*Maryland Gazette* 1728, 3–10 Dec.)

> A boy died not long ago, notwithstanding all the physical assistance that could be given him, of a canine appetite, with which he had been affected above a twelve month . . . that he daily ate from 50 to 60 pounds, liquid and solid; and if not supplied fast enough, would eat the flesh from his own shoulders. (*Maryland Gazette* 1747, 10 March)

> A sample of seed was brought to the market which fell from the clouds in a storm of hail the same week. . . . It is like hempseed in form, but larger and of several colors and tassels. A seed being boiled in water, swelled pretty large, and being opened, produced a fine flour like that of wheat. A gentleman in that neighborhood has gathered a bushel, in order to sow. (*Maryland Gazette* 1750, 4 July)

> Several persons of both sexes convicted of witchcraft, have been condemned to be burnt alive, but before they were executed they put them upon the following trials. . . . The first was to tie their hands and feet and throw them into the water, who as sorcerers used to do, swam like a piece of wood; after which they were put into scales, when it appeared that a large woman weighed but an ounce, and her husband but 5 drams, . . . whereupon they were burnt alive. . . . There were among 'em a midwife who had baptized 2000 children in the name of the devil. (*Maryland Gazette* 1728, 17–24 Dec.)

> We have a very unaccountable story here concerning a school boy that was found dead in a ditch. . . . About three weeks after, the boy appeared in the school in his usual place, and a coffin behind him. . . . His brother said to the other boys, who all saw him, here's our Jack; and because he did not speak, threw at him, and immediately he vanished, and all the church and school gallery were dark two minutes, to their great surprise; upon which they ran downstairs. . . . About three days after, he was seen by a man in the field where he was found dead. . . . The coroner, who caused the body to be taken up and viewed by surgeons, . . . found he was strangled and the jury brought in willful murder. (*Maryland Gazette* 1728, 3–10 Dec.)

> They write . . . of a very facetious affair. . . . A butcher of the town sent his apprentice boy to drive home a black ram he had bought; but it being late in the night and very dark, the ram gave him a slip through a dark entry, and

then into a little back court of a house, and seeing the glimmering light of a candle . . . he pushed with all his might against the window, and broke in a whole light, and his head and his horns only appearing to those within, they were so terrified, they took to their heels . . . being firmly persuaded it was the devil. . . . The inhabitants . . . watched all night in order to wait the return of this supposed devil. (*Maryland Gazette* 1753, 11 Jan.)

Peasants . . . have been lately struck with a strange kind of panic, arising from the appearance of great numbers of mice of different colors, in various parts of the country; which they consider as a never failing presage of the march of foreign troops of various nations through the places where they appear, which they fancy has been frequently confirmed by experience . . . and notwithstanding all the pains that can be taken, there is no getting the foolish notion out of their heads. (*Maryland Gazette* 1750, 28 Feb.)

We learn that the country people . . . are still so full of ignorance and superstition, that they imagine there are several witches and wizards in the neighborhood; and that they have tied up two or three old people in sheets, with cords round their middles, and flung them into the rivers, to see if they could save themselves; but whether the cords held them up, or providence supported the poor wretches, it's certain they got safe on shore. This has confirmed their opinion, and to them they attribute the loss of cattle, bad harvest, etc. and insist that the poor wretches shall be tried by the church Bible . . . but the clergy in that neighborhood are too wise to listen to them, or to suffer such nonsensical trials. (*Maryland Gazette* 1753, 2–7 Jan.)

Notes

1. Much of this information on the interaction of iron, clay, and sand was provided from consultation with Wayne Clark, a prehistoric archaeologist who has worked in Maryland for many years.

2. The information in the appendix was gathered by Marlys Pearson.

CHAPTER 12

Dexterous Creation

MATERIAL MANIFESTATIONS OF INSTRUMENTAL SYMBOLISM IN THE AMERICAS

Christopher C. Fennell

In a larger-scale study, entitled *Crossroads and Cosmologies*, I examined multiple data sets of material culture uncovered at African American occupation sites in the historic period (Fennell 2007b). That larger study utilized theories concerning modes of symbolic expression, formation and maintenance of social group identities, and the role of individual creativity and innovation. I applied these analytic frameworks to the past creation and use of material expressions of core symbols within the diasporas of particular African and European cultures, such as the BaKongo, Yoruba, Fon, and Palatine German, among others. I explored the divergent ways those creative processes played out at sites in North America, the Caribbean, and South America. A multitude of independently developed beliefs and practices from Africa and Europe came to meet at the many crossroads of the Americas.

The selected case study examined in this chapter involves theoretical concepts that I developed in *Crossroads and Cosmologies*. Anthropologists have articulated concepts concerning the operations of "core" symbols within culture groups, which have also been referred to as "key" or "dominant" symbols (Ortner 1973; Schneider 1980; Turner 1970, 1973). Such core symbols express fundamental elements of a culture group's cosmology and sense of identity within the world. Core symbols are communicated in myriad ways, including expression in ritual performances, spoken words, and tangible renderings in material culture (Fennell 2007b).

Such material representations of key symbols span a spectrum of expressive modes within each culture. This continuum extends from emblematic communications to more instrumental versions of the same core symbols (Fennell 2007b; Firth 1973; Ortner 1973; Turner 1970, 1973). Emblematic versions of such key symbols summarize the identity of a culture group as a cohesive order, and are illustrated by symbols such as the Star of David for Judaism, a national flag, or the crucifix for Christianity. An instrumental expression of a culture's core symbol is typically abbreviated in composition and employed for more individual purposes. For example, a member of the Christian faith performs an instrumental representation of a key symbol when she moves her hand across heart and brow to gesture a cross as a sign of individual prayer and self-protection. Emblematic expressions of social group identities are usually deployed in settings of public ceremonies celebrating group solidarity. In contrast, the abbreviated, instrumental expressions of those core symbols are more often employed in private settings for individual purposes (Fennell 2007b).

This chapter examines the contours of such expressive processes through a study of small hand figures discovered at several African American archaeological sites from the eighteenth and nineteenth centuries. The sample size in this exercise is quite small—just twelve of these artifacts have been reported and documented in archaeological reports concerning African American residential and work spaces. Scholars in African Diaspora archaeology have viewed these artifacts as among "the most evocative" (Heath 2003: 12), the "most enigmatic" (Thomas 1998: 546), and highly challenging to interpret (Singleton 1991: 162–163). Due to the limitations of such a small data set, this chapter is not intended to offer conclusive explanations or interpretations of the meanings and uses of these particular artifacts. Rather, my goal is to open a series of research questions with which archaeologists can investigate these types of artifacts with more detailed and complex historical processes in mind.

I first provide a description of the hand figures uncovered archaeologically, based on the limited data published about them. I next ask a series of questions as to how, and for what purpose, those items were manufactured, and what may have influenced the design choices of those producers. These possible design influences entail a number of instances of core cultural symbols expressed as instrumental forms and later transformed into popular culture configurations for mass-production ornaments. The final sections of this chapter examine possible meanings that persons of African descent could have read into these objects, turning manufactured commodities into "found symbols" that related to separate lines of beliefs within African Diaspora cultures. Such found symbols consist of manufactured objects that include ornamentation attractive to an end-user who acquires and reinterprets the ornamental element as standing for a meaningful symbol within his or her belief system. Thus, the end-user did not purposefully manufacture this item with that ornamental element, but rather acquired an object that was manufactured by someone else, and the end-user reinterpreted the ornamental element for new purposes.

Functions and Puzzles in Small Things Recovered

A number of artifacts uncovered at nineteenth-century archaeological sites in the United States present evidence of both parallel and intersecting facets of European and African belief systems (see also Gundaker, Leone et al., both this volume). Several sites of the living and work areas of enslaved African Americans in the 1800s have contained the remains of small hand figures manufactured of copper alloy. For example, Anne Yentsch (1994: 32–33) and her archaeology team recovered a small fastener in the shape of an enclosed hand from residential fill at the site of the Charles Calvert House in Annapolis, Maryland. The Calverts were wealthy Anglo-Americans, and they occupied this house for several decades starting in 1719. The Calvert House was also occupied by enslaved African Americans who worked there as servants. This hand figure artifact was only 1.3 cm in size, and Yentsch speculated that it functioned as a hook assembly to a clothing fastener. She further observed that a person of African American heritage may have interpreted such a figure as providing a symbolic invocation to protect against malevolent witchcraft. The archaeological context at the Calvert House site, however, did not provide evidence that this item was deposited in a location primarily occupied by African American laborers or by the Anglo-Americans in residence at the house (ibid.: 32–33).

Archaeologists working at several other sites have uncovered hand figure artifacts in contexts more specifically associated with the occupation and work areas of African Americans in the early to middle 1800s. These items exhibit similar characteristics: a hand closed in the form of a fist is set within an encompassing circle, and a crossbar bisects that circle perpendicular to the base of the wrist. The closed hand typically grasps a smaller circlet that extends out from the larger circle (figure 12.1a1).[1] This design was rendered in a single stamped figure, 1.3 cm or less in diameter, cut out of a sheet of brass or copper alloy. Hand figures of this configuration have been uncovered from the fill material within the living and work spaces

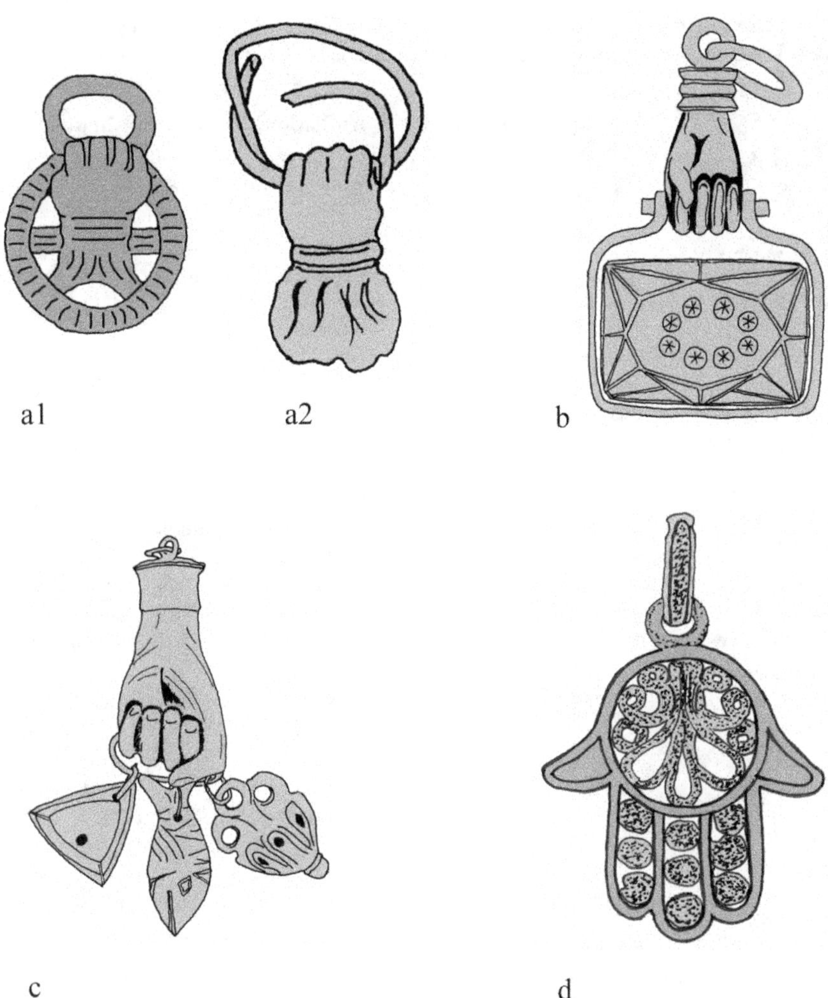

FIGURE 12.1 (a–d). Hand figures, images adapted by the author: a1, a2. types of small hand figures uncovered at archaeological sites in the United States; b. a nineteenth-century watch charm; c. a sixteenth-century European jewelry charm; d. a *Khamsa* or Hand of Fatima amulet.

once occupied by African American laborers at the Maynard Burgess House sites in Annapolis, Maryland; Thomas Jefferson's Poplar Forest plantation in Virginia; Andrew Jackson's Hermitage plantation in Tennessee; the Hildebrand and Wynnewood plantation sites in Tennessee; and the Zephania Kingsley Plantation in Florida (J. Davidson, pers. comm., Feb. 2013; Heath

Table 12.1. Summary of locations in which small metal hand figures have been recovered in archaeological contexts.

Site Name and Location	Site Description	Artifact Location	Occupant Affiliation	Date Range	Citations
Maynard Burgess House, Annapolis, Md.	Urban house	Residential fill	Free African Americans	Early to middle 19th C.	Leone 2005
Charles Calvert House, Annapolis, Md.	Urban colonial house	Residential fill in cellar crawlspace	European Americans and enslaved African Americans	Early to late 18th C.	Yentsch 1994
Zephania Kingsley Plantation, Ft. George Island, Fla.	Slave quarters	Middens adjacent to slave cabins	Enslaved African Americans	Early to middle. 19th C.	J. Davidson, pers. comm., Feb. 2013; Lee 2013
Hildebrand Plantation, near Memphis, Tenn.	Slave quarters	Residential fill	Enslaved African Americans	Early to middle 19th C.	Heath 2003; Heath et al. 2004
Hermitage Plantation, near Nashville, Tenn.	Slave quarters	Residential fill	Enslaved African Americans	Early to middle 19th C.	McKee 1995; Russell 1997; Thomas 1998
Wynnewood Plantation, Sumner County, Tenn.	Slave quarters	Residential fill	Enslaved African Americans	Early to middle 19th C.	Heath 2003; Heath et al. 2004; Lee 2013
Thomas Jefferson's Poplar Forest Plantation, Forest, Va.	Slave quarters	Residential fill above chimney base	Enslaved African Americans	Early to middle 19th C.	Heath 2003; Heath et al. 2004

2003; Heath et al. 2004; Lee 2013; Leone 2005; McKee 1995; Russell 1997; Yentsch 1994). Another hand figure artifact (figure 12.1a–2), discovered in a similar context at the Hermitage plantation in Tennessee, was different. This item was made of molded metal, with a slightly larger, closed hand that holds a loop of wire (McKee 1995; Russell 1997). Table 12.1 summarizes these locations of archaeological sites and the contexts in which such artifacts have been uncovered and reported.

At this juncture, it would be reasonable to ask for a similar summary of archaeological sites where these hand figures have been uncovered and associated solely with European-American occupants. Comparisons and contrasts could then be examined with such additional evidence. Unfortunately, I am not aware of any such sites in published reports. This chapter thus proceeds on limited data, and seeks to expand available considerations of possible historical and cultural connections without drawing conclusive inferences. These small artifacts raise a number of inquiries: Were these items simply utilitarian objects? What was the purpose of each of these items as a manufactured object? If these were "popular culture" items of manufactured clothing ornaments or jewelry, what inspired manufacturers to utilize a design which included such a hand figure? How were these items perceived and utilized by the African American individuals who acquired and possessed them?

The examples of items with a hand set inside a circle (figure 12.1a1) were most probably a form of manufactured adornment called "stampings." Consumers could sew these products onto clothing and accessories as ornaments or use them as part of hook-and-eye fastener assemblies (Bury 1991: 355–359). The second type of hand figure from the Hermitage site, consisting of a larger, molded figure holding a loop of wire (figure 12.1a2), was very likely a manufactured watch charm or jewelry amulet. A smaller metal or glass ornament was likely held by that loop of wire as part of this composition. This was one of a type of commercially produced watch charm during the nineteenth century (figure 12.1b; Fales 1995: 165, 368; Israel [1897] 1968: 419). Hand figures have been incorporated in the design of manufactured jewelry for hundreds of years throughout Europe. Notable examples, dating from the fifteenth century onward, consist of hand-shaped clasps for necklaces and of charms with the design of a hand figure holding a loop of wire from which smaller ornamental items were suspended (figure 12.1c; see Fales 1995: 165, 182, 368; Hansmann and Kriss-Rettenbeck 1966; Hinks 1975: 36).

If these artifacts uncovered at archaeological sites were such commercially produced items of popular culture, what would have inspired the manufacturers of jewelry and clothing ornaments to employ such a design? Manufacturers often assimilated symbolic motifs derived from religious beliefs or emblems of guilds and benevolent societies when creating decorative designs for mass-produced, commercial ornaments and charms (Fales 1995; Hansmann and Kriss-Rettenbeck 1966; Israel [1897] 1968: 419–422; Mackey 1919: 317). Three symbolic repertoires from Christianity and related European folk religion practices provide primary candidates for the past design inspirations of such enclosed or clenched hand figures: the *mano fica, Manus Dei,* and crucifixion of Christ.

GESTURES OF FERTILITY AND VITALITY

A *mano fica* charm (also called a *higa* or *figa*) is typically shaped as a hand closed into a fist with the thumb inserted between the first two fingers in a gesture connoting copulation and reproductive vitality (Deagan 2002: 89–99). The fertility symbolism of this charm is also evident in its name. The Italian word *fica* denotes a vulva, and was derived from the Latin word *ficus,* which denotes the fruit of the fig tree (Moss and Cappannari 1976: 8). *Figas* served as popular talismans across the Mediterranean region for hundreds of years, and because they were believed to possess supernatural powers, were frequently employed as protection against the perceived dangers of "evil eye" maledictions (Elworthy 1900: 176–177; Tait 1986: 211–213). Beliefs in a form of evil eye imprecation have been widespread across numerous cultures for thousands of years (Allen 2009; Dundes 1981). This conviction consists of the perception that individuals can invoke curses based on malevolent intent and motivations of envy, deployed by a fixed gaze cast upon a targeted person, livestock, or parcel of crops (Maloney 1976: v–vii; Roberts 1976: 221–226). Protections against such expressions of malevolence include regular wearing of amulets such as a *figa* to deflect evil.

The *figa* symbol was likely assimilated as a form of apotropaic charm because of its association with vitality. Parents often placed *figas* on their children to protect them during vulnerable periods of youth (Deagan 2002: 89; Elworthy 1895: 255–258). Spanish colonization of the Americas introduced *figas* to locations in the New World. Examples of these items have been uncovered at archaeological sites throughout the Spanish colonial sphere, dating from the sixteenth century onward, at locations ranging from South Carolina and Florida to the Caribbean and South America (Deagan 2002: 89, 95–99). Did *figa* charms supply the historic referent that adornment manufacturers had in mind when they designed the hand figures that were later uncovered at African American sites in Maryland, Virginia, Tennessee, and Florida? It seems improbable. Jewelers certainly knew how to manufacture them, and those commercial operations produced many over several centuries with the distinctive gesture of the thumb thrust between two fingers (Elworthy 1900: 176–177; Tait 1986: 211–213). That design configuration is not incorporated in the enclosed hand figures of interest here (figure 12.1a).

OMNIPOTENCE AND GRACE

Symbolic representations of the wounds of Christ and the *Manus Dei* provide more probable sources for the design inspiration of such manufactured charms depicting an enclosed hand within an encompassing circle (Stafford 1942: 32–34; Webber 1971: 140–144). A symbolic motif utilized by Catholic denominations and related vernacular religion invocations, the wounds of Christ consist of the piercing of the messiah's heart, feet, and hands in the course of crucifixion (Deagan 2002: 83–84; Strauss 1975: 62–63; Webber 1971: 140–144). These representations of the passion of Christ's sacrifice are employed in devotional art to symbolize the creation of grace as a pervasive source of spiritual power and benevolence made manifest by the messiah's crucifixion (see Wagner 1986: 96–125). In such compositions, the image of the hand is often depicted with the fingers closing over the wound created by a spike hammered through the palm into the cross (see Yoder 1990: 81, 100).

Talisman symbols incorporating an *open* hand have been employed to connote messages of sacredness, benediction, and power in a number of cultures for thousands of years (Elworthy 1900: 169–174; Webber 1971: 49–54). For example, the "Hand of Fatima" is the name within denominations of Islam for a symbolic composition consisting of an open, extended hand, communicating abundance, benevolence, and good fortune (see below). This motif, and similar ones that predated Islam, were later integrated into personal, apotropaic talismans utilized to ward off malevolent forces such as the evil eye (Hansmann and Kriss-Rettenbeck 1966: 197; Hildburgh 1906: 459).

The *Manus Dei* (or "Hand of God") has been rendered within Christian symbolic traditions as an open, extended hand overlaying a tri-radiant nimbus (Stafford 1942: 33; Webber 1971: 49–54). The three rays of this composition represent the Holy Trinity and bisect one half of a circular nimbus (an encompassing halo), which is in turn a representation of divinity and sanctity (Stafford 1942: 33; Webber 1971: 50). The contours of the open hand fill the other half of the nimbus and partially overlay the tri-radiant motif. A similar symbol of God's benevolence, expressed by an open, extended hand framed against a tri-radiant nimbus, was carved as an emblem in the twelfth century over the main door of the Cathedral of Ferrara in Italy (Elworthy 1900: 195). In the following centuries, such earlier key symbols of Christianity, which focused on a direct relationship with the Godhead, were "obviated" and displaced by new symbols concerning the sacrifice and wounds of Christ, as well as the related concept of grace as a free-flowing pool of spiritual power created by the crucifixion (Wagner 1986: 96–125).

Christian symbolism that focused on the sacrifices of the messiah more directly employed renderings of an *enclosing* hand. For example, strings of *paternoster* (denoting "Our Father") beads included small metal figures of an enclosed hand. *Paternoster* beads were a predecessor of rosary beads within Catholic liturgical practices (Deagan 2002: 65; Lightbrown 1992: 528–529; Winston 1993: 621) and of the Islamic prayer beads called *tesbih*.

These bead strings—held in the hand, worn about the neck, arm, or wrist, or attached to clothing with a brooch—were used in the practice of repeated prayers as acts of devotion (Deagan 2002: 65–66; Winston 1993: 621–622). In Catholic rituals, prayers typically consisted of the Lord's Prayer and Ave Maria (Hail Mary), and devotees repeated those prayers while meditating on the experiences of the messiah (Winston 1993: 620–22, 631–632). An example of such *paternoster* beads created in the late 1400s to early 1500s consisted of small wooden beads surrounding several small metal figures, including a hammer, three spikes, an enclosed hand, a cloak, and the head of the messiah bearing the circlet of thorns (Lightbrown 1992: 528–529).

Most likely based on the symbolism of the wounds of Christ, many vernacular religious amulets were created in southern and central Europe, at least from the 1400s onward, which consisted of an enclosed hand holding a loop of wire on which subsidiary items were appended. The smaller charm elements attached to these compositions varied greatly, but often included other symbols of Christianity (such as a cross, fish, church censor, or triangle shape for the Trinity), fertility (such as phallic figures), or images of human anatomy or livestock for which cures and protection were sought (figure 12.1c; Hansmann and Kriss-Rettenbeck 1966: 162–167, 199, 211).

Archaeologists who peeled back the layers of soil in the sites in Maryland, Virginia, Tennessee, and Florida revealed such small hand ornaments, thereby uncovering items that were very likely the product of symbolic iterations extending far back into European history. Emblematic symbols within Christian denominations were incorporated into the instrumental, vernacular amulets of Europeans over hundreds of years. Manufacturers of mass-produced commodities in the 1800s assimilated popular images from these vernacular religion talismans into small items stamped out by a machine or molded as watch charms. Many consumers in North America likely acquired such mass-produced goods from their local merchants because they viewed the ornamentation as attractive, and not necessarily because they interpreted it with any of the past symbolism that could have been read from the composition.

Potential African American Reinterpretations of Manufactured Designs

At those house and work sites in Maryland, Virginia, Tennessee, and Florida, these small hand-shaped ornaments appear to have been possessed and used by African American individuals. What meanings might someone of African descent in the early and middle 1800s have associated with these figures? Such free and enslaved African Americans may have obtained these items by purchasing them from local merchants or through barter and trade with others in their communities (Heath 1999: 50–58; Thomas 2001: 20–23). These African Americans may have utilized the ornaments as attractive adornments without assigning them particular symbolic significance. Such persons may also have subscribed to Christian beliefs and viewed the hand-shaped items as expressive of a related religious theme, such as one of those discussed above. The following discussion explores several other ways these ornaments may have been viewed by African Americans at those sites. The strength of these potential interpretations is limited by the scant documentary evidence available for each archaeological site as to the particular cultural heritage of its African American occupants.

FIGAS AND SELF-PROTECTION

Some analysts have offered the conjecture that an African American possessor of one of these figures may have used it as an apotropaic amulet because it resembled a *figa* charm (McKee 1995: 40; Singleton 1991: 162). *Figas* were in use in the Americas by the middle 1800s (Singleton 1991: 162–163). African Americans in the areas of Maryland, Virginia, Tennessee, or Florida could have learned of the beliefs accompanying *figas* if they had spent time in more southerly plantations that had been impacted by Spanish colonial influences, or had socialized with others who practiced such beliefs (Russell 1997: 67). The hand figures uncovered at these archaeological sites, however, lacked the *figa*'s distinctive gesture of thumb inserted between two fingers (see figure 12.1a). This notable difference of configurations in the compositions makes an interpretation focusing on *figas* less persuasive.

POTENTIAL ISLAMIC INFLUENCES

Analysts have also proposed that the African American bearers of these small hand figures may have viewed them as expressive of a symbolic motif referred to as the Hand of Fatima or *Khamsa* (Allen 2009: 84; McKee 1995: 40; Russell 1997: 67). Thousands of West Africans of Islamic heritage were abducted into the transatlantic slave trade, and they may have eventually transmitted knowledge of Islamic beliefs and amulets to others with whom they associated in the plantations of North America (Allen 2009; Chireau 2003: 46; Diouf 1998; Fett 2002: 42). The artifacts from these Maryland, Virginia, Tennessee, and Florida sites, however, were quite distinct in appearance from talismans that depict the open and extended Hand of Fatima (figure 12.1d). This difference in configuration also makes this potential explanation less persuasive.

MULTIVALENCE AND INDIVIDUAL ACTION

An historical analysis focusing on potential phonemic and phonetic associations of these hand-shaped artifacts provides another possible interpretation of their perceived significance. These artifacts may have been viewed as symbolic for a form of "conjuration" composition that was itself called a "hand" in some African American vernacular religions in the 1800s (McKee 1995: 40; Singleton 1991: 163). Within these African American cultural traditions, such compositions were created as part of an apotropaic invocation to deflect malevolent spiritual forces. The records of interviews with formerly enslaved persons frequently included accounts referring to such material compositions by a number of terms, including mojo, jack, hand, and gris-gris (Chireau 2003: 47; Russell 1997: 66–67; Singleton 1991: 163). These small hand-shaped ornaments may have been viewed as symbolic substitutes for another material composition that would have been called a hand.

Such punning idioms were a prominent feature of African American vernacular religion and spiritual practices in the 1800s, and continue today (see Gundaker, this volume). When creating a material composition to make supplication to spiritual forces, African American practitioners often selected elements based on similarities in the shapes or names of those items with characteristics of the dangers or maladies to be deflected or cured (e.g., Brown 1990: 22). If such a punning association of symbolic elements was involved in the utilization of these hand-shaped adornments, the process could have also involved continuing developments of particular African cultural beliefs.

In fact, as many chapters in this volume show, punning techniques were a prominent feature of the rituals of the African populations in Western Africa and the African Diaspora groups. For example, the BaKongo ritual specialists often employed such methods to create material compositions as part of their supplications for protection and healing (Jacobson-Widding 1979: 140; Janzen and MacGaffey 1974: 6; MacGaffey 1991: 5; 2000a: 44). The BaKongo people inhabited an area in West Central Africa (see map 1.1), a multiethnic cultural area known as the Kongo region (Janzen 1977: 112; MacGaffey 2000a: 35). A part of this network of ethnic groups and chiefdoms in the region shared the KiKongo language and were united under the Kingdom of Kongo starting in approximately the fourteenth century. Portuguese colonial interests began operation in the Kongo in the late fifteenth century. In the course of the transatlantic slave trade, millions of BaKongo people were abducted into bondage and transported to plantations throughout the Americas (Fennell 2007b: 48–54). In the period 1700–1866 alone, over 100,000 captives from the region of West Central Africa were brought into North America (Eltis 2009). BaKongo people accounted for high percentages of the captured Africans brought into the areas of Maryland, Virginia, and the plantations of the mid-Atlantic region of the United States (Holloway 1990; Walsh 2001).

The phonetic root of "hand" resonates with relevant terms of the BaKongo culture. The KiKongo words *vanda* and *handa* denote meanings of "activation" and "to operate" (Janzen and MacGaffey 1974: 6, 46). Similarly, the "word magician, *nganga,* comes from *vanga,* to make, and could be translated 'operator'" (MacGaffey 1970: 28). An additional phonetic resonance can be found in the KiKongo word *kànda,* which means "palm of the hand" (Denbow 1999: 418; MacGaffey 1986: 126). Employment of the word "hand" for a ritual composition could thus have involved a punning derivation from phonetically similar KiKongo words to represent an act of dexterous creation to invoke the protection of spiritual forces. Indeed, *wanga* was another term for conjuration objects among African Americans in North America, and that phrase was derived in this manner from the KiKongo language (G. M. Hall 1992: 302; Long 2001: 4, 39).

African Diaspora historians might also propose that persons of BaKongo heritage would have perceived Christian imagery in the small figure of an enclosing hand. Many of the BaKongo people abducted into the transatlantic slave trade had been introduced to Catholicism by Portuguese missionaries while in the Kongo. Little evidence exists, however, to indicate that those missionaries employed such images of the hand in the course of their proselytizing. Missionaries in the Kongo instead focused primarily on symbols such as the water of baptism and the cross of the crucifixion (Fennell 2007b: 54–63; Thornton 1977: 513–514). Christian denominations in North America also typically deployed a similar focus on symbols of baptism and the crucifix (Fennell 2007b: 92–95; Raboteau 2004: 34; Stuckey 1987: 34–35).

A key cultural symbol of the BaKongo people was called *dikenga dia Kongo* or *tendwa kia nza-n' Kongo* in the KiKongo language (Fu-Kiau 2001: 22–23; Janzen and MacGaffey 1974: 34; Thompson and Cornet 1981: 43). This core symbol, which I refer to as the *dikenga*, served as a fundamental summarizing symbol for the BaKongo cosmology from the fourteenth through the early twentieth centuries (Janzen 1977: 81; MacGaffey 2000b: 8–11; Thompson and Cornet 1981: 27–30, 44–45; Thornton 1998a: 251). In its fullest expression, the *dikenga* operated as an emblematic representation of the BaKongo people and their culture, and summarized an array of concepts that comprised their sense of identity within the world (Gundaker 1998b: 8–10; MacGaffey 1986: 136, 169–171; Thompson 1997: 29–30).

A full rendering of the *dikenga* consists of intersecting horizontal and vertical lines, set within an ellipse or circle, with smaller circles at the four ends of those crossed lines (figure 12.2; Jacobson-Widding 1991: 182–83; MacGaffey 1986: 43–46; Thompson 1997: 29–30). This emblematic composition summarized a remarkable array of layered, metaphoric meanings for the BaKongo people, and only a limited sample of those interrelated meanings is described here (Fennell 2007b). The small disks represent the "four moments" of the cosmos and cycles of existence, with the top symbolizing (among other things) the land of the living, a masculine element, and the height of a person's life and exercise of power within the land of the living. The bottom disk symbolizes (among other things) a female element, the land of the dead and the spirits, and the greatest extent of a person's exercise of spiritual powers. The right-hand disk stands for the power of potentiality and transition, the nascence of the spirit, soul, and earthly life in a cosmic cycle. In turn, the left-hand disk connotes movement from the living to the spirit world, and the power and transformations of death. The horizontal axis represents the "Kalunga" boundary line between the land of the living and the realm of the spirits, and the intersecting vertical axis connotes that the living may make supplication to summon the aid of the ancestors and spiritual forces to cross that permeable boundary. Such entreaties were usually made by a ritual specialist, an *nganga*, who created material compositions as part of those invocations for aid and wisdom (Fennell 2007b: 31–33; Gomez 1998: 148–149; Janzen and MacGaffey 1974: 34; Thompson 1983: 108–109; Thompson and Cornet 1981: 27–30).

Consider again the shape and design of the small hand ornaments uncovered at African American sites in Maryland, Virginia, Tennessee, and Florida (figure 12.1a1). An individual who subscribed to aspects of BaKongo heritage might have acquired and used one of those ornaments as a ritual symbol because she or he perceived a significance to the figure of a creative hand operating within an encompassing circle. These small hand figures

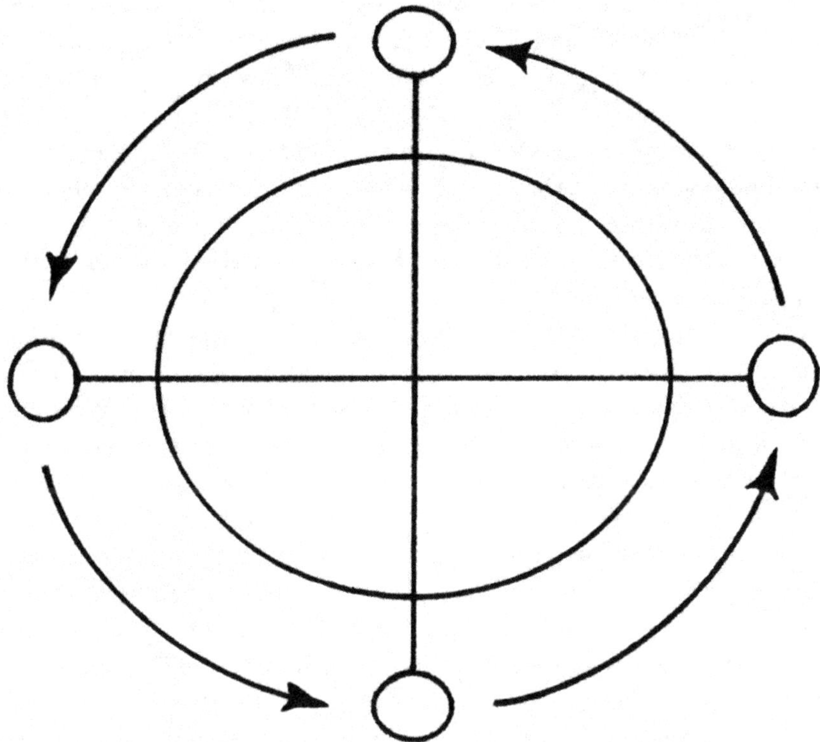

FIGURE 12.2. *Dikenga dia Kongo,* a key cultural symbol of the BaKongo people. *Courtesy of the author.*

would have been of engaging interest to an individual who subscribed to facets of BaKongo cosmological beliefs. The hand figure, representative of the creative capabilities of the *nganga,* is centered within an encircling cycle of the cosmos and rests on a horizontal crossbar (figure 12.1a1) that could be interpreted as expressing the permeable boundary line between the living and spirit worlds. Moreover, the hand within that composition reaches up from that horizon and grasps the top point of the encompassing circle, which is a position within the BaKongo cosmic cycle that represents the powerful actions of the living (Fennell 2007b: 77–78; R. F. Thompson, pers. comm., Sept. 2005).

Some analysts may view it as questionable to look for such particular cultural connections between specific African cultures and the beliefs and practices of African Americans in the 1800s in the United States. Historians have often contended that the 1808 abolition of international slave trading by the United States dramatically curtailed the arrival of newly captive Africans after that time (e.g., Genovese 1976: 211). They have, in turn, argued that, in the absence of newly arriving Africans, the connections between particular African cultures and the beliefs and practices of African Americans in the 1800s became increasingly attenuated, with African components decreasing over time. Recent research, however, demonstrates that slave traders engaged in extensive smuggling of captive African laborers into the United States after 1808.

For example, the DeWolf family operated extensive plantation holdings with facilities in Rhode Island, the Caribbean, and West Africa, and managed slave vessels that transported over ten thousand captive Africans to North America. Studies show that the DeWolfs continued those operations into the 1820s, bringing slave vessels with newly abducted Africans into Rhode Island ports by bribing officials and through other illicit means (Coughtry 1981; Farrow et al. 2005). Similarly, hundreds of newly captured Africans from the Kongo area were brought into South Carolina on a single slave vessel as late as 1858 (Baldwin 1993: 82–83). Obviously, these accounts are not directly connected to the sites in Maryland, Virginia, Tennessee, and Florida in which hand figures have been uncovered archaeologically. But these examples contribute to a growing body of evidence of the continuing importation of Africans into the United States after the 1808 ban. In addition, the cultural beliefs and practices of earlier-arriving captive Africans could have influences among African Americans in particular locations for generations, and not become as quickly attenuated as some historians would contend.

LEGACIES OF *IKENGA*

The figure of an enclosing hand also could have resonated with the expressive configuration of a West African symbolic motif—the *ikenga* of Igbo culture (figure 12.3). The historic-period cultures of Igbo-speaking peoples were located in what is today southeastern Nigeria. British, French, and Portuguese commercial interests in the slave trade focused on this area starting in the sixteenth century, creating an exacerbation of regional conflicts (Kolapo 2004; Okpoko and Obi-Ani 2005; Walsh 2001: 145). A pattern of intergroup conflicts, raids, kidnappings, and contrived criminal charges led to a stream of captives flowing out of the slave ports located along the Bight of Biafra (Eltis 2009; Gomez 1998: 132; Hall 2005: 129–130). In the period 1700–1866, over 75,000 captives from that region were brought to the

FIGURE 12.3. *Ikenga,* Igbo culture, wood composition with a representation of a machete in the right hand and ivory tusk in the left, 61 cm, adapted by the author from Boston 1977: 29.

plantations of North America (Eltis 2009). Like the BaKongo, the Igbo people made up significant percentages of the captured Africans brought into the areas of the Chesapeake and mid-Atlantic regions (Chambers 1997: 73–77; Gomez 1998: 115; Northrup 2000: 14; Walsh 2001: 145–149, 156–159). Many of those enslaved Africans carried with them knowledge of a rich cultural repertoire that included the "cult of the hand" represented by the symbolic expressive motifs of personal *ikenga* figures and household shrines.

The *ikenga* expression of the cult of the hand celebrates an individual's accomplishments and aspirations of achievement (figure 12.3; Cole 2013: 24–28; Dean 1983: 33; Lorenz 1987: 71–72; Vogel 1974: 2–4). This cultural tradition among the Igbo and neighboring cultural groups, especially the Edo, extends back to at least the fifteenth century in West Africa (Ben-Amos 1995: 80–81; Boston 1977: 2; Dean 1983, 33; Lorenz 1987: 71–72; Odita 1973: 76; see also Ogundiran, this volume). *Ikenga* sculptures varied in size from several centimeters to a meter or more in height. Many figures of this type were made by members of Igbo households, or by specialist carvers within their communities, for use in personal altars maintained in private dwellings (Boston 1977: 14; Dean 1983: 33; Vogel 1974: 4). Such a form of symbolic composition focusing on individual accomplishment and employed within private spaces comprised a form of instrumental expression of a key cultural symbol (Fennell 2007b: 28–31).

In the design of *ikenga* figures, both the right and left hand grasped objects that, in turn, conveyed statements concerning the aspirations of the individual's capabilities and accomplishments. The right hand of an *ikenga* usually closed around the hilt of a machete or other weapon, while the left hand held objects of wealth, such as an ivory tusk (Bentor 1988: 70; Boston 1977: 29, 41, 68; Dean 1983: 33). As seen in this example, elongated horn elements extended off of a headdress component, symbolizing power and vitality. *Ikenga* were not used solely to symbolize aspirations of victory in arms and aggression; they were also employed as supplications for success in subsistence, household health and vitality, protection against malevolent forces, and overall social and spiritual competence (Bradbury 1961: 133–134; Boston 1977: 78; Dean 1983: 33; Ottenberg 1983: 51; Peek 1986: 47; Vogel 1974: 2).

The symbolic tradition of the cult of the hand also manifests as an element in the *ukhurhe* compositions among the Edo people of Benin. The *ukhurhe* was an ornate, carved wooden staff with a segmented design. These staffs, which often included rattle components as well, were usually incorporated into private altars within dwellings (Dean 1983: 37–40; Von Luschan

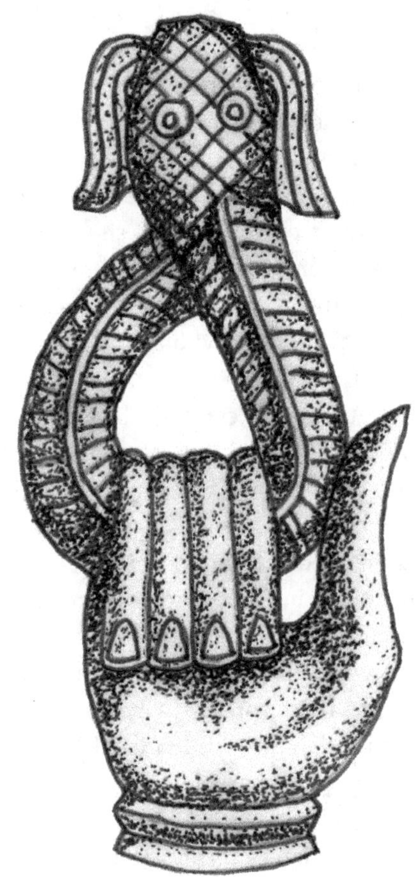

FIGURE 12.4. *Ukhurhe* rattle staff (Benin), showing a hand holding a mudfish, 19 cm, adapted by the author from Dean 1983: 40.

[1919] 1968). An element in the *ukhurhe* design among higher-status individuals included the figure of an enclosing hand holding a mudfish (figure 12.4; Dean 1983: 40, figure 26; Von Luschan [1919] 1968: figure 716). This element represented the owner's capacity to control spiritual forces as symbolized by the coiled and dynamic form of the mudfish (Dean 1983: 37). Such compositions as the *ikenga* and *ukhurhe* among the Igbo and Edo respectively "explicitly refer to individual power as symbolized by the hand" (ibid.). Many individuals of Igbo heritage undoubtedly worked as enslaved laborers in the regions in which small hand ornaments were later recovered at archaeological sites in Maryland, Virginia, Tennessee, and Florida. Persons with such cultural heritage may have found the small hand ornaments of engaging interest due to these past referents among West African cultures.

Concluding Observations

This case study arrives at no conclusive account for these small hand-shaped figures uncovered at African American sites dating from the early and middle 1800s. By posing a systematic series of questions and exploring possible answers, however, I hope this analysis has pointed to intriguing potentials. A spectrum of data sources show that these small ornaments likely embodied intersecting lines of history reaching from the symbols of Christ's passion spreading across the Mediterranean to the expressions of self-determination through individualized ritual invocations by enslaved Africans in the Americas.

An analyst can often be more confident with some interpretations than others. As the title for this chapter indicates, these manufactured figures were very likely shaped by European design choices derived from instrumental symbolism within Christian traditions. This cultural connection became attenuated in time as a shift occurred from individually created charm compositions in Europe to mass production of a popular cultural commodity shipped out to merchants in North America. Yet, shifts from the individually sacred to the profane can later be reversed. Commercially produced objects can be reinterpreted by persons choosing to utilize them as found symbols within their own individual expressions, derived from distinct cultural repertoires. Until we obtain more data and contexts to explore the set of probabilities outlined above, the linear argument that a core cultural symbol of a messiah's sacrifice in Europe was transformed into a profane clothing commodity in the Americas, and that this was in turn redeployed as an instrumental symbol analogous to the dexterous force of an *nganga* or *ikenga* to ward off malevolence, will have to remain a conjecture. Some archaeologists also propose that the hand figures were viewed by African Americans as resembling a hand in a shackle. The figures thus could have served as expressions of protest against enslavement and of hope for abolition (Lee 2013). Such interpretations require additional evidence to be persuasive.

Hopefully future investigations will yield an expansion of the data set under consideration here. Interpretations of the meaning and function of such hand figures at particular sites will be aided by more documentary and contextual evidence concerning the site occupants and their particular cultural heritages. Only with multiple lines of evidence concerning each site can we confidently infer whether such an artifact was utilized simply as a fastener, as a social adornment, or as an expression of ideological convictions.

Notes

I extend sincere thanks to Kofi Agorsah, James Davidson, Lori Lee, Mark Leone, Larry McKee, Akin Ogundiran, Robert Farris Thompson, and Anne Yentsch for their comments on this analysis.

1. There are two versions. The first (figure 12.1a1) depicts a type of stamped brass fastener or ornament, usually .1 to 1.2 cm tall across both circles combined. The second (figure 12.1a2) depicts a likely watch charm, made of molded metal holding a loop of wire, approximately 1.9 cm tall from the base of the wrist to the top of the hand, uncovered at the Hermitage site.

CHAPTER 13

Ritualized Figuration in Special African American Yards

Grey Gundaker

> The larger, the more human, the less technical the problem of practice, the more open-eyed and wide-viewing the corresponding method. I do not say that all things that have been called philosophy participate in this method; I do say, however, that a catholic and farsighted theory of the adjustment of the conflicting factors of life *is*—whatever it is called—philosophy.
>
> —JOHN DEWEY ([1910] 1997: 44)

This paper explores the placement and ritualized use of statuary of animals, religious figures, and mythic beings in special African American yards to contribute to the philosophical "adjustment of the conflicting factors of life" (Dewey [1910] 1997: 44). Practitioners who make these yards call the spaces around their homes "yards" and view them as exceptional; certainly, they are not typical of African American domestic landscapes. Figuration in these yards is ritualized because, by drawing on a stable visual and material repertoire and recurring spatial practices, practitioners work toward, as John M. Janzen puts it, "the amplification of layers and layers of meaning, . . . [and] the addition of more lines of communication to those normally used between individuals" (1992: 174).

All the yard makers discussed here were over fifty years old when we met in the late 1980s, retired or working as contractors, nurses, pastors, and industrial workers. Age correlates with property ownership and perhaps more free time, but its main significance is that community leadership and role modeling require maturity. All also grew up under segregation in the

South, which probably honed their skills in composing the layered messages and double entendres, which many yards contain. Figures used in the yards range from commercial statuary to abstract ensembles. Some were initially produced as "toys," a topic that I return to later. The makers discussed here, however, move beyond decoration to make philosophical, spiritual, and political statements in material form, using a well-documented repertoire of material signs that mixes Black Atlantic and Christian imagery (Gundaker and McWillie 2006; Thompson 1983). This chapter situates figures in relation to this repertoire, ritualization, and landscape ideology. It privileges participants' own terms and the indirect language they use about their work. Although I focus on contemporary sites, I suggest that archeologists keep landscape ideologies and figuration in mind as they investigate earlier sites.

Figuring Theories in African Diaspora Anthropology

Art historian Robert Farris Thompson inspired this chapter by identifying *figuration* as a principle in African American yard shows (1993), and arguing that they build on the philosophical foundations of transatlantic arts from Kongo, Cross River, and other peoples who have informed cultural production in the Americas (Thompson 1983; Thompson and Cornet 1981). This position, however, is greatly at odds with prevailing attitudes in anthropology, which Andrew Apter summarizes as follows:

> Unless critically deconstructed, the idea of African origins is decidedly out of favor. On methodological grounds alone, criteria for establishing African provenance have remained controversial since the Herskovits-Frazier debate, demanding strict functional correspondences that can never realistically be found (Smith [1957] 1984), involving essentialized tribal designations that should be abandoned (Mintz and Price 1992), or invoking a play of tropes within a historically situated discursive field that can never be transcended (Scott 1991, 1997). According to these methodological strictures, African cultural practices may well exist in the Americas, but they cannot be known with any specificity. They lie beyond the limits of anthropological reason. (2002: 234)

Despite this, Apter argues for African origins to resolve a narrow debate about creolization in Haiti. He does not claim that the evidence demands a change of outlook or that anthropological theories have often obscured Diasporic complexity (Gundaker 1998b). Rather, he suggests that with due caution, the "limits of anthropological reason" can be pushed—just a little.

While caution is wise, anthropologists also routinely project speculative generalizations onto the peoples they study and call it "theory" (Mudimbe 1988). To counter this, anthropologists can emulate Susan Sontag (1961) and John Szwed (2011) by forgoing interpretation as much as possible, or frame research as cultural history, which proponents argue is non- or less speculative (Matory 2005: 14; Palmié 2002; Thornton 1998a). But this can mask knowledge built on material practices, including ritual and performance. As participants' *accounts* of their experiences, these practices must be theorized as carefully as any other source (Garfinkel 1991), lest scholars default to the position that Richard Rorty (1981) critiques as the "mirror" theory of representation.

This takes us full circle because *any* theory involves speculation (Kuhn 1996). But anthropologists can still flag the more speculative portions of their arguments (Bateson [1972] 2002: 87) and incorporate participants' own theories of their actions on a par with, or, better yet, over and against, academic theories (Myhre 2006; Turner et al. 1992). This move is also a corrective in the wider context of the African Diaspora. For to date, nothing approaching parity—narration from the perspectives of everyone concerned—has been achieved. Despite years of critical intervention, European-oriented dominance has continued because it has also shaped the intellectual climate in which even critics of this situation do their work (Miller 1999).

Given that, we can emphasize plausibility over proof when necessary, aim for more complex understandings of cultural practices that share cognates across wide areas, and ask how those considered transatlantic fit into *modes of use* (Wittgenstein 2009: 238). For modes of use persist for two main reasons: either nothing in a "new" environment meets the purpose at hand, or "old" and "new" recalibrate in relation to each other. The figuration that I discuss below is not reducible to either the "new" or the "old," or to the Protestant Christianity of its users and makers. Rather, it recalibrates new and old because Christian theology makes no sanctioned place for ritualized ancestral commemoration or protective signs. My aim is not to find "African origins," but to stay as open to transatlantic and local resources as to the assumed "European origins" or ahistorical "creativity" of African Diaspora cultures.

Considerable work is underway to achieve parity: this volume, for example. But dominant anthropological theories have resisted Africa-centered approaches to the study of African Diaspora cultural formation. They have also discouraged ethnographic research in the United States, at least since

Sidney Mintz and Richard Price's *Birth of Afro-American Culture* (1976, 1992) began circulating in the mid-1970s. Mintz and Price asserted that culture is carried through institutions, and that no African institutions could survive the Middle Passage intact (1992: 19, 57–59). Enslaved individuals were no more than cogs in an economic machine, but their humanity could be rehabilitated by showing their creativity and resistance. Thus, causation depended either on the plantation system or on "informal" arenas of marginal importance. Philip Morgan offers an example of this outlook when he states that "slave societies"

> were impoverished in formal recreations. But this very diminution encouraged more informal creativity. Precisely because of, as Mintz and Price [1976: 26] have argued, "the relentless assault on personal identity, the stripping away of rank, the treatment of people as nameless ciphers" its victims cultivated "an enhanced appreciation for exactly those most personal, most human characteristics which differentiate one individual from another." (1998: 594)

In sum, hard labor for life limited recreation, which in turn caused more creativity and more appreciation of individual differences—and, as a result, recovery of humanity, which the enslaved never lost. Would such logic be accepted for any other group?

The "birth" metaphor offered a fixed starting point, but variation and change are cultural constants, not aberrations. In the Diaspora, rupture and dislocation amplify the experience of change not because drastic transitions are uncommon but because dislocation rips apart contexts of sense-making that are inseparable from and integral to participation in the world as we know it (Bateson [1972] 2002; Garfinkel 1991). Because these contexts are part and parcel of the practices that comprise them, even the Middle Passage cannot simply erase the past and clear the way for the "new." Certainly, new ways of framing experience emerge—especially with respect to racial and local solidarities—but, when rupture is involuntary, it is reasonable to also expect a strong pull toward cultural conservatism to ground experience in the familiar and outflank the oppressor. There have been anthropological critiques of Mintz and Price, but these have recommended only minor adjustments to their theory of creolization. Much stronger critique has come from historians, but they emphasize continuity of experience and practice between Africa and its Diaspora rather than theory.

Another gaping hole in the theorizing of African Diaspora cultural formation is the near-absence of the African American experience. None of the theorists of the African Diaspora, including Melville Herskovits, the progenitor of these debates, conducted sustained fieldwork within the United States. Yet their dictums are applied to the United States and their positions remain largely unchallenged within anthropology (e.g., Yelvington 2006). Indeed, Africanists who have not worked anywhere in the Americas render verdicts on African Diaspora scholarship that would be vociferously challenged in reverse. Is this because fieldwork in Benin or Kenya fits the old anthropological saw of the farther away the better? Or do Africanists accrue authority from working on the home continent of those very "African origins" that lie "beyond the limits of anthropological reason"? Do they gain an aura of "authenticity" even when most agree that authenticity itself is produced through participants' own strategic narratives of origins? Ironically, though important, this insight has also diverted attention away from investigating longer-term transatlantic resources, which is now regarded as passé, in favor of more recent appropriations, which are more easily tracked. If we already knew as much about African contributions to the Americas as we know of European contributions, this would be reasonable. Unfortunately, we do not. So, much more remains to be "deconstructed" (or reconstructed) in the theory-politics of anthropology.

Toy Blindness, African American Yards, and Ritualized Vision

Marginalization of the African cultural Diaspora in the United States necessitates clearing a path through anthropological debates. But this can also divert attention from "real world" occasions where differences in theoretical orientations manifest. This chapter stems from one such occasion, when the approach critiqued above confronted multivalent figuration in African American yards, with rather humorous results. As soon as my work started to circulate in the 1990s, scholars unfamiliar with African Diaspora practices, except perhaps through texts, began insisting that certain figures I mentioned could only be "toys." For example, a noted historian of American slavery dismissed Mrs. Ruby Gilmore's claim that a stuffed Snoopy she placed beside a "Keep Out" sign on her garage roof (figure 13.1) was now her "watchdog" after bootleggers poisoned her live dog, Chip (Gundaker 1998b: 68). The historian stated that Snoopy "toys" are icons of American popular culture and could be nothing more.[1] Underlying this assertion was the bias that documents outweigh human voices, as well as the notion that ordinary people use only transparent semiotic repertoires and live lives largely

FIGURE 13.1. Mrs. Ruby Gilmore's stuffed Snoopy watchdog.

determined by economic modes of production and consumption (Myhre 2006; Rancière 2003), a philosophical flatness only amplified by a history of oppression and slavery. Thinking otherwise would mean extensive revision of his scholarly practice.

For the past twenty-three years, I have worked as an ethnographer in the United States and Anglophone Caribbean. It soon became clear that failing to consider "African cultural practices" among the historical foundations of American life would leave me with the thoroughly unanthropological proposition that numerous people, like Mrs. Gilmore, were doing similar things that could set them at odds with their peers and even make them the butt of jokes—and that they did this for purely idiosyncratic reasons. To map recurring practices in yards geographically and thematically, I created a data base of about three thousand images, which, along with site maps and oral accounts, is the basis for my analysis and claim that certain practices amplify "layers and layers of meaning." Methodologically, I follow a simple rule of redundancy. To warrant claims about meanings beyond first impressions, the context requires, minimally, at least *three* signs that signify in the same way (Peirce 1998). Thus, the argument that Mrs. Gilmore's Snoopy is not "just a toy" depends on her words, the figure's placement beside the Rosetta Stone "Keep Out" sign, and her copious use of other warnings against intrusion which foreground sensory acumen.

Makers like Mrs. Gilmore often use ordinary objects to disturb the margins of visibility and sort those who can see deeply from those who cannot. Thus, they stress the both/and layering of vision that a mature person must master. Dominant classifications like "toy" mask multivalent object-coding. Even terms like "chair," "hub cap," and "statue" trigger preconceptions so that members of the so-called dominant culture may resist the idea that they are missing something. This complacency has probably helped African Americans mask activities in plain sight for generations. Further, conventional material culture research usually focuses on handmade objects or spheres of consumption in which designers, producers, and users share similar expectations. When different cultural orientations intersect in the Black Atlantic, however, multilayered resources from Europe, Africa, and the Americas undercut such expectations and expose their biases. The same transformative dynamics of code- and style-switching that African Diasporans have used to define themselves through performance extend into the material world. Combining materials with different cultural histories and associations also undermines the very notion of discrete "material culture," for the "culture(s)" are patently not apparent from the "material."

Yard makers use object coding that is equally at home with spiritual and pragmatic concerns, and shift among words and material signs through visual translations, puns, icons, and indexical signs. For example, Mrs. Gilmore put a blue wooden cat on her grandson's grave: "He was quite a cat and I'm blue that he was killed." Not all object coding is so precise, but the principle holds that the entire material world has potential to tell us who we are and who we should become. Further, rather than comprising a genre in itself, with a recognized name and audience, yard work draws on other genres of ritual and performance: songs, proverbs, tales, sermons, films, parades, labor practices, legal proceedings, burial practices, and much more. Figurative language translates readily into physical form, including religious phrases like "rock of ages," "Jacob's ladder," etc. (Ahlo 1976), and from verbal arts such as "bug-eye," "puzzle-gut," "shovel-head," and so on (Hurston 1942: 104). The results often fit what Zora Neale Hurston called "decorating a decoration" ([1926] 1997: 59), a layering of materials that in turn echoes West and Central African recursive, fractal patterning (Eglash 1999) and an "accretive" quality like that of, for example, Mande *boli* figures, whose power increases with the accumulation of sacrificial matter (McNaughton 1993).

Although such patterns seem clear if one has the luxury to travel, most makers say their work is unique. This is also true. Each yard is deeply personal and rarely collaborative. Yard makers say that they do not see their work as part of a tradition because their parents worked too hard to spend time "decorating." Neighbors and even spouses may regard certain types of yard work as messy or inappropriate. Mrs. Mary Smith asked me to urge the city to bulldoze arrangements her husband, Johnson Smith, had spread over the property, including a replica ancestral burial ground with broken vessels, shells, and pipes. She saw them as a poor reflection on her housekeeping.[2] These differences in perception worried me. If even some family members did not see yard contents as valuable, were recurring patterns an illusion? Finally, after numerous conversations with participants about their theories of "right living," I realized that they regarded *all* individual destinies as unique because God created each person for a special purpose that we cannot always know, and that may seem at odds with our own views in this inherently troubled world.

Although there are usually no more than two or three high-profile yards in any urban neighborhood or small town, the building blocks of grander visions are everywhere: boundaries and thresholds clearly marked; symmetrical contrasted with more random areas; antiques used as memorials; figures watching paths; plants treated as individuals (Westmacott 1992); and surfaces given thoughtful attention so that that the property is "sealed" against negativity (Abrahams 1983). Such ritualizations are the baseline for a philosophy of "doing things right," which binds individuals to communities and cosmologies through performance (Gundaker and McWillie 2006: 96–136). In this way, commonplace practices address the same basic concerns as special yards: mediating access to the property, asserting moral authority, and claiming good standing in the community. But special yards take these further by encapsulating in one landscape the most important cosmological relationships in a just and balanced world: among persons, the community, and God; and among the living, dead, and unborn. Thus, makers work to illustrate key components of a well-lived life.

Caring for the front yard so that it looks like a freshly ironed apron attests to *cultivation*—the accomplishment, maturity, and vigilance—of the maker and the household. Wilder parts of the yard, often at the back or side, contain herbs and antiques tucked among the plants: pots, tools, plows, chairs, and even animal skulls. Such areas may also be used as places for prayer, recalling the wilderness where Jesus prayed. Parallels with the body and behavior are legion because a yard is a presentation of self (Goffman 1959). Some contexts call for cool formality and predictable comportment; others for greater flexibility and higher, hotter energy.[3] Like ritual in some churches, the front part of the yard, like the first part of the service, is more controlled. The service begins with standard biblical texts; the front yard focuses on formal plantings and statuary. Areas that look wilder parallel the transition when services become more emotionally charged through call-and-response as the body moves with the spirit (Pitts 1989). Cultivated areas are like churchgoers arriving, crisply groomed; wilder parts call and respond with powers of the spirit, forest diversity, and the past. Cultivation and wildness, formality and unpredictability, have their own places in a balanced world. The former shows behavior necessary for an ethical life; the latter ensures that order remains in touch with changing conditions. So, when both combine in the design, rather than being mere domestic landscapes, these yards are many places at once, holding in balance the tensions and diversity that make up the community, the world, and the cosmos.

Cultivated Modes of Poise and Accomplishment

Cultivation stands out less than wildness because it fits expectations about proper upkeep of one's home. Still, some yards foreground cultivation so forcefully they command attention—like that of Mrs. Jackie Jones, a nurse in Chattanooga, committed to healing in all aspects of her life (figure 13.2). When a wilderness of crack houses and deteriorating property encroached on her street, she confronted them with a vibrant assertion of love, paving a path to her door with one "Welcome" mat after another. Every plant thrives, each stone is spotless white, and an angel presides over all to model well-being within the "safety zone"[4] of cultivated, Christian living. Most displays of cultivation share features with Mrs. Jones's yard: beds and borders marked, plants trimmed, and statuary glistening. Many contain subtler

FIGURE 13.2. Home of Mrs. Jackie Jones, Chattanooga.

signs like vessels of water near doorways as reminders of purification. Calm, composed figures like Mrs. Jones's angel or Jesus and Mary, Greek gods, and heroic role models like Dr. Martin Luther King, Jr., embody the cool, philosophical centeredness from which the wise person takes stock of situations before acting (Thompson 1973). Since they project an ideal demeanor for facing the world, it makes sense that they occupy visible spots. Usually these figures are white, though Jesus is sometimes red and white, as befits an active power in the world. Such figures double as watchers and signs of moral authority, challenging misbehavior in their presence. Thus, yards like Mrs. Jones's also align cultivation with respectability and leadership (Abrahams and Szwed 1983; Wilson 1995).

An emphasis on cultivation, however, can take forms less compatible with conventional expectations. Victor Melancon, who surrounded his house with watchers and hemmed both sides with wilder memorial areas, also filled his living room with figures built of items associated with valuable professions: white shoes, a folded white dress, a stethoscope, and a striped cap for nurses; black shoes, blue pants and jacket, and an airline cap topped with a model airplane for a pilot; and on and on. His "little people" comprised a diverse "congregation" of contributors to making the world "work the way it's supposed to."[5]

Placed to suggest the movement of a house, the omniscience of God, personal centeredness, and the encompassing knowledge of a mature person, wheels can also signal cultivation (see also Thompson 1989). In addition, lighthouses warn against life's shoals as they wheel God's sight around 360 degrees.[6] Although they do not seem figural initially, a number of men—in my fieldwork, only men—use lighthouses and whirligigs to show that their roles as leaders entail cultivating knowledge that comes from, and moves out, in all directions.

Ancestor Figures

Knowledge from ancestors is essential to leadership, as tributes in the yards of these same men make clear. Further, like ancestors buried in a cemetery, ancestor figures in the yard ground the right of the residents to justice and full citizenship, however unwilling national, state, and local authorities are to recognize this fact. A leader must enforce these rights. At death, the spirit seeks respect from the living through proper burial. As memories of individual qualities fade over time, those worthy transition to the more general status of ancestor (cf. K. M. Brown 2001). Along the way, the power of the dead intensifies from that of a single soul to that of a collective, known in the United States as "the old folks," "slavery-time people," or "people back then." As the familiar feel of these phrases suggests, ancestors remain part of the family. In the Protestant areas that dominate most of the South except Louisiana, no Catholic saints serve as intercessors, but the wisdom of ancestors passes down through memory, and proverbs bridge heaven and earth with a legacy that must not be ignored (Jacobs and Kaslow 1991). The Jordan River in Christian imagery is a two-way conduit. The saved soul crosses over to heaven and a seat at God's table (like one under the tree in figure 13.3), while guidance comes back to the living through prayer and remembered advice.

Most ancestor figuration is away from foot traffic. Even if a yard contains no wilder area, the association of ancestors with special trees like cedars creates one in itself (Thompson and Cornet 1981: 186–194). Sculptor Ralph Griffin explained that he used twisted wood from streams because it held "old experience ages" (McWillie and Lockpez 1989: 11). Luisa Teish has

FIGURE 13.3. Packnett family tree.

written of the energy of the ancestors in "wood that groans" (1989: 68). In Mississippi, Gyp Packnett tied a hemlock he called his "family tree" with chains and the weights from an old cotton scale to show that his ancestors endured the weight of slavery and "came on through" (figure 13.3). Clearly, trees like these are abstract forms of figuration in which a living being becomes the body-trunk of an object-portrait.

Links between trees and the dead are also ritualized by placing a wheel around a dead branch. Robert Farris Thompson (pers. comm., Sept. 1990) has identified the hole as a gateway to the other world. Dead wood passes

FIGURE 13.4. Mrs. Olivia Humphrey's dedicatory rituals to female ancestors.

through the hole as the soul leaves its husk to "cross over." This sign, thus, warns thieves of their fate and invokes ancestors in one move. In the Caribbean, such holes appear near provision gardens and fruit trees. Mrs. Olivia Humphrey used it in her side-yard, along with other allusions to burial and the dead (figure 13.4). Some figural trees and posts have shining wheels, hub-caps, or silver gazing-balls for faces. These also imply mastery, but unlike spinning whirligigs and fans, whose motion pulls inward and outward, these concentrate bright light in one spot to suggest centripetal distillation and a lens focused on the other world. Just as use wears down the face on a coin to a silver disk, the individuality of the ancestors coalesces into brightness. Here, a halo does not *surround* the head as in European art; its radiance *is* the head. Thus, Jesus has two personas. Ready-made figures are role models of divine cultivation. But Jesus also shines as the ultimate ancestor, his face distilled to the sun of Resurrection mornings. Other ancestor tributes in wilder areas look like miniature cemeteries of the African American past, with small statues, headstones, shells, vessels, pipes, whiteness, and silvery allusions to water (Thompson and Cornet 1981: 181–203). Although these objects are "real things," they too become more abstract and remote from ordinary life when relocated near old trees and brushy areas away from a house.

Memorials to Recently Deceased Persons

In contrast to the abstraction of ancestor figures, tributes to the recently deceased aim for specificity while showing death's transformation of a loved one into a new being. Dolls, especially baby dolls, surrounded by mementos fit this purpose well, integrating the person born again in heaven with the image of the soul as a little person led into God's presence by Jesus, an angel, or other spiritual guide. Unlike ancestor figures, these memorials are usually close to the pathways of the living. Gyp Packnett's tribute to his late wife began as a vacant seat with mirrors, flowers, her work shoes, and silver chains of pop tops she strung together. Later, he reworked the arrangement with a flying baby doll at the center. It would be hard to imagine using a mere "toy" for such a serious purpose. Mr. Packnett built this tribute on the carport he used as a patio, where he could see it from his favorite armchair. When guests joined him, Mrs. Packnett was also present through her memorial.

Conversion visions provide background for dolls and small, vulnerable animals like rabbits in memorials. Writing about the "Afro-Baptist sacred cosmos" of coastal Georgia, Mechal Sobel (1979) points out the recurring figure of a "little me inside the big me," which took the form of a little white man in the conversion narratives of *God Struck Me Dead,* a collection of interviews compiled by Fisk University researchers in the 1920s (Rawick 1972: vol. 18). Sobel argues that the little person reconfigured the multiple souls of West African cosmologies to fit a Christian worldview. Samuel Miller Lawton's interviews (1939) in the Sea Islands contain twenty-five references to little white people in visions (see also Lester 1972; Bass 1935). The color white here refers to snow white, a sign of purity, not to Caucasian skin, which African American artists usually paint pink. It also echoes the coloration of the ancestors like *mpembe,* the Kongo zone of the dead, with *mpembe* doubling as the term for white kaolin clay (Thompson and Cornet 1981: 40). With the assistance of his wife, Lawton, who was blind, quantified his findings. He found that whiteness appeared more often than any other feature of grave offerings and vision narratives. Mrs. Olivia Humphrey composed a tribute to the women of her family with her mother's cast iron Dutch oven suspended from an arch (threshold) spanning a larger bowl containing water and vessels, surrounded by inverted white vases and a little girl's shoes. A tree stump forms the base of the arrangement, which she dusted liberally with white powder (lower left in figure 13.4). When Sam Hogue made a memorial to his wife, he rearranged the ornaments already in his yard into circles within circles and painted everything white (see Gundaker and McWillie 2006: 7). Indoors, he made a smaller memorial to his late son, using diplomas, photos, and toy cars. Like Mr. Packnett's arrangement, this one was colorful. These examples suggest that brighter and more diverse colors are often used in tributes to the recent dead; varied colors situate the deceased within the activities of everyday life. Ancestors are always, in my experience, white or silver.

Watchers

Figures at thresholds and boundaries can represent protective forces, who watch over the household, like Mrs. Gilmore's "watchdog" Snoopy. Whereas the vision of mature people is flexible and that of God omnidirectional, watchers gaze intensely in one direction with eyes *always* aligned with approaches to the property. Many watcher figures depict creatures known for their loyalty and sensory powers like dogs and geese (cf. Brewer 1958). Even in yards with little other figuration, eagles are popular near doors. On a superficial level, an eagle plaque is a legacy of the Colonial Revival style, with the patriotic eagle lingering beyond the demise of the style. But, like the Fourth of July, patriotic symbols are often more ambiguous for African Americans than for European Americans. A passage from Reverend C. L. Franklin's famous sermon *The Eagle Stirreth Her Nest* stresses the eagle's extraordinary vision, not patriotic forms:

> Another thing about the eagle is that he has extraordinary sight. . . . He can rise to a lofty height in the air and look in the distance and see a storm hours away. That's extraordinary sight. And sometimes he can stand and gaze right in the sun because he has extraordinary sight. I want to tell you my God has extraordinary sight. . . . He can look behind that smile on your face and see that frown in your heart. God has extraordinary sight. (1989: 48)

God's sight gives believers guidance and protection from the traps human beings lay for each other—thus eagles share qualities with lighthouses. Given the vigilance required for the exercise of black citizenship, placing eagles above doors adds an African American "coded" aspect to the patriotic American eagle.

No matter how cultivated the design of a threshold may appear, all are crossroads where negativity and unpredictable change can enter. Many watchers seem merely decorative at first, the cool, neutral demeanor of cultivation. A house in Chattanooga has busts of Beethoven, Michelangelo's David, and Moses gazing out and down from the roof. Since trouble takes intangible forms like gossip and ill will, watchers watch the unseen as well as the visible. Thus, the creatures selected are often known for their mediatory movement and vision across different types of environments: birds, amphibians, and reptiles (Thompson 1993: 75–91). Other watchers look like empty chairs that imply invisible bodies or, at Johnson Smith's gate, a stained washbasin that makes a face with cross mark/taps for eyes (Gundaker 1993).

Yet, most are recognizably figurative. Toys and stuffed animals are common, like Snoopy. Victor Melancon put stuffed animals on the front porch of a vacant house because he worried that children would hurt themselves playing on the rotten floorboards. I wondered how he knew the "toys" would keep children away instead of attracting them, so I asked neighborhood kids if they played there. "No way," one said. "See that stuff? That man put a power out on it." Protection through figuration and other means also fits a Christian interpretation of the Lord's Prayer, which several yard makers expressed as the rule, "Do not lead others into temptation" through unguarded property. One criticized me when I left a camera on the seat of my car: "That looks expensive. Don't want to tempt some soul to take it. Then it's you, not them that cross the line."

Hot Watcher Guardians

Some threshold guardians would make anyone think twice about entering. A hot blue homemade figure near Augusta, Georgia, wore a ghoulish Halloween mask and held a vacuum cleaner that could suck up anything negative that came its way (Gundaker and McWillie 2006: 132; cf. Doris 2011). A propeller blew its power in all directions. Mrs. Ruby Gilmore hung a gorilla mask and a skeleton at her front door. Grand master of the visual pun, Johnson Smith used an old football helmet on a gatepost as the head/skull of a figure with pruning saws for arms. In southeastern Virginia, a resident mounted a plastic skull on the knob of his chain link gate. If a would-be visitor missed this cue, a black cloth figure was strapped to the mesh of the fence, which also enclosed a live pit bull. Edward Houston used an old armchair to double as a throne of justice beside the path to his door.

On each side he set a post capped with a large white stone to suggest a skull or decapitated human head (photo in Gundaker 1993).

"Toys" make aggressive hot guardians. Victor Melancon posed an Incredible Hulk doll in a chair by his door and taped the drawing of a very toothy Jack-O-Lantern to the screen. It was there in May; it was not for Halloween. Robert Farris Thompson included a pair of female doll hot guardians carrying a real gun in the exhibition *Face of the Gods* (1993: 95). Their character was not lost on airport security when he carried them home from Louisiana. Previously, they had hung directly to the left of Gyp Packnett's back door at eye level. The eyes of hot watchers glare aggressively. If the faces of these figures were African masks, the pupils of the eyes would be surrounded entirely in white and they would bulge—like the quintessential ceramic hot guardian of "spirits" in the U.S. south, the face jug (Thompson and Cornet 1981: 159).

While cooler watchers stand closer to porch edges and fences, hot figures are posted where an intruder might actually gain entry. Not all hot guardians say "go away," but their ferocity promises punishment for transgressions. Perhaps this threat is why I have not seen hot guardians in yards like Mrs. Jones's, where saturated cultivation confronts wildness outside the property. Yet, in keeping with the trickster side of deep vision, creative people like Johnson Smith and Gyp Packnett enjoyed making these figures and looked forward to visitors' reactions. In contrast to the ancestral memorials these men made, they did not mind talking about their hot watchers. Because the most fearsome figures are also closest to the houses' entrances, they bring the violent side of wildness into cultivated territory. The coolest, brightest figures—ancestors—have the most moral authority but are farther from the house and not directly discussable. In effect, then, hot guardians embody the ancestral and divine justice, which backs the makers' demand that they, their families, and property be respected. Like Hurston's ritual insults and other forms of indirection, visitors to whom hot watchers' warnings do not apply can take them as jokes—but ancestors demand seriousness and so are appropriately far from casual access and casual talk.

Discussion

I grew up near several of the African American yards in Chattanooga mentioned in this paper and knew other people in the same neighborhoods. I first noticed a special yard on the way to the grocery store while home from graduate school over Thanksgiving in 1986. At that point, I was thoroughly skeptical about African influences in the United States. Shortly before break, I had remarked to my advisor, John Szwed, after a class he cotaught with Robert Farris Thompson, "You guys aren't going to get *me* out there chasing Africa!" I soon realized, however, that ignoring this vast part of the American cultural mix also meant refusing to accept that certain forms of behavior and practice could serve purposes and show competencies beyond those already familiar to me. Resting with familiar categories and interpretations means, in effect, failing to give the benefit of the doubt necessary for mutual understanding.

Mrs. Olivia Humphrey's yard (figure 13.4) initially appeared to my uneducated eyes as a well-planned junkyard, with rusting metal and dead wood to the left and right of the house and a neat white graveled area with a white birdbath and white wrought iron bench in front. What caught my eye initially were sparks of reflected light—flash—adjacent to this area. Even the most hardened skeptic who has just read a book called *Flash of the Spirit* could not fail to notice that. As I got to know Mrs. Humphrey over the years, I found her, like other yard makers, reticent to speak directly about her "junk" areas—a term which in the United States, as among the BaKongo and perhaps other groups as well, is sometimes used as a coded reference to the grave or belongings of the dead (MacGaffey 1977). As I later learned, such areas bristle with signs of ancestors and those who have recently passed.

When I came to write about her memorial, I went over my interpretation with Mrs. Humphrey, asking if this was what she would want people to read long after we were gone. She said "yes" but added no more explanation. Given the politics of race in America, some would argue that black people tell white people anything they want to hear. But, how could I know what to "want to hear" when the significance of the materials was invisible to me until I saw it elsewhere, similarly configured many times? Also, today this strategy does not extend to the print media, for yard makers want accurate recognition for their achievements—hence, I also use their real names. Further, yard makers energetically corrected many of my interpretations, and some, like Gyp Packnett, spoke freely about areas with deep content once he realized I could "see" them. Ancestor areas do not contradict Christian values, but they do draw on another resource pool associated with the dead and spirits that surely involves transatlantic trajectories, like BaKongo vision in which the power of the creator manifests in twisted wood and gnarled growth (Brown 2002), along with a host of cognate practices from

Senegambia through Central Africa that signal spirits through whiteness. Practitioners Mrs. Laverne Spurlock of Long Island and Eddie Bowens of Sunbury, Georgia, called this resource pool "the old way that's not in the Bible," and used oblique language when referring to it because it included not only positive practices but also invocation of the dead for potentially malign purposes in hoodoo and conjuration. The Old Way also resonates with biblical themes. For example, ritually calling the names of the dead can figure in negative spells, but also maps onto ancestral genealogies in the Bible. Thus, naming is invoking and so requires caution and maturity. Thus, the Old Way and Christianity inform each other in a complex relationship to which shallow either/or, "European"/"African," cannot do justice.

The practices of figuration and placement discussed above show consistencies in my database from northern Connecticut to southern Louisiana, and in many more sites than I can mention here. Material signs without explicit figuration also span this distance, with parallels in the Bahamas, Barbados, St. Lucia, and Trinidad. Archaeologists have found what I take to be earlier versions of these signs in and around African American living and work spaces. Permutations of the figuration discussed here, thus, seem plausible to reach as far back as the African descendant presence in what is now the United States. To give just one example of a watcher, "In 1861 a tar-baby was painted above the door of a blacksmith shop on the McDowell plantation near Sumter, S.C. It was for good luck, or to guard the shop against ill luck. Thus, the tar-baby has other uses than to catch B'rer Rabbit" (Puckett [1926] 2003: 41).

High-profile yard arrangements demonstrably existed in the early twentieth century. For example, a white local color writer in Kansas, Effie Graham (1912), described the yard of an ostensibly fictional character named "Aunt June" so precisely that she must have observed a similar place. Since Kansas was home to the Exoduster migration, the state has a long history of African American property ownership (Painter 1976). But obviously the iconography that Aunt June employed predates these settlements.

Among the recurring Black Atlantic material signs that Graham mentions are bright colors, which she calls "childlike" but Thompson (1983) terms "high-affect"; flashing surfaces; broken and inverted vessels surrounding an upright pipe like those found in old-time graveyards (Thompson and Cornet 1981: 193–194; see also Matternes and Richey, this volume); and a white baby-buggy filled with white flowers that Aunt June assembled as a memorial to a deceased white infant (Graham 1912). The book even contains an illustration of the pipe and broken vessel. Since the pipe and baby buggy imply unseen bodies, they fall under the broad sense of figuration used here, and their placement also follows the pattern proposed above: the baby buggy, commemorating a particular, remembered person, is closer to the front, more visible and accessible than the pipe. The book also mentions how the buggy quieted the dead baby's talkative brother and touched the mother of both children emotionally, suggesting it alludes to a sister and daughter. The pipe and broken pottery are farther back in a tangle of plants. Their placement and abstraction suggest a memorial to ancestors who died farther back in time.

Nothing in this account, or the yards I have studied, implies property ownership as a requirement for material ritualization. What property ownership does affect is scale. Apartment dwellers put watchers and other mediatory materials at thresholds. A memorial need be no larger than a photo, an old watch, or a pile of pebbles from home. The enslaved would need no more than a found locus for remembering and way of seeing materials philosophically instead of literally in order to situate self-worth beyond the tunnel-vision of toil—a profound challenge, certainly, but one that, there is no doubt, many met.

Turning back to "toys," all this suggests that if an archaeologist finds a scatter across a yard, the toys were probably used as playthings. If they occur near a boundary or threshold, however, they may have been reminders to those who approached of their accountability. Fierce, animal, or ambiguous figures like the tar-baby also imply moral authority. Those hidden or buried may have been active agents in *medicating* the dwelling, as when power objects are used to protect, heal, or harm (see Saunders, this volume). An assemblage that mixes one "toy" with objects that could be associated with a particular person—pots, shoes, tools, and the like—may commemorate a known individual. Finally, if the assemblage is remote from everyday traffic, and if its content and layout emphasize abstraction, directionality, breakage, flash, vessels, and plant or animal materials, an ancestor memorial or shrine seems likely (Samford 1996).

This analysis also has relevance for other findings reported in the archaeological literature. Space does not permit a review; however, archaeologists have found deposits near thresholds containing pins, shells, twisted wood, emblems of flight, flash like bits of mirror and beetle wings, and special earths like kaolin and white sand, and have invoked Kongo *nkisi* to explain them (Leone et al., this volume). Bear in mind that *nkisi*—as well as Dahomean *boccio* and other power complexes like the *caldera* of Palo Monte—were not made as static assemblages but rather as forms of figuration that mimicked the actions of a live being, whether or not the assemblage physically resembles a figure. These figures contain medicinal materials and are forms of medicine themselves as they watch or actively chase down prey to heal the same kinds of social imbalance that African American figuration addresses today. Such assemblages miniaturize in one efficient package what now might comprise an entire yard, with allusions to wildness and cultivation, dead and living, and the qualities of each needed to perform a designated purpose. Thus, though scale varies, the drive to medicate imbalanced environments and model balanced ones continues unabated and undiminished in the Black Atlantic United States.

Issues like this, and the tight bond between philosophy of life and figuration, illustrate subjects well worth investigating that do not lend themselves to claims of documentary "proof" over behavioral plausibility. Ritualized use of materials offers a window on a much wider network of ways that African Americans have both theorized and acted upon situations. As Ingold argues, "things are active not because they are imbued with agency but because [properties of materials] . . . are caught up in . . . currents of the lifeworld. . . . To describe these properties means telling their stories" (2007: 1). Further, as Garfinkel points out, every indexical expression channels what happens next in producing the "routine grounds of everyday life" (1991). John Dewey noted long ago that a values orientation is built into every action, comparing better with worse ways of carrying it out (1939: 58). Thus, "stories" build relationally, and these relations feed back into what the lifeworld is. Far from being "noninstitutional practices" that do not really matter, the semiotic repleteness of African Diaspora landscapes and material practices is a thicket of instructions, of pushes and pulls toward the better over the worse, and the physical instantiation of a moral high ground in the face of oppression. Because yard makers expressed no interest in finding or projecting explicit Africanity through this aspect of their lives, and because yard work can involve both Christian and Old Way trajectories into the past, I see these yards as support for Sterling Stuckey's (1987) argument for a "circle of culture," which philosophically sustained individuals under slavery through rituals like the Ring Shout and through rituals of ancestral protection and commemoration today. While this view is consistent with evidence that figuration fits into and reconstitutes older cultivated/wild landscape distinctions, it weighs heavily against the cultural "stripping" of the enslaved Africans for which Mintz and Price (1992), Price (2006), Philip Morgan (1998), and, more recently, Ira Berlin (2004) have argued.

Despite the consistencies emphasized here, however, yard figuration does not comprise an interpretive recipe, independent of practices on the ground, all the more because makers use figures as reminders that surface appearances can be deceiving. Further, there is an improvisational dimension to all "work"—in the broad sense of both labor and medication—that encourages exceptions, variations, and innovations. Thus, yard figuration has more in common with multimedia cultural performances like masquerades—initiatory, ancestral, juridical—than with static categories like "sculpture" or "landscape design." Indeed, figuration makes yard *shows* in the fullest sense.

Notes

Many thanks for research and writing support to the estate of Nell Dorsey Turner, and fellowships in Garden and Landscape Studies at Dumbarton Oaks in 1992–1993 and 2009–2010, the Center for the Study of American Religion at Princeton in 1997–1998, Fulbright Fellowship at the University of Haifa in 2000–2001, and the W. E. B. Du Bois Institute of African and African American Research at Harvard in 2010–2011. For sustaining insights and encouragement, I am especially grateful to Robert Farris Thompson, John Szwed, Judith McWillie, Martha Gundaker, Johnson Smith, Flossie Bailey, Ruby Gilmore, and Gyp Packnett; and for thoughtful comments on this manuscript thanks to Neil Norman, John Szwed, Rachel Reynolds, and Brad Weiss.

1. It is not uncommon for figural forms used as playthings in various African cultures to have parallels in ritualized figuration or to serve a dual role. For example, see Béart (1955), Hechter-Schulz (1966), Roy (1981), Dagan (1990), Cameron (1997), and Cameron and Ross (1996).

2. Mrs. Mary Smith, Interview, Lumberton, Mississippi, April 1989. Photographs in Gundaker (1993).

3. "Asymmetry is a definite feature of Negro art. . . . It is the lack of symmetry which makes Negro dancing so difficult for white dancers to learn. The abrupt and unexpected changes. . . . There is always rhythm, but it is the rhythm of segments. Each unit has a rhythm of its own, but when the whole is assembled it is lacking in symmetry" (Hurston [1926] 1997: 60).

4. This phrase comes from the gospel song "Standing in the Safety Zone," for example as recorded by the Fairfield Four (1992).

5. Victor Melancon, Interview, Hammond, Louisiana, June 1991.

6. I am grateful to Ywone Edwards Ingram for sharing this insight.

CHAPTER 14

"I Cry 'I Am' for All to Hear Me"

THE INFORMAL CEMETERY IN CENTRAL GEORGIA

Hugh B. Matternes and Staci Richey

The conclusion of the Civil War was a major turning point in African American history. For the first time since they or their ancestors were brought from Africa, recently emancipated African Americans were in a position to take charge of their lives and explore freedoms that they had previously been denied. Few of them, however, had the social and economic resources to take advantage of freedom's opportunities. African Americans faced the challenges of building stable, functioning communities that were capable of providing the materials and services needed to survive in the postbellum South within and around a largely Anglo-American social context. These needs included ensuring that death did not disrupt the social network and providing the dead a stable and meaningful place in their community. To achieve these goals, some African Americans adopted traditional, institution-based burial grounds modeled after (and sometimes controlled by) the Anglo-American community. When these could not meet the freed African Americans' needs, they created cemeteries that lacked an overseeing authority. In this chapter, we suggest that some African American communities explored alternative burial areas. These informal cemeteries developed in communities where no single institution was responsible for the entire cemetery. The Old School Cemetery in Wilkes County, Georgia, is an example of an informal cemetery.

Death is an agent of social disintegration, preventing the departed from contributing their labor, experience, wisdom, and genes to the community's well-being. Death eventually removes all community members, and communities must adjust their organizational structure to compensate for these losses. In their ancestral homelands, parent communities developed rituals designed to lessen the damage done by death (see Norman, Ogundiran, both this volume). Many African funerary traditions were labeled as primitive and pagan by Christian overseers in America. When not outright forbidden, their African practices were generally dismissed. Despite these suppressions, African mortuary traditions were not completely lost; instead, they merged with other traditions, including Anglo-American and Native American practices, to form new mortuary behaviors (Genovese 1976: 198; see also Blouet, this volume).

Burial grounds were a material focus for these transformations. In the antebellum South, the slaveholder ultimately decided the final resting place of a deceased enslaved person. While most slave owners were aware that dissolution of enslaved African mortuary rituals would result in anomie and even revolt, they also held the power to limit the amount of ritual practiced by their property. Fate of the body ranged from heinous to humanitarian. The most degrading option was abandonment, with the deceased treated as expended property with no regard paid to his or her humanity. The practice was common enough that in colonial Charleston, South Carolina, local ordinances forbade open-air abandonment (Rauschenberg 1990: 41). The dead were sometimes provided an expedient burial, frequently near the place of death (Blassingame 1977: 260, 575, 716; Diamond 2006: 51). Expedient burials addressed the dead as biological hazards and provided a minimal avenue for social response. More commonly in the South, property was set aside for burial purposes. Enslaved Africans, particularly on smaller holdings, were buried outside or adjacent to the slaveholder's burial ground (Blassingame 1977: 734; Mattson 1992: 16; Matternes and Gillet 2007: 10–12). These graves recognized the enslaved as human beings, but spatial segregation and minimal surface decoration emphasized their social position as subservient. Larger holdings dedicated lands for use as burial grounds (Lange and Handler 1985: 21–25; Crist et al. 2000: 3). These parcels usually occupied less productive lands. Allowing burial in the slave's domestic areas consciously or unconsciously provided links with their homeland's traditions (Huffman 1997: 152; Armstrong and Fleischman 2003: 39). In urban settings, the sheer volume of dead people generated health issues, and public lands were set aside for the burial of African Americans. Enslaved people in an urban setting were sometimes denied burial in these grounds. Sometimes, the fate of deceased slaves in urban areas was that of burial in poorly marked graves discreetly placed on owners' lots (Gus 2004: 143; Matternes

2008). Some churches recognized enslaved Africans as humans and worthy of burial on church grounds, as long as funerary rites were dictated by the church (Roedinger 1981: 170–171). These rites, however, were independent of the deceased person's cultural heritage.

Although there were also free African Americans in the antebellum South, they had limited death care options. The sociopolitical climate of the South restricted the choices of "freedmen" about the ways they performed their burial rituals. Free expression was restricted to those fortunate enough to own property where burial was allowed (Jackson 1997: 197). More commonly, freedmen's graves were allowed in grounds set aside for African Americans (Diamond 2006: 50; Matternes et al. 2010: 334–335). Freedmen's subordinate status was emphasized by limiting their burial choices to grounds used to inter enslaved Africans.

By the latter part of the nineteenth century, death care options began to change as part of the effects of the Emancipation Proclamation and the 13th Amendment to the Constitution. The range of burial options expanded for both recently emancipated slaves and established freedmen. If property was owned, a private cemetery could be established. Some communities allowed African Americans to be buried in communal grounds; however, this required the purchase of a plot. These cemeteries were segregated, and the range of services provided varied along racial lines. With membership or permission, one could be buried on church grounds. Mutual aid and burial associations emerged to help with burial costs and even established private cemeteries. Sympathetic landowners allowed unused land and grounds used by former enslaved people to be used for burial purposes. Unfortunately, these privileges could be terminated when property changed hands.

Freedom in life did not exactly equate to freedom in death. With each option there was always an institution that exercised control over mortuary expression. This control ultimately included permission to bury and regulation over funeral practices. The informal cemetery provided an opportunity to bury the dead without these institutional controls.

The Old School Cemetery

The Old School Cemetery is located on the outskirts of Washington, in Wilkes County, Georgia (map 14.1). Washington was settled in 1773 on lands originally belonging to the Creek and Cherokee Indians. The cemetery grounds were not originally in Washington and hence were not part of the

MAP 14.1. Map of Old School Cemetery. *Courtesy of Shawn Patch, 2007.*

original town plan laid out in 1783 by the Georgia state legislature (Kissane 1998: 31). The property was part of a several-thousand-acre estate owned by planter Sanders Walker. In the late 1700s, Walker sold the cemetery's future site to planter Osborne Stone, who built a private burial ground (Lindsey 1959: 12–16). While its exact location is unknown, deeds from 1870 grant purchase exemption and easement to a burial ground in or near the Old School Cemetery (Wilkes County Deed Book 1870: 357; 1890: 719). Stone's cemetery likely became the Old School Cemetery.

It is unclear when the first African Americans settled in the area, but enslaved Africans were undoubtedly brought there to maximize the region's agricultural output. Census records indicated that slave-based manpower was important to Wilkes County's economy. A significant number of ex-slaves left Wilkes County after emancipation, however, a sizeable contingent remained in and around Washington. In the 1840s, Nicholas Wylie began purchasing parcels in the vicinity, including much of the old Stone plantation (Wilkes County Wills Book 1841: 54–56; Bowen 1950: 115). By 1867, he owned 3, 500 acres. Recognizing opportunity, he sold four-acre lots to freedmen on Washington's west side. Wylie encouraged land ownership in the fledgling community by selling lots for $100 each. Deed records indicated that debts were settled in cash, barter, and labor. Grateful freedmen named their community Wylieville in his honor. Later, the area was called Freedmanville, Freedman, and finally Whitehall (Wilkes County Deed Books 1868–1872; Willingham 1969: 192). The Old School Cemetery was nestled within this community, but no records have been found to indicate that Wylie ever sold the Old School Cemetery grounds.

Wylieville was a thriving Reconstruction-era community. In 1867 and 1868, the Jackson African Methodist Episcopal Chapel Church and the Springfield Baptist Church were founded. Neither church established cemeteries, but Jackson Chapel likely used the Old School Cemetery (Richey et al. 2008: 9). In 1868, the Freedman's Bureau built a school adjacent to Springfield Baptist Church and in 1893, Washington High School was added (Willingham 1969: 197–199, 234–235). The school and its 1933 replacement were built east of the cemetery. It is unclear what the burial ground was called before these schools were built, but after construction the graveyard was referred to as the Old School Cemetery.

Gravestone inscriptions indicate that the Old School Cemetery was used in the 1890s. Community members, however, believe that the cemetery originated in the 1870s or perhaps a little earlier, with its beginnings correlating with the rise of Wylieville. While many antebellum tracts in Wilkes County lack slave cemeteries, there were no indications that enslaved Africans were buried in the Old School Cemetery. In the 1990s, the city of Washington determined that the last legal ownership of the cemetery dated to Wylie's purchase in the 1840s. Wylie or his descendants never exerted any recorded formal control over the property. They may have opportunistically sold plots when approached, but there was no evidence that the cemetery was developed as a commercial venture. While legally considered abandoned, the grounds are an active part of the African American community landscape.

Rituals of Death: A Conceptual Framework

Early considerations of the emancipated African American cemetery by nineteenth- and twentieth-century researchers noted that many southern African American funerary customs deviated from mainstream American patterns (e.g., Anderson 1937; Courlander 1996; Georgia Writers Project 1940; Puckett 1926; Shepard 1888; Smiley 1919; Torain 1943; Waring 1894). While interviewers were concerned with obtaining pre-emancipation narratives, details on post-emancipation rituals were invariably recorded (Waters 2000: xviii). Early analysts tended to view African American culture as a relatively recent construct with little to no ties to its African heritage (Russell 1997: 63). Melville Herskovits ([1941] 1990), however, contended that African traditions survived as core elements of African American culture. Works epitomized by John Blassingame (1972), Robert Farris Thompson and Joseph Cornet (1981), Robert Farris Thompson (1983), and John Vlach (1990) demonstrated that the material and ideological symbolism associated with African American mortuary behavior had direct ties with West African traditions (see Gundaker, LaRoche, both this volume). More recently, Leland Ferguson's (1992) "creolization of material culture" has been applied by James Davidson (2004b; 2010) to interpret how objects with no African foundation were used to address traditional African cultural fears of spirits and magic. Davidson (2004a) also considered economic models to develop a new understanding of the mortuary dynamics based on Raymond Garman's use of reception theory (1994) to interpret changes in the forms and meanings of African American gravestone inscriptions. Likewise, grave furniture and inclusions at Philadelphia's First African Baptist Church have been used to investigate African American ethnic identity formation (McCarthy 1997). Charlotte King (2010) has also used ethnic identity to interpret form and placement in the New Philadelphia (Illinois) African American Cemetery.

Public awareness of African American history shifted the focus of cemetery studies from academic to more popular venues, and research questions about these sites now include those posed by descendant communities. Likewise, scholars of all stripes are increasingly paying attention to the self-understanding of African American descendant communities about these sites. Archaeological projects, including the Philadelphia First African Baptist Church, Dallas Freedman Cemetery, the New York African Burial Ground, and the Avondale Burial Place have demonstrated that the importance of these mortuary deposits for understanding the history and cultural formation processes of African American communities (Parrington et al. 1989; Peter et al. 2000; Perry et al. 2006; Matternes et al. 2012). Moreover, African American cemeteries are now recognized as cultural landmarks (Wright and Hughes 1996) and commemorative sites (see LaRoche, this volume), and are among the grounds included in the National Register of Traditional Cultural Properties (Meader 2002).

While emancipation was a catalyst for change, it did not trigger a complete reinvention of African American mortuary traditions. Burial relied on newly developed concepts as well as those of pre-emancipation communities. Determining the origins of ideas is not a simple task because detailed pre-emancipation-era records on enslaved Africans in Wilkes County are practically nonexistent. What has survived provides estimates of numbers and ages of enslaved people, but no record of where they originated or their ethnicities. Without strong foundations illuminating the ethnicities of slave community members, precise ethnographic ties among African, slave, and post-emancipation mortuary traditions cannot be made.

Enslaved Africans did not come from one place or follow one cultural tradition. Instead, they came from diverse cultural and ethnic origins; they were frequently shipped from the west coast of Africa, but captives were taken to virtually every port granting Europeans access. Michael Gomez (1998) and Gwendolyn Hall (2005) note that within regions where enslaved Africans were captured, there were hundreds of societies, each expressing distinct cultural traditions. There are few records for most groups that chronicle their burial rites from the times when enslaved Africans were drawn from their communities. Additionally, many enslaved Africans were influenced by non-African burial practices at various times, and many also were either not born in Africa or had no knowledge of African funerary rites. Thus, direct correlates cannot be demonstrated between slave-era African society and the mortuary customs followed by their American descendants. Some analysts question whether cultural evolution has compromised comparisons of African American practices with those followed by contemporary versions of the parent society (Thomas 1995). While a tradition's pedigree may not be determinable, common themes provide some notion of concepts that may have survived to the post-emancipation era.

In addition to the lack of information on African cultural origins, Hall (2005) has pointed out that factors including the African port of departure, American port of entry, and the moment in history when enslaved Africans were acquired resulted in ethnic and cultural clusters in regions employing slave labor. Gomez (1998: 150–151) has emphasized that the regions of Senegambia, West Central Africa, and Sierra Leone were primary contributors to slave populations in Georgia and South Carolina. Almost half the enslaved Africans brought to South Carolina were from the BaKongo region (Ferguson 1992: 114). While the enslaved communities contained many people from the same parts of Africa, they were rarely homogenous. Slaveholders held stereotypical views that physical abilities, personality, and skills varied by African society and tailored purchases of captive Africans to meet specific needs (Bell 1987). Knowledge of cotton agriculture led to a demand for enslaved Africans from Sierra Leone, while other slaveholders favored Gambians because of their experience with cattle (Wood 1996; Gomez 1998). The Mande were stereotypically viewed as excellent house servants, and the robust physique of Angolans was considered ideal for field labor (Holloway 1990). This mixture of people generated a mix of ideas and cultural practices in the African Diaspora. Thus, mortuary traditions rarely came from one African society but rather exhibited contributions from all groups who were members of the burial community. The African sources of Old School Cemetery's burial traditions included input from virtually all ancestral societies represented in the burial community. For example, customs from Senegambia, West Central Africa, and Sierra Leone were likely among those ancestral to at least some of the Old School Cemetery's burial traditions.

Emancipation, job loss in the South's agricultural economy, and news of opportunities elsewhere provided impetus for many freed slaves to pull up roots. Industrialists in the Northeast and Midwest recognized formerly enslaved people as an important labor resource and encouraged African Americans to leave the South (Wilkerson 2010). Our research has shown that migration occurred within the South as well (Matternes et al. 2012; Matternes and Smith 2014). By tracing African American family roots, patterns of movement to take advantage of opportunities available in the South become visible. Post-emancipation African American communities were not simply the descendants of local slave populations. They also contained people from other parts of the South, who brought and used their own funerary repertoire to help bury their dead. The range of mortuary traditions available to communities like those in Washington was not limited to those practiced locally but included ideas introduced by these newcomers.

Mortuary rituals associated with Old School Cemetery were not static, although some of the cemetery's material representations lack historical precedence because the ideas and means of expression originated within the burial community. Each death assembled a new presentation team, who brought their own concepts of appropriate expression and provided a means for integrating new interpretations. This creation of new ideas that incorporated African, Anglo-American, African American, and other belief systems enabled funerary rituals to evolve. The rituals used after emancipation were not simply different mixes of earlier concepts; they included changes in ideas and expressions to meet the needs of changing social environments.

In every community, death requires a social response. Surviving members of the community assume culturally prescribed social roles and perform rituals designed to influence how others think and feel about death. This is accomplished by grounding rituals in community belief systems (McGuire 1988: 440). Ritual participants are defined as the deceased, members of presentation teams, or viewers in an audience (Goffman 1959). The ritual is composed of ideas integrated by the interaction of these roles, and is an ideological construct defining the place of the living and dead in the social matrix, reaffirming group cosmologies, and identifying important community constructs. A successful ritual is supportive of both the dead and the living community (O'Shea 1984: 287).

Mortuary rituals help the living adjust to life without the deceased, and they continue for as long as survivors need them. As players become decedents, the cemetery becomes the primary medium for conveying the ritual's messages. The cemetery therefore serves as a multi-planed communication medium. Since graves usually represent independent deaths and rituals, they record independent sets of ritual messages. Graves and their messages can be combined with others to emphasize or convey ideas about the decedent, the dead as a whole, and the depositing community. These corporate statements may apply to specific groups of graves or convey information about the whole cemetery. Cemeteries with formal presentation teams tend to convey messages differently from those without such teams. As would be expected, these cemeteries also tend to have different kinds of audience, and the contents and forms of their messages accordingly differ from one another. The contrast between the formal and informal cemeteries is used below to further explore the processes of messaging and materialization of message.

FORMAL CEMETERY

Formal cemeteries are those that are regulated by cemetery institutions. These institutions include various organizations, such as churches, burial associations, governments, and commercial enterprises who oversee and regulate the range of expressions applied to a cemetery as a whole. Their sphere of influence is greater than that of the individual grave's presentation team associated with informal burials. Cemetery institutions recognize that cemeteries act as social feedback loops, where inclusion in a cemetery communicates information about the dead, and likewise the dead communicate ideas about the whole cemetery population. To ensure that socially appropriate messages are conveyed, formal cemeteries adopt norms that are generally more restrictive than those found in the community as a whole, and there are important consequences from this. First, formal cemeteries are exclusive. Inclusion of the deceased is limited to those who meet the institution's criteria. Burial in a formal cemetery may be limited by membership in the institution, economic status, belief system, moral character, or race and ethnicity, among other factors. Second, grave placement follows a predetermined structure. Access to burial space in the cemetery is not equal because space is used to transmit information. Different areas communicate specific meanings, including family affiliation, age, group membership, or national origin. Grave and plot placement must compliment these messages, following a predetermined, long-term plan by the institution. Finally, funerary expressions are limited to prescribed ranges. The variety of potential mortuary behaviors, particularly material expressions, available to a presentation team is limited to those deemed acceptable by the cemetery institution. The information communicated by the gravesite must be appropriate and intelligible to the formal cemetery's audience. The cemetery institution acts as a filter to ensure that mortuary expressions are complementary not just of the dead but of the community as a whole.

INFORMAL CEMETERY

In the rural postbellum South, particularly in places where use of property was not rigidly defined, the opportunity arose for less "controlled" cemeteries to emerge. Absence of a single overseer-institution is a primary feature of the informal cemetery. Instead, informal cemeteries develop under the eyes of multiple, coexisting groups. These groups exert control only over individual graves or portions of a burial ground, not the entire facility. Informal cemetery groups comprise many small clusters of individuals, whose members include individual families or decedent social networks. No single group exerts more control over the whole cemetery than other groups. There are two broad outcomes from this.

First, social communication feedback loops in the informal cemetery are extremely limited. There is little conscious effort to convey unified messages. While messages can be interpreted by examining individual graves and plots, very little of it is used to generalize about the community as a whole. The cemetery, therefore, is not a critical focus for gleaning information about each decedent. This knowledge comes from interpreting the individual grave. Second, the norms governing mortuary behavior are less restrictive. Informal cemeteries lack institutional filters to exclude the "inappropriate." In addition, placement of the dead is less exclusive and instead based more on a specific grave's or plot's appropriateness than on the cemetery as a whole. Informal cemeteries display wide varieties of mortuary behavior, which translate into greater freedom of artistic and symbolic expression than that found in more formal cemeteries. As long as expressions do not violate the community's values, there are no use restrictions. As a result, informal cemeteries lack the unified appearance of most formal cemeteries.

The Old School Cemetery as an Informal Cemetery

African Americans in the Washington area had a variety of potential cemeteries to choose for burial. Some were under commercial or city regulation. Inclusion required the purchase of space, and African Americans were restricted to specific portions of the grounds. Material expression was limited to a narrow range of media. As noted earlier, not all African American churches had cemeteries, but those with cemeteries gave parishioners first priority. Alternatively, some kin groups opted to develop family cemeteries on their owned land. The restrictive nature of these formal cemetery alternatives could be avoided by pursuing burial in an informal cemetery, and the Old School Cemetery provided that opportunity.

Old School was likely an informal cemetery for most of its existence. Grounds ownership was not formally recognized, and no single institution oversaw grave placement, expression, or maintenance. These respon-

Table 14.1. Marker distribution in the Old School Cemetery.

Form	Count	Proportion
Unmarked	810	0.470
Commercial Markers	177	0.103
Temporary Metal Markers	20	0.011
Fieldstone Markers	135	0.078
Other Nontraditional Markers*	584	0.338
Total	1726	1.000

Note:
* Includes bricks, tiles, cinderblocks, wood, metalwork, glass, ceramics, and noncommercial concrete markers.

sibilities were largely left up to those who opted to use it. So how was this cemetery used? The Old School Cemetery occupies a 7.7-acre tract forming an irregular polygon along the western slope of an unnamed ridge (see map 14.1). Much of this slope has been landscaped to form family plots. While plots appear to form terraces, they vary in size and are leveled to different heights. Plot forms do not follow a master plan; rather, they are the result of at least ninety different building episodes. One common feature is that plot margins are clearly identified, with boundaries delineated by edging, earth and masonry walls, and ground covers, as well as varying degrees of maintenance. Plot boundaries did not always abut one another. Scattered between clearly demarcated plots were solitary and ungrouped graves. Rows of undifferentiated, unmarked graves were evidence that the cemetery was not a families-only domain. It was open for use wherever unclaimed space could be found. While most graves shared a common east-west orientation and loose tendency toward placement in rows, there were no indications that a formal plan was followed. Row arrangements were contiguous within individual plots, but not between plots, and rows outside of family group areas were not consistent over larger areas.

As of 2008, there were 1,726 graves within the cemetery. The high degree of variability found in an informal cemetery was emphasized by how graves were marked. Graves in Washington's formal cemeteries that were placed at the same time as those in Old School indicate that commercially made stone markers were available to Washington's burial community. They are the dominant marker form in formal cemeteries but account for only about 10 percent of the Old School assemblage. Representing the single largest marker group in the cemetery, about a third of the graves have nontraditional markers. Commonplace objects never designed for use in a mortuary setting were pressed into service as memorials and markers. For example, bricks, cinderblocks, chimney flues, drain tiles, iron bars, and glass and stoneware vessels are among the more common forms. Nontraditional markers can be distinguished from other decorations by placement near the head in the grave's western wall. They tend to be larger and more prominently positioned than other surface decorations.

While some custom and handmade markers conform to the shape and style of mainstream American vertical and horizontal memorials, others bear profoundly different shapes. These are testaments that the cemetery provided an avenue for creative expression to communicate ideas not addressed by commercial memorials. While the choice to use some nontraditional markers may have been economically based, these nonconventional forms indicate that the communication of nonmainstream messages was also a driving force. Some markers, including those made of wood and fieldstone, had their roots in America's frontier period. Most communities abandoned these forms when commercially made monuments became available (Hijiya 1983: 342–343). This pattern, however, was not universally followed in the South. Almost 8 percent of Old School's graves are marked by unmodified fieldstones. Undressed chunks of milky quartzite and slabs of gneiss and schist were available from numerous local outcrops and employed as head- and footstones. Wooden markers, used in pre-emancipation cemeteries, are evidence that less durable materials were considered acceptable markers (Blassingame 1977: 734; Jordan 1982: 47; Stuckey 1987; Vlach 1991: 47, 1990: 145). Almost half of the assemblage has no surviving markers. While some of these originally sported markers that were lost over time, mortuary traditions may not have required graves to have markers.

Lack of markers does not mean that grave surfaces are barren. Many graves are outlined using bricks, cinderblocks, garden edging, and fieldstones, while others are paved. Some grave covers are commercially made ledger stones and modern vault covers. More commonly, concrete covers were brought to the gravesite or poured directly over the grave, occasionally sealing the marker in the cover. Names and decorations were hand inscribed in some covers, and white pebbles embedded in the surface of others. Alternatively, gravel and sand were used to cover burial sites. Grave covers are not limited to inanimate objects but also include planted flora. Markers and covers are forms of material communication that disclose a grave's location and serve as media for ideas and symbols. Less permanent grave decorations (or offerings) also serve as vehicles for information transmission. Objects not intended for cemetery use, including personal possessions, kitchen and household goods, construction materials, toys, wild and domesticated plants, broken and whole glass, and ceramics, are placed on and around the graves (see also Ogundiran, this volume). These objects are smaller and more centrally located than nontraditional markers, while others are placed on the interior facing sides of markers.

A list of features at the Old School Cemetery that stray away from mainstream American mortuary traditions is well beyond the scope of this chapter, but these examples emphasize a burial ground where material expression could be more fully explored. The resulting cemetery is not a flowing integration of grave and plot architecture with landscape. Its lack of uniformity sends few cohesive messages about the community, and its wide array of surface materials provides a seemingly cluttered, unstructured appearance.

Symbolic and Social Meanings in the Old School Cemetery

No church, town, association, or family lay physical claim to the Old School Cemetery. There are no sections reserved for religious, fraternal, veteran, ethnic, children, economic, or social groups, nor are there walls defining its margins or paths dividing it into sections. In fact, the only cohesive structural message conveyed by the cemetery is that it is an African American space and even this message lacks a common banner. It is a message expressed by many voices all speaking at once. Like other aspects of mortuary ritual, graves in the Old School Cemetery conveyed information about the dead in a manner that an audience could perceive. The nineteenth and twentieth centuries saw the rise of death-care industries intent on providing mass-produced cemetery wares to a predominantly Anglo-American market. Grave markers, covers, and decorations were among the objects manufactured to convey Victorian and post-Victorian notions of secular achievement and conspicuous displays of grief. These goods, however, saw limited use in the Old School Cemetery and then only on more recent interments. Since presentation teams affiliated with the Old School Cemetery were rarely the target market for death-care industry products, the texts, material messages, and symbols associated with these products were not always suitable for the Wilkes County African American community.

Old School's presentation teams were more interested in expressing other, more personal ideas. The absence of materials capable of communicating appropriate messages meant that alternative media were used to get these points across. Social, geographic, and economic isolation in the South were factors behind longstanding traditions where everyday objects were used as tools of funerary communication (Jeane 1978, 1989; Jordan 1980; Milbauer 1989). Rural audiences were familiar with these traditions, and an object's physical qualities corresponded with recognizable symbols. One example is the fieldstone marker. Slabs were selected or modified to generally resemble traditional marker shapes. In keeping with traditional, less secular views of human's relationship with God, surfaces may have remained unmarked or minimally scribed (Hijiya 1983: 342–343; Jeane 1978: 896). This was also part of the southern African American funeral tradition. Objects whose physical qualities offered multiple lines of symbolic information and whose meaning varied when viewed by different audiences were of particular value to African American presentation teams.

What were the messages and how were they conveyed? As noted, the most visible structures in the cemetery are family plots. Kinship ties represented one of the strongest messages communicated. Bonds established by marriage and blood were translated into space defined by the family and not a regulating authority. Many graves are grouped by shared walls or edgings, placed on common prepared platforms or covered by pavements. These features physically and symbolically merged graves into units separate from the assemblages around them. In this way, individual families acted as micro-institutions. They standardized messages within their plot by sharing monument forms, edgings decorations, and surnames to emphasize the strength of their relationships and the idea that the people in a plot were part of a network built around family ties.

The strength of these bonds was also reflected in surface representations. Both in the past and present, many African Americans share deep-rooted desires to be interred with their families. When kinsmen moved away, provisions were made to ensure interment in the family burial ground (Georgia Writers Project 1940: 62–63, 77, 195–197; Holloway 2002: 201; Politzer 1999: 141–142). In the Old School Cemetery, this tradition is visible among concrete markers made by Eldren Bailey for Atlanta-based African American funeral homes (Henderson 2009). Bailey's markers bear the names of these funeral homes, and they frequently accompanied the dead from Atlanta to the burial site. They were distinctive and readily recognized by the Washington community as nonlocal gravestones. Bailey's markers are mediums that emphasized how a decedent's family bonds remained intact despite having left to seek his or her fortunes elsewhere.

Many plots in the Old School Cemetery receive regular maintenance by family and friends of the deceased. Weeds are removed, trash collected, monuments and decorations restored, surfaces scraped clean, and pavements repaired. These actions ensure that a family plot's message remains coherent. Maintenance also emphasizes that bonds between kinsmen are not severed by death. For example, placing cut flowers and temporary decorations in a plot indicates that the dead are not forgotten and that familial bonds are regularly renewed. In the South, tangible signs of frequent visitation convey a respect for the dead (Jeane 1989: 162).

Individual graves utilize a variety of material languages to express the deceased's personality. The most obvious forms are marker and ledger stone inscriptions. The decedent's name and death date are common texts, but other information, including birth date, age at death, marital status, gender, and profession, might also be recorded. In addition, portrait photos on the memorial poignantly humanize the deceased's social characteristics. Unique marker forms identify qualities of a decedent's life. Grave markers not only include text to outline military service, but their distinctive forms identify the dead as veterans. Some graves are marked with three chain links welded to an iron rod. These chains are icons of the Independent Order of Odd Fellows, and they also symbolize friendship, love, and truth. Fenn (1985: 44) suggests that the tools and images of tools found on some of these graves portray the deceased's occupation, much like tools of deceased craftsmen such as blacksmiths accompanied their burial in West Africa (for example, Armstrong and Fleischman 2003; see also Ogundiran, this volume). The use of a screw jack to mark a grave probably conveyed the decedent's knowledge of mechanics or construction.

Portrayals of Christian faith are the most frequently recorded personality features. Located on a high ground, the cemetery links the dead with Judeo-Christian concepts of heaven as a place "in the sky" or at least above the physical world (Cottle 1997: 17). Within the cemetery, most graves are oriented east-west with the head positioned to the west. In this context, this orientation likely symbolizes resurrection as it allows the Christian to rise and face Christ during the second coming (Crissman 1994: 6). The east-west grave orientation may reflect not only Christian concepts but also aligns the dead with African cosmological and philosophical metaphors (Dickens and

Blakeley 1978: 313; Pollitzer 1999: 142). Crosses are also common motifs in the Old School Cemetery. While they are associated with biblical verses on Christian concepts of spiritual immortality, heaven, forgiveness, and charity with the dead, it is important to also open up to the possibilities of what these crosses may have represented in relation to the West Central African cosmogram, an important foundation for African Diaspora symbolism (Thompson 1983: 109; Thompson and Cornet 1981: 152; see also Fennell, Gundaker, both this volume).

In the South, there is the African-influenced belief that the sun's setting into a watery horizon is a metaphor for transition between life and death (Parrington et al. 1989: 122; Thompson and Cornet 1981: 1, 44). Hence, water symbolized the return home or reunion with departed kinsmen (Capozzoli 1997: 331). The water pitchers, bottles, jars, washtubs, and other containers found in association with particular graves in the Old School Cemetery illustrate the widely held belief in the South that graves are a nexus between life and death. The Old School's drainage pipe grave markers were also water-related idioms (Fenn 1985: 45). Anchors inscribed on gravestones and ledger stones textured with undulating lines symbolize the sea and its waves on which many African American men made respectable livings during their lifetimes as seamen (Bolster 1998; figure 14.1).

Black, the color associated with death in mainstream America, is almost nonexistent in the Old School Cemetery. Some West and Central African cultures use white to symbolize the newly released spirit's innocence and purity of death and to emphasize ritual purity (Thompson and Cornet 1981: 40, 43; see also Ben-Amos 1986: 62). White marble, granite and quartzite (fieldstone), and whitewashed concrete markers are media that communicate this color. Surface decorations including bleached seashells, milk glass, plain china, and salt glazed stoneware are also common. White blooming yucca, dogwood, and lilies were grown, and white wild flowers such as daisies, fleabane, and Queen Anne's lace were likewise promoted at the Old School Cemetery.

While nineteenth- through early twenty-first-century mainstream America viewed the worlds of the living and dead as permanently divided, African American perspectives included movement of spirits between both planes. The dead were important members of the living. Physical and metaphysical preparations of gravesites were important parts of funeral rituals. Graves were sources of spiritual emanation requiring control to protect both the living and the dead. The surfaces around many African American graves

FIGURE 14.1. Jordan Bell gravestone with an anchor motif in relief, 1892. *Courtesy of the authors, 2007.*

were enclosed and reminiscent of West Central African structures designed to protect ritual spaces from physical and supernatural forces (Fenn 1985: 43; Thompson 1983: 139). Enclosures contained the spirit at the grave and correspondingly protected it from outside agents. Edgings in the Old School Cemetery, made of quartzite, brick, garden fencing, and other materials, not only define graves but also draw protective lines around them. Ledger stones may have also been designed to act as physical and spiritual barriers. Cacti were likely means of protection against witchcraft (Thompson and Cornet 1981: 146–147).

Objects within the enclosure helped to keep the decedent's spirit in and others out. Bottles acted as traps to contain supernatural powers (Davidson 2010). Like the grave's soil, possessions last used by the dead were also metaphysically charged (Capozzoli 1997: 330; Fenn 1985: 43). Toys, combs, drinking glasses, plates, medicines, and other objects were left on graves to prevent the spirit's return to retrieve them. Sometimes they were broken to release their spirits, a metaphor of the transition from life to death (Burrison 1983: 27). Bits of glass and pottery, mirrors, foil, and metallic- or silver-colored objects were left on grave surfaces. When struck by sunlight, the resulting shimmer provided a conduit to the world of the dead (Fenn 1985: 46). Shiny objects also acted as charms that caught and held the spirit within the grave (Capozzoli 1997: 330; Evans et al. 1969: 80; Puckett 1926: 106). Davidson (2010) notes that, conversely, reflective objects captured malevolent spirits before they harmed the decedent. Glass oil lamp chimney sherds symbolically lit the way to the spirit world (Thompson 1983: 139). The shimmering light metaphor was duplicated by the application of metallic paint (Jeane 1989: 166). The monuments and interior walls in one of Old School's plots are painted silver. This "shimmering" space symbolized a supernatural area and emphasized that graves were in themselves sacred charms designed to influence the spirit world.

Some symbols expressed local perceptions of their ancestral African home. Informants noted that graves were planted with giant reeds because they resembled plants growing along African waterways. Yuccas were also reminiscent of African flora. West and Central African use of anthropomorphic grave furniture has been linked to Cyrus Bowen's early twentieth-century grave art (Thompson 1977b; Vlach 1990: 146). In the Old School Cemetery, anthropomorphic figures, reminiscent of West and Central African motifs, were created from iron bars bent to form stylized shoulders and heads (figure 14.2).

FIGURE 14.2. Anthropomorphic iron bar and salt-glazed stoneware grave decorations. *Courtesy of the authors, 2007.*

The nineteenth- and early twentieth-century formal cemeteries were showcases designed to communicate power and opulence. Their target audience was not only the local community but the world at large. The media used for material communication was intelligible within the parameters of Euro-American culture. Formal cemetery graves were hallmarked with text inscribed on durable monuments, decorated with Judeo-Christian and Greco-Roman symbols, and placed in plots organized into informative sections. There was limited use of nonstandardized media, and the focus was on conformity throughout the facility so that local and nonlocal visitors could translate material forms into understandable ideas and concepts.

Without institutional management, the informal cemetery's messages were less aimed at the world at large. Instead, its target audience was the local community. These were people who knew how to translate its community-specific and personalized symbolism. Very few enslaved Africans and freedmen were literate, and even fewer received an inscribed monument at death. Knowledge of the decedent was recorded in the community's oral tradition, linked by mnemonic clues using the color, shape, texture, and composition of objects left at the grave. They were intended to communicate to a local, largely African American audience because the African-descended people were not valued as social entities. Focus was rarely on the outside world. These roots perpetuated as freedmen communities developed their own senses of identity. Freedom enabled exploration of a wider range of material expression than was previously available.

Many of the Old School Cemetery's graves cannot be interpreted within the material language of mainstream America, because they reflect ideologies that are foreign to most Americans. Southern African American mortuary practices emphasized a greater alliance between the living and spirit worlds than was seen in most American funeral rituals at the time. In a sense, expression of the bonds between the living and spirit worlds served as a kind of broad ethnic marker. It emphasized pride in the individual and strength in a kinship network, and grounded the decedent's place with their distant ancestors. Lacking a commercial material language to address and convey these ideas, individuals used more vernacular objects to express them.

Some of the ideas demonstrated in the Old School Cemetery emphasized concepts that were incompatible with more institutionally controlled facilities. Symbols that openly promoted African and African American ancestry were at odds with an Anglo-dominated vision of southern culture.

The materiality of the rituals of burial practices reflected both Christian and non-Christian viewpoints, which were viewed as quaint, backward, and evidence of African American inferiority. While discretely used on some African American graves in formal cemeteries, the range of expression is limited in those contexts. The iconography used at Old School Cemetery reflected a kind of double vision, where symbols communicated one idea when viewed from a Western cultural perspective and a different concept from a more African viewpoint. Absence of institutional control in the informal cemetery meant that the ritual did not have to address the agendas represented by those institutions. The informal cemetery provided avenues to define and explore ethnicity as positive components of individual and community identities.

The Old School Cemetery as an informal burial ground made important social statements about the community and its relationship with deceased members. It was not saddled to existing Anglo-American cemeteries; rather, it was an independent cultural landmark. It visibly conveyed that the African American community was a part of Washington and Wilkes County, as well as helped to shape the identity of a postslavery African American community. Its spatial and material symbols provide important insights into the social relations, ideology, and worldviews of that community.

CHAPTER 15

Spatial and Material Transformations in Commemoration on St. John, U.S. Virgin Islands

Helen C. Blouet

In 1862, missionary Brother Badham visited St. John's Bethany Moravian Church and cemetery. During his trip, he wrote,"[the cemetery] is the resting place of members of the Mission family, . . . [it is] still the custom to bury laborers on the estates . . . [where] they . . . previously resided" (Moravian Periodical Accounts 1862: 425). The members of the mission family were, for the most part, German- and English-descent Moravian missionaries. The laborers to whom Badham refers were the free blacks (Africans) who worked on St. John's estates. By this time, the majority of African–St. Johnians were Moravian and regularly attended services at Bethany and Emmaus churches. Although the churches included members of European and African descent, Badham affirms that the two broad ethnic groups often used separate burial sites. This chapter explores the use of burial sites and commemorative rituals for mediating race relations between St. John's African and European Moravians and on the island as a whole between 1718 and the 1950s. The study presents documentary and material evidence for two church cemeteries and over fifty interment areas within household and estate properties (map 15.1a). While this is only a fraction of the number of grave sites created during the time period, the data provide significant information for the distinctions and similarities in commemoration over time. I contextualize mortuary sites and material culture through the application of Creole transformation theory (Armstrong 2003) and genealogies of place and practice (McAnany 1995; Mills and Walker 2008; Rakita and Buikstra 2005) to develop an understanding of St. John's social and commemorative histories and the implications for Moravian race relations in the larger society.

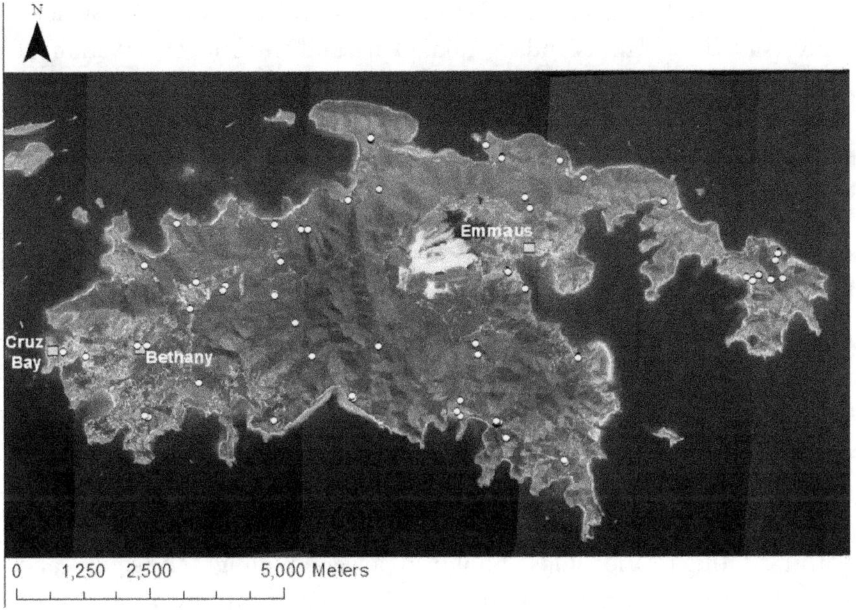

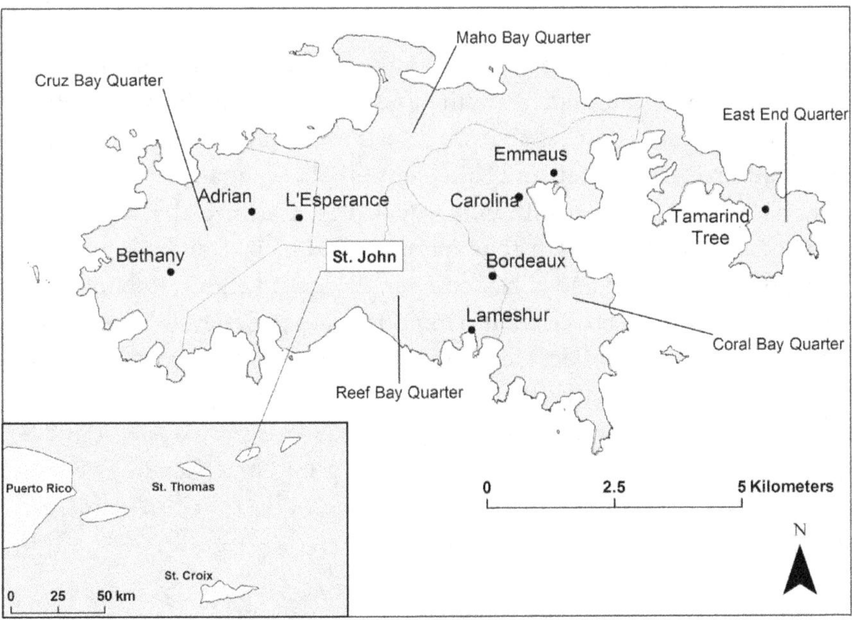

MAP 15.1. St. John, U.S. Virgin Islands. a. Locations of burial sites in the study (top); b. Caribbean context and political divisions (bottom). *Courtesy of Helen C. Blouet.*

This study, based on the collaborative research conducted by Syracuse University, the Virgin Islands National Park and Historic Preservation Office, and the local St. Johnian community, reveals that burial sites existed as continual and transformative symbols of heritage within fluid constructs of St. Johnian identity. Furthermore, it emphasizes the involvement of enslaved and free people of African descent in the alteration of Virgin Island and Moravian burial practices. Therefore, I interpret eighteenth-century St. Johnian mortuary practices within the context of the arrival of enslaved Africans, as well as in their experiences in captivity and forced labor in agriculture, manufacture, and trade in the Atlantic world. I also analyze mortuary changes and continuities in relation to the introduction of Africans to Moravian Protestant missions. In particular, I consider the impact of emancipation in 1848, and the post-emancipation era, when St. Johnian blacks enhanced their status as free citizens. Through an examination of connections between changeable mortuary practices and social identities within shifting relationships of political power, I highlight the significance of burial sites and commemorative practices to dynamic processes of community building and maintenance within culturally diverse and complex societies on St. John.

Mourning, burial, and funerary acts, otherwise known as mortuary practices, impact the understanding and enactment of life and death in socially charged ways (Chesson 2001; Silverman and Small 2002: 1–11; see also Matternes and Richey, and LaRoche, both this volume). Archaeological research reveals that a community's quotidian and specialized mortuary practices are often shaped by the experience and social contexts of the people who coordinated them (Chesson 2001; Rakita et al. 2005; Robben 2005). Differential access to resources also impacts how people develop meaningful mortuary practices for deceased family and community members (Binford 1971; Brown 1971). Yet such differences do not necessarily limit people of particular backgrounds to commemorate the dead in expected ways (Hodder 1982; McGuire 1988). Rather, individual and group practices transform in unique and varied forms as social experiences alter over time and space (Chesson 2001; Silverman and Small 2002).

Creolized Genealogical Frameworks

I frame my interpretations within genealogies of practice (Mills and Walker 2008: 12), genealogies of place (McAnany 1995), and Creole transformation theory (Armstrong 2003) in order to illustrate social transformations that emerged from the African–St. Johnian community's fluid creation and use of burial sites and commemorative practices. Genealogies of practice- and place-making recognize that people utilized known references and meanings in novel and diverse ways to craft and reconstitute mortuary sites, objects, and behaviors in order to connect or disconnect themselves to particular deceased, ancestral, and spirit populations (Adams and King 2011; McAnany 1995; Mills and Walker 2008). By addressing shifting material and social legacies of the living and their treatment and perceptions of the deceased and their ancestors, this interpretive scheme highlights processes of community building, personhood, and belonging over time and space in St. John's colonial and slave societies, societies built on tensions of sociopolitical domination and subordination.

Evidence for material and social legacies appear in a variety of burial sites across St. John. These include residential and nonresidential burial sites. Residential burial sites are those that appear in a place or locality used as daily and nightly living space by members of one or more households. Nonresidential burial sites refer to interment spaces removed from quotidian household living spaces and include sites such as church cemeteries (Adams and King 2011: 3). These different kinds of burial sites coexisted on St. John between 1718 and the 1950s, and were influenced by the construction of shared and unique identities. This examination of diverse burial sites, grave markers, and commemorative practices enables a robust interpretation of the dynamic situations experienced by members of the African–St. Johnian community.

This study is also backed by a commitment to Creole transformation theory. As stated by Armstrong, Creole transformation examines "modal patterns" and "internal variation" through the interpretation of material residues to evaluate intersections among diverse people and their shifting commemorative and cultural behaviors, physical environments, sociopolitical relationships, and economic contexts (Armstrong 2003: 68; see also Giddens 1984). Creole transformation stems from transculturation (Ortiz 1940, 1995), ethnogenesis (Deagan 1998; Hill 1998), and creolization (see Lenik 2009 for an overview). Such theories are distinct from acculturation, assimilation, and replacement models that utilize a "whole culture" approach (Orser 1989).

The whole culture approach views culture as a "set of traits, characteristics, and behaviors" that are shared, changed, and omitted by a group or majority over time (Armstrong 2003: 63; Orser 1989). But the concept misses signs of internal variation due to its emphasis on group similarity and normalcy. Furthermore, group culture change and broad transitions in material culture are defined by replacements of one set of practices for another, often due to external influences, such as the diffusion of cultural practices from one group to another (Armstrong 1998, 2003: 63–64). In contrast, Creole transformation theories interpret material and behavioral change within complex historical settings populated by vibrant people of diverse socioeconomic and cultural backgrounds (Armstrong 2003). They complement genealogy approaches that emphasize how senses of identity, belonging, and community impact and are affected by behavioral and material changes over time and space. St. John's eighteenth-, nineteenth-, and twentieth-century societies provide important examples of the significance of mortuary sites and practices in the fluid formation and transformation of identities and senses of belonging in complex and shifting multicultural and socioeconomic contexts.

St. John's Physical and Sociocultural Genealogies

In 1671, the Danish West India Company commenced Caribbean colonies for Denmark by acquiring St. John and St. Thomas. Having once supported Native American settlements, by 1718 the two islands included small farms and communities developed by European colonists who moved there before the Danish colonies materialized (De Booy and Faris [1918] 1970: 46–47). Denmark purchased St. Croix from France in 1733, and the three islands primarily remained under Danish control until 1917, when they became and remain American territories known as the U.S. Virgin Islands (Dookhan 1974; N. Hall 1992).

St. John, covered by rolling hills, steep ravines, and rocky soils, extends about 48 square km (30 square miles). It is the smallest of the three islands (map 15.1b). Today, St. John's north, central, and west portions contain tropical plants, nutrient soils, and good rainfall that in the eighteenth and nineteenth centuries supported sugar cane. The island's east and south interior and coastal regions, with less-nutrient-rich soils and lower amounts of rain, were favorable to sustained cotton and livestock production.

St. John's challenging topography impeded the growth of agriculture and settlements. Initially, land speculators plotted out small parcels of land for agricultural development, but the properties did not produce as much as expected. By 1800, landowners consolidated sugar cane estates and focused most of their attention on plantations in the island's arable west, central, and north sections. Despite St. John's arduous living and economic conditions, the island possessed a diverse population of European- and African-descended inhabitants. From 1718 to 1815, St. John's enslaved population doubled from about one thousand to its peak of just over two thousand. This forced labor increased agricultural and maritime production (Armstrong 2003; Dookhan 1974; N. Hall 1992; Olwig 1985). Within the free citizenry, the multicultural population developed a society tolerant of different faiths, mortuary sites, and commemorative practices. However, this society restricted the mortuary practices of enslaved Africans (see also Matternes and Richey, this volume). Danish colonial officials enforced laws that restricted the open use of non-Christian mortuary practices by enslaved Africans and disallowed integrated burial sites for most Africans and Europeans (Carstens 1994: 14–15; N. Hall 1992: 56–59). Similar laws emerged elsewhere in the Caribbean and North America (Brown 2008; Jamieson 1995). As the number of enslaved Africans grew, restrictions and punishments for laborers intensified.

In 1733, Gardelin's Code enforced cruel punishments for slaves who did not follow the law, including regulations on leisure and ritual behaviors (N. Hall 1992: 56–59). During funerals, enslaved Africans could not dance, play drums, sing, or perform traditional rituals. Burial sites for enslaved Africans remained separate from those of plantation owners, confined to areas near their residences and unsuitable for large-scale agricultural production. From the planters' perspective, the restrictions of the code were necessary for racial segregation in order to maintain authority and control over the enslaved (ibid.: 56–59). Yet, while the government intended Gardelin's Code to inhibit the collective power of the enslaved, it was actually one of the contributing factors to an eight-month slave rebellion in 1733, the first large-scale Caribbean slave insurrection (Norton 2012).

Funeral and religious monitoring continued after Europeans regained control on the island. In 1755, when Denmark supported the Christianization of enslaved laborers, King Frederik V established a Reglement that required all children born to enslaved mothers to be baptized at birth and exposed to Christianity over their lifetimes (N. Hall 1992: 60). Other measures soon followed. In 1765, St. Thomas's commandant, Peter de Gunthelberg, forbade the practice of wakes by enslaved people (ibid.: 63). In 1774, Governor Peter Clausen restricted the number of mourners at enslaved Africans' Christian funerals to twelve people, plus the pall bearers. Before the law's enactment, African funerals could attract over three hundred mourners, enslaved and free, black and white. Yet in the 1770s, large gatherings of African-descended people were declared illegal out of fear that the enslaved might incite rebellion (ibid.: 64).

Regardless of their subjugation by Europeans, enslaved and free people of African descent on St. John and throughout the Caribbean partially maintained commemorative and funerary traditions they knew in their West and Central African homelands. These included burying kin and community members on or near residential land and erecting a variety of grave markers from diverse materials placed atop graves or constructed into durable markers and monuments (Blouet 2013; see also Matternes and Richey, this volume). The enslaved sustained such mortuary customs because they believed they appropriately honored and remembered the fallen and the ancestors in their Caribbean and African homelands. They also valued the symbolic meanings of the rituals related to kinship, religion, and social status. The new Caribbean contexts, however, made it impossible for most Africans, as well as Europeans, to replicate the customs. Instead, enslaved and free residents prepared new objects and places in foreign lands to enact their mortuary obligations. By the mid-eighteenth century, for example, enslaved Africans incorporated Moravian mortuary practices. While Europeans could freely reorganize their daily and ceremonial practices in the Americas to suit their own tastes and new environments, Africans faced the challenge of creating appropriate mortuary customs that fit their cultural norms, reflect their experiences, and at the same time satisfied standards of European acceptability.

From the mid-eighteenth century, many free colonists who owned land on St. John were interred on their property while others were buried on St. Thomas. Some of the deceased were transported to Europe and buried in their home or ancestral communities. Therefore, the use of diverse cemeteries off island minimized their need on St. John. Nevertheless, white Moravian missionaries predominantly used Bethany and Emmaus cemeteries from the 1750s until the mid- to late nineteenth century. The historic Moravian churches and cemeteries remain in use today by the island's majority African–St. Johnian population. Despite the existence of a few church cemeteries, the majority of St. John's enslaved and early free black population buried their dead on family property to avoid the arduous transport of bodies to church cemeteries. Furthermore, two of the four eighteenth-century church cemeteries primarily serviced Moravian congregations, specifically Moravian missionaries and their families. Thus, only a small number of free blacks utilized church cemeteries. This pattern of usage, similar to trends in rural North America (LeeDecker 2009; Sloane 1991), continued in St. John throughout the nineteenth and twentieth centuries as families and households—Europeans and free Africans—successfully managed and protected burial sites within their property boundaries.

Among St. John's European and free black residents in the eighteenth and nineteenth centuries, survivors of the deceased established monuments based on what they could afford or preferred, including an array of horizontal and vertical gravestones, headstones, and above-ground tombs, as well as loose stone collections. Some families commissioned inscriptions that described the deceased by name, age, occupation, marital status, and kinship (Carstens 1994; Taylor 1970: 53). The markers and burial sites, tokens of remembrance that represented and influenced identities and senses of belonging, reflect the resources that landholders, including those of African descent, used to commemorate their dead.

When emancipation for all enslaved subjects of the Danish West Indies occurred on 3 July 1848 (N. Hall 1992: 208; Olwig 1985: 1), the freed African-descended population increasingly enacted mortuary practices within church and municipal cemeteries in addition to yard spaces and village burial grounds. Numbers of burial sites for whites drastically reduced as many whites moved off the island. In the post-emancipation era, the increasing population of African–St. Johnians expanded mortuary practices across varied sites, thereby signalling a broader and freer sense of community and belonging.

African–St. Johnian and Moravian Interactions

The Moravian influence on St. John's past is complex. It involved inclusion and exclusion, tolerance and objection. Moravian missionaries believed everyone, no matter their status or background, could live in a Christian community, yet they accepted that Christian communities could be divided by class, race, and gender hierarchies. As a result, their views received both support and contempt among St. Johnian colonists. Among the early supporters of the Moravian church were enslaved and free blacks, many of whom benefited from the privileges of mission membership, such as learning how to read and write. While the missionaries did not expedite the end of slavery, mission and church privileges grew increasingly valuable to the pursuit of freedom and the maintenance of helpful social and economic networks among the African–St. Johnian population.

Moravian missionaries came from a Protestant background, developed in Eastern Europe and Germany, whose adherents strove to live lives of service, prayer, and love for Jesus Christ (Atwood 1997; Wood 2010). In the eighteenth century, backed by the support of German Count Nikolas Ludwig von Zinzendorf, the Moravian Church established a missionary movement of "international ambassadors for evangelical Protestantism" (Sensbach 1998: 19; Weinlick 1956: 93), and started their mission work to Africans in the Danish West Indies. They opened the Bethany and Emmaus missions on St. John in 1754 and 1782 respectively (Oldendorp [1977] 1987). In the mission's early period, some owners allowed missionaries to convert their slaves because they believed Christianity would instill obedience. Many owners, however, were hesitant, for they feared religious conversion would produce rebellion, especially after the island's 1733 slave uprising. Yet on 18 August 1747, the Danish authority passed a royal ordinance of legal protection for Moravian missionaries in its Caribbean colonies (Hamilton 1967).

Despite their inclusion in the missions, Moravian African–St. Johnians were not fully embraced as equals to whites. After all, Moravians did not object to the institution of slavery, and the Bethany and Emmaus missions themselves owned slaves (Furley 1965: 6; Wood 2012: 120). Although some European missionaries believed spiritual equality could exist for both groups, others remained skeptical as some questioned the converts' ability to understand and adopt the faith (Richards 2007). One missionary in 1798 suggested that contact between African-Moravians and non-Christian Africans would undermine mission work and harm the congregation (Moravian Periodical Accounts 1798: 57). In 1847, another lamented that converts were more concerned with receiving Christian burials than with learning to live by the church's principles (Moravian Periodical Accounts 1847: 411). Such doubts may have influenced the onset of separate burial sites and different grave markers for European and African Moravians before the end of slavery. Separate burial sites also emerged as a result of the missionaries' need to establish their own identity on St. John, as well as their desire to appease those in the plantocracy who opposed including the enslaved as full mission members. Furthermore, before and after the end of slavery, African–St. Johnians maintained separate burial sites for their own reasons.

Commemorative Genealogies before 1862

According to Brother Badham's 1862 statement quoted at the beginning of the chapter, the majority of enslaved black Moravians in St. John were buried outside Moravian churchyards. The Moravian mission's burial registers confirm this. As far back as the 1730s, people of African descent were predominantly buried on estates rather than in the church cemeteries. This is, however, different from multiethnic Moravian communities elsewhere in the Americas, such as in Bethlehem, Pennsylvania, and Salem, North Carolina, where throughout the eighteenth century, the majority of black Moravians were buried alongside white Moravians (Ferguson 1994; Sensbach 2000). Integrated cemeteries continued in Bethlehem throughout the nineteenth century, while in Salem, racial segregation entered the congregation and cemetery in 1816 (Ferguson 2011). "National helpers"—baptized and literate black Moravian missionary teachers charged with evangelizing, recruiting, and mentoring duties among the black population—however, received burial in the Moravian churchyards on St. John (Oldendorp [1777] 1987: 605; Sensbach 2005: 74–75, 158–161).

The black members of the church who did not attain national helper status were excluded from the church graveyard. They were interred underneath house floors, within house yards, or in areas designated for enslaved community cemeteries (Jamieson 1995). For example, in the mid-eighteenth century, Johan Lorentz Carstens, a Danish planter, described the following: "When they have carried the body through all their streets, they take him back to his own house, where they have dug a grave in the middle of the floor" (1994: 15; see also Haagensen 1994; Kellar 2004: 203–205). African–St. Johnians used a variety of objects, including stones, bricks, shells, food, drink, ceramics, tobacco pipes, and jewelry as grave markers and offerings for the deceased (Carstens 1994: 15). In some cases, they constructed masonry grave markers. These diverse markers are consistent with what was used elsewhere in the Caribbean, such as in Jamaica (Armstrong and Fleischman 2003: 43, 47) and Montserrat (Pulsipher and Goodwin 2001: 196). Landscape surveys on St. John of over fifty house yard and community burial sites identified a common use of grave markers fashioned from loose stones, bricks, shells, and to a lesser extent masonry and mortar (Blouet 2013).

While the loose stone and shell markers, and scant numbers of masonry gravestones may reflect a lack of economic, political, and commemorative resources by enslaved households, they also represent African-derived commemorative practices, as illustrated by Neil Norman and Akinwumi Ogundiran in chapters 3 and 4 respectively. In the 1760s, Moravian missionary C. G. A. Oldendorp learned that a number of enslaved Africans traditionally interred family and household members close to their homes because when they died, their souls did not give up their lived needs and relationships ([1777] 1987: 177–179, 199). Rather, souls experienced a period of time during which they wandered on earth and maintained social connections with the living before they moved on to live with gods and spirits, a point also discussed in chapters 9 and 13. These connections required the living to remain close to the graves so that they could provide foods and beverages to the souls. Survivors took a soul's previous personal belongings to the graveside for the soul's benefit. The display of such goods at gravesides reflected the love and respect survivors held for the deceased. In addition, many Niger-Congo language communities, from which almost all of the enslaved Africans in St. John originated, believed that the souls of good people reincarnated into newborn babies, so it was crucial for good souls to stay close to the living (ibid.: 192). Due to such social and supernatural contexts, burial sites and practices contributed to the management and protection of relationships between living people, souls, ancestral spirits, and deities.

Based on Oldendorp's accounts, his enslaved informants came from well-established religious foundations that recognized connections among spirits, the deceased, and the living. People believed that they possessed immortal souls that must be protected and nourished in life and death. An array of mortuary practices therefore served as meaningful mechanisms to cope with human loss and soul management. The diverse grave markers used in the house yard and residential burial sites symbolize the ways in which household and community members identified and related to the dead (Armstrong and Fleischman 2003: 58). As in many human societies over time and space (Chapman and Randsborg 1981; Parker Pearson 1999), people create grave treatments based on their worldviews, cosmological beliefs, and ideas about the relationships between the living and the dead, and the need to satisfy the deceased's identities and positions within the household, estate, and community. Burial sites and burial practices provide important ways for the living to maintain relationships with ancestors and deities. Such relationships help people to negotiate and assert group presence and a sense of belonging in surrounding landscapes. Despite challenging living situations and social contexts that existed on St. John during slavery and in the following decades, enslaved and free people of African descent found diverse ways to meaningfully commemorate deceased relatives in their communities. Indeed, commemorative practices represented resistance to the colonial regime that sought to strip the enslaved of their humanity.

Commemorative Genealogies after 1862

After slavery was abolished in the Danish West Indies in 1848, the African–St. Johnian community experienced gradual changes in social practices and in their relationships to the colonial institutions of law, church, and state. Many St. Johnians left for St. Thomas but not all. Some families from the British Virgin Islands moved to St. John to settle on available property. St. John's African-descended population increasingly assumed roles and identities outside slavery, such as landowners and leasers, farmers, traders, artisans, pastors, and educators (Armstrong 2003: 45–46; Olwig 1985: 38). As Brother Badham's statement and Moravian burial registers from the 1860s to the 1880s show, house yard and estate burials in the decades following emancipation prevailed. House yard and estate grave markers were still fashioned from stone and shell, such as the markers at Johnny Horn Sites 1 and 2. Some residents, such as the Davis family at Brown Bay, created masonry monuments alongside stone and shell markers (figure 15.1). Other households such as those occupied by the Beverhoudt, Lindquist, and Francis families erected masonry markers only. This evidence indicates that differences in commemoration were based on resource access and how the living chose to portray the deceased's lived identities and roles.

Post-1881 burial registers are not available, but oral accounts indicate that house yard and estate burial sites were common across the island. Guy Benjamin, an East End and Coral Bay elder, stated that the use of house yard burial sites remained important because, as in earlier generations, many African–St. Johnians imbued significant kin, spiritual, and protective meanings into such sites (Olwig 1985: 156–157; Olwig 1994; see also Gundaker 2001: 32). His statements are supported by the existence of early twentieth-century house yard burial sites from East End, Reef Bay, Concordia, and Maho Bay where masonry and stone/shell markers still stand.

In addition to continuing house yard and estate burial sites in the late nineteenth and early twentieth centuries, Moravian congregations and ac-

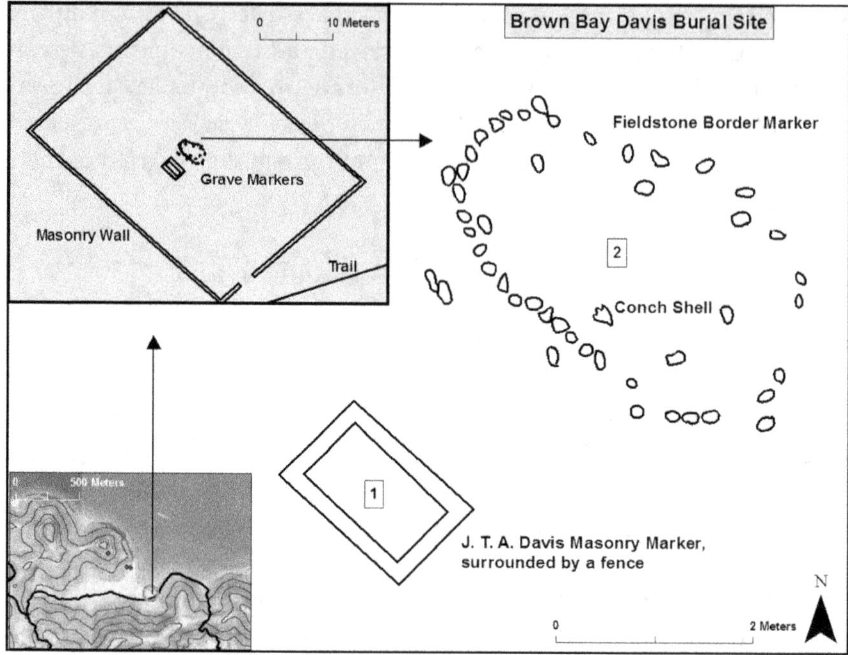

FIGURE 15.1. Davis family burial site, Brown Bay. *Courtesy of Helen C. Blouet.*

tivities were increasingly overseen by African–St. Johnians. As the regular presence of white Moravians decreased due to a lack of funding to pay for their travel from Europe, North America, and other Caribbean islands, black Moravians shaped the congregations and cemeteries into the period of American control (Moravian Periodical Accounts 1911: 275; 1914: 61). During this time, the majority of people interred in Moravian cemeteries were African Moravians, indicating that the norms for who could be buried in the churchyards had changed locally (Wood 2012: 130).

Grave markers from the 1880s to the 1950s differ from the older ones in the cemeteries. Stone and shell markers were more numerous in the churchyards for this period, and the types of masonry markers also changed. Twentieth-century masonry markers consisted of whitewashed horizontal rectangular slabs that measured approximately 1 × 2 m. The gravestones possessed vertical headstones on the east or west end, and the shapes of headstones were usually triangular (figure 15.2). The "bed markers," as they are called locally because the triangular headstones resemble pillows, reflected popular

FIGURE 15.2. Moravian square marker in the foreground with a Moravian "bed marker" in the background. *Courtesy of Helen C. Blouet.*

grave marker resources and designs, as well as symbolized the decedents' peaceful sleep with Jesus, a meaning reminiscent of the heavenly and pious unity expressed by earlier white, square markers. The "bed marker" design also appeared in contemporary house yard burial sites alongside stone/shell markers outside church cemeteries.

Conclusion

This chapter interprets diverse burial and commemorative sites and practices in relation to post-Columbian Caribbean identity formation and community building. Considering them through the lenses of Creole transformation and genealogies of place and practice, St. John's commemorative patterns and transitions before and after 1862 indicate that the African peoples on the island created diverse burial sites to enact religious, political, economic, and social relationships within local and transcontinental contexts. The transformation of mortuary practices and social contexts on St. John derived from decisions and influences of enslaved and free St. Johnian residents with complex and dynamic African-, European-, and Creole-derived backgrounds. St. Johnians created burial sites for practical and symbolic reasons while navigating and negotiating the colony's political, economic, and social structures.

In the eighteenth and early nineteenth centuries, the majority of free and enslaved islanders buried their dead near homes or within property boundaries because churchyards were too far and the terrain too tough for most people to effectively travel with deceased bodies. Church cemeteries were also too small to comfortably inter all of St. John's deceased. And race-based discrimination prevented the black Moravian majority from being buried in church cemeteries. Yet small numbers of free black St. Johnians, especially the so-called national helpers, were interred in church graveyards. All of these factors, as well as the commitment of most blacks in St. John, enslaved and free, to African-based worldviews, prompted them to utilize diverse household and community spaces for interring and commemorating the dead. Those sites created effective and important senses of belonging and cohesion during the egregious stress under which they lived. Despite sociopolitical, racist, and environmental constraints that impeded enslaved African burials, land on which dwellings and burials coexisted held sacred value because it connected living and deceased relations in social and spiritual support and protection (Armstrong 1998; Besson and Olwig 2005; Jamieson 1995; Olwig 1994).

At the same time, this practice bore significance as a West and Central African–derived custom maintained and transformed in the face of European-dominated plantocracy (Gomez 1998). Although burying the dead close to the living is not unique to African Diaspora communities (see Adams and King 2011; Catédra 2004), the practice of burying individuals who were respected, admired, and loved near one's home was important to maintaining hope and integrity in enslaved communities that relentlessly protected their humanity. Indeed, the enslaved and free African physical and spiritual connection to land sustained ancestral lineages (Olwig 1994). In the post-emancipation period, formerly enslaved people and their descendants used these ancestral ties in lieu of deeds to legitimate ownership in the landscape (Olwig 1985: 41). In fact, the identification of burials continues to validate land ownership for current families in the U.S. Virgin Islands and throughout the Caribbean (Besson and Olwig 2005; Olwig 1994).

Note

The research presented in this chapter would not have been possible without the support of the following: on St. John, the Virgin Islands National Park, the Friends of the National Park, the Virgin Islands Department of Natural Resources, and the St. John Moravian churches and local community; at Syracuse University, the anthropology department, the Program on Latin America and the Caribbean, the Maxwell School of Citizenship and Public Affairs, and the Graduate School. Paul Peucker and Lanie Graf, archivists for the Moravian Archives in Bethlehem, Pennsylvania, helped me identify historic documents pertinent to this study.

CHAPTER 16

"As Above, So Below"

RITUAL AND COMMEMORATION IN AFRICAN AMERICAN ARCHAEOLOGICAL CONTEXTS IN THE NORTHERN UNITED STATES

Cheryl J. LaRoche

Ritual objects excavated from African American archaeological sites blend elements of ancestral culture, spiritual intent, memory, and modern philosophy in revealing the dynamics of spiritual and cultural continuity (Idowu [1962] 1994; Mills and Walker 2008; Ogundiran and Falola 2007). Simultaneously, modern ceremonial expressions at sites such as New York's African Burial Ground and Philadelphia's President's House sites stir deep expressions of public emotion in tribute to once-forgotten ancestors. Contemporary actors engaged with these sites honor ancestors to effect the present and influence the future.

In historic contexts such as the African Burial Ground, excavated objects of tribute establish evidence of ritual or ceremony later interpreted by archaeologists. For the most part, spiritual intent must be inferred through the written record, intentional artifact or skeletal placement, sequencing, and/or three-dimensional patterning (Mills and Walker 2008). Artifacts of ritual or spiritual expression recovered from archaeological sites, however, consign discussions of spiritual mediation to the past. From this temporal distance, the efficacy, spirituality, and intent of past ritual acts are hypothesized and theorized in the present. By theorizing ritual within historical frames and archaeological contexts, one need not confront the question of spiritual potency or the purported efficacy of objects or practices. This chapter questions the efficacy and consequences of ritual practices beyond the ritual itself. Ritual acts tend to be seen, teleologically, as part of pre-Enlightenment, premodern practices that either lacked or have lost their potency in the present. Bringing the discussion of "non-empirical powers" or ritual efficacy into contemporary moments and our lives necessitates acknowledging or, at the very least, questioning the potential "power from unknown sources" that are implied in ritual performance (Turner 1970: 54). Modern ritual and ceremonies held at archaeological sites force professionals and the public alike to assess their relationship with spiritual mediation. "Layers of complexity," according to Mills and Walker, exist at the intersections between and within "memory and materiality, knowledge and practice, subjects and objects, and the past and the present" (2008: 5).

In comparing two archaeological sites, the African Burial Ground in New York City and the President's House site in Philadelphia, this chapter combines a dialectical approach between the historic and the contemporary with an empirical, observational exploration that is based on personal narratives of individuals who participated in the present-day rituals. By examining ritual and commemoration within the archaeological idiom, primarily in the northern United States, this chapter bridges the fissure between archaeological indications of ritual and modern-day commemorative and ritual expressions. Engaging with the archaeological evidence of historic ritual and then entwining that evidence with my own participation in contemporary rituals had a profound effect on my own belief about the place and power of spirit.

Relying on examples drawn from the two sites provides material evidence of spiritual intent associated with ritualistic acts at historic sites. Ritual in contemporary commemoration and ceremonial performances can serve psychically ameliorating, culturally regenerative, and racially restorative purposes. The two sites hold little in common other than their importance to the history and archaeology of the African Diaspora and their location in large urban centers in the northern United States. Yet, they are bound by modern acts of commemorative expression honoring and incorporating ancestors into the living realm of the present.

Although I have written about public engagement in articles and site reports (LaRoche 2002, 2007a, 2011, 2012; LaRoche and Blakely 1997; Leone et al. 2005), here I consider spiritual and ritual practices in modern and historic contexts. I began my work as a rather detached scientist preserving and conserving artifacts from the African Burial Ground site. But the intense dedication and reverence of the public toward the site and its artifacts caught me off guard, and forced me to reconsider and question the intangible, extrinsic properties of the artifacts I was treating. More pointedly, the African American public repeatedly voiced concern for the protection of the spiritual and physical well-being of the burials, the sanctity of the artifacts, and, by extension, the disruption of archaeology on the intentions of the past. Ritual performances of ceremonial acts, cultural production, commemoration, and meaning emerged as salient topics. I witnessed concerned New York coalitions of elderly African Americans, archaeologists, politicians, activists, and government workers moving beyond scientific knowledge and infusing space, place, and artifacts with symbolic meaning and ancestral spiritual heritage.

Ritual, Spirituality, and Symbolic Expressions

Ritual elongates tradition. Cathartic in nature and communal in structure, ritual and ceremony are portals through which one touches the sacred and nourishes the soul. Nebulous in form and varied in definition, ritual exists within "persistent and enriching spheres of social action where African and African Diaspora communities in the Atlantic World created and negotiated their values, ideas, beliefs, spirituality, and sociopolitical/ideological interests" (Ogundiran and Saunders, this volume), often in an effort to gain favor with supernatural forces. Claude Lévi-Strauss distinguished ritual as "the attempt to overcome any break or interruption in the continuity of lived experience, the discontinuous made continuous" (1981: 674–675). On the other hand, Catherine Bell states, "There is no clear and widely shared explanation of what constitutes ritual or how to understand it" (1997: x). Rituals, simultaneously self-referential and canonical, embody performance, observation, and practice. The condensed, symbolic actions associated with rituals create special relationships among the immediate, material, social, cultural, spiritual, and natural worlds. Such actions also create relationships between individuals or corporate groups and larger society, as well as between the past and the present. Through ritual, practitioners expect to influence, transcend, and transform commonplace sociocultural relationships, the materiality of contemporary existence, and one's relationship with the world of ancestors, deities, and powerful forces (malevolent and benevolent). Implied within ritualistic practices are the expectations of securing advantages to the individual or group involved in ritual making (De Coppet 1992; Holloway 2005; Innis 2004; Mills and Walker 2008; Thompson 1983, 2005; Tishken et al. 2009; Turner 1969).

Ritual acts delineate significance in a bid to affect the culture and consciousness of individuals, as well as the collective unconscious of communities. Ritual is often narrowly conceived as a formal rite repeated within a cultural or religious tradition and practiced across time as it is passes from generation to generation. In recognizing the unprecedented discoveries at both the African Burial Ground and the President's House, the contemporary African American public invoked and invented forms of ritual expression intended to honor the rich legacies that the archaeological discoveries seemed to demand. For the communities in New York and Philadelphia, ritual acts of remembrance necessarily compensated for the perceived lack of tribute deemed essential for the important moments of past lives. Ritual and commemoration guarantee survival of memory, ensuring the historic populations that what archaeology brings to light will not be easily forgotten. Memory enables one to participate posthumously in the ongoing life of the ancestral community, to retain a place in its rituals, to bring the past to modern consciousness, and to coexist within that continuing existence (Mills and Walker 2008; Van Dyke and Alcock 2003).

The African Burial Ground, New York City

In 1991, during the process of constructing a federal office building at 290 Broadway in lower Manhattan, construction workers began unearthing what had been the largest colonial-era cemetery for enslaved Africans in America. The cemetery once occupied more than five acres of low-lying, undeveloped land in lower Manhattan, and contained the burials of approximately twenty thousand Africans from about the mid-1600s to 1795. Represented among the dead were members of colonial Manhattan's earliest African community of varying status. Throughout the nineteenth and twentieth centuries, sections of the burial ground were destroyed, as buildings, streets, subways, and parking lots were constructed over and through the site. Discovery of the burials at the building site led to protracted struggles among the federal government, local politicians, and an engaged coalition composed of many different stakeholders. Construction work at the site was halted in the summer of 1992. Archaeological investigation was undertaken, and the excavated remains were then sent to Howard University for scientific study. At the end of the bioanthropological analysis, the remains were returned to New York City in 2003 for reinterment. With great ceremony, the grave goods along with the human skeletal remains were reburied at the cemetery site at Broadway, Duane, Elk, and Reade streets.[1]

The study demonstrates that funerary rites and ritual practices were important to the Africans burying their deceased relatives in the lower Manhattan burial ground during the height of its use throughout much of the eighteenth century. The location of the cemetery near the Collect Pond may have imparted spiritual significance for some African people who used the burial ground. In various coastal communities in West and West Central Africa, burial grounds were associated with bodies of water where spirits reside (Ferguson 1992, 1999; Perry et al. 2006; Thompson 1983: 135–138; Thompson and Cornet 1981: 197–198; see also Matternes and Richey, this volume).

The funeral practices of black New Yorkers using the cemetery encompassed an Atlantic African world of enormous complexity and scope (African Burial Ground 2009). According to Edna Medford, "ethnically diverse Africans shared agreed-upon traditions that had been created by drawing on the similarities of many African customs and adapting to the circumstances they found in New York" (2009: 88). "The Heathenish rites . . . performed at the graves of their countrymen" mentioned by European observers tell us of the ritual expressions, the tumult of large night gatherings with drumming, great funeral corteges, and pall-draped coffins with pall bearers of African-descended populations (Sharpe 1880: 341–363; Valentine 1860: 567). These funerary rites became highly regulated, however. Legislation limiting gatherings to "not more than twelve slaves" sought to prevent "great numbers of slaves assembling and meeting together" at funerals (Minutes of the Common Council 1731: 4:86–89). The law mandated whipping as the punishment for members of large assemblages that attempted to come together to honor the dead.

RITUAL AND MATERIAL CULTURE

For my own work, there is a direct connection between my experience of the African Burial Ground and my larger fluency with the healing powers of spiritual practices. Working as one of the conservators for the burial ground site placed me in an intimate relationship with the artifacts, as well as with the people who came to view them. I was primarily entrusted with the conservation of artifacts and material objects recovered from the graves of more than four hundred enslaved eighteenth-century men, women, and children excavated at the cemetery. The shroud pins, buttons, pipes, shells, ox shoes, beads, adornments, crystals, and pieces of iron either worn on the body or placed in the graves accrued meaning well beyond their primary function. The New York public, as well as visitors from around the world, treated the artifacts excavated from the cemetery with deep reverence by offering frequent blessings and prayers; on occasion, these observers were moved to tears. The public prayed and cried over the artifacts; they also blessed them and offered blessings to those of us working on the project. By extension, my work became part of the spiritual process. I quickly learned that past denial of power for deceased individuals does not necessarily mean an absence of power. While those buried in the cemetery were denied power in their lifetimes, they had a great influence on those of us who are their cultural—if not biological—descendants.

At the African Burial Ground, material culture confirmed the continuity of socioreligious beliefs linking the past with the present (see Van Dyke and Alcock 2003). A variety of African traditions no doubt motivated the burial practices of New York's eighteenth-century Africans. Arguably, New York's African Burial Ground ranks as one of the most compelling North American archeological finds of the twentieth century. Personal adornments and intimate effects among the grave goods were presumably the important artifacts necessary for the journey to the spirit world (see also Ogundiran, Matternes and Richey, both this volume). Coins placed on eye sockets, beads adorning the body, or artifacts such as crystals and shells placed on or with the body for ritual purposes may well have been votive offerings intended to attract the attention of the spirits, as well as gain favor with supernatural forces. As conduits for spiritual intervention and ritual practices, artifacts imbued with spiritual power ensure access to the deeper corridors of contact with the invisible spiritual realm of ancestors, gods, and spirits. Within that context, the burial of a woman with a strand of 112 beads and 7 cowrie shells around her waist, in addition to a strand of 41 green and yellow beads around one of her wrists, and evidence of additional beads around her other wrist, represented one of the most significant individuals within that mortuary population (LaRoche 1995). The power of beads and other materials, such as shells and iron, function as emblems of spiritual mediation. The social, religious, and status connotations associated with the materials and class of artifacts that were important to New York's African population no doubt have West African cultural antecedents (see Norman, Ogundiran, both this volume).

For America's earliest Africans, beads would have symbolized royal inheritance or divine power (LaRoche 1995; Ogundiran 2002b: 448). Similar to shell and iron, this class of artifact possesses the power to bring good fortune. New York's first Africans would have understood and acknowledged the status and rank imparted in the wearing of beads, which distinguished the wearer and alerted the observer to matters of position, knowledge, and spiritual power (Drewal and Mason, 1998). The intimate nature of burial practices suggests that those preparing the body understood the symbolism of interring the body with beads, cowries, and other objects of adornment.

Coral and shell represented water-related artifacts recovered among the grave goods at the cemetery. In African Diaspora sites, the relics connected with the ocean were associated with Africa, the Middle Passage, and the spirits of the ancestors (African Burial Ground 2009; Thompson 1983: 135–138; Thompson and Cornet 1981: 197–198). Cowries functioned as "embodiment of transformative/ritual potency" (Ogundiran 2002b: 440), as well as a signifier of wealth and life's fortunes. As part of the grave goods recovered from the cemetery, cowrie shells were important material symbols, perhaps suggesting, as they would have in Yorubaland, fertility, abundance, and self-realization (Ogundiran, this volume). In an act of cultural recollection, seashells can be found on graves from the United States to Haiti and beyond (Thompson 1983: 135). In analogous African contexts, grave goods such as beads and cowries have functioned as "supplications to ancestors and the dead for good fortune-money, children, long life, and good health" (Ogundiran 2002b: 452).

CONTEMPORARY RITUALS AT THE AFRICAN BURIAL GROUND: EVOKING THE ANCESTORS FOR THE LIVING

Honoring the ancestors was a constant refrain heard at the African Burial Ground. In the prevalent Yoruba-based African cosmology that informed contemporary ritual practices at both sites discussed in this chapter, human physical existence is the consequence of the actions and determinations of deities and ancestors, and is being continually influenced by them. This imprint persists today in many contemporary expressions of the arts, and in a variety of African American faith traditions that have arisen in the Caribbean, South America, and United States. Certainly, the contemporary ritual practices evident at the African Burial Ground in New York City reflect those lasting sociocultural influences. According to Henry Drewal and others, "Yoruba philosophical, religious, and artistic tenets, ideas, and icons have transformed and continue to transform religious beliefs, practices, and the arts of persons far beyond Africa's shores" (1989: 13–14).

In contemporary practices, shrines, prayer vigils, and ritualistic practices reveal spirituality in the modern idiom. For many African Americans associated with the New York Burial Ground project, the archaeological discovery formed a critical missing link in their historical genealogy. Considering the Middle Passage and American slavery as sources of discontinuities of social memory and interrupted cultural lineage, the spiritually attuned individuals among the African American New York public struggled to fill the empty spaces of the temporal and cultural void slavery had wrought. Feeling the necessity of addressing the ancestors buried in the cemetery, and driven by a profound quest for a healing ritual based on an African centered culture and religion, activist Emilyn Brown began to address these needs by searching for a ritual practitioner to perform the necessary ceremonies.[2]

After expressing her concerns to Yoruba practitioners, Brown was directed to Chief Elegba, a priest prepared for ancestral work at the Kingdom of Oyotunji African Village in South Carolina. Chief Elegba was brought onto the archaeological site to perform a Yoruba-based ritual and construct a shrine. Prayer is at the heart of life for Yoruba and other African ethnic groups, and shrines are an important extension of religious expression. Archaeologists working at the site at the time of Chief Elegba's visit stopped their work and participated in the ritual along with the public. Ritual performances honored the various deities invoked for protection or blessings. In lieu of traditional animal sacrifice, Elegba made an offering of honey and other ritual expressions in honor of the Yoruba god Sango. This customized, impromptu ceremony contained African traditional elements that were transformed to meet the needs of African Americans whose ancestors had been in the United States for several generations.[3]

Following the ritual, Emilyn Brown, Joyce Jenkins Jones, and Miriam Francis (who has now gone to join the ancestors) helped Chief Elegba build an altar at the burial site, which included Francis's artwork (figure 16.1). As the number of excavated skeletal remains increased, climbing from the original estimate of fifty to more than four hundred specimens, the bones were stored in a gymnasium at Lehman College in the Bronx (LaRoche and Blakely 1997). Numerous individuals from the New York community, fronted by Jones, Brown, and Francis, helped to build a second altar and shrine among the human remains stored at the college. Mirroring religious practices in the African Diaspora, the women gathered paraphernalia, charms, votive offerings, and other treasures requested by Chief Elegba to construct the beautiful altar, and Miriam Francis again enhanced the shrine with her artwork.

In recollecting the ceremonies at Lehman College, anthropologist Diana di Zigara Wall reported that she had never seen anything like it. Despite her general lack of knowledge on these rituals, Wall found them moving,

FIGURE 16.1. Ancestral shrine at the African Burial Ground, New York. *Courtesy of Emilyn Brown.*

"primarily because other people were moved."[4] Filmmaker Eric V. Tait, Jr., producer/director of the multiple award-winning film *Then I'll Be Free to Travel Home,* also attended and filmed the ceremonies. He, too, recalled how strongly he felt the need to participate in the ritual, rather than remain the distant observer behind the camera.[5] Brown observed further, "With the rituals came a sense of reverence. These acts were meant to be neither spectacle nor performance as they have been perceived by some, but rather heartfelt ceremonies intended to elevate to the stature of the project," as well as to meet the needs of the global community interested in the project. The inevitable detractors did nothing to diminish her understanding of ritual as compelling "in the sense that rituals are always for the living and have great power for the living."[6] The public experienced a high degree of emotional investment in the rituals, as well as in small, individual, and personal rites. Brown recalled the literally hundreds of spontaneous individual acts of tribute. She remained grateful to Chief Elegba for putting the shrines in place and for shifting the primary emphasis away from scientific analysis and toward a greater recognition of the humanity of the people who were buried at the cemetery. Their African American descendants created the opportunity to both witness and participate in the process of reclaiming the humanity of their ancestors, connecting with past generations, and honoring the humanity and dignity of the living. As one of the scientists associated with the project, I, too, experienced a deeply transformative shift toward spirituality and connection with the ancestral legacy, as did many others working on the project. Honoring the humanity of the many people interred at the cemetery in the manner of their African origins resonated deeply with many archaeologists working at the site.

Twenty years later, Brown continues to believe in the power of ritual performances to sustain social memory. She stated, "The African Burial Ground represents a confirmation of all that we accomplished as a community; something we were called to do in the same way that someone is called to preach or to bear witness."[7] For Wall, the rituals allowed her to be a part of a larger community, "like the creation of a historical community, a congregation, a created spiritual community talking about ancestors, talking about the people who lived in the past." She became a part of "the community of the past, as well as the community of the present."[8] In expressing the dedication of so many who worked steadfastly to honor those buried in the cemetery, Brown added, "whenever I go by the African Burial Ground, I say: I will not forget, I have not forgotten, I will never forget."[9]

In 1992, thousands of people came to pay tribute during a twenty-six-hour candlelight remembrance vigil. For the New York public, the site transcended archaeological significance—the burial ground had become sacred space. Spiritual leaders from various faith traditions came to honor the dead, each in their own ways. Christians, Yoruba, Muslims, and the many religious traditions of Africa all recognized and treated the archaeological site as sacred ground. Merging the past with the present, both ancestors and newborns were honored through the pouring of libations and other ceremonies. Renowned international photographer Chester Higgins, Jr., witnessed, initiated, and photographed solemn moments of ceremony at the African Burial Ground. He observed that "spiritual people commonly use ceremonies to draw them closer to the spirit and give voice to their individual and collective souls." As a student of Egyptology and as an Africanist, Higgins's photo-documentation of Egyptian tombs drew him to include this New York community of burials within the "various historical footprints of Af-

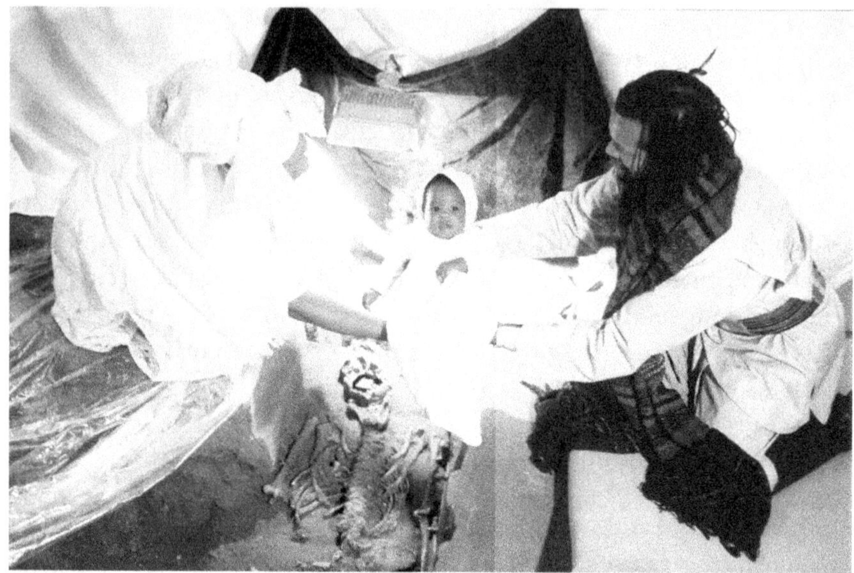

FIGURE 16.2. Ceremony of Continuity. *Courtesy of Chester Higgins, Jr.*

rican people, across time and space." Higgins recognized that "the grave and how . . . people are interred is a statement about the survivors and how they committed the body to the earth."

Because Higgins, like Brown, viewed ritual as the means to pay proper respect to the ancestral remains as the site was closing, he "wanted to find people who worshipped the ancestor's religion of Naturalism to perform the closing rites before the last burials were removed." In using a Khamite priest representing ancient Egypt and a Yoruba priestess representing West Africa, the closing "Ceremony of Continuity" was intended to bring a "spiritual bridge and closure to a burial ground that had been served by these ancient beliefs." Higgins continued, "Among West Africans and enslaved African Americans, the midnight burials would engage the newest born in the 'ritual of continuity' at the burial by passing the child, back and forth, over the deceased for three times. The first pass in the 'ceremony of continuity' is for an acknowledgment of the spirit of the ancestors, whose blood continues to flow within us. The second pass is an acknowledgment of the spirit of the living present, and the third pass is a prayer to the expectation of the spirit of the future (see figure 16.2).[10]

After the initial honoring of the ancestors through a wide variety of rituals, the federal government eventually acceded to public demands that the human remains be sensitively studied by African American bioanthropologists at Howard University. The public rejoiced as the remains were transported from New York City and arrived in Washington, D.C., where the homage continued. Great ceremonies marked the departure of the skeletal remains from New York as they were moved to Howard University, where they were welcomed with jubilant celebration and ceremony. Toward the end of the project, after years of scientific investigations, the public insisted on the reburial of all human remains and artifacts. On 3 October 2003, during the "Rites of Ancestral Return" ceremony, the remains of more than four hundred enslaved Africans were returned from Howard University for reinterment at the site. Multitudes of people participated in the multicity tribute when the remains were transported from Washington, D.C., to Baltimore and then on to Wilmington, Delaware. Fittingly, the entourage was received at Mother Bethel African Methodist Episcopal (AME) Church in Philadelphia, the mother church of that historic denomination, before arriving by boat at the Wall Street pier in New York City. For this homecoming, the remains were brought ashore near where newly arrived African captives—once destined for enslavement—had been auctioned two hundred years before. The funeral procession accompanied the remains up Broadway to their final resting place at the African Burial Ground, where they had been removed more than twelve years earlier. An overnight vigil concluded the ancestors' final hours among us, before the remains were returned to their rightful resting place. On that clear, windy day, the bones and artifacts, resting in wooden coffins hand carved in Ghana, made one last journey. Once at the site, they were greeted by actors, singers, drummers, politicians, and all manner of celebrities who had fought to pay proper tribute to the ancestral legacy. Many of the activists were "motivated by a special reverence for and gratitude to their ancestors" (Mazama 2005: 33).

The cemetery is currently part of the National Park Service system. In an enduring act of commemoration, a memorial with a spiraling, sunken granite court now marks the site of the African Burial Ground as an icon of public memory. Award winning designer Rodney Leon explained the spiraling symbolism of the monument as a jutting "ancestral chamber" that represents "the soaring African spirit embracing and comforting all those who enter" (Associated Press 2007). Leon further noted the significance of the structure, observing that "The African Burial Ground represents a unique opportunity and responsibility for all of us to tell our story to the world and to specifically honor the memories of the ancestral Africans. . . . Our generation has been entrusted with this awesome responsibility and we're honored" (Leon 2005). This perceived responsibility to the ancestors explains the depth of emotional reaction one often encounters at archaeological sites where the African American public defines significance. In an ongoing gesture of respect and commemoration, visitors to the cemetery site continue to leave tributes on the graves, which the National Park Service collects and curates.

The President's House, Philadelphia

Philadelphia's President's House marks the site where the nation's first president, George Washington, and the first lady, Martha, are remembered for enslaving nine African captives throughout the presidential years between 1790 and 1797. The archaeological excavations of the President's House took place at Sixth and Market streets between March and July 2007. The public interest influenced the decision to conduct archaeological investigations at the site once it was discovered that the remnants of the President's House lay buried in front of the new Liberty Bell Pavilion. Particularly galling for the public was the revelation that contemporary visitors to the pavilion would walk and stand atop the "slave quarters" for Washington's enslaved liverymen in order to visit the ultimate antislavery symbol, the liberty bell (Lawler 2002). Equally troubling, in holding nine Africans captive in Philadelphia, Washington actively circumvented Pennsylvania personal liberty laws, which stated that any enslaved person who resided in Pennsylvania for longer than six months was entitled to freedom.

The ten-year period between 1790 and 1800 represented the potential temporal focus of the project. No artifacts, however, were recovered definitively from that period, and nothing suggestive of the two presidents who occupied the building—George Washington and John Adams—was discovered. Similarly, no artifacts owned or handled by the enslaved Africans can be associated with the site. As a result, the foundations of the house became the major interpretative component, particularly remnants of the kitchen where the enslaved people toiled and may have slept. Focus also centered on the bow window that Washington added to the house as presidential ceremonial space, and a passageway between the kitchen and the main house where the enslaved would have moved between the spaces of slavery and the domain of the presidency. More than 300,000 visitors watched the archaeological excavations from a public viewing platform, and discussed the now-visible relationship between freedom and slavery exposed by archaeologists. Rather than a historic site of ritual, the President's House revealed how modern societies mark and use archaeological sites in acts of remembrance.[11]

RITUALS OF MEMORY

Mirroring the African Burial Ground, the public in Philadelphia also staged modern acts of homage, inspiration, and healing at the President's House. Before the site opened to visitors in 2007, present-day Philadelphians were moved to pay tribute to those who had been enslaved there. Charged protests also communicated public concerns for the historical resource and its African American ancestral legacy. On 3 July 2002, the eve of Independence Day and years before the excavations began, five hundred people gathered outside the Liberty Bell Pavilion in remembrance of those who had been held captive at the President's House, as well as those subjected to slavery throughout the Diaspora. Avenging the Ancestors Coalition (ATAC), an advocacy group for the President's House, condemned slavery as "a crime against humanity." Comparing the atrocities of slavery to a crime scene, "protesters wove yellow police tape through their assembly" (Achrati 2002). Speakers also repeated a symbolic litany, ceremonially invoking the names of the nine Africans known to have been enslaved by Washington in Philadelphia. The call struck a responsive chord with participants paying homage to the people who had once toiled and lived at the site (ibid.).

In an act of cultural reclamation and recollection, ATAC has marked 3 July every year since 2002 as "Black Independence Day" by holding annual demonstrations at the Market Street site, much in the spirit of Frederick Douglass's "What to the Slave Is the Fourth of July?" (Douglass 1852). As part of the ceremony, ATAC members carried symbolic coffins and released black balloons signifying a metaphorical release from bondage. The ever-present American flag, reinterpreted in black, green, and red, symbolizes Africa in America. The ATAC members and other advocates finally won support and funding for archaeological investigations at the site, aimed at understanding the contributions of enslaved Africans to the making of the young American republic. The young and old among the crowd—largely African Americans—gathered at the ground-breaking to listen to speeches, take pictures, and touch the ground that would eventually bear a monument

FIGURE 16.3. Closing ceremony at the President's House, Philadelphia, Penn., July 2008. *Courtesy of Patrice Jeppson.*

to those once enslaved by Washington. We witnessed in that moment the transformation of the site to something beyond archaeology as the rocks and the soil became artifacts infused with meaning. For National Park Service archaeologist Jed Levin, it was one of several events at the President's House site that "strengthened his feelings about the power of culture to transform and give our lives meaning; we can feel as though we are part of something that is going to live on."[12]

In addition to the visitor site opening and the 3 July ceremonies, the most powerful celebration and acts of ritual came at the end of the excavation phase of the project. Two Yoruba practitioners were invited by ATAC to pour libations at the closing ceremonies (figure 16.3). Mixing water and sand from the banks of the River Nile with the soil from places where Washington and those enslaved by him would have walked, Ayoka Quinones and Mukasa Afrika prayed to uncover the truth and gave praise to the enslaved ancestors. Raised in the Yoruba tradition, Quinones was crowned priestess of Obatala in 1999, and Afrika is an African-centered activist, educator, author, and lecturer. Quinones and Afrika poured libations in honor of the ancestors.[13] In a moving tribute, Quinones offered a blessing for the earth and for the dead by praying, singing, and chanting her homage to God. She also gave "praise to the ancestors and enslaved Africans who once toiled here and were being recognized by their descendants of yesterday and today. May they bask in healing light as we commemorate their struggles, their plight, and their journey, and their dream deferred." Her prayer continued, "May our memories be not a stagnant temporary fixture in our hearts and minds but a permanent national memory and living testimony of our culture, our ancestral ties that will never be forgotten; may their spirits empower us and change our nation." Adding a pan-Africanist element to the libation ceremonies, Afrika expanded beyond the Yoruba tradition in recognition "that our African ancestors came from continental Africa; we remember the names for the spiritual connection through pouring libations."[14] Using water from the Nile and sand from its banks, the pair offered a blessing for the earth and for the dead who once tread upon that soil. The libation ceremony particularly honored the nine enslaved Africans who were held by the Washingtons at the site—Hercules, Oney Judge, Paris, Richmond, Austin, Moll, Joe, Giles, and Christopher Sheels—and commemorated all those who had been held in bondage.

Similar to Brown's observations about the rituals associated with the African Burial Ground, Levin found deep significance in the "ad hoc rituals" at the President's House. These rituals were performed throughout the closing ceremonies through personal tributes, such as the tossing of coins or flowers that required no formal sanction. The archaeologists participated directly by inventing acts of commemoration. One such act was the burying of a 2007 Washington quarter and an Adams dollar coin, along with small brass name plaques that were impressed with the names of each of the nine enslaved Africans and wrapped in cloth to act as place holders until the memorial excavation phase of the project unearthed the newest artifacts.[15] Levin observed that the public invented "new rituals to mark what happened more than 200 years ago and to mark what happened over the last several months." The project shifted his perspective away "from archaeology as a science that uncovers the past to a notion of engaging in a project that gave a shared heritage. In that moment, the past and the present merged, there was no distinction. The past, still present and unfolding, was present in seeing people inventing rituals."[16]

Similar to the African Burial Ground site, the President's House site is etched permanently in the landscape of American memory. Again, the activist public found three elements of the foundation particularly evocative: the kitchen, the bow window, and the passageway mentioned above. The public insisted that these archaeological elements be incorporated into the design of a planned memorial monument. This important gesture provided a permanent physical reminder of the people enslaved at the President's House. Philadelphia activist Edward Robinson, Jr., an author and educator, expresses a repeated sentiment: "We want to memorialize the fact that our ancestors in and around Sixth and Chestnut were brought there, forced there by a white man, George Washington. He bought them, body and soul, and we want to memorialize them, not just as our ancestors, but as people" (Salisbury 2002). Attorney Michael Coard, founding member of ATAC, was equally powerful: "We want a monument, a memorial, a bold, serious structure that people can see and touch, just like they touch the Liberty Bell."[17] That monument, now a National Park site, stands at Sixth and Market streets in downtown Philadelphia.

Afterword

French historian Pierre Nora, in his suggestion that we pay attention to the spaces between memory and history, gives voice to the modern dilemma: "The remnants of experience still lived in the warmth of tradition, in the silence of custom, in the repetition of the ancestral, have been displaced under the pressure of a fundamentally historical sensibility" (1989: 7). Modern populations resort to ritual practices that honor the memory of ancestors and claim a heritage of dignity and self-discovery for the living. Critical African American archaeological projects have also been among the most potent, evocative sites for these ritual practices. Seeking to situate themselves within enduring wisdom traditions, contemporary practitioners use rituals to bridge the cultural disruptions brought on by slavery and the displacement of millions of Africans (see Reed 2004). At the two sites discussed here, the formal rites engaged in by priests and the informal practices of the interested public are older and deeper than individualist consciousness, and "unfold from a deeper more subtle order of consciousness that at its root is African in origin," according to the Afrocentric psychoanalyst Edward Bynum (1999). For practitioners, remembering and reclaiming a unifying social consciousness and a shared spirituality exist in dynamic juxtaposition to the disruptions of slavery and the displacements throughout the diaspora. Bynum locates these strivings within the Africanism tradition, revealing the notion of consciousness as encompassing not only the present generation, but also incorporating several generations in the past and one generation in the future (ibid.).

As I worked at these historic African American archaeological sites, I witnessed expressions of social consciousness in similar public commemorative practices across a twenty-year span between the tumultuous discovery of the African Burial Ground and the publicly driven archaeological project at Philadelphia's President's House site. I have observed contemporary constructions of ritual, meaning, and ceremony at modern-day archaeological sites where the public refused to settle for the mere collection of information and the exploitation of data, by consistently demanding and infusing meaning through ritualistic and commemorative practices. The placing of the Burial Ground on the National Register of Historic Places and awarding it National Historic Landmark status signaled its significance to the preservation world and the historic community. Similarly, landmark status reinforced its secular significance for those who felt an affinity to these sites. Rites, rituals, and ceremonies transformed the sites into sacred and spiritual spaces.

History can only organize a small subset of the past. It is the sweep of memory and ritual that reinvent tradition, turning the sacred spotlights to the unsung, the neglected, and the forgotten. Bringing a measure of honor and sanctity to those who were trapped in the dishonorable practice of slavery, rituals substantiated the lives of those consigned to the oblivion that accompanies forgetting. The meaning of the African Burial Ground and the President's House projects crossed multiple planes. The building of monuments at archaeological sites that are significant to African American history literally altered the landscape of American memory. The African Burial Ground today functions as "a place that tells the story of a people, their struggle for freedom, and their immeasurable contributions to a city and a nation [where] thousands of people have participated in traditional African ceremonies or American-style memorials at the site" (NPS Archaeology Program 2007).

Public demonstrations and protests at both the African Burial Ground and the President's House site were intended to heal those affected in the past through acts in the present. The goal of ATAC's annual 3 July commemorative event may not reside in the sacred realm or in the realm of ritual as it is traditionally understood, but the group's commemorative acts are designed to influence memory, honor the dead, and ensure that the cycle of ancestral memory will not be again lost. Public reactions to the African American archaeological sites have tangible, explainable elements, as well as abstract spiritual and emotional components, which are difficult to quantify. Ritualized expressions of remembrance, both in the monuments and in the acts of participants, bring about shared expressions of emotion that are a fundamental part of the healing experience. Tait's experience at the African Burial Ground site mirrored the sentiment of others: "I was not an ancestral person before the burial ground [but] once the burial ground gets hold of you it never lets go. . . . You don't just visit the burial ground, it gets inside of you—it gets hold of you. And you interpret just about any other experience using that yard stick."[18] For Wall, her experience with the African Burial Ground site changed the course of her research life and moved her to consider the black presence in early New York.

For me, the burial ground and the President's House infused a level of ancestral awareness and spiritual practice that altered the shape and direction of my life (LaRoche 2007b). I came away from these sites with a depth of understanding about spiritual intent, both in the past and present, recognizing that the efficacy and power of ritualistic acts are impacted by one's belief system. Rituals transcend empirical and self-evident matters of fact. Rather, ritual concerns itself with the metaphysical designed to permeate intangible objects with sacred meaning, to imbue the inert with significance and events with profundity, to honor ancestors, and to alter the course of both spiritual events and the mundane social world.

Archaeological studies cannot determine the efficacy of spiritual actions. Ritual validates the nonmaterial in an attempt to "realize a divine order in mundane time" (Innis 2004: 202). Therefore, one—whether archaeologist, descendant, or other interested party—must be prepared to examine the value and potency of the spiritual world beyond the logical, linear, and scientific realms. This calls for reflexivity and the need to ponder some important questions. Should we as investigators question the belief systems we bring to our work around ritual with the same rigor we bring to the interrogation of the belief systems of the practitioners we study? This question is particularly viable in light of observations that "academics have tended to have a distrustful view of the faithful" (Tishken et al. 2009: 5). Should we, as archaeologists, embark on our own spiritual journeys when we uncover evidence of spiritual practices in our work? Do dispassionate observation and objectivity preclude or inhibit emotional participation? Can we effectively understand ritualistic practices we encounter in the ground if we do not engage with the fundamental intentions, primarily effective mediation and negotiation of the spiritual, natural, and social worlds? What happens when we do not believe in the object of our study? Does it have an impact on the outcome of our research? Can we responsibly study things dispassionately without somehow being affected? As Chester Higgins, Jr. observed, witnessing and participating in events and ceremonies "made many African American New Yorkers feel spiritually fortunate and left them with a deep sense of responsibility. Since the respect and care for the remains of the dead is beyond the control of the deceased, only a living constituency with memory or a bonded cause is obligated to affect the behavior of the living on their behalf."[19]

Thus, as I began my own journey from detached scientist to spiritually attuned actor and believer, these were the questions that awaited me as I handled the artifacts from the African Burial Ground. I began to realize that ritual acts impart spiritual power to artifacts with which I had been entrusted. How was I to treat and honor the nonspecific, immaterial properties of the artifacts I conserved? My beliefs began to shift as I engaged with the intangible dimensions of the objects. Routinely, I approached my work with greater reverence, largely the result of my interactions with the spiritually conscious public and its insistent requirements. When we, as archaeologists, are entrusted with objects suffused with sacredness in the historic context and valued for that same sacredness in the modern world, we have an obligation to honor that original intent and treat the objects with the greatest dignity possible in the contemporary realm.

Notes

1. For complete details about the excavations, the politics, and the findings, visit http://www.gsa.gov/portal/content/249941

2. Emilyn Brown and Howard Wright kept the New York public informed through a grass-roots newsletter, "Ground Truth." Brown, Interview, 3 December 2010. Transcript on file with the author.

3. Brown, Interview.

4. Diana Di Zerega Wall, Interview, 1 March 2010. Transcript on file with the author.

5. Eric Tait, Interview, 12 March 2010. Transcript on file with the author.

6. Brown, Interview.

7. Brown, Interview.

8. Wall, Interview.

9. Brown, Interview.

10. Chester Higgins, Jr., Interview, New York, 24 August 2010.

11. For complete details about all aspects of the project, see "The President's House," www.ushistory.org.

12. Jed Levin, Interview, 11 August 2010. Transcript on file with the author.

13. Avenging the Ancestor Coalition Reburial Ceremony, 31 July 2007, http://www.ushistory.org/presidentshouse/news/ataco73107.htm; Rites of Ancestral Return, African Burial Ground, http://www.nypl.org/research/sc/afb/shell.html.

14. Avenging the Ancestors Coalition Closing Ceremony, 31 July 2007, http://avengingtheancestors.com/releases/july_31_2007.htm.

15. The brass name plaques have become an official part of the material record of the project and been accessioned into the President's House collection.

16. Levin, Interview.

17. See "The President's House," www.ushistory.org.

18. Tait, Interview.

19. Higgins, Interview.

CHAPTER 17

Cape Coast Castle and Rituals of Memory

Brempong Osei-Tutu

The materialization of memory through landscape and structural designs has proliferated over the past two decades, and the study of memory-making and commemoration has become an important meeting point for several disciplines (Araujo 2012; Connerton 1989; Linenthal 1995; Macdonald 2005; Nora 1989; Reinhardt 2005; Ruffins 1997, 1998; Young 1993). Some of the best-known memorials include the Vietnam Veterans War Memorial and the Holocaust Memorial Museum, both in Washington, D.C., and recently the National September 11 Memorial and Museum in New York City. In particular, the Holocaust memorials in Europe and the United States have provided models for commemorating other episodes of collective trauma (Ruffins 2006: 424; Young 1993). A significant development in this emerging trend is the establishment in July 2001 of the International Committee of Memorial Museums in Remembrance of the Victims of Public Crimes by the International Council of Museums (Murphy 2005: 75). Since the 1990s, UNESCO's Slave Route Project has sought to connect significant sites and events associated with the transatlantic slave trade. This and other efforts have sparked debates and policy actions on the memorialization of slavery, particularly in Africa, where that subject has largely been sequestered from public discourse. UNESCO's initiative has bolstered the Ghanaian authorities' efforts to restore Cape Coast and Elmina castles, two of Ghana's seventeen extant European fortifications—designated as World Heritage Sites by UNESCO in 1979—as memorials to transatlantic slavery.

This chapter interrogates the intersection of African American activism, Ghana's memorial entrepreneurism, and the sacralization and ritualization of Cape Coast Castle. A pilgrimage framework is the thread that connects the central themes of the chapter, including commodification, representation, ritualization, and African Americans' quest for African roots, identity, and authenticity with the notions of the power of a place. The quest for special places, irrespective of their underlying religious or spiritual values, ultimately leads to commodification and contestation, as disparate groups interact and make their constructions and interpretations of the significance of those locations (see Dubisch 1995; Eade and Sallnow 2000; Feld and Basso 1996).

Biography of Cape Coast Castle

Such an interrogation warrants a brief biographical sketch of Cape Coast Castle. The structure is one of numerous fortified trading posts built by rival European companies along the West African Atlantic seaboard, mostly between the fifteenth and eighteenth centuries, to protect trade with various African polities as well as to accommodate commercial and military staff involved in the Atlantic trade (Anquandah 1982: 131, 1999: 11; Lawrence 1963: 25; Van Dantzig 1980: iv; Walker 1998: 17–18). This commercial enterprise was dominated by the Danes, Dutch, English, French, German Brandenburgers, Portuguese, and Swedes.

These competing powers ranked their structures as lodges or forts or castles depending on the buildings' architectural and structural complexity. Lodges represented the simplest structures, while castles constituted the most complex fortifications. Forts were intermediate structures between lodges and castles. The only three structures designated as castles by the Europeans—Cape Coast Castle in Cape Coast, Christiansborg Castle in Accra, and Elmina Castle in Elmina—also became the respective headquarters of British, Danish, and Portuguese/Dutch imperial, trading, and colonial interests in West Africa (Van Dantzig 1980: i).

There is no certainty about the exact number of these structures because some have disappeared without trace, but various estimates suggest between sixty and one hundred (Anquandah 1999: 20; Lawrence 1963: 42). The vast majority of the buildings were constructed along a 240-km stretch of Ghana's coastline, a unique phenomenon that has been attributed to the country's advantageous physical setting (e.g., DeCorse 2001: 21; St. Clair 2006: 1; Van Dantzig 1980: i, vii–viii). Ghana's irregular and rocky coastline with its natural harbors provided not only safe anchorage for ships but also quarriable stone for the construction of the fortifications. In addition, the coastline's numerous promontories added to the buildings' defensive capabilities. Further, Ghana is the only area on the West African seaboard with abundant gold deposits close to the coast, a commodity that initially drew the Europeans to the region. On the other hand, fewer fortifications were constructed further east and west of Ghana, where the landscapes were characterized by low sandy coasts and dangerous surfs.

During the era of the transatlantic trade, these structures typically contained residential quarters, offices, and storerooms for merchandise. While the buildings' top floors were reserved as residences for high officials, their ground floors were generally used as storerooms or garrisons for the lower officers. The onset of the transatlantic slave trade led to the intensification of fort construction; at the same time, existing ones were adapted for prisons/dungeons to accommodate captives awaiting shipment (Lawrence 1963: 86). By the end of the eighteenth century, only three European nations—Britain, Denmark, and the Netherlands—controlled the fortifications. From 1872 through 1957, however, when they were ceded to Ghana on attainment of political independence, the buildings were under the sole jurisdiction of Britain (DeCorse 2001: 28). For their roles as administrative headquarters, these fortifications came to be known as *aban* (a term synonymous with government) by the surrounding local Akan communities (see Van Dantzig 1976: 53). For example, Cape Coast Castle was the colonial headquarters of the British Gold Coast until 1877 when the administrative capital was relocated to Accra. Since that date, Christiansborg Castle, which Ghanaians refer to as the "Osu Castle," or simply as "the Castle," has been the seat of Ghana's colonial and postcolonial governments.

Together, these structures became centers of European administrative, economic, and political power in West Africa, and an integral component of the intricate network of ships and entrepôts that characterized the transatlantic trade and ensuing colonial enterprise (see St. Clair 2006: 2). The resulting complex web of economic, political, and sociocultural interactions among Africa, Europe, and the Americas contributed significantly to the conditions of the modern world (see Thornton 1995; Walvin 2002: 49–50). In restoring and memorializing Cape Coast Castle, the Ghanaian authorities sought to emphasize the structure's unique role in these complex events, as well as the continuing encounters between Ghanaians and the rest of the global community, particularly Africans in the Diaspora (Arhin 1995: 6).

Cape Coast Castle's Memorial Landscape and Ghana's Magnetic Pull for African Americans

While the restoration and memorialization of Cape Coast Castle was designed for the global community, it was particularly aimed at what the Ghanaian authorities characterized as the "40 million strong middle-income African Americans" (see Asmah 1997; Boateng 1999). The initiative was part of a broader integrated development project to stimulate socioeconomic development, particularly in the Central Region where the castle is located (Hyland 1995; Kreamer 2006). Ghanaian policy makers hoped to increase national revenues through African Americans' spiritual journeys to the slave dungeons that are housed in the castle (Mosk 2000). The Ghanaian authorities understood the special place Ghana holds in the hearts of African Americans, and the significance of the slave dungeons on Diaspora Africans' pilgrimages to Africa, their ancestral homeland (Finley 2004: 114).

As some authors have observed, certain landscapes seem to possess spiritual magnetism that draws people to their locations (see Andriotis 2008: 72; Dubisch 1995). Ghana features prominently in Diaspora Africans' quest to experience Africa, the ancestral homeland. In addition, for decades, African Americans from all walks of life, including Maya Angelou, Martin Luther King, Jr., Malcolm X, and Richard Wright, have gone on pilgrimages to Ghana. In October 1961, the great pan-Africanist W. E. B. Du Bois immigrated with his wife, Shirley Du Bois, to Ghana where both are entombed. African Americans go to Ghana with a multiplicity of motivations, including a quest for identity, sanctuary, and roots (see Okafor 2004: 143; Washington 1992). Lindsay Barrett (1997), a Diaspora African pilgrim, describes the pilgrimage to Ghana as an ancestral call. For most contemporary African Americans, Ghana's slave castles—the symbolic cradle of transatlantic slavery—constitute significant sites of history and memory of their ancestral lineage in Africa and the cause of their diasporic condition (Finley 2004: 114). The density of these structures on Ghana's coastline convinces some of these constituents that their ancestors may have exited the continent through one of the structures' "Doors of No Return" (see Phillips 2000: 205). These monuments, therefore, represent some of the most powerful sites on African Americans' spiritual journeys to Africa (Davis 1997: 160).

To encourage these constituents to visit Ghana, in July 2000, the authorities there launched twice-weekly direct flights between Accra, Ghana's capital city, and the Baltimore-Washington International Airport (BWI) in

FIGURE 17.1. Cape Coast Castle's spacious courtyard with marked graves. *Courtesy of the author.*

Maryland, reputed as the "home to one of" America's "largest populations of middle and upper-class blacks" (Mosk 2000: B1). This was in addition to an existing service between Accra and New York City. Ghana Airways, the now-defunct national airline, carried 2,700 passengers between the Accra and BWI destinations in its first month of operation alone (ibid.).

In the initial planning for memorializing the castle in the late 1980s, the Ghanaian authorities had envisaged the building's spectacular courtyard (figure 17.1) as a multipurpose production and performance space for pan-African events (Hyland and Intsiful 2003). The project was, therefore, linked with Pan-African Historical Theater Festival (PANAFEST), which is a cultural event held in Ghana every two years that showcases music, drama, poetry, and other performances. This biennial event was originally proposed in 1980 by the pan-Africanist and playwright the late Efua Sutherland. It was designed to commemorate transatlantic slavery and to reunite African peoples dispersed as a result of that trauma. Born in Cape Coast and married to William Sutherland, an African American activist who lived and worked in Ghana in the 1950s, Efua Sutherland was well positioned to understand the links among Cape Coast Castle, homeland Africans, and African descendants of slavery. She, therefore, suggested that Cape Coast should be the venue for the celebration of PANAFEST, and when the Ghanaians implemented Sutherland's proposal in 1992, they chose Cape Coast Castle as the symbolic center for the event (Salm and Falola 2002: 70). By that time, the castle had already established itself as a popular venue for artistic performances and other commemorative events (see Cole 1996: 193; Holsey 2008: 160; Hyland and Intsiful 2003).

The Ghanaians also sought to address the diverse motivations of pilgrims and visitors, including those who focus on the building's architectural history and splendor (Finley 2004: 111; Teye and Timothy 2004: 152; Woolfork 2009: 103). This focus on visitors' interests is highlighted on a panel in the exhibition room, which is devoted to the building's structural history, where all are entreated to reflect on the following narrative:

> Cape Coast Castle as it exists today was built over a period of 300 years. . . . You are invited to explore its fascinating history and discover how and why and when it took the shape and the form that it has today. And when you walk around the castle, enter its dungeons, visit some of its many rooms, and climb to its bastions, let its walls speak to you of the splendor and the sorrow and the suffering and the shame of those who had lived and died here.

For most contemporary African American pilgrims, however, the dungeons that are housed in the castle represent a shrine where they expect decorum to prevail. They are adamant that rituals and sacred activities, not mundane events, be associated with the shrine. For this reason, two decades prior to the inauguration of PANAFEST, a group of expatriate African Americans, led by the late Dr. Robert Edward Lee, formed African Descendants Association Foundation (ADAF) to restore Fort Amsterdam, located about 24 km east of Cape Coast Castle. This building was meant to serve as a shrine comparable to the Muslims' Mecca and the Jewish Wailing Wall, where African Americans can return and "cleanse their spirits" (Phillips 2000: 206–207; see also "Shrine to Slaves" 1972). ADAF's initiative, however, did not come to fruition due to a lack of funding. An inaugural pilgrimage in 1987 to Ghana, consisting of a group of Afrocentric African American activists who called themselves the returning African descendants or ascendants (Okofu 1999: 274), was meant to invigorate the spirit behind ADAF's initiative. This inaugural group included the late Ben Robinson (later known as Nana Okofo Ababio II), Vienna Robinson (subsequently IMAHKUS Okofu), and Rabbi Kohain Nathanyah HaLevi.

The ascendants told me in 2002 that, prior to their inaugural journey, they were neither aware of ADAF's plans nor of the existence of the slave dungeons. The discovery of the castle and its dungeons in 1987 was a defining moment for these ascendants. The structures' deplorable state of disrepair at the time gave them an evocative sense of authenticity. They saw the structures as part of their historical experience in Atlantic Africa (Osei-Tutu 2009: 109). One of them, Vienna Robinson, reflects on her experience:

> When I visited the Cape Coast Castle/Dungeons in 1987, it was my first trip to the continent of "Mother" Africa. As I stood transfixed in the Women's dungeon, I could feel and smell the presence of our ancestors. From the dark, damp corners of that hell-hole I heard the whimpering and crying of tormented mothers and sisters being held in inhumane bondage, never knowing what each new day (which is difficult to discern in the dungeons) would bring. . . . As I stood there in the center of that dungeon I felt a tightness at the base of my scalp as though someone had grabbed me by the back of my neck, causing me to fall to my knees. Shortly thereafter, as I knelt crying and terrified, a warmth slowly crept across my shoulders, the fear that had previously wretched my gut was replaced by a serenity and calm I had never experienced before. Many hands caressed me, stilling my fears, wiping away my tears and welcoming me home to "Mother" Africa and Ghana, in one of the many dungeons along the West Coast of Africa, where it all began for Africans born in the Americas and the Diaspora. (1994: 48–49)

The ascendants believed, albeit erroneously, that they had found the castle and its dungeons in the same condition in which the last African captives had left them. Unknown to them, torrential rains, high humidity, salt spray, and lack of maintenance had caused the decay they witnessed. This included cracked walls, leaking roofs, and defective windows with missing casements, which had allowed rainwater into some rooms. Further, much of the building's exterior walls had not been lime-washed for many years, resulting in black mold. Similarly, most of the exterior woodwork in the doors and windows had not been painted for many years.

The castle seemed to derive its authenticity from this degree of decay and tarnish. By contrast, barely two decades earlier, Jack Moore, a white American visitor, had described the same structure as "a dazzling, hot white castle" with "blinding bright white walls" (1972: 167). The Ghana Museums and Monuments Board (GMMB) had lived up to its mandate as the statutory national institution responsible for maintaining the castle and other national monuments until the 1970s, when Ghana's deteriorating economic conditions left the board with no funds to even stop the building's decay. That problem had created the condition in which the ascendants found the castle during their visit.

They subsequently repatriated to Ghana determined to preserve the structure's historical integrity (Okofu 1999: 217). They soon, however, found out that Ghana's slave castles, like most memorials, are contested sites because of the diversity of vested interests associated with such commemorations. For example, the Vietnam Veterans War Memorial in Washington, D.C., one of America's most powerful symbolic sites, was also one of the most controversial memorials in the nation's history (Hess 1983; Sturken 1991). As Susan-Mary Grant observes, the more traditional soldier group statue was erected as both an addendum to and criticism of Maya Lin's dramatic, "understated and unrealistic design" (2006: 20). Similarly, the Holocaust Memorial Museum in Washington, D.C., took almost fifteen years to complete because the presidential commission mandated by President Jimmy Carter sought a compromise between claims of uniqueness and those of universality (Flanzbaum 1999: 5).

Likewise, the memorialization of Cape Coast Castle was contested because of the differing visions, viewpoints, and expectations Ghanaians and African Americans brought to the project. In particular, rather than focusing solely on the building's slavery heritage, as desired by African Americans, the Ghanaians sought to address that subject as one of many components of the structure's complex, five-hundred-year web of political, economic, and sociocultural interactions with Africa, Europe, the Americas, and the rest of the world. During this lifespan, the castle has served as a residential trading post, a military fortification, slave dungeons, a colonial administrative center, a prison, a school, offices, and a pilgrimage site. In addition, when the Ghanaians dealt with slavery, they presented it as a problem for African Americans, instead of as a subject for mutual interrogation by both groups (see Schramm 2005: 133). As a result, the Ghanaian treatment of slavery has been problematic (Hasty 2002: 62). The conundrum is a product of the Ghanaians' and African Americans' disparate historical experiences (see Appiah 1992: 6–7; Bruner 1996: 293). According to the ascendant IMAHKUS Okofu, only the descendants of transatlantic slavery and those who have experienced American racism "can relate to the significance of our return" (1999: 268).

Until the restoration and memorialization of the castle, most Ghanaians associated the structure with colonialism and governance; they did not perceive it as a symbol or icon of transatlantic slavery and its legacy (see Tolliver 2000: 113). While slavery is an integral part of African Americans' collective memory, most Ghanaians have not internalized that tragedy as part of their historical experiences. As Alasdair Pettinger (1998: ix) has cautioned, transatlantic slavery should not be conceptualized as a monolithic experience but as a complex one in different parts of the Black Atlantic, crisscrossed by people with different ideas and experiences.

As several writers (e.g., Bruner 1996, 2005; Kreamer 2006; Osei-Tutu 2002, 2004, 2006, 2007, 2009) have shown, the differing visions of the ascendants and Ghanaians resulted in a combative memorial landscape that produced several layers of complexity. The ascendants were activists from the United States who adopted a variety of strategies to draw attention to their cause. When they relocated to Ghana in the early 1990s, they pitched their homes and businesses at the coastal village of Iture, near Elmina, where they are now sandwiched by Cape Coast and Elmina castles. From this vantage, the ascendants have positioned themselves as the de facto "gatekeepers" of the castles, a role they have carried out with passion.

According to Christine Kreamer (2006: 466) and Katharina Schramm (2010: 91–95), the ascendants initially contacted GMMB with proposals about their vision for preserving the castle and the role they could play in its realization. Unlike GMMB, which sought to project the castle's complex life, the ascendants' proposal focused solely on the building's slavery lifespan. Kreamer (2006: 450) observes that African Americans felt marginalized when GMMB ignored their proposals and also failed to formally involve them in the project. When their initial strategy did not produce the desired results, the ascendants staged a sit-in protest by fasting and sleeping in the castle's dungeons for days. One of them, Rabbi Kohain Nathanyah HaLevi, told me in 2002 that, even though the ascendants' actions were for sacred and serious reasons, the Ghanaians accused them of overreacting. The ascendants also understood the power of the written word and used the print media to contest their marginalization from the project, insisting that they and other African descendants of slavery deserved a role in determining how the castle was managed. Vienna Robinson summed up the frustration of the ascendants thus: "Where is our input, both financial and otherwise? Where is our voice? This is a traumatic and staggering experience, but very important in our reconnection with our roots" (1994: 49). The ascendants and other critics characterized the project as "Disneyfication" and desecration of shrines as well as "whitewashing" of slavery (e.g., Deku 1993; Robinson 1994). They incited African descendants of slavery for action:

> Are flowers being planted in the ovens at Auschwitz where millions of Jews perished? Have the death chambers of horror been brightly painted to somehow camouflage or silence the cries and screams of people who were brutally tortured and murdered? Think about that and then think about the Cape Coast and Elmina Castle/Dungeons on the Gold Coast of West Africa, where you can still hear and feel the presence of our African ancestors when you enter the dark dungeons and tunnels. But will this be true when they finish renovating the castles and painting the insides of the dungeons? Restore, preserve, renovate, maintain? Exactly what is being done? And right under our noses. If I sound in a panic . . . I am. Concerned?; definitely. Seeking collective help and responsibility to prevent an action that cannot be reversed . . . or can it? But we must do something before it's too late. . . . Here I am today witnessing the "White Wash" of African History. But I cannot sit in idleness and watch this happen without sounding an alarm and praying that African American and other Africans of the Diaspora will hear, wake-up and get involved before it's too late, if it's not too late already. (Robinson 1994: 48–49)

These concerns attracted wide international attention, and the ascendants' actions garnered support among African descendants of slavery from around the world (see Norton 1995; Ransdell 1995). The intensity of African American activism compelled the Ghanaians to schedule a conference in the castle in May 1994 to address the issues of concern to both parties. Following considerable debate, the conference produced a document that provides guidelines for managing Cape Coast Castle and similar structures in Ghana (National Commission on Culture 1994). In addition, the stakeholders endorsed Cape Coast Castle's complex lifespan and agreed on the multiple representations of its historical uses, as well as contemporary meanings for a diverse audience. In addition, they agreed that transatlantic slavery should be marked as the building's main historical significance. That decision effectively underscored the castle's significance as a pilgrimage site for African descendants of slavery whose ancestors were taken via this and similar sites along the West and Central African coast. Since decorum is observed at pilgrimage sites, there were suggestions to curtail inappropriate activities in the building. These included relocating restrooms, shops, and a restaurant that was located directly on top of the Male Dungeons.

The building's spaces of special historical significance, such as the Male and Female dungeons, were subsequently highlighted with labels and signs (Finley 2004: 116; MacGonagle 2006: 252). Similarly, a new sign was erected in front of the building's main entrance that identified the building as a castle while also drawing attention to its dungeons. In response, however, Ghanaians continue to refer to the structure as a castle or anachronistically as a "slave castle." For the most part, only the ascendants religiously refer to the architectural edifice as "Castle/Dungeons" (Osei-Tutu 2003: 16). The Male and Female dungeons, as well as the "Door of No Return," have become the castle's most powerful evocative spaces for Diaspora African pilgrims, the tours of which, as I demonstrate below, have become intensely ritualized.

Ritualized Tour of the Castle

Today, pilgrims and other visitors can take a guided tour of Cape Coast Castle. The guides have varied backgrounds; some are permanent GMMB employees with considerable knowledge about the castles, while others are polytechnic and university students who can spare the time to earn extra money. These part-time guides, who rarely go through formal training, usually learn by observing other guides, as well as through independent readings. The guides are at liberty to embellish their presentations because they are not required to follow rigidly structured narratives. The guides have, "through the exchange of backstage anecdotes and experience gained from actual tours," learned how to handle diverse groups (Richards 2005: 627). For instance, they recognize that most African American pilgrims desire tours of the dungeons organized exclusively for African descendants of slavery. During my research on the castles, however, I have also encountered African Americans who do not object to interracial groupings, provided the tours are conducted with sensitivity. The guides respond to this conundrum by conducting exclusive tours on request and interracial/mixed group tours for those who are willing.

Today, the ritual tour of Cape Coast Castle typically begins at the entrance of the Male Dungeons where pilgrims are invited to reflect on the words engraved on a commemorative plaque that serves to memorialize the victims of the transatlantic slave trade:

In ever lasting memory
Of the anguish of our ancestors
May those who died rest in peace
May those who return find their roots
May humanity never again perpetrate
Such injustice against humanity
We, the living, vow to uphold this.

From this location, pilgrims have to tread carefully through an angled ramp into the dungeons, which are composed of five vaults with arched ceilings that were hollowed out of the rocky coastline. The chambers are dark and also damp because their walls perspire, which make them look like tombs. The dampness is aggravated by rainwater, which enters through tiny air vents located some 6 m above ground level and close to the brick roof. The only light that illuminates these claustrophobic chambers filters through these air vents, which barely illuminates the space. Electric lighting is sometimes provided for illumination, but it is also turned off for brief moments during the ritualized tours so that the pilgrims can experience the utter darkness the captives lived in while they were held there, prior to being shipped to the Americas. Khephra Burns, an African American pilgrim who experienced the dungeons in 1992, captured the essence of significant parts of the tour narrative:

> It takes a visit to Cape Coast Castle to bring home the horror of the word *dungeon.* The cell where male slaves were kept, sometimes for months, is underground and as close to hell as human beings have come on earth. It is hot down there, and there is no light and no air. People were branded, thrown into these unsanitary holes with their open wounds, and starved, some shackled to the walls. And there they waited in their own waste, waste which after 200 years had raised the floor two feet. That is what you walk on when you visit the dungeon at Cape Coast. It is a place filled with the moans and crying of ghosts. The screams of those who were driven insane echo down through the centuries from the scratches they made in the walls with their fingers. Many died and their bodies were thrown into the sea outside the castle. A thousand men were crowded into a space that would make 150 panic. (1992: 102)

This narrative is most likely derived from diverse sources. For instance, the reference to "the moans and crying" as well as shackles recall Quobna Ottobah Cugoano's recapitulations of his childhood experiences in one of Ghana's slave holds in his *Thoughts and Sentiments on the Evil of Slavery,* published in 1787. In this antislavery narrative, Cugoano (cited in Hartman

2007), an eighteenth-century African abolitionist in England, referred to the groans and cries of his fellow inmates who were in chains and handcuffs in his rare account of an enslaved African's experience of the Middle Passage in Atlantic Africa. The French traveler and writer Jean Barbot is the likely source of the narrative's reference to a "thousand men" crowded into the dungeons. When Barbot visited Cape Coast Castle in 1679, he noted that the dungeons were "divided into several apartments which can easily hold a thousand slaves" (Hair et al., 1992: 392).

The narrative on the other horrible conditions, such as the captives living in their own waste, likely originated from accounts of conditions in slave ships, which were described as unsanitary and smelly (see Falconbridge 1788; Simmonds 1973: 267; Taylor 2006: 20). These poor conditions prompted the castle's resident surgeon to make recommendations in 1718 to improve the conditions of the captives (Taylor 2006: 20). These suggestions included constructing platforms for the captives to sleep on, providing sanitary tubs for their use as toilets, protecting them from the damp walls, cleaning the dungeons with citrus and green herbs, and allowing the captives to smoke in order to reduce the stench (Hartman 2007: 120–121; Taylor 2006: 20). The horrific conditions, however, likely persisted until the British abolition of the trade of African captives in 1807, when the entire dungeon complex was disinfected and sanitized with sand and lime (Simmonds 1973: 268).

While still in the Male Dungeons, pilgrims encounter the shrine of the local deity, Nana Tabir, whose habitation is believed to be the rock out of which the dungeons were carved. The alteration of the rock to build the dungeons is believed to have dislodged the deity, much in the same way that the captives who occupied the created space had been displaced from their homes and families. Similarly, just like the homecoming of Diaspora African pilgrims, Nana Tabir was relocated to the dungeons in 1979 (Holsey 2008: 186). Here, the shrine's attendant, dressed in all-white apparel, offers a reverential libation with Aromatics Schnapps gin and invites the pilgrims to pray to the ancestors, as well as make monetary offerings. After the departure of the pilgrims, the candles, Schnapps bottles, and other tokens and offerings left behind on the shrine's altar attest to the rituals that took place there (see figure 17.2).

The visit to the Female Dungeons follows that of the Male Dungeons. Unlike the latter, the Female Dungeons comprise two separate ground-level vaulted rooms that are located next to the "Door of No Return." The tour

FIGURE 17.2. Memorials left by pilgrims in the Cape Coast Castle dungeons. *Courtesy of the author.*

narratives here tend to depict the horror and humiliation faced by female captives, especially when they were in their menstrual periods and did not have any means of cleaning themselves. From the Female Dungeons, the pilgrims proceed to the "Door of No Return," which is represented by an archway with wooden double doors that open out literally into the Atlantic Ocean, with the usual view of local fisher folk engrossed in their daily activities. According to Van Dantzig (1980: 60) this space, which was originally designated as the castle's Sea Gate, was constructed in the second half of the eighteenth century to facilitate the movement of merchandise and supplies to and from the castle. It is not certain whether it also served as an exit point for captives. William St. Clair (2006: 38) observes that the castle's original "Door of No Return" was a narrow gate located on the structure's seaward side, which opened from the Male Dungeons directly onto the stony beaches. He suggests that it was through this narrow gate that both captives and merchandise were ferried in canoes to and from the castle before the eighteenth century. This original passage was sealed by the British following the abolition of the trade in 1807. The ascendants were concerned about the absence of a "Door of No Return" in the building because that space symbolized the crossing of an important threshold for enslaved Africans—the Middle Passage. As part of the ritualization of the castle, GMMB implemented a suggestion by the ascendants to redesignate the Sea Gate as the "Door of No Return."

The guides encourage the pilgrims to exit and reenter this space to dramatize the experience of departure of the captives and the return of contemporary Diaspora Africans to the motherland. Tour narratives present this location as the departure point for captives as they exited the dungeons to board ships for the unknown and difficult journey to the Americas. The horrors of the Middle Passage are recounted here, including narratives on how the bodies of captives who died on the high seas were usually unceremoniously dumped into the sea. Pilgrims also learn that the same space has become the symbolic "Door of Return" for Diaspora African pilgrims since 1998, marked by the return of Samuel Carson and Crystal, two enslaved Africans whose remains were taken through it to further enhance its significance.

Samuel Carson's remains were recovered from the Brooklyn Naval Yard Cemetery in New York, while those of Crystal were uncovered from the eighteenth-century African-Jamaican enslaved settlement at the Seville Plantation in Jamaica (Singleton 2006: 249). There is not much information available about these individuals. The late Sonny Carson (1999), a black nationalist of New York City, claimed Samuel as his great-great uncle. Samuel Carson was said to be a U.S. Navy seaman who escaped to New York City from South Carolina in the aftermath of the planned Denmark Vesey rebellion around 1822. Crystal, on the other hand, was the only female among four skeletal remains of enslaved Africans who were uncovered during collaborative archaeological investigations between the Jamaica National Heritage Trust (JNHT) and Syracuse University's Anthropology Department between 1988 and 1995. The researchers named her after a pecked crystal stopper that was associated with her burial because of lack of information about her identity (Armstrong and Fleischman 2003: 47). It was estimated that she died a teenager, around the age of sixteen to nineteen, probably as a result of chronic anemia.

The repatriation of the remains of these two individuals to Ghana resulted from the collective efforts of the New York–based Committee to Honor Black Heroes, the government of Ghana, and JNHT. The committee, led by Sonny Carson, advocated the repatriation of the remains of enslaved

Africans to their ancestral homeland for reburial. It had hoped to negotiate with the directorate of the African Burial Ground (ABG) project in New York City to release some of the over four hundred human skeletal remains of enslaved Africans recovered from this seventeenth- to eighteenth-century burial site of free and enslaved Africans for reinterment in Ghana (Carson 1999; see also LaRoche, this volume). When the negotiations with the ABG directorate failed, the committee arranged for the remains of Carson and Crystal to be repatriated to Ghana for reburial (ibid.).

Carson's and Crystal's caskets were transported to Accra onboard Ghana Airways on 29 July 1998. A thirty-member delegation led by Sonny Carson and Minion Phillips, a Jamaican businesswoman and activist who represented Crystal, accompanied the remains to Ghana. From Accra, Carson's and Crystal's caskets were transported to Cape Coast Castle, where they were carried through the building's "Door of No Return"/"Door of Return" to dramatize how the captives may have exited, as well as to symbolically reverse the original dispersal that gave birth to the African Diaspora in the Americas (see Schramm 2004: 143).

To mark this important return, Ghanaian chiefs poured libations to atone for the role their ancestors played in the trade of captives. Thereafter, Carson and Crystal continued their journey to their final resting place at Assin Manso, a site along the slave route, located about a half an hour's drive inland from Cape Coast Castle. Assin Manso is believed to be the site where the captives had their last bath before being taken to the castles for holding, prior to departure to the Americas. Here, Carson and Crystal were given a state and royal burial involving several rituals, the firing of guns, the singing of dirges, traditional drumming and dancing, and the offering of libations. Thus, in death, Carson and Crystal were accorded the dignity that slavery had denied them. Assin Manso has since become a pilgrimage center for Diaspora Africans.

Ritual Reenactments

Six years after the inauguration of PANAFEST in 1992, the Ghanaian authorities appropriated the commemoration of Emancipation Day. This event celebrates the end of slavery in the British colonies and highlights other forms of political, economic, and social struggles for African-descended populations worldwide. But whereas Emancipation Day is celebrated annually, PANAFEST is a biennial affair. The two events are usually commemorated together every two years in the last week of July through the 1st of August, with the proclamation of emancipation at midnight. The conjoining of the two festivals sought to strengthen Ghana's claim as the gateway to the homeland of people of African descent in the Diaspora.

The commemoration of these events is preceded by a candlelight procession on 31 July by enthusiastic pan-African participants. These participants congregate at Mfantsipim School and process through the town's Kotokuraba Street and eventually to the castle. Dr. Mohammad Ben Abdallah, the government appointee who implemented PANAFEST, explained to me in an interview (2004) that the purpose of the procession is to encourage participants to relate the town's history with the imposing castle. Mfantsipim School's role in the procession likely reflects its status as the first and one of the leading secondary schools in Ghana. In addition, the school's location assures the shortest route through one of Cape Coast's principal streets to the castle.

The candlelight procession is followed by musical and dramatic performances, including ritualistic reenactments of the capture of Africans and their experiences in captivity in the castle's spacious courtyard by artists from the continent and its Diaspora. One such performance is the Ghana National Dance Company's ritual dance drama called *Musu: Saga of the Slaves. Musu,* a taboo word in Ghana, is significant here because it highlights the interrogation of an abominable subject (slavery) that has largely been sequestered from public discourse. During these ritual reenactments, Ghanaian performers who portray white enslavers sometimes wear masks of recent American presidents, such as Ronald Reagan, possibly to link the castle to slavery in the United States and perhaps to modern-day neocolonial practices (see Finley 2004: 121). Just before midnight, representatives of Diaspora African pilgrims and top Ghanaian government officials, including the minister of tourism, enter the dungeons to pay homage to the ancestors. The rituals here begin with a reverential libation with Aromatic Schnapps gin by the shrine's attendant, which is then followed by the invocation of the names of prominent pan-African figures, including some of those who have been immortalized in the Ghanaian landscape. These include W. E. B. Du Bois, Marcus Garvey, Martin Luther King, Jr., Kwame Nkrumah, George Padmore, and Malcolm X. After the invocations, the pilgrims and the Ghanaian dignitaries emerge from the dungeons into the courtyard where the government minister or his or her representative proclaims emancipation at midnight to the cheers of the teeming crowd. The emancipation proclamation marks the climax of the celebration, and thereafter participants disperse to their various destinations.

In addition to these ceremonies, both Ghanaians and the African American ascendants conduct ritual reenactments in the castle at various times in between the annual commemorative activities of Emancipation Day, during which their disparate historical experiences surface (see Appiah 1992: 6–7; Bruner 1996: 293). One of these activities is a performance by One Africa Tours and Specialty Services Ltd. (OATSSL), owned by the ascendants IMAHKUS Okofu and her late husband, Nana Okofo, as well as reenactments directed by Ghanaians.

OATSSL's three-part narrative of slavery called "Through the Door of No Return, the Return," is performed by the local Tweampong Traditionals and mainly targets Diaspora African pilgrims. This performance depicts an initial horror of capture, Diaspora African resistance, and a joyous return to Africa, the motherland. Following this performance, the pilgrims are led into the respective Male and Female dungeons for candlelight vigils. Here, the pilgrims hold hands, sing, chant, and scream, culminating in varied emotional responses. In addition, some pilgrims become possessed and roll on the floor, while others remain quiet and pensive (Okofu 1999: 255–260, 268). Thereafter, the pilgrims emerge from the dungeons and exit through the castle's "Door of No Return," which with their reentry is metaphorically transformed into the "Door of Return." The pilgrims then proceed back to the dungeons at a high tempo, to signify their return to the motherland as they sing in unison and with the accompaniment of intense drumming:

> We are home once more
> We are home once more
> Glory be to God we are home once more
> We were in that part of sin
> And King Alpha put us in
> We said glory, glory be to God
> We are home once more
> Hallelujah
> Boom . . . boom . . . boom.

This ritual enables Diaspora African pilgrims to collapse the past and present into mutually constitutive spheres as they internalize the suffering of their ancestors through re-memory and experiential connection, culminating in a therapeutic return (Woolfork 2009: 4–5, 102). As IMAHKUS Okofu forcefully articulates, "The reconnection, the re-birth hurts but it's necessary" (1999: 268). On the other hand, reenactments directed by Ghanaian groups, including the National Dance Company, show slight differences. Unlike the performances by the ascendants, the Ghanaian reenactments are not restricted to only Diaspora African pilgrims as their audience. In addition, the Ghanaian-directed performances end in the dungeons without a candlelight vigil. Further, such performances do not include the component on the symbolic return of Diaspora African pilgrims through the "Door of Return" (see Bruner 2005: 111). According to Saidiya Hartman (2007: 104), however, initiatives by another local company to incorporate this segment in its performance immediately sparked a copyright dispute between the Ghanaian company and OATSSL. Moreover, the ascendants seem to have the conviction that only they, born out of the historical experience of slavery, can produce an "authentic" ritual for Diaspora African pilgrims (see Okofu 1999: 268).

Discussion and Conclusion

For many decades, the ritualization of the transatlantic slave trade has been part of annual festivals commemorated by communities in southeastern and northern Ghana whose ancestors were victims of this trauma (see Bailey 2005; Greene 1997; Holsey 2008: 84–87; Howell 2007; Isichei 2002). But commemoration and ritualization of the transatlantic slave trade within the Ghanaian national landscape has emerged only within the last three decades. In this national, transatlantic agenda, the Ghanaian leadership and African Americans have collaborated to produce new memories in shaping the commemoration of the transatlantic trade, in spite of their disparate historical trajectories. As Susan Benson and Tom McCaskie observe, in doing so, the Ghanaians and African Americans have combined "cross-Atlantic identification with spatial and temporal displacement" in the Ghanaian landscape (2006: 107).

This has resulted, for instance, in relabeling spaces in Cape Coast Castle, so that the "Sea Gate" has been redesignated as the "Door of No Return." It has also resulted in the repatriation of ancestral remains from the Diaspora for reburial in Ghana. Critics might question the basis for selecting Ghana for the reinterment, since Carson and Crystal or their ancestors could have originated from other parts of Africa such as Senegal or Angola. In any case, these ancestors would have had no consciousness of a bounded Ghana at the time of their transplantation to the Americas. Like most states in Africa, modern Ghana (formerly the Gold Coast) came into existence only after the partition of Africa in 1884–1885. And given the diversity and complexity of diasporic African identity constructs, the question arises whether these ancestors would have preferred to be reburied in Africa; not all Diaspora Africans desired to repatriate to the continent.

This conundrum raises a debate regarding the link between historical truth and memory (see Benson and McCaskie 2006: 93). In his monumental work *Les lieux de mémoire* (sites of memory), Pierre Nora (1989) points to the link between memorials and interest in memory since the 1980s. And according to Maurice Halbwachs (1992), collective memories are shaped by commemorative events through differential editing by individuals and groups. As a result, memory is constantly evolving new configurations of meaning (Carrier 1996: 438). In the ritualization and sacralization of Cape Coast Castle, Ghanaians and African Americans, like other groups, have developed stories or narratives to highlight issues they consider most meaningful about their past experiences. What is important is not the accuracy of these narratives but the complex social forces behind them, as well as the meanings attached to them (see Gray and Oliver 2001: 14; Ruffins 1992: 510–513; Sturken 1997: 9). As the African American Janet Butler emphasized in a 2002 interview, Diaspora Africans on a pilgrimage to Cape Coast Castle are not interested in facts and figures; instead, they just want to be there to experience it.

The tension over the memorialization of Cape Coast Castle highlights the competing visions Ghanaians and African Americans brought to the project as a result of differing perceptions, attitudes, and historical experiences. The Ghanaian state sought to address the legacy of slavery within a complex history of political and economic interactions with Europeans, Ghana's struggle for self-determination, and contemporary Ghanaian cultural production. Underpinning the entire project was commodification in anticipation of increased revenues through tourist arrivals.

While the ascendants' activism may not have produced all the desired results they had hoped for, it nonetheless generated a productive dialogue with Ghanaians (Layton and Thomas 2001). Both groups recognized the multiple historical events that took place in the castle and also agreed that transatlantic slavery should be marked as its main historical significance. This agreement saved the castle from being adapted for hotel accommodations and other inappropriate uses that would have diminished the building's historical significance. In addition, it led to the intensification of the building's sacralization and ritualization by both groups. The tension over the memorialization of the castle underscores the complexity and contestation over the making of memorials (see Devenish 1997; Woolfork 2009), how to sacralize spaces of trauma and multiple historical experiences (such as the Cape Coast Castle), and how sacred spaces should be memorialized as a pilgrim and tourist site.

REFERENCES

Aaronson, D., and K. Kwan. 2008. *Luck: The Essential Guide*. New York: Morrow.

Aberle, D. F. 1966. "Religio-Magical Phenomena and Power, Prediction, and Control." *Southwestern Journal of Anthropology* 223: 221–230.

Abimbola, K. 2006. *Yoruba Culture: A Philosophical Account*. Birmingham, England: Iroko Academic Publishers.

Abiodun, R. 1994. "Understanding Yoruba Art and Aesthetics: The Concept of Ase." *African Arts* 27 (3): 68–78.

Abrahams, R. D. 1983. *The Man of Words in the West Indies: Performance and the Emergence of Creole Culture*. Baltimore: Johns Hopkins University Press.

Abrahams, R. D., and J. F. Szwed. 1983. *After Africa*. New Haven, Conn.: Yale University Press.

Achrati, N. 2002. "Seek Slave Memorial at Liberty Bell." *Philadelphia Inquirer,* 4 July, http://www.ushistory.org/presidentshouse/news/inq070402.htm.

Act 24 of 1760. 1771. In *Acts of Assembly Passed in the Island of Jamaica; from the Year 1681 to the Year 1769, Inclusive,* vol. 2, 52–55. Saint Jago de la Vega, Jamaica: Lowry and Sherlock.

Act 91 of 1781. 1786. In *Acts of Assembly Passed in the Island of Jamaica from 1770 to 1783, Inclusive,* 277. Kingston, Jamaica: Lewis and Eberall.

"An Act for the More Effectual Punishment of Persons Convicted of Dealing in and Practicing Obeah and Myalism." 1856. In *The Laws of Jamaica, Passed in the Nineteenth Year of the Reign of Queen Victoria,* 512. Kingston, Jamaica: S. M. Samuels.

Act of 1809. 1816. "An Act for the Protection, Subsisting, Clothing, and for the Better Order, Regulation, and Government of Slaves; and for Other Purposes." In *British Parliamentary Papers* (House of Commons), *Miscellaneous Papers,* session 1 February–2 July, vol. 19 (Colonial Laws Respecting Slaves), 124–125.

"An Act to Alter and Amend the Slave Laws of This Island." 1826. In *British Parliamentary Papers, State Papers,* session 21 Nov. 1826–2 July 1827, vol. 25 (Papers Respecting the Enslaved Population in the West Indies: Jamaica), 80–90.

"An Act to Explain the Fourth Victoria, Chapter Forty-Two, and the Nineteenth Victoria, Chapter Thirty, and for the More Effectual Punishment of Obeah and Myalism." (1857) 1890. In *The Statutes and Laws of the Island of Jamaica, Revised Edition,* vol. 4, edited by C. Ribton Curran, 44–46. Kingston, Jamaica: Government Printing Establishment.

"Acts Causing or Tending to Cause Danger to Life, or Bodily Harm." (1864) 1889. In *The Statutes and Laws of the Island of Jamaica: Revised Edition,* vol. 4, edited by C. Ribton Curran, 306–309. Kingston, Jamaica: Government Printing Establishment.

Acts of Jamaica. 1774. CO 139/30, British National Archives, Kew, England.

Acts of Jamaica. 1799. CO 139/49, British National Archives, Kew, England.

Acts of Jamaica. 1802. CO 139/51, British National Archives, Kew, England.

Adams, R., and S. King. 2011. "Residential Burial in Global Perspective." In *Residential Burial: A Multiregional Exploration,* edited by R. Adams and S. King. Special issue of *Archaeological Papers of the American Anthropological Association* 20 (1): 1–16.

African Burial Ground. 2009. Introduction to the Electronic Versions of the Final Reports. The New York African Burial Ground: Unearthing the African Presence in Colonial New York. http://www.gsa.gov/portal/content/249941.

Agha, A., and N. M. Isenbarger. 2011. "Recently Discovered Marked Colonoware from Dean Hall Plantation, Berkeley County, South Carolina." *Historical Archaeology* 45 (2): 184–187.

Agorsah, E. K. 1975. "Unique Discoveries from Efutu." *Ghana Sankofa* 1: 88.

———. 1994. *Maroon Heritage: Archaeological, Ethnographic and Historical Perspectives.* Kingston, Jamaica: Canoe Press.

———. 2007. "The Scars of Brutality: Archaeology of the Maroons in the Caribbean." In *Archaeology of the Atlantic Africa and the African Diaspora,* edited by A. Ogundiran and T. Falola, 332–354. Bloomington: Indiana University Press.

———. 2010. *Religion, Ritual and African Tradition.* Bloomington, Ind.: Authorhouse.

Agorsah, E. K., and T. Butler. 2008. "Archaeological Investigation of the Historic Site of Kormantse." *African Diaspora Archaeology Newsletter,* September, 1–22.

Agorsah, E. K., and G. T. Childs. 2005. *Africa and the African Diaspora: Cultural Adaptation and Resistance.* Bloomington, Ind.: Authorhouse.

Ahlo, O. 1976. *The Religion of the Slaves: A Study of the Religious Tradition and Behavior of Plantation Slaves in the United States, 1830–1865.* Helsinki: Folklore Fellows.

Akindele, A., and C. Renaud. 1953. *Contribution à l'étude de l'histoire de l'ancien Royaume de Porto-Novo.* Dakar: Institut Fondamental d'Afrique Noire.

Akinjogbin, I. A. 1967. *Dahomey and Its Neighbors 1708–1818.* Cambridge: Cambridge University Press.

"An Alleged Obeahman Arrested." 1899. *The Daily Gleaner,* 7 September, 2.

Allen, K. 2009. "Looking East: Muslim Identity in the Archaeological Record of American Enslavement." *African Diaspora Archaeology Newsletter,* September, http://www.diaspora.uiuc.edu/news0909/news0909.html#2.

Allen, W. S. 1868. Christian Missionary Society Journal, 25 October. CA2/O series, file 19, microfilm, Birmingham University Library, Birmingham, England.

Alleyne, M. 1988. *Roots of Jamaican Culture.* London: Pluto Press.

Allman, J., and J. Parker. 2005. *Tongnaab.* Bloomington: Indiana University Press.

"The Allman Town Obeah Case." 1907. *The Daily Gleaner,* 24 October, 9.
Allsworth-Jones, P. 1996. "Continuity and Change in Yoruba Pottery." *Bulletin of the School of Oriental and African Studies* 592: 312–322.
Anderson, J. E. 2008. *Hoodoo, Voodoo, and Conjure: A Handbook.* Westport, Conn.: Greenwood Press.
Anderson, U. 1937. "A Comparative Study of Some of the Older Beliefs and Usages of East Tennessee." *Tennessee Folklore Society Bulletin* 31: 1–7.
Andriotis, K. 2008. "Sacred Site Experience: A Phenomenological Study." *Annals of Tourism Research* 36 (1): 64–84.
Anquandah, J. 1982. *Rediscovering Ghana's Past.* Harlow, England: Longman.
———. 1987. "Stone Circle Sites of Komaland, Northern Ghana, in West African Archaeology." *African Archaeological Review* 5: 171–180.
———. 1998. *Koma-Bulsa: Its Art and Archaeology.* Rome: Istituto Italiano per l'Africa e l'Oriente.
———. 1999. *Castles and Forts of Ghana.* Paris: Atalante.
Appadurai, A. 1986. "Introduction." In *The Social Life of Things: Commodities in Cultural Perspective,* edited by A. Appadurai, 3–63. Cambridge: Cambridge University Press.
Appiah, K. 1992. *In My Father's House: Africa in the Philosophy of Culture.* Oxford: Oxford University Press.
Apter, A. 1992. *Black Critics and Kings: The Hermenutics of Power in Yoruba Society.* Chicago: University of Chicago Press.
———. 2002. "On African Origins: Creolization and Connaissance in Haitian Vodou." *American Ethnologist* 29 (2): 233–260.
Araujo, A. L. 2012. *Politics of Memory: Making Slavery Visible in the Public Space.* New York: Routledge.
Argenti, N. 2006. "Remembering the Future: Slavery, Youth and Masking in the Cameroon Grassfields." *Social Anthropology* 14: 49–69.
Argyle, W. J. 1966. *The Fon of Dahomey: A History and Ethnography of the Old Kingdom.* Oxford: Clarendon Press.
Arhin, K. 1995. "Cape Coast and Elmina in Historical Perspective." In *The Cape Coast and Elmina Handbook: Past, Present and Future,* edited by K. Arhin, 1–12. Legon, Ghana: Institute of African Studies.
Armah, A. K. 1979. *Two Thousand Seasons.* Chicago: Third World Press.
Armitage, D. 2002. "Three Concepts of Atlantic History." In *The British Atlantic World, 1500–1800,* edited by D. Armitage and M. J. Braddick, 11–30. New York: Palgrave Macmillan.
Armstrong, D. 1998. "Cultural Transformation among Caribbean Slave Communities." In *Studies in Culture Contact: Interaction, Culture Change, and Archaeology,* edited by J. Cusick, 378–401. Carbondale: Southern Illinois University Press.
———. 2003. *Creole Transformation from Slavery to Freedom: Historical Archaeology of the East End Community, St. John, Virgin Islands.* Gainesville: University of Florida Press.
Armstrong, D., and M. Fleischman. 2003. "House-Yard Burials of Enslaved Laborers in Eighteenth Century Jamaica." *International Journal of Historical Archaeology* 7 (1): 33–65.

Arno, A. 2005. "Cobo and Tabua in Fiji: Two Forms of Cultural Currency in an Economy of Sentiment." *American Ethnologist* 32 (1): 46–62.

Asmah, G. F. 1997. "Ghana Goes for the Afro Tourists." *New African,* April, 33.

Associated Press. 2007. "African Burial Ground Opens in Manhattan." http://www.msnbc.msn.com/id/21150548/.

Atwood, C. 1997. "The Joyfulness of Death in Eighteenth-Century Moravian Communities." *Communal Societies* 17: 39–58.

Atwood, T. 1791. *History of the Island of Dominica.* London: J. Johnson.

Awolalu, J. O. 1973. "Yoruba Sacrificial Practice." *Journal of Religion in Africa* 5 (2): 81–93.

Baduel-Mathon, C. 1971. "Le langage gestuel en Afrique occidentale: Recherches bibliographiques." *Journal de la Société des Africanistes* 41: 203–249.

Bailey, A. C. 2005. *African Voices of the Atlantic Slave Trade: Beyond the Silence and Shame.* Boston: Beacon Press.

Baldwin, C. K. 1993. *Great and Noble Jar: Traditional Stoneware of South Carolina.* Athens: University of Georgia Press.

Banbury, T. 1894. *Jamaica Superstitions; or, The Obeah Book.* Kingston, Jamaica: Mortimer C. DeSouza.

Baneong-Yakubu, B., P. M. Nude, and Y. S. Anku. 2006. *Petrography and Provenance of Rocks in Selected Shrines in the Tengzug Shrine, Upper East Region.* Legon: Department of Geology, University of Ghana.

Barber, K. 1995. "Money, Self-Realization, and the Person in Yoruba Texts." In *Money Matters: Instability, Values, and Social Payments in the Modern History of West African Communities,* edited by J. Guyer, 205–224. Portsmouth, N.H.: Heinemann.

Barnes, S., ed. 1997. *Africa's Ogun: Old World and New.* 2nd ed. Bloomington: Indiana University Press.

Barrett, J., and K. Fewster. 1998. "Stonehenge: Is the Medium the Message?" *Antiquity* 72: 847–852.

Barrett, L. 1997. "The Long Homecoming." *West Africa,* 11–17 August, 1300–1301.

Bascom, W. 1973. *African Art in Cultural Perspective: An Introduction.* New York: Norton.

Bass, R. 1935. "Death Is a Little Man." *Scribners' Magazine* 97: 120–123.

Bates, W. C. 1896. "Creole Folk-Lore from Jamaica, I: Proverbs." *Journal of American Folklore* 9: 38–42.

Bateson, G. (1972) 2002. *Steps to an Ecology of Mind.* Reprint ed. Chicago: University of Chicago Press.

Baum, R. 1999. *Shrines of the Slave Trade: Diola Religion and Society in Precolonial Senegambia.* Oxford: Oxford University Press.

Bay, E. G. 1998. *Wives of the Leopard: Gender, Politics, and Culture in the Kingdom of Dahomey.* Charlottesville: University Press of Virginia.

———. 2008. *Asen, Ancestors, and Vodun: Tracing Change in African Art.* Urbana: University of Illinois Press.

Béart, C. 1955. *Jeux et joets de l'Oest Africain.* 2 vols. Dakar: Institut Fondamental d'Afrique Noire.

Beckwith, M. 1969. *Black Roadways: A Study of Jamaica Folk Life.* New York: Negro Universities Press.

Beier, G. 1980. "Yoruba Pottery." *African Arts* 8 (3): 48–53, 92.

Belasco, B. 1980. *The Entrepreneur as Culture Hero: Preadaptations in Nigeria Economic Development.* New York: Praeger.

Bell, C. 1992. *Ritual Theory, Ritual Practice.* Oxford: Oxford University Press.

———. 1997. *Ritual: Perspective and Dimensions.* Oxford: Oxford University Press.

Bell, H. H. J. 1889. *Obeah: Witchcraft in the West Indies.* London: Sampson, Low, Marston, Searle and Rivington.

Bell, M., Jr. 1987. *Major Butler's Legacy: Five Generations of a Slaveholding Family.* Athens: University of Georgia Press.

Ben-Amos, P. G. 1986. "Artistic Creativity in Benin Kingdom." *African Arts* 19 (3): 60–63.

———. 1995. *The Art of Benin.* Washington, D.C.: Smithsonian Institution Press.

———. 1999. *Art, Innovation, and Politics in Eighteenth-Century Benin.* Bloomington: Indiana University Press.

Benson, S., and T. C. McCaskie. 2006. "Asen Praso in History and Memory." *Ghana Studies* 7: 93–113.

Bentor, E. 1988. "Life as an Artistic Process: Igbo Ikenga and Ofo." *African Arts* 21 (2): 66–71, 94.

Berlin, I. 2004. *Generations of Captivity: A History of African-American Slaves.* Cambridge, Mass.: Harvard University Press.

Besson, J., and K. Olwig. 2005. *Caribbean Narratives of Belonging.* Oxford: Macmillan.

Bilby, K. 1994. "Maroon Culture as a Distinct Variant of Jamaican Culture." In *Maroon Heritage: Archaeological, Ethnographic, and Historical Perspectives,* edited by E. K. Agorsah, 72–93. Kingston, Jamaica: Canoe Press.

———. 1995. "Oral Traditions among Two Maroon Societies: The Windward Maroons of Jamaica and the Aluku Maroons of French Guiana and Suriname." In *Born out of Resistance: On Caribbean Cultural Creativity,* edited by W. Hoogbergen, 169–180. Utrecht, Netherlands: ISOR Publications.

Bilby, K., and J. Handler. 2004. "Obeah: Healing and Protection in West Indian Slave Life." *Journal of Caribbean History* 38 (2): 1–31.

Binford, L. R. 1971. "Mortuary Practices and Their Potential." In *Approaches to the Social Dimensions of Mortuary Practices,* edited by J. A. Brown, 6–29. New York: Society for American Archaeology.

Bisnauth, D. 1996. *History of Religions in the Caribbean.* Trenton, N.J.: Africa World Press.

Blake, F. I. R. 1995. *The Trinidad and Tobago Steel Pan: History and Evolution.* Molins de Rei, Spain: Grafiques.

Blassingame, J. 1972. *The Slave Community: Plantation Life in the Antebellum South.* New York: Oxford University Press.

———, ed., 1977. *Slave Testimony: Two Centuries of Letters, Speeches, Interviews and Autobiographies.* Baton Rouge: Louisiana State University Press.

Blier, S. 1987. *The Anatomy of Architecture: Ontology and Metaphor in Batammaliba Architectural Expression.* Cambridge: Cambridge University Press.

———. 1991. "King Glele of Dahomè Part Two: Dynasty and Destiny." *African Arts* 24 (1): 44–103.

———. 1995a. *African Vodun: Art, Psychology, and Power.* Chicago: University of Chicago Press.

———. 1995b. "Vodun: West African Roots of Vodou." In *Sacred Arts of Haitian Vodou,* edited by D. J. Cosentino, 60–87. Los Angeles: Fowler Museum of Cultural History, University of California at Los Angeles.

Blouet, H. 2013. "Interpretations of Burial and Commemoration in Moravian and African Diasporas on St. John, Virgin Islands." *International Journal of Historical Archaeology.* 17: 731–781.

Boateng, O. 1999. "Back to the Roost: Ghana Woos Diaspora Africans with PANAFEST." *New African,* June, G6.

Boivin, N. 2008. *Material Cultures, Material Minds: The Role of Things in Human Thought, Society and Evolution.* Cambridge: Cambridge University Press.

———. 2009. "Grasping the Elusive and Unknowable: Material Culture in Ritual Practice." *Material Religion* 5: 266–287.

Bolland, N. 2001. *The Politics of Labour in the British Caribbean: The Social Origins of Authoritarianism and Democracy in the Labour Movement.* Kingston, Jamaica: Ian Randle Publishers.

Bolster, W. J. 1998. *Black Jacks: African American Seamen in the Age of Sail.* Cambridge, Mass.: Harvard University Press.

Bosman, W. 1705. *A New and Accurate Description of the Coast of Guinea, Divided into the Gold, the Slave, and the Ivory Coasts.* London: J. Knapton.

Boston, J. 1977. *Ikenga Figures among the North-West Igbo and the Igala.* Lagos, Nigeria, and London: Federal Department of Antiquities and Ethnographica.

Bowen, E. A. 1950. *The Story of Wilkes County, Georgia.* Marietta, Ga.: Continental Book Company.

Bradbury, R. E. 1961. "Ezomo's Ikegobo and the Benin Cult of the Hand." *Man* 61: 129–138.

Bradley, R. 2000. *An Archaeology of Natural Places.* London: Routledge.

———. 2005. *Ritual and Domestic Life in Prehistoric Europe.* London: Routledge.

Brandon, G. 1997. *Santeria from Africa to the New World: The Dead Sell Memories.* Bloomington: Indiana University Press.

Brasio, A. 1960. *Monumenta Missionaria Africana Africa Occidental 1631–1642.* Vol. 1. Lisbon: Academia Portuguesa de Historia.

Breslaw, E. G. 2000. *Witches of the Atlantic World: A Historical Reader and Primary Sourcebook.* New York: New York University Press.

Brewer, J. M. 1958. *Dog Ghosts and Other Texas Negro Folk Tales.* Austin: University of Texas Press.

Brown, D. F. 1990. "Conjure/Doctors: An Exploration of a Black Discourse in America, Antebellum to 1940." *Folklore Forum* 23 (1–2): 3–46.

Brown, D. H. 2003. *Santeria Enthroned: Art, Ritual, and Innovation in an Afro-Cuban Religion.* Chicago: University of Chicago Press.

Brown, J. 1971. "The Dimensions of Status in the Burials at Spiro." In *Approaches to the Social Dimensions of Mortuary Practices,* edited by J. Brown, 92–112. Washington, D.C.: Society for American Archaeology.

Brown, J. W. 2004. "The Illusory and the Real." *Matter and Mind: An International Interdisciplinary Journal of Mind-Matter Research* 2 (1): 37–59.

Brown, K. L. 1994. "Material Culture and Community Structure: The Slave and Tenant Community at Levi Jordan's Plantation, 1848–1892." In *Working toward Freedom: Slave Society and Domestic Economy in the American South,* edited by L. E. Hudson, Jr., 95–118. Rochester, N.Y.: University of Rochester Press.

———. 2001. "Interwoven Traditions: Archaeology of the Conjurer's Cabins and the African American Cemetery at the Jordan and Frogmore Plantations." In *Places of Cultural Memory: African Reflections on the American Landscape,* edited by L. D. Hudson, 99–114. Washington, D.C.: National Park Service.

———. 2004. "Ethnographic Analogy, Archaeology, and the African Diaspora: Perspectives from a Tenant Community." *Historical Archaeology* 38 (1): 79–89.

Brown, K. L., and D. C. Cooper. 1990. "Structural Continuity in an African-American Slave and Tenant Community." *Historical Archaeology* 24 (4): 7–19.

Brown, K. M. 2001. *Mama Lola: A Vodou Priestess in Brooklyn.* 2nd ed. Berkeley: University of California Press.

Brown, L. A., and W. H. Walker. 2008. "Prologue: Archaeology, Animism and Non-Human Agents." *Journal of Archaeological Method and Theory* 15: 297–299.

Brown, R. M. 2002. "Walk in the Feenda: West-Central Africans and the Forest in the South Carolina–Georgia Lowcountry." In *Central Africans and Cultural Transformations in the American Diaspora,* edited by L. M. Heywood, 289–318. Cambridge: Cambridge University Press.

Brown, V. 2008. *The Reaper's Garden: Death and Power in the World of Atlantic Slavery.* Cambridge, Mass.: Harvard University Press.

Brück, J. 1999. "Ritual and Rationality: Some Problems of Interpretation in European Archaeology." *European Journal of Archaeology* 2: 313–344.

Bruner, E. 1996. "Tourism in Ghana: The Representation of Slavery and the Return of the Black Diaspora." *American Anthropologist* 98 (2): 290–304.

———. 2005. *Culture on Tour: Ethnographies of Travel.* Chicago: University of Chicago Press.

Burdett, W. 1800. *Life and Exploits of Mansong, Commonly Called Three-Fingered Jack, The Terror of Jamaica in the Years of 1780 & 1781: with a Particular Account of the Obi.* Sommers Town, London: A. Neil.

Burns, K. 1992. "Land of Gold: Ghana—Through Slavery's Darkest." *Essence,* 23 October, 102–103.

Burrison, J. A. 1983. *Brothers in Clay: The Story of Georgia Folk Pottery.* Athens: University of Georgia Press.

Burton, R. (1864) 1966. *A Mission to Gelele, King of Dahome.* London: Routledge and Kegan Paul.

Bury, S. 1991. *Jewellery 1789–1910: The International Era.* Woodbridge, England: Antique Collectors' Club.

Bynum, E. B. 1999. *The African Psychological Lineage on Dream States, Family Dynamics, the Unconscious and Beyond.* Amherst: University of Massachusetts Health Series. Also available at http://www.obeliskfoundation.com/articles/artdreams.html.

Caltanisseta, L. de, and F. Bontink. 1970. *Diarie Congalais, 1690–1701.* Kinshasa: Publications de l'Université Lovanium de Kinshasa.

Cameron, E. L. 1997. "In Search of Children: Dolls and Agency in Africa." *African Arts* 30 (2): 18–33, 93.

Cameron, E. L., and D. H. Ross. 1996. *Isn't S/He a Doll: Play and Ritual in African Sculpture*. Los Angeles: Fowler Museum of Cultural History, University of California at Los Angeles.

Campbell, J. 1976. *Obeah: Yes or No? A Study of Obeah and Spiritualism in Guyana*. Georgetown (Huay), Guiana: Autor.

Capozzoli, M. M. 1997. "A Rip in the Flesh, A Tear into the Soul: An Ethnography of Dissection in Georgia." In *Bones in the Basement: Post-Mortem Racism in 19th Century Medical Training*, edited by R. L. Blakely and J. M. Harrington, 313–339. Washington, D.C.: Smithsonian Institution Press.

Carey, B. 1997. *The Maroon Story: An Authentic and Original History of the Maroons in the History of Jamaica 1490–1880*. Kingston, Jamaica: Agouti Press.

Carney, J. A. 2001. *The African Origins of Rice Cultivation in the Americas*. Cambridge, Mass.: Harvard University Press.

Carrier, P. 1996. "Historical Traces of the Present: The Uses of Commemoration." *Historical Reflections/Reflexions Historiques* 22 (2): 431–445.

Carson, S. 1999. "Emancipation Day in Ghana." *New York Daily Challenge*, 13 July.

Carstens, J. L. 1994. "General Description of the Danish, American, or West Indian Islands." In *Kamina Folk: Slavery and Slave Life in the Danish West Indies*, edited by G. Tyson and A. Highfield, 1–18. St. Croix: Virgin Islands Humanities Council.

Carvalho, M. J. 1998. "To Catch a Duppy." *Kaos Magick Journal* 1 (2): 6–8.

"Case under the Obeah Law." 1909. *The Daily Gleaner*, 16 April, 13.

Cassidy, F. G., and R. B. LePage, eds. 2002. *Dictionary of Jamaican English*. Kingston, Jamaica: University of the West Indies Press.

Catédra, M. 2004. "Kinds of Death and the House." In *Death, Mourning, and Burial: A Cross-Cultural Reader*, edited by A. Robben, 77–90. Malden, Mass.: Blackwell.

Chambers, D. B. 1997. "'My Own Nation': Igbo Exiles in the Diaspora." *Slavery and Abolition* 18 (1): 72–97.

———. 2001. "Ethnicity in the Diaspora: The Slave Trade and the Creation of African 'Nations' in the Americas." *Slavery and Abolition* 22 (3): 25–39.

———. 2005. *Murder at Montpelier*. Jackson: University Press of Mississippi.

Chaplin, J. E. 2001. *Subject Matter: Technology, the Body, and Science on the Anglo-American Frontier, 1500–1676*. Cambridge, Mass.: Harvard University Press.

Chapman, I. K., and K. Randsborg, eds. 1981. *The Archaeology of Death*. Cambridge: Cambridge University Press.

"Charge of Obeah." 1907. *The Daily Gleaner*, 2 August, 3.

"Charges of Theft and Obeah." 1902. *The Daily Gleaner*, 5 September, 13.

Chesson, M. ed. 2001. *Social Memory, Identity and Death: Ethnographic and Archaeological Perspectives on Mortuary Rituals*. Arlington, Va.: American Anthropological Association.

Chireau, Y. 2003. *Black Magic: Religion and the African American Conjuring Tradition*. Berkeley: University of California Press.

Clapperton, H. 1829. *Journal of a Second Expedition into the Interior of Africa, from the Bight of Benin to Soccatoo*. London: John Murray.

Clarke, W. H. 1972. *Travels and Explorations in Yorubaland 1854–1858*. Edited with an introduction by J. A. Atanda. Ibadan, Nigeria: Ibadan University Press.

Cochran, M. D. 1999. "Hoodoo's Fire: Interpreting Nineteenth Century African-American Material Culture at the Brice House, Annapolis, Maryland." *Maryland Archaeology* 35 (1): 25–33.

Cole, C. M. 1996. "Reading Blackface in West Africa: Wonders Taken for Signs." *Critical Inquiry* 23 (1): 183–215.

Cole, H. M. 2013. *Igbo.* Milan: Five Continents.

"Commentary on the New Slave Law." 1827. In *The Consolidated Slave Law, Passed on the 22d December, 1826,* p. x. 2nd ed. Kingston, Jamaica: Courant Office.

Connah, G. 1975. *The Archaeology of Benin: Excavations and Other Researches in and around Benin City, Nigeria.* Oxford: Clarendon Press.

Connerton, P. 1989. *How Societies Remember.* Cambridge: Cambridge University Press.

Cooksey, S., R. Poynor, and H. Vanhee, eds. 2013. *Kongo across the Waters.* Gainesville: University Press of Florida.

"A Coolie Obeahman." 1899. *The Daily Gleaner,* 17 June, 2.

Cottle, R. K. 1997. Cemetery Siting in the Bluestone Reservation Area, Summers County, West Virginia, 1750–1997. M.A. thesis, Virginia Polytechnic Institute and State University.

Coughtry, J. 1981. *The Notorious Triangle: Rhode Island and the African Slave Trade, 1700–1807.* Philadelphia: Temple University Press.

Courlander, H. 1960. *The Drum and the Hoe: Life and Lore of the Haitian People.* Berkeley: University of California Press.

———. 1996. *A Treasury of Afro-American Folklore.* New York: Marlow Company.

Crissman, J. K. 1994. *Death and Dying in Central Appalachia.* Urbana: University of Illinois Press.

Crist, T. A., W. R. Henry, J. W. Joseph, R. H. Pitts, W. P. Catts, A. Caton, A. Washburn, and S. P. Norris. 2000. *With Death Came Liberty: The Archaeology and History of the Sam Goode Cemetery, Mecklenburg County, Virginia.* Report prepared for U.S. Army Corps of Engineers, Savannah District, by New South Associates, Stone Mountain, Ga.

Crossland, L. B., and M. Posnansky. 1978. "Pottery, People, and Trade at Begho, Ghana." In *The Spatial Organization of Culture,* edited by I. Hodder, 77–89. London: Duckworth.

Crowley, D. 1956. "The Traditional Masques of Carnival." *Caribbean Quarterly* 3: 42–90.

"The Crusade against Obeah." 1901. *The Daily Gleaner,* 18 January, 7.

Cudjoe, D. 1971. "The Du-Legba Cult among the Ewe of Ghana." *Baessler-Archiv* 19 (2): 187–206.

Dagan, E. A. 1990. *African Dolls: For Play and for Magic.* Montreal: Galerie Amrad.

Dallas, R. C. 1803. *History of the Maroons.* London: T. N. Longman and O. Rees.

Dance, D. C. 1985. *Folklore from Contemporary Jamaicans.* Knoxville: The University of Tennessee Press.

Dapper, O. 1686. *Description de l'Afrique, contenant les noms, la situation & les confins de toutes ses parties, leurs rivieres, leurs villes & leurs habitations, leurs plantes & leurs animaux, les moeurs, les coûtumes, la langue, les richesses, la religion & le gouvernement de ses peoples.* Amsterdam: Wolfgang, Waesberge, Boom and van Someren.

Datta, A. K., and R. Porter. 1971. "The Asafo System in Historical Perspective." *Journal of African History* 12 (2): 279–297.

David, M. 1983. "Poterie domestique et rituelle du Sud-Bénin: Etude ethnoarchéologique." *Archives suisses d'anthropologie générale* 47 (2): 121–184.

Davidson, J. M. 2004a. Mediating Race and Class through the Death Experience: Power Relations and Resistance Strategies on an African-American Community, Dallas Texas (1869–1907). Ph.D. dissertation, University of Texas, Austin.

———. 2004b. "Rituals Captured in Context and Time: Charm Use in North Dallas Freedman's Town 1869–1907, Dallas, Texas." *Historical Archaeology* 38 (2): 22–54.

———. 2009. "African Spiritualities in the New World: Conjuring and Counter Charms at Kingsley Plantation, Fort George Island, Duval County, Florida 1814–1839." Paper presented at the Conference on Society for Historical and Underwater Archaeology, Toronto, 6–11 January.

———. 2010. "Keeping the Devil at Bay: The Shoe on the Coffin Lid and Other Grave Charms in 19th and Early 20th Century America." *International Journal of Historical Archaeology* 14 (4): 614–649.

Davis, O. 1997. "The Door of No Return: Reclaiming the Past through the Rhetoric of Pilgrimage." *Western Journal of Black Studies* 21 (3): 156–161.

Deagan, K. 1998. "Transculturation and Spanish American Ethnogenesis: The Archaeological Legacy of the Quincentenary." In *Studies in Culture Contact: Interaction, Culture, Change, and Archaeology,* edited by J. Cusick, 23–43. Carbondale: Center for Archaeological Investigations, Southern Illinois University Press.

———. 2002. *Artifacts of the Spanish Colonies of Florida and the Caribbean, 1500–1800,* Vol. 2, *Portable Personal Possessions.* Washington, D.C.: Smithsonian Institution Press.

Dean, C. 1983. "The Individual and the Ancestral: *Ikegobo* and *Ukhurhe.*" In *The Art of Power, The Power of Art: Studies in Benin Iconography,* edited by P. Ben-Amos and A. Rubin, 33–40. Los Angeles: Museum of Cultural History, University of California at Los Angeles.

De Barros, J. 2007. "Dispensers Obeah and Quackery: Medical Rivalries in Post-Slavery British Guiana." *Social History of Medicine* 20 (2): 243–261.

De Barros, P. 1986. "A Quantified, Chronologically Controlled, Regional Approach to a Traditional Iron Production Center in West Africa." *Africa* 56 (2): 148–174.

De Booy, T., and J. Faris. (1918) 1970. *The Virgin Islands: Our New Possessions and the British Islands.* Westport, Conn.: Negro University Press.

De Coppet, D., ed. 1992. *Understanding Ritual.* London: Routledge.

DeCorse, C. 2001. *An Archaeology of Elmina: Africans and Europeans on the Gold Coast, 1400–1900.* Washington, D.C.: Smithsonian Institution Press.

De Groot, S. W. (1973) 1996. "Bush Negro Chiefs Visit Africa: Diary of an Historic Trip." In *Maroon Societies: Rebel Slave Communities in the Americas,* edited by R. Price, 389–398. 3rd ed. Baltimore: The Johns Hopkins University Press.

Deku, A. 1993. "The Truth about Castles in Ghana and Africa." *Weekly Spectator,* 8 May, 5.

Denbow, J. 1999. "Heart and Soul: Glimpses of Ideology and Cosmology in the Iconography of Tombstones from the Loango Coast of Central America." *Journal of American Folklore* 112 (445): 404–423.

De Sandoval, A. (1627) 1956. *Instauranda aethiopum salute; el mundo de la esclavitud negra en América.* Edited by Angel Valtierra. Bogotá: Empresa Nacional de Publicaciones.

Desch-Obi, T. J. 2008. *Fighting for Honor: The History of African Martial Art Traditions in the Atlantic World.* Columbia: University of South Carolina Press.

Deschamps, H. 1960. *Les religions de l'Afrique Noire.* Paris: Presses universitaires de France.

Descola, P. 2009. "Human Natures." *Social Anthropology* 17 (2): 145–157.

Desmangles, L. 1992. *The Faces of the Gods: Vodou and Roman Catholicism in Haiti.* Chapel Hill: University of North Carolina Press.

Devenish, D. 1997. "Exhibiting the Slave Trade." *Museum International* 49, 3: 49–52.

Devisch, R. 1991. "Symbol and Symptom among the Yaka of Zaire." In *Body and Space,* edited by A. Jacobson-Widding, 283–302. Uppsala, Sweden: Uppsala University Press.

Dewey, J. (1910) 1997. *The Influence of Darwin on Philosophy and Other Essays.* Amherst, N.Y.: Prometheus Books.

———. 1939. *The Theory of Valuation.* Chicago: University of Chicago Press.

Diamond, J. E. 2006. "Owned in Life, Owned in Death: The Pine Street African and African-American Burial Ground in Kingston, New York." *Northeastern Historical Archaeology* 35 (1): 47–62.

Dickens, R. S., and R. L. Blakeley. 1978. "Preliminary Report on Archaeological Investigations in Oakland Cemetery, Atlanta, Georgia." *Conference on Historic Site Archaeology Papers* 13: 286–314.

Dietler, M. 2001. "Theorizing the Feast: Rituals of Consumption, Commensual Politics, and Power in African Contexts." In *Feasts: Archaeological and Ethnographic Perspectives on Food, Politics, and Power,* edited by M. Dietler and B. Hayden, 65–114. Washington, D.C.: Smithsonian Institution Press.

Diouf, S. A. 1998. *Servants of Allah: African Muslims Enslaved in the Americas.* New York: New York University Press.

———. 2003. *Fighting the Slave Trade: West African Strategies.* Athens: Ohio University Press.

Dookhan, I. 1974. *A History of the Virgin Islands of the United States.* Kingston, Jamaica: Canoe Press.

Doris, D. T. 2011. *Vigilant Things: On Thieves, Yoruba Anti-Aesthetics, and the Strange Fates of Ordinary Objects in Nigeria.* Seattle: University of Washington Press.

Douglass, F. 1852. "What to the Slave Is the Fourth of July?" http://teachingamericanhistory.org/library/index.asp?document=162.

D.P.W. 1851. "Replies to Minor Queries: Obeahism." *Notes and Queries: Medium of Inter-Communication for Literary Men, Artists, Antiquaries, Genealogists, etc.* 3 (69): 150.

Drewal, H. J. 1996. "Mami Wata Shrines: Exotica and the Construction of Self." In *African Material Culture,* edited by M. J. Arnoldi, C. M. Greary, and K. L Hardin, 308–333. Bloomington: Indiana University Press.

———. 1997. "Art or Accident: Yoruba Body Artists and Their Deity Ogun." In *Africa's Ogun: Old World and New,* edited by S. Barnes, 235–259. 2nd ed. Bloomington: Indiana University Press.

———. 2008. *Sacred Waters: Arts for Mami Wata and Other Divinities in Africa and the Diaspora.* Bloomington: Indiana University Press.

Drewal, H. J., and J. Mason. 1998. *Beads, Body, and Soul: Art and Light in the Yoruba Universe.* Los Angeles: Fowler Museum of Cultural History, University of California at Los Angeles.

Drewal, H. J., H. Pemberton, and R. Abiodun. 1989. *Yoruba: Nine Centuries of African Art and Thought.* New York: Center of African Art and H. Abrams.

Drewal, H. J., and E. Schildkrout. 2009. *Dynasty and Divinity: Ife Art in Ancient Nigeria.* New York: Museum of African Art.

Drewal, M. T. 1992. *Yoruba Ritual: Performers, Play, Agency.* Bloomington: Indiana University Press.

Dubisch, J. 1995. *In a Different Place: Pilgrimage, Gender, and Politics of a Greek Island Shrine.* Princeton, N.J.: Princeton University Press.

Du Bois, W. E. B. (1903) 1982. *The Souls of Black Folk: Essays and Sketches.* New York: New American Library.

Dundes, A., ed. 1981. *The Evil Eye: A Folklore Casebook.* New York: Garland.

Durkheim, É. (1912) 1961. *The Elementary Forms of the Religious Life.* Translated by Joseph Ward Swain. New York: Collier Books.

Eade, J., and A. Sallnow. 2000. "Introduction." In *Contesting the Sacred: The Anthropology of Christian Pilgrimage,* edited by J. Eade and A. Sallnow, 1–29. Urbana: University of Illinois Press.

Echard, N. 1992. "A propos de le metallurgie systeme, technique organization sociale et histoire." *Etudes Nigeriennes* 52: 1–38.

Edwards, Y. 1998. "'Trash' Revisited." In *Keep Your Head to the Sky: Interpreting African American Home Ground,* edited by G. Gundaker, 245–329. Knoxville: University of Tennessee Press.

Eglash, R. 1999. *African Fractals: Modern Computing and Indigenous Design.* New Brunswick, N.J.: Rutgers University Press.

Ehret, C. 2002. *The Civilizations of Africa: A History to 1800.* Charlottesville: University of Virginia Press.

Elder, J. D. 1988. *African Survivals in Trinidad and Tobago.* London: Karia Press.

Elliott, J. H. 2006. *Empires of the Atlantic World: Britain and Spain in America, 1492–1830.* New Haven, Conn.: Yale University Press.

Eltis, D. 2000. *The Rise of African Slavery in the Americas.* Cambridge: Cambridge University Press.

———. 2009. Voyages: The Trans-Atlantic Slave Trade Database, http://www.slavevoyages.org/tast/database/search.faces.

Eltis, D., and D. Richardson, eds. 1997. *Routes to Slavery: Direction, Ethnicity, and Mortality in the Atlantic Slave Trade.* London: Frank Cass.

Eluyemi, O. 1977. "Excavations at Isoya." *West African Journal of Archaeology* 7: 97–115.

Elworthy, F. T. 1895. *The Evil Eye: An Account of This Ancient and Widespread Superstition.* London: John Murray.

———. 1900. *Horns of Honour and Other Studies in the By-Ways of Archaeology.* London: John Murray.

Epperson, T. 2001. "'A Separate House for the Christian Slaves, One for the Negro Slaves': The Archaeology of Race and Identity in Late Seventeenth-Century Virginia." In *Race and the Archaeology of Identity,* edited by C. E. Orser, Jr., 54–70. Salt Lake City: University of Utah Press.

Espenshade, C. 2007. "A River of Doubt: Marked Colonoware, Underwater Sampling, and Questions of Inference." *African Diaspora Archaeology Newsletter,* March, http://www.diaspora.uiuc.edu/news0307/news0307.html#2.

Essabal, P. 1961. "The Door and the Threshold in Armenian Folklore." *Western Folklore* 204: 265–273.

Evans, D., D. R. Rice, and J. K. Partin. 1969. "Parallels in West African, West Indian and North Carolina Folklore." *North Carolina Folklore* 1969: 77–84.

Evans-Pritchard, E. 1929. "The Morphology and Function of Magic: A Comparative Study of Trobriand and Zande Ritual and Spells." *American Anthropologist* 31: 619–641.

Eyo, E. 1974. Recent Excavations at Ife and Owo, and Their Implications for Ife, Owo, and Benin Studies. 3 vols. Ph.D. dissertation, University of Ibadan, Nigeria.

Fairfield Four. 1992. *Standing in the Safety Zone.* Audio CD. Los Angeles: Warner Brothers.

Falcolnbridge, A. 1788. *An Account of the Slave Trade on the Coast of Africa.* London: J. Philips.

Fales, M. G. 1995. *Jewelry in America, 1600–1900.* Woodbridge, England: Antique Collectors' Club.

Falola, T., and A. Adebayo. 2000. *Culture, Politics and Money among the Yoruba.* New Brunswick, N.J.: Transaction.

Falola, T., and M. D. Childs. 2004. *The Yoruba Diaspora in the Atlantic World.* Bloomington: Indiana University Press.

Farrow, A., A. Lang, and J. Frank. 2005. *Complicity: How the North Promoted, Prolonged, and Profited from Slavery.* New York: Ballantine Books.

Feld, S., and K. Basso. 1996. "Introduction." In *Senses of Place,* edited by S. Feld and K. Basso, 3–11. Santa Fe: School of American Research Press.

Feng, P. 2002. "Rituals of Rememory: Afro-Caribbean Religions in Myal and It Begins with Tears." *MELUS* 27 (1): 149–175.

Fenn, E. 1985. "Honoring the Ancestors: Kongo-American Graves in the American South." *Southern Exposure* 13 (8): 42–47.

Fennell, C. C. 2000. "Conjuring Boundaries: Inferring Past Identities from Religious Artifacts." *International Journal of Historical Archaeology* 44: 281–313.

———. 2007a. "Bakongo Identity and Symbolic Expression in the Americas." In *Archaeology of Atlantic Africa and the African Diaspora,* edited by A. Ogundiran and T. Falola, 199–232. Bloomington: Indiana University Press.

———. 2007b. *Crossroads and Cosmologies: Diaspora and Ethnogenesis in the New World.* Gainesville: University Press of Florida.

———. 2011. "Early African America: Archaeological Studies of Significance and Diversity." *Journal of Archaeological Research* 19: 1–49.

Ferguson, L. 1992. *Uncommon Ground: Archaeology and Early African America, 1650–1800.* Washington, D.C.: Smithsonian Institution Press.

———. 1994. "Hidden Testimony: A Perspective from Historical Archaeology on African Americans and Cemeteries in Old-Salem, Retrospect and Results of the 1993 Project." Old Salem, Inc., Winston-Salem, N.C.

———. 1999. "'The Cross Is a Magic Sign': Marks on Eighteenth-Century Bowls from South Carolina." In *"I, Too, Am America": Archaeological Studies of African-*

American Life, edited by T. Singleton, 116–131. Charlottesville: University Press of Virginia.

———. 2007. "Comments on Espenshade's 'A River of Doubt: Marked Colonoware, Underwater Sampling, and Questions of Inference.'" *African Diaspora Archaeology Newsletter,* March, http://www.diaspora.uiuc.edu/news0307/news0307.html#3.

———. 2011. *God's Fields: Landscape, Religion, and Race in Moravian Wachovia.* Gainesville: University Press of Florida.

Fett, S. M. 2002. *Working Cures: Healing, Health and Power on Southern Slave Plantations.* Chapel Hill: University of North Carolina Press.

Finley, C. 2004. "Authenticating Dungeons, Whitewashing Castles: The Former Sites of the Slave Trade on the Ghanaian Coast." In *Architecture and Tourism: Perception, Performance, and Place,* edited by D. M. Lasansky and B. McLaren, 109–126. New York: Berg.

Firth, R. 1973. *Symbols: Public and Private.* Ithaca, N.Y.: Cornell University Press.

Flanzbaum, H. 1999. "Introduction: The Americanization of the Holocaust." In *The Americanization of the Holocaust,* edited by H. Flanzbaum, 1–17. Baltimore: Johns Hopkins University Press.

Fogelin, L. 2007. "The Archaeology of Religious Ritual." *Annual Review of Anthropology* 36: 55–71.

"Folklore of the Negroes of Jamaica." 1904a. *Folklore* 15 (1): 87–94.

"Folklore of the Negroes of Jamaica, II." 1904b. *Folklore* 15 (2): 206–214.

"Folklore of the Negroes of Jamaica Continued." 1905. *Folklore* 16 (1): 58–77.

Fortes, M. 1934a. Unpublished Notebook, Golib 2, Book 37. Manuscripts Room, University Library, University of Cambridge.

———. 1934b. Unpublished Notebook, M3 Golib. Manuscripts Room, University Library, University of Cambridge.

———. 1945. *The Dynamics of Clanship among the Tallensi.* Oosterhout, Netherlands: Anthropological Publications.

———. 1987. *Religion, Morality and the Person.* Edited by Jack Goody. Cambridge: Cambridge University Press.

Fowler, F. G., and H. W. Fowler. 1986. *The Oxford Handy Dictionary.* London: Chancellor Press.

Fowler, I. 1990. Babungo: A Study of Iron Production, Trade and Power in a Nineteenth Century Ndop Plain Chiefdom Cameroon. Ph.D. dissertation, University College London.

Franklin, C. L. 1989. *Give Me This Mountain: Life History and Selected Sermons.* Edited by J. T. Titon. Champaign: University of Illinois Press.

Fu-Kiau, K. K. B. 2001. *African Cosmology of the Bantu-Kongo: Tying the Spiritual Knot, Principles of Life and Living.* 2nd ed. Brooklyn: Athelia Henrietta Press.

Furley, O. 1965. "Moravian Missionaries and Slaves in the West Indies." *Caribbean Studies* 5: 3–16.

Gadamer, H. 1976. *Philosophical Hermeneutics.* Berkeley: University of California Press.

Games, A. 2006. "Atlantic History: Definitions, Challenges, and Opportunities." *American Historical Review* 111 (3): 741–757.

Gardner, W. 1878. *A History of Jamaica from Its Discovery by Christopher Columbus to the Present Time*. London: Elliot Stock.

Garfinkel, H. 1991. *Studies in Ethnomethodology.* Boston: Polity Press.

Garlake, P. 1974. "Excavations at Obalara's Land, Ife, Nigeria." *West African Journal of Archaeology* 4: 111–148.

———. 1977. "Excavations on the Woye Asiri Family Land in Ife." *West African Journal of Archaeology* 7: 57–95.

Garman, R. 1994. "Viewing the Color Line through the Material Culture of Death." *Historical Archaeology* 28 (3): 74–93.

Gaspar, D. 1993. *Bondmen and Rebels: A Study of Master-Slave Relations in Antigua.* Durham, N.C.: Duke University Press.

Gazin-Schwartz, A. 2001. "Archaeology and Folklore of Material Culture, Ritual, and Everyday Life." *International Journal of Historical Archaeology* 5 (4): 263–280.

Geertz, C. 1973. *The Interpretation of Culture.* New York: Basic Books.

Gell, A. 1998. *Art and Agency: An Anthropological Theory.* Oxford: Clarendon Press.

Genovese, E. 1976. *Roll, Jordan, Roll: The World the Slaves Made.* New York: Vintage Books.

Georgia Writers Project. 1940. *Drums and Shadows: Survival Studies among the Georgia Coastal Negroes.* Athens: University of Georgia Press.

Geschiere, P. 1997. *The Modernity of Witchcraft: Politics and the Occult in Postcolonial Africa.* Charlottesville: University Press of Virginia.

Giddens, A. 1984. *The Constitution of Society: Outline of the Theory of Structuration.* Berkeley: University of California Press.

Gillespie, S. D. 2008. "History in Practice: Ritual Deposition at La Venta Complex A." In *Memory Work: Archaeologies of Material Practices,* edited by B. J. Mills and W. H. Walker, 109–136. Santa Fe: School for Advanced Research Press.

Gilroy, P. 1993. *The Black Atlantic: Modernity and Double Consciousness.* Cambridge, Mass.: Harvard University Press.

Goffman, E. 1959. *The Presentation of Self in Everyday Life.* New York: Anchor.

Gomez, M. A. 1998. *Exchanging Our Country Marks: The Transformation of African Identities in the Colonial and Antebellum South.* Chapel Hill: University of North Carolina Press.

———. 2006. "Introduction—Diasporic Africa: A View from History." In *Diasporic Africa: A Reader,* edited by M. A. Gomez, 1–23. New York: New York University Press.

Gómez, P. F. 2010. Bodies of Encounter: Health, Illness and Death in the Early Modern African Spanish Caribbean. Ph.D. dissertation, Vanderbilt University.

———. 2013. "The Circulation of Bodily Knowledge in the Seventeenth-Century Spanish Caribbean." *Social History of Medicine* 26: 383–402.

Gordon, R. B. 1996. *American Iron, 1607–1900.* Baltimore: Johns Hopkins University Press.

Gosden, C. 2005. "What Do Objects Want?" *Journal of Archaeological Method and Theory* 12: 193–211.

Goucher, C. 1993. "African Metallurgy in the Atlantic World." *African Archaeological Review* 11: 197–215.

Goucher, C., and E. K. Agorsah. 2011. "Excavating the Roots of Resistance: The Significance of Maroons in Jamaican Archaeology." In *Out of Many, One People: The Historical Archaeology of Colonial Jamaica*, edited by J. Delle, M. Hauser, and D. Armstrong, 144–159. Tuscaloosa: University of Alabama Press.

Goucher, C., C. Herbert, and C. Saltman. 1986. *The Blooms of Banjeli: Technology and Gender in African Ironworking.* Video. Watertown, Mass.: Documentary Educational Resources.

Graham, E. 1912. *The Passin' on Party.* Chicago: McClurg.

Grant, S. 2006. "Landscapes of Memory." *History Today* 56 (3): 18–20.

Gray, P., and K. Oliver. 2001. "The Memory of Catastrophe." *History Today* 51 (2): 9–15.

Green, E. C. 1978. "Winti and Christianity: A Study of Religious Change." *Ethnohistory* 25 (3): 251–276.

Greene, S. 1997. "Crossing Boundaries/Changing Identities: Female Slaves, Male Strangers, and Their Descendants in Nineteenth- and Twentieth-Century Anlo." In *Gendered Encounters: Challenging Cultural Boundaries and Social Hierarchies in Africa*, edited by M. Grosz-Ngate and O. H. Kokole, 23–41. London: Routledge.

Gundaker, G. 1993. "Tradition and Innovation in African American Yards and Gardens in the Southeastern United States." *African Arts* 26 (2): 58–71, 94–96.

———. 1998a. *Keep Your Head to the Sky: Interpreting African American Home Ground.* Charlottesville: University Press of Virginia.

———. 1998b. *Signs of Diaspora/Diaspora of Signs: Literacies, Creolization, and Vernacular Practice in African America.* New York: Oxford University Press.

———. 2001. "At Home on the Other Side: African American Burials as Commemorative Landscapes." In *Places of Commemoration: Search for Identity and Landscape Design*, edited by J. Wolschke-Bulman, 27–54. Washington, D.C.: Dumbarton Oaks.

———. 2011. "The Kongo Cosmogram in Historical Archaeology and the Moral Compass of Dave the Potter." *Historical Archaeology* 45 (2): 176–183.

Gundaker, G., and J. McWillie. 2006. *No Space Hidden: The Spirit of African American Yards.* Knoxville: University of Tennessee Press.

Gus, J. W. 2004. *Savannah's Laurel Grove Cemetery.* Charleston: Arcadia Publishers.

Guyer, J. 1993. "Wealth in People and Self-Realization in Equatorial Africa." *Man*, new series, 28 (2): 243–265.

———. 2004. *Marginal Gains: Monetary Transactions in Atlantic Africa.* Chicago: University of Chicago Press.

Guyer, J., and E. Belinga. 1995. "Wealth in People as Wealth in Knowledge: Accumulation and Composition in Equitorial Africa." *Journal of African History* 36: 91–120.

Haagensen, R. 1994. "Description of the Island of St. Croix." In *Kamina Folk: Slavery and Slave Life in the Danish West Indies*, edited by G. Tyson and A. Highfield, 29–46. St. Croix: Virgin Islands Humanities Council.

Hair, P. E., A. Jones, and R. Law, eds. 1992. *Barbot on Guinea: The Writings of Jean Barbot on West Africa 1678–1712, Volume II of II.* London: Ashgate.

Halbwachs, M. 1992. *On Collective Memory.* Chicago: University of Chicago Press.

Hall, G. M. 1992. *Africans in Colonial Louisiana: The Development of Afro-Creole Culture in the Eighteenth Century.* Baton Rouge: Louisiana State University Press.
———. 2005. *Slavery and African Ethnicities in the Americas: Restoring the Links.* Chapel Hill: University of North Carolina Press.
Hall, N. 1992. *Slave Society in the Danish West Indies.* Baltimore: Johns Hopkins University Press.
Hallam, E., and J. Hockey. 2001. *Death, Memory and Material Culture.* Oxford: Berg.
Hallett, R., ed. 1984. *The Niger Journal of Richard and John Lander, Travelers and Explorers.* London: Routledge and Kegan Paul.
Hallgren, R. 1995. *The Vital Force.* Lund, Sweden: Lund Studies in African and Asian Religions.
Hamilton, J. 1967. *History of the Moravian Church: The Renewed Unitas Fratrum, 1722–1957.* Bethlehem, Penn.: Interprovincial Board of Christian Education, Moravian Church in America.
Hansmann, L., and L. Kriss-Rettenbeck. 1966. *Amulett und Talisman: Erscheinungsform und Geschichte.* Munich: Callwey.
Hardin, K. L., and M. J. Arnoldi. 1996. "Introduction: Efficacy and Objects." In *African Material Culture,* edited by M. J. Arnoldi, C. M. Greary, and K. L Hardin, 1–28. Bloomington: Indiana University Press.
Harms, R. 1981. *River of Wealth, River of Sorrow: The Central Zaire Basin in the Era of the Slave and Ivory Trade.* New Haven, Conn.: Yale University Press.
Harris, C. L. G. 1994. "The True Traditions of My Ancestors." In *Maroon Heritage: Archaeological, Ethnographic and Historical Perspectives,* edited by E. K. Agorsah, 36–63. Kingston, Jamaica: Canoe Press.
Hart, R. 1985a. *Slaves Who Abolished Slavery: Blacks in Bondage.* Vol. 1. Kingston, Jamaica: Institute of Social and Economic Research, University of the West Indies.
———. 1985b. *Slaves Who Abolished Slavery: Blacks in Rebellion.* Vol. 2. Barbados: University of the West Indies Press.
Hartman, S. V. 2007. *Lose Your Mother: A Journey along the Atlantic Slave Route.* New York: Farrar, Straus and Giroux.
Hartsinck, J. J. 1770. *Beschrijving van Guyana of de Wilde Kustin Zuid Amerika.* Amterdam: Gerrit Tielenburg.
Hasty, J. 2002. "Rites of Passage, Routes of Redemption: Emancipation Tourism and the Wealth of Culture." *Africa Today* 49 (3): 47–76.
Hazoumé, P. 1956. *Le pact de sang du Dahomey: Travaux et mémoires de l'Institut d'Ethnologie.* Paris: Institute d'Ethnologie.
Heath, B. 1999. *Hidden Lives: The Archaeology of Slave Life at Thomas Jefferson's Poplar Forest.* Charlottesville: University Press of Virginia.
———. 2003. "Archaeology at Thomas Jefferson's Poplar Forest." *Council for Northeast Historical Archaeology Newsletter* 56: 11–13.
Heath, B., R. Lichtenberger, K. Adams, L. Lee, and E. Paull. 2004. "Poplar Forest Archaeology: Studies in African American Life; Excavations and Analysis of Site A, Southeast Terrace and Site B, Southeast Curtilage, June 2003–June 2004." Report to the Public Welfare Foundation, June 15, 2004. Forest, Va.: Corporation of Jefferson's Poplar Forest.

Hechter-Schulz, K. 1966. "Fertility Dolls: Cults of the Nguni and Other Tribes of the Southern Bantu." *Anthropos* 61 (3–4): 516–528.
Henderson, D. 2009. "Balancing Cultural Considerations and Preservation Priorities in African American Cemeteries." Paper presented at the Nationwide Cemetery Summit, Nashville, Tennessee, 19–21 October.
Herbert, E. 1993. *Iron, Gender, and Power: Rituals of Transformation in African Societies.* Bloomington: Indiana University Press.
Herbert, E., and C. L. Goucher. 1987. *Resource Guide: The Blooms of Banjeli: Technology and Gender in African Ironworking.* Watertown, Mass.: Documentary Educational Resources.
Herskovits, M. J. 1932. "Some Aspects of Dahomean Ethnology." *Africa* 5 (3): 266–296.
Herskovits, M. J. (1941) 1990. *The Myth of the Negro Past.* Boston: Beacon Press.
Herskovits, M. J., and F. Herskovits. 1933. *An Outline of Dahomean Religious Belief.* Menasha, Wis.: American Anthropological Association.
Hess, E. 1983. "A Tale of Two Memorials." *Art in America* 71: 120–127.
Heywood, L. M., ed. 2002. *Central Africans and Cultural Transformations in the American Diaspora.* Cambridge: Cambridge University Press.
Hicks, D., and M. C. Beaudry. 2010. "Introduction: Material Culture Studies: A Reactionary View." In *The Oxford Handbook of Material Culture Studies,* edited by D. Hicks and M. C. Beaudry, 1–21. Oxford: Oxford University Press.
Hijiya, J. A. 1983. "American Gravestones and Attitudes toward Death: A Brief History." *Proceedings of the American Philosophical Society* 127 (5): 339–363.
Hildburgh, W. L. 1906. "Notes on Spanish Amulets." *Folklore* 17 (4): 454–471.
Hill, J. D. 1998. "Violent Encounters: Ethnogenesis and Ethnocide in Long Term Contact Situations." In *Studies in Culture Contact: Interaction, Culture, Change, and Archaeology,* edited by J. Cusick, 146–171. Carbondale: Center for Archaeological Investigations, Southern Illinois University Press.
Hinks, P. 1975. *Nineteenth Century Jewellery.* London: Faber and Faber.
Hodder, I. 1982. *Symbolic and Structural Archaeology.* Cambridge: Cambridge University Press.
———, ed. 1987. *The Archaeology of Contextual Meanings.* Cambridge: Cambridge University Press.
———. 2012. *Entangled: An Archaeology of the Relationships between Humans and Things.* Malden, Mass.: Wiley-Blackwell.
Hogendorn, J., and M. Johnson. 1986. *The Shell Money of the Slave Trade.* Cambridge: Cambridge University Press.
Holl, A. 2000. "500 Years in the Cameroons: Making Sense of the Archaeological Record." In *West Africa during the Slave Trade: Archaeological Perspectives,* edited by C. R. DeCorse, 152–178. New York: Continuum.
Holloway, J. E. 1990. "The Origins of African-American Culture." In *Africanisms in American Culture,* edited by J. E. Holloway, 1–18. Bloomington: Indiana University Press.
———. 2005. *Africanisms in American Culture.* 2nd ed. Bloomington: Indiana University Press.
Holloway, K. F. C. 2002. *Passed On: African American Mourning Stories.* Durham, N.C.: Duke University Press.

Holsey, B. 2008. *Routes of Remembrance: Refashioning the Slave Trade in Ghana.* Chicago: University of Chicago Press.
Hoogbergen, W. 1990. "A History of the Suriname Maroons." In *Resistance and Rebellion: Old and New,* edited by G. B. Shute, 65–102. Studies in Third World Societies, No. 43. College of William and Mary, Williamsburg, Va.
Hopwood, A. 2006. "Measure to Deter *Duppies.*" *Jamaica Gleaner,* 20 April, http://jamaica-gleaner.com/gleaner/20060420/news/news6.html.
House of Commons. 1859. Accounts and Papers: Colonies. West Indies Immigration, vol. 20, session 2, 31 May–13 August, British National Archives, Kew, England.
Howell, A. M. 2007. "'Showers of Arrows': The Reactions and Resistance of the Kasena to Slave Raids in the 18th and 19th Centuries." In *The Transatlantic Slave Trade: Landmarks, Legacies, Expectations,* edited by J. K. Anquandah, 189–209. Accra: Sub-Saharan Publishers.
Huffman, T. 1997. "Architecture and Settlement Patterns." In *Encyclopedia of Pre-Colonial Africa,* edited by J. Vogel, 149–158. Walnut Creek, Cal.: Alta Mira Press.
Hurston, Z. N. (1926) 1997. *Sweat.* Edited by C. A. Wall. New Brunswick, N.J.: Rutgers University Press.
———. (1938) 1990. *Tell My Horse: Voodoo Life in Haiti and Jamaica.* Reprint ed. New York: Harper and Row.
———. 1942. *Dust Tracks on a Road.* Philadelphia: Lippincott.
Hutton, P. 1981. "The History of Mentalities: The New Map of Cultural History." *History and Theory* 20 (3): 237–259.
Hyland, A. D. C. 1995. "Monuments Conservation Practice in Ghana: Issues of Policy and Management." *Journal of Architectural Conservation* 2: 45–62.
Hyland, A. D. C., and G. Intsiful. 2003. "When the Castles Were White, II." Paper presented at the 14th International Council on Monuments and Sites General Assembly and International Symposium, Victoria Falls, Zimbabwe, 27 –31 October.
Idowu, E. B. (1962) 1994. *Olodumare: God in Yoruba Belief.* New York: Wazobia.
Ingold, T. 1988. *What Is an Animal?* London: Unwin Hyman.
———. 2007. "Materials against Materiality." *Archaeological Dialogues* 14 (1): 1–16.
Innis, R. E. 2004. "The Tacit Logic of Ritual Embodiments: Rappaport and Polany between Thick and Thin." *Social Analysis* 48 (2): 195–212.
Insoll, T. 2004. *Archaeology, Ritual, Religion.* New York: Routledge.
———. 2006. "Shrine Franchising and the Neolithic in the British Isles: Some Observations Based upon the Tallensi, Northern Ghana." *Cambridge Archaeological Journal* 16: 223–238.
———. 2007. *Archaeology: The Conceptual Challenge.* London: Duckworth.
———. 2009a. "Materialising Performance and Ritual: Decoding the Archaeology of Shrines in Northern Ghana." *Material Religion* 5: 288–311.
———. 2009b. "Materiality, Belief, Ritual: Archaeology and Material Religion: An Introduction." *Material Religion,* 5: 261–264.
———. 2010a. "Meyer Fortes and Material Culture: The Published Image and the Unpublished Resource." *Journal of the Royal Anthropological Institute,* new series, 16: 572–587.
———. 2010b. "Pots and Earth Cults: The Context and Materiality of Archaeological Ceramics amongst the Talensi of Northern Ghana and Their Interpretive Impli-

cations." In *Heureux qui comme Ulysses a fait un beau voyage: The Movements of People in Space and Time,* edited by B. De Vries, 93–112. Bergen, Norway: Bric Press.

———, ed. 2012. *The Oxford Handbook of the Archaeology of Ritual and Religion.* New York: Oxford University Press.

Insoll, T., B. Kankpeyeng, and R. MacLean. 2009. "The Archaeology of Shrines among the Tallensi of Northern Ghana: Materiality and Interpretative Relevance." In *Shrines in Africa,* edited by A. Dawson, 41–70. Calgary, Alb.: University of Calgary Press.

Insoll, T., B. Kankpeyeng, and S. Nkumbaan. 2012. "Fragmentary Ancestors? Representing Bodies and Persons in a Koma Mound." In *Archaeology of Spiritualities,* edited by C. Morris, A. Peatfield, and K. Rountree, 25–45. New York: Springer.

Isichei, E. 2002. *Voices of the Poor in Africa.* Rochester, N.Y.: Rochester University Press.

"Is Obeahism Increasing." 1893. *The Daily Gleaner,* 23 December, 4.

Israel, F. L., ed. (1897) 1968. *1897 Sears Roebuck Catalogue.* New York: Chelsea House.

Jackson, H. 1997. "Race and the Politics of Medicine in Nineteenth Century, Georgia." In *Bones in the Basement: Post-Mortem Racism in 19th Century Medical Training,* edited by R. L. Blakely and J. M. Harrington, 184–205. Washington, D.C.: Smithsonian Institution Press.

Jacobs, C. F., and A. J. Kaslow. 1991. *The Spiritual Churches of New Orleans: Origins, Beliefs, and Rituals of an African-American Religion.* Knoxville: University of Tennessee Press.

Jacobson-Widding, A. 1979. *Red-White-Black as a Mode of Thought: A Study of Triadic Classification by Colours in the Ritual Symbolism and Cognitive Thought of the Peoples of the Lower Congo.* Uppsala, Sweden: Acta Universitatis Upsaliensis.

———. 1991. "The Encounter with the Water Mirror." In *Body and Space: Symbolic Models of Unity and Division in African Cosmology and Experience,* edited by A. Jacobson-Widding, 177–216. Uppsala, Sweden: Upsaliensis Academiae.

Jadin, L. 1966. *Rivalités luso-néederlandaises au Sohio, Congo, 1600–1675: Tentatives missionaires des récollets flamands et tribulations des capucins italien, 1670–1675.* Brussels: Academia Belgica.

Jadin, L., and C. R. Boxer. 1961. *Le Congo et la secte des Antoiniens: Restauration du royaume sous Pedro IV et la "Saint Antoine" congalaise.* Brussels: Institut Historique Belge de Rome.

Jamieson, R. 1995. "Material Culture and Social Death: African-American Burial Practices." *Historical Archaeology* 29 (4): 39–58.

Janzen, J. M. 1977. "The Tradition of Renewal in Kongo Religion." In *African Religions: A Symposium,* edited by N. S. Booth, Jr., 69–116. New York: NOK Publishers.

———. 1992. *Ngoma: Discourses of Healing in Central and Southern Africa.* Berkeley: University of California Press.

Janzen, J. M., and W. MacGaffey. 1974. *An Anthology of Kongo Religion: Primary Texts from Lower Zaire.* Occasional Publications in Anthropology, No. 5. University of Kansas, Lawrence.

Jeane, D. G. 1978. "The Upland South Cemetery: An American Type." *Journal of Popular Culture* 11 (4): 895–903.

———. 1989. "Folk Art in Rural Southern Cemeteries." *Southern Folklore* 46 (2): 159–174.

Johnson, C., and P. Smith. 1998. *Africans in America: America's Journey through Slavery.* New York: Harcourt Brace.

Johnson, K. 2008. "African Spirit Bundle Found, Hints at U.S. Slave Ritual." *National Geographic News,* 31 October, http://news.nationalgeographic.com/news/2008/10/081031-annapolis-artifact.html.

Johnson, S. 1921. *The History of the Yorubas: From the Earliest Times to the Beginning of the British Protectorate.* Edited by O. Johnson. London: Routledge and Kegan Paul.

Jones, A., and G. MacGregor. 2002. *Colouring the Past: The Significance of Colour in Archaeological Research.* Oxford: Berg.

Jordan, T. G. 1980. "'The Roses So Red and the Lilies So Fair': Southern Folk Cemeteries in Texas." *Southwestern Historical Quarterly* 83 (3): 227–258.

———. 1982. *Texas Graveyards: A Cultural Legacy.* Austin: University of Texas Press.

Joseph, J. W. 2007. "One More Look Into the Water—Colonoware in South Carolina Rivers and Charleston's Market Economy." *African Diaspora Archaeology Newsletter,* June, http://www.diaspora.uiuc.edu/news0607/news0607.html#2.

———. 2011. "'All of Cross'—African Potters, Marks, and Meanings in the Folk Pottery of the Edgefield District, South Carolina." *Historical Archaeology* 45 (2): 134–155.

Joyce, R., and J. Pollard. 2010. "Archaeological Assemblages and Practices of Deposition." In *The Oxford Handbook of Material Culture Studies,* edited by D. Hicks and M. C. Beaudry, 291–309. Oxford: Oxford University Press.

Kamara, G. 2000. "Regaining Our African Aesthetics and Essence through Our African Traditional Religion." *Journal of Black Studies* 304: 502–514.

Kankpeyeng, B. W., and S. N. Nkumbaan. 2008. "Rethinking the Stone Circles of Koma Land: A Preliminary Report on the 2007/2008 Fieldwork at Yikpabongo, Northern Region, Ghana." In *Current Archaeological Research in Ghana,* edited by T. Insoll, 95–102. Oxford: Archaeopress.

———. 2009. "Ancient Shrines? New Insights on the Koma Land Sites of Northern Ghana." In *Crossroads/Carrefour Sahel: Cultural and Technological Developments in First Millennium BC/AD West Africa,* edited by S. Magnavita, L. Koté, P. Breunig, and O. A. Idé, 193–202. Frankfurt: Africa Magna Verlag.

Kankpeyeng, B. W., S. N. Nkumbaan, and T. Insoll. 2011. "Indigenous Cosmology, Art Forms and Past Medicinal Practices: Towards an Interpretation of Ancient Koma Land Sites in Northern Ghana." *Anthropology and Medicine* 18: 205–216.

Kea, R. 1982. *Settlement and Trade and Politics in the Seventeenth Century Gold Coast.* Baltimore: Johns Hopkins University Press.

Kellar, E. 2004. The Construction and Expression of Identity: An Archaeological Investigation of the Laborer Villages at Adrian Estate, St. John, USVI. Ph.D. dissertation, Syracuse University.

Keller, J. D., and C. M. Keller. 1996. *Cognition and Tool Use: The Blacksmith at Work.* Cambridge: Cambridge University Press.

Kelly, J. D., and M. Kaplan. 1990. "History, Structure, and Ritual." *Annual Review of Anthropology* 19: 119–150.

Kelly, K. G. 1995. Transformation and Continuity in Savi, a West African Trade Town: An Archaeological Investigation of Cultural Change on the Coast of Bénin during the Seventeenth and Eighteenth Centuries. Ph.D. dissertation, University of California at Los Angeles.

———. 2001. "Change and Continuity in Coastal Bénin." In *West Africa during the Atlantic Slave Trade: Archaeological Perspectives,* edited by C. R. DeCorse, 81–100. London: Leicester University Press.

Kelly, K. G., and N. L. Norman. 2004. "Medium Vessels and the Longue Durée." In *African Re-Genesis: Confronting Social Issues of the African Diaspora,* edited by J. Haviser and K. McDonald, 223–234. London: University College of London Press.

King, C. 2010. "Separated by Death and Color—The African-American Cemetery at New Philadelphia, Illinois." *Historical Archaeology* 441: 125–137.

King, J. A. 2006. "Historical Archaeology, Identities and Biographies." In *The Cambridge Companion to Historical Archaeology,* edited by D. Hicks and M. Beaudry, 293–313. New York: Cambridge University Press.

Kingsley, C. 1887. *At Last: A Christmas in the West Indies.* London: Macmillan.

The King v. Jack and Prince. 1824. 7 April. St. George General Slave Court, 2/18/6, Jamaica Archives, Spanish Town.

The King v. Polydore. 1831. 28 July. Special Slave Court, St. Dorothy, CO 137/209, British National Archives, Kew, England.

Kissane, J. A. 1998. Wilkes County Georgia Historic Resources Survey. Mary Willis Library, Washington, Ga.

Kolapo, F. J. 2004. "The Igbo and Their Neighbors during the Era of the Atlantic Slave-Trade." *Slavery and Abolition* 25 (1): 114–133.

Kopytoff, I. 1986. "The Cultural Biography of Things: Commodification as Process." In *The Social Life of Things: Commodities in Cultural Perspective,* edited by A. Appadurai, 64–91. Cambridge: Cambridge University Press.

Kreamer, C. M. 2006. "Shared Heritage, Contested Terrain: Cultural Negotiation and Ghana's Cape Coast Castle Museum Exhibition 'Crossroads of People, Crossroads of Trade.'" In *Museum Frictions: Public Cultures/Global Transformations,* edited by I. Karp, C. A. Kratz, L. Szwaja, and T. Ybarra-Frausto, 435–468. Durham, N.C.: Duke University Press.

Kreinath, J., J. Snoek, and M. Stausberg, eds. 2006. *Theorizing Rituals: Issues, Topics, Approaches, Concepts.* Vol. 1. Leiden: Brill.

Kröger, F. 1982. *Ancestor Worship among the Bulsa of Northern Ghana.* Munich, Germany: Klaus Renne.

Küchler, S. 2005. "Materiality and Cognition: The Changing Face of Things." In *Materiality,* edited by D. Miller, 206–231. Durham, N.C.: Duke University Press.

Kuhn, T. 1996. *The Structure of Scientific Revolutions.* 3rd ed. Chicago: University of Chicago Press.

Kyriakidis, E., ed. 2007a. *The Archaeology of Ritual.* Los Angeles: Cotsen Institute of Archaeology, University of California at Los Angeles.

———. 2007b. "Finding Ritual: Calibrating the Evidence." In *The Archaeology of Ritual,* edited by E. Kyriakidis, 9–22. Los Angeles: Cotsen Institute of Archaeology, University of California at Los Angeles.

———. 2007c. "In Search of Ritual." In *The Archaeology of Ritual,* edited by E. Kyriakidis, 1–8. Los Angeles: Cotsen Institute of Archaeology, University of California at Los Angeles.

Labat, J. B. 1730. *Voyage du chevalier des Marchais en Guinée, Isles Voisines, et à Cayenne, fait en 1725, 1726 & 1727.* Paris: Chez Saugrain.
Labouret, H., and P. Rivet. 1929. *Le royaume d'arda et son évangélisation au XVIIe siècle.* Paris: Institut d'Ethnologie.
"The Land We Live In." 1890. *The Daily Gleaner,* 15 November, 4.
Lange, F., and J. S. Handler. 1985. "The Ethnohistorical Approach to Slavery." In *The Archaeology of Slavery and Plantation Life,* edited by T. Singleton, 15–32. Orlando, Fla.: Academic Press.
LaRoche, C. J. 1995. "Beads from the African Burial Ground: A Preliminary Assessment." *Beads: Journal of the Society of Bead Researchers* 6: 3–20.
———. 2002. *Conservation of Materials from the African Burial Ground and the Non-Mortuary Contexts of the 290 Broadway Block (Block 154), Foley Square, Lower Manhattan, New York.* Report prepared for Edwards and Kelcey Engineers, New York, and U.S. General Services Administration, Region 2, New York, by John Milner Associates.
———. 2007a. "Public History at Sites of Protest: Citizenship on the President's House Viewing Platform." *Cross Ties: Mid-Atlantic Regional Center for the Humanities Newsletter* 2 (3): 1–2.
———. 2007b. "Walk with the Ancestors." *Philadelphia Inquirer.* 4 July, http://articles.philly.com/2007-07-04/news/24994685_1_oney-judge-freedom-and-slavery-george-washington.
———. 2011. "Archaeology, the Activist Community, and the Redistribution of Power in New York City." *Archaeologies* 7 (3): 619–634.
———. 2012. "The Anthropology of Archaeology: The Benefits of Public Intervention at African American Archaeological Sites." In *The Oxford Handbook of Public Archaeology,* edited by J. Carman, C. McDavid, and R. Skeates, 629–658. Oxford: Oxford University Press.
LaRoche, C. J., and M. L. Blakely. 1997. "Seizing Intellectual Power: The Dialogue at the New York African Burial Ground." *Historical Archaeology* 31 (3): 84–106.
Latour, B. 1993. *We Have Never Been Modern.* Translated by Catherine Porter. Cambridge, Mass.: Harvard University Press.
———. 1999. *Pandora's Hope: Essays on the Reality of Science.* Cambridge, Mass.: Harvard University Press.
———. 2005. *Reassembling the Social: An Introduction to Actor-Network Theory.* Oxford: Oxford University Press.
Lave, J., and E. Wenger. 1991. *Situated Learning: Legitimate Peripheral Participation.* Cambridge: Cambridge University Press.
Law, R. 1977. *The Oyo Empire c.1600–c.1836: A West African Imperialism in the Era of the Atlantic Slave Trade.* Oxford: Oxford University Press.
———. 1989. "'My Head Belongs to the King': On the Political and Ritual Significance of Decapitation in Pre-Colonial Dahomey." *Journal of African History* 30 (3): 399–415.
———. 1991. *The Slave Coast of West Africa, 1550–1750: The Impact of the Atlantic Slave Trade on an African Society.* Oxford: Clarendon Press.
———. 1995. "Cowries, Gold, and Dollars: Exchange Rate Instability and Domestic Price Inflation in Dahomey in the Eighteenth and Nineteenth Centuries." In *Money*

Matters: Instability, Values, and Social Payments in the Modern History of West African Communities, edited by J. Guyer, 53–73. Portsmouth, N.H.: Heinemann.

———. 2004. *Ouidah: The Social History of a West African Slaving Port, 1727–1892.* Athens: Ohio University Press.

Law 5 of 1898 (Obeah Law). 1898. In *The Laws of Jamaica Passed in a Session Which Began on the 15th Day of March, and Adjourned Sine Die on the 29th Day of August, 1898,* 1–3. Kingston, Jamaica: Government Printing Office, 1898.

Lawal, B. 1996. *Gelede Spectacle: Art, Gender, and Social Harmony in African Culture.* Seattle: University of Washington Press.

Lawler, E., Jr. 2002. "The President's House in Philadelphia: The Rediscovery of a Lost Landscape." *Pennsylvania Magazine of History and Biography* 126 (1): 6–95.

Lawrence, A. W. 1963. *Trade Castles and Forts of West Africa.* London: Jonathan Cape.

Lawrence, R. 1898. *The Magic of the Horseshoe and Other Folk-lore Notes.* Boston: Houghton, Mifflin.

Lawton, S. M. 1939. The Religious Life of South Carolina Coastal and Sea Island Negroes. Ph.D. dissertation, George Peabody College for Teachers.

Layton, R., and J. Thomas. 2001. "Introduction: The Destruction and Conservation of Cultural Property." In *Destruction and Conservation of Cultural Property,* edited by R. Layton, P. G. Stone, and J. Thomas, 1–21. New York: Routledge.

Lazarus-Black, M. 1994. *Legitimate Acts and Illegal Encounters: Law and Society in Antigua and Barbuda.* Washington, D.C.: Smithsonian Institution Press.

Leach, M. 1961. "Jamaican *Duppy* Lore." *Journal of American Folklore* 74 (293): 207–215.

Lee, L. 2013. "Beads, Coins, and Charms at a Poplar Forest Slave Cabin (1833–1858)." *Northeast Historical Archaeology* 40: 104–122.

LeeDecker, C. 2009. "Preparing for an Afterlife on Earth: The Transformation of Mortuary Behavior in Nineteenth-Century North America." In *International Handbook of Historical Archaeology,* edited by T. Majewski and D. Gaimster, 140–157. New York: Springer.

Lenik, S. 2009. "Considering Multiscalar Approaches to Creolization among Enslaved Laborers at Estate Bethlehem, St. Croix, US Virgin Islands." *International Journal of Historical Archaeology* 12 (1): 12–26.

Lentz, C., and P. Nugent. 2000. "Ethnicity in Ghana: A Comparative Perspective." In *Ethnicity in Ghana,* edited by C. Lentz and P. Nugent, 1–28. Basingstoke, England: Macmillan.

Leon, R. 2005. "Rodney Leon Tapped to Design National Historic Landmark; Winner to Create Memorial for 17th- and 18th-Century Africans." EXODUS Online, 9 May, http://www.exodusnews.com/HISTORY/History025.htm.

Leone, M. P. 2005. *The Archaeology of Liberty in an American Capital: Excavations in Annapolis.* Berkeley: University of California Press.

Leone, M. P., and G. Fry, 1999. "Conjuring in the Big House Kitchen: An Interpretation of African American Belief Systems Based on the Uses of Archaeology and Folklore Sources." *Journal of American Folklore* 112 (445): 372–403.

Leone, M. P., G. Fry, and T. Ruppel. 2001. "Spirit Management among Americans of African Descent." In *Race and the Archaeology of Identity,* edited by C. E. Orser, Jr., 143–157. Salt Lake City: University of Utah Press.

Leone, M., C. LaRoche, and J. Babiarz. 2005. "The Archaeology of Black Americans in Recent Times." *Annual Review of Anthropology* 34: 575–598.

Lester, J. 1972. *The Knee High Man and Other Tales.* New York: Penguin.

Levine, L. 2007. *Black Culture and Black Consciousness: Afro-American Folk Thought from Slavery to Freedom.* New York: Oxford University Press.

Lévi-Strauss, C. (1949) 1971. *The Elementary Structures of Kinship.* Richmond, Va.: Beacon Press.

———. 1981. *The Naked Man.* New York: Harper and Row.

Lewis, G. 1980. *Day of Shining Red.* Cambridge: Cambridge University Press.

———. 2002. "Magic, Religion and the Rationality of Belief." In *Companion Encyclopedia of Anthropology,* edited by T. Ingold, 563–590. London: Routledge.

Lewis, M. G. 1861. *Journal of Residence among the Negroes in the West Indies.* London: John Murray.

Libretto, H. R. M. 1990. "The Maroon in Cuban and Jamaican Literature." In *Caribbean Literature in Comparison,* edited by J. Pereira, 9–30. Kingston, Jamaica: Institute of Caribbean Studies, University of the West Indies.

Lightbrown, R. W. 1992. *Mediaeval European Jewellery.* London: Trustees of the Victoria and Albert Museum.

Lindsay, A., ed. 1996. *Santeria Aesthetics in Contemporary Latin American Art.* Washington, D.C.: Smithsonian Institution Press.

Lindsey, W. C. 1959. *A History of Washington, Wilkes County, Georgia.* Washington, Ga: N.p. Copy on file in the Mary Willis Library Special Collections, Washington, Ga.

Linebaugh, P., and M. Rediker. 2000. *The Many-Headed Hydra: Sailors, Slaves, Commons and the Hidden History of Revolution Atlantic.* Boston: Beacon Press.

Linenthal, E. T. 1995. *Preserving Memory: The Struggle to Create America's Holocaust Museum.* New York: Viking.

Little, B. J. 1992. "Explicit and Implicit Meanings in Material Culture and Print Culture." *Historical Archaeology* 26 (3): 85–94.

Liverpool, H. 2001. *Rituals of Power and Rebellion: The Carnival Tradition in Trinidad and Tobago, 1763–1962.* Chicago: Research Associates School Times Publications.

Long, C. M. 2001. *Spiritual Merchants: Religion, Magic, and Commerce.* Knoxville: University of Tennessee Press.

Long, E. (1774) 1970. *The History of Jamaica; or, General Survey of the Antient and Modern State of That Island with Reflections on Its Situation, Settlements, Inhabitants, Climate, Products, Commerce, Laws, and Government.* 3 vols. London: T. Lowndes. Reprint London: F. Cass.

Lorenz, C. A. 1987. "The Ishan Cult of the Hand." *African Arts* 20 (4): 70–91.

Lovejoy, P. 1997. "The African Diaspora: Revisionist Interpretations of Ethnicity, Culture, and Religion under Slavery." *Studies in the World History of Abolition and Emancipation,* 2 (1), http://ejournalofpoliticalscience.org/diaspora.html.

Macdonald, S. 2005. "Commemorating the Holocaust: Reconfiguring National Identity in the Twenty-First Century." In *The Politics of Heritage: The Legacies of Race,* edited by J. Littler and R. Naidoo, 49–68. London: Routledge.

MacGaffey, W. 1970. "The Religious Commissions of the BaKongo." *Man,* new series, 5 (1): 27–38.

———. 1977. "The Black Loincloth and the Son of Nzambi Mpungu." In *Forms of Folklore in Africa: Narrative, Poetic, Gnomic, Dramatic,* edited by B. Lindfors, 144–151. Austin: University of Texas Press.

———. 1986. *Religion and Society in Central Africa: The BaKongo of Lower Zaire.* Chicago: University of Chicago Press.

———. 1991. *Art and Healing of the BaKongo, Commented by Themselves: Minkisi from the Laman Collection.* Stockholm: Folkens Museum-Etnografiska.

———. 2000a. "The Kongo Peoples." In *In the Presence of Spirits: African Art from the National Museum of Ethnology, Lisbon,* edited by F. Herreman, 35–59. New York: Museum for African Art.

———. 2000b. *Kongo Political Culture: The Conceptual Challenge of the Particular.* Bloomington: Indiana University Press.

MacGonagle, E. 2006. "From Dungeons to Dance Parties: Contested Histories of Ghana's Slave Forts." *Journal of Contemporary African Studies* 24 (2): 249–260.

Mackey, A. G. 1919. *An Encyclopedia of Freemasonry.* New York: Masonic History Company.

Madden, R. 1835. *Twelvemonth's Residence in the West Indies during the Transition from Slavery to Apprenticeship.* Vol. 2. Philadelphia: Carey, Lead, and Blanchard.

Magnavita, S., and C. Pelzer. 2000. "Tombs of Kissi: Archaeological Evidence of Early Trade Contacts in Northern Burkino Faso." Paper presented at the 15th Biennial Meeting of the Society of Africanist Archaeologists, Cambridge, England, 12–15 July.

Mali, J. 2003. *Mythistory: The Making of a Modern Historiography.* Chicago: University of Chicago Press.

Malinowski, B. 1948. *Magic, Science and Religion and Other Essays.* Boston: Beacon Press.

Maloney, C. 1976. *The Evil Eye.* New York: Columbia University Press.

Manuel, J. 1998. *Chokwe!: Art and Initiation among Chokwe and Related Peoples.* New York: Prestel-Verlag.

Marcus, G. E., and M. M. J. Fischer. 1999. *Anthropology as Cultural Critique: An Experimental Moment in the Human Sciences.* Chicago: University of Chicago Press.

Maryland Gazette. 1728, 1747, 1750, 1753. Microfilm vols. 1007, 1278, 1279, Maryland State Archives, Baltimore.

Matory, J. L. 2005. *Black Atlantic Religion: Tradition, Transnationalism, and Matriarchy in the Afro-Brazilian Candomblé.* Princeton, N.J.: Princeton University Press.

Matternes, H. B. 2008. "Recovery and Analysis of Burial 1, 93 Queen Street, Charleston. South Carolina." Report prepared for Charleston College Housing by New South Associates, Stone Mountain, Ga.

Matternes, H. B., V. Davis, J. Coco, S. Richey, and S. Lowry. 2012. Hold Your Light on Canaan's Shore: A Historical and Archaeological Investigation of the Avondale Burial Place (9BI164), Bibb County, Georgia. Report prepared for Atkins Global, Inc., Atlanta, Ga., and Georgia Department of Transportation, Atlanta, by New South Associates, Stone Mountain, Ga.

Matternes, H. B., V. Davis, S. McIntyre, M. Umberger, F. Cadle, and K. Lockerman. 2010. "Shimmering Glimpses of the Spirit World: Archaeological Recovery and

Relocation of Two Historic Cemeteries 9CH875 and 9CH1168 at Hunter Army Airfield, Chatham County, Georgia." Report prepared for U.S. Army Corps of Engineers, Savannah District, by New South Associates, Stone Mountain, Ga.

Matternes, H. B., and T. Gillet. 2007. "A Historical and Archaeological Investigation of Possible Cemetery Areas in the Connelly Nature Park, City of East Point, Georgia." Report prepared for City of East Point by New South Associates, Stone Mountain, GA.

Matternes, H. B., and G. C. Smith. 2014. Cemetery Preservation Plan for the Dunwoody Cemetery, McIntosh County, Georgia. Report prepared for The Ceylon Cemetery Trust, Darien, Ga., and Georgia Department of Transportation, Atlanta, by New South Associates, Stone Mountain, Ga.

Mattson, R. C. 1992. "An Architectural Resources Survey and Evaluation for NC-16 Lucia to NC-150 Gaston, Lincoln and Catawba Cemeteries." Report prepared for Post, Buckley, Schuh, and Jernigan, Charlotte, N.C., by Mattston and Associates, Charlotte.

Maupoil, B. 1943. La géomancie à l'ancienne Côte des Esclaves. Thesis, Université de Paris.

May, A. F. 1982. *Surinaams Kruidenboek Sranan Oso Dresi.* Paramaribo, Suriname: Vaco.

Mazama, A. 2005. "The African Burial Ground Project." In *Encyclopedia of Black Studies,* edited by M. K. Asanti and A. Mazama, 33–34. Thousand Oaks, Cal.: Sage Publications.

Mbiti, J. (1969) 1990. *African Religions and Philosophy.* Portsmouth: Heinemann.

McAnany, P. 1995. *Living with the Ancestors: Kinship and Kingship in Ancient Maya.* Austin: University of Texas Press.

McCarthy, J. P. 1997. "Material Culture and the Performance of Sociocultural Identity." In *American Material Culture—The Shape of the Field,* edited by A. S. Martin and J. R. Garrison, 339–379. Knoxville: University of Tennessee Press.

McGuire, R. 1988. "Dialogues with the Dead: Ideology and the Cemetery." In *The Recovery of Meaning: Historical Archaeology in the Eastern United States,* edited by M. P. Leone and P. B. Potter, Jr., 435–480. Washington, D.C.: Smithsonian Institution Press.

McIntosh, R. J., and S. K. McIntosh. 1981. "The Inland Niger Delta before the Empire of Mali: Evidence from Jenne-Jeno." *Journal of African History* 22: 1–22.

McKee, L. 1995. "The Earth Is Their Witness." *The Sciences* 35 (2): 36–41.

McNaughton, P. 1993. *The Mande Blacksmiths: Power, Knowledge and Art in West Africa.* Bloomington: Indiana University Press.

McWilliams, J., and E. Papenfuse. 1969. Final Report Appendix F, "Lot Histories and Maps." NEH Grant H69-178, MD, Maryland Hall of Records, Annapolis.

McWillie, J., and I. Lockpez, ed. 1989. *Another Face of the Diamond: Pathways through the Black Atlantic South.* New York: INTAR Latin American Gallery.

Meader, J. F. 2002. "A Traditional Cultural Property Evaluation for Taylors Creek, Pleasant Grove and Strum-Bay-Stewart Town Cemeteries, Ft. Stewart, Georgia." Report prepared for U.S. Army Corp. of Engineers, Savannah District, by New South Associates, Stone Mountain, Ga.

Medford, E. G., ed. 2009. *Historical Perspectives of the African Burial Ground New York Blacks and the Diaspora.* Vol. 3. Washington, D.C.: Howard University Press, http://www.gsa.gov/graphics/regions/V013HistoricalPerspectivesOfTheNYABG.pdf.

Medical Times and Gazette: A Journal of Medical Science, Literature, Criticism, and News. 1858. Vol. 17. London: John Churchill.

Médiohouan, G. O. 1993. "Vodoun et littérature au Bénin." *Canadian Journal of African Studies* 27 (2): 245–258.

Mendonsa, E. 1982. *The Politics of Divination.* Berkeley: University of California Press.

Mercier, P. 1960. "The Fon of Dahomey." In *African Worlds: Studies in the Cosmological Ideas and Social Values of African Peoples,* edited by D. Forde, 210–234. Oxford: Oxford University Press.

Merrifield, R. 1987. *The Archaeology of Ritual and Magic.* New York: New Amsterdam Books.

Meskell, L., ed. 2005. "Introduction: Object Orientations." In *Archaeologies of Materiality,* edited by L. Meskell, 1–17. Oxford: Blackwell.

Meskell, L., C. Nakamura, R. King, and S. Farid. 2008. "Figured Lifeworlds and Depositional Practices at Çatalhöyük." *Cambridge Archaeological Journal* 18: 139–161.

Meyer, M. W., and R. Smith. 1994. *Ancient Christian Magic: Coptic Texts of Ritual Power.* Princeton, N.J.: Princeton University Press.

Milbauer, J. A. 1989. "Southern Folk Traits in the Cemeteries of Northeast Oklahoma." *Southern Folklore* 46 (2): 175–185.

Miller, J. C. 1999. "History and Africa/Africa and History." *American Historical Review* 104: 1–32.

Mills, B. J., and W. H. Walker. 2008. "Memory, Materiality, and Depositional Practice." In *Memory Work: Archaeologies of Material Practices,* edited by B. J. Mills and W. H. Walker, 3–23. Santa Fe: School for Advanced Research Press.

Mintz, S., and R. Price. 1976. *An Anthropological Approach to the Afro-American Past.* Philadelphia: Institute for the Study of Human Issues.

———. 1992. *The Birth of African-American Culture: An Anthropological Perspective.* Boston: Beacon Press.

Minutes of the Common Council of the City of New York. 1731. Vols. 3–4, New York Public Library.

Mitchell, W. J. T. 2005. *What Do Pictures Want? Essays on the Lives and Loves of Images.* Chicago: University of Chicago Press.

Mitchem, S. Y. 2007. *African American Folk Healing.* New York: New York University Press.

Monroe, J. C., and A. Ogundiran, eds. 2012. *Power and Landscape in Atlantic West Africa: Archaeological Perspectives.* Cambridge: Cambridge University Press.

Moore, B. L., and M. A. Johnson. 2004. *Neither Led nor Driven: Contesting British Cultural Imperialism in Jamaica, 1865–1920.* Kingston, Jamaica: University of the West Indies Press.

Moore, J. B. 1972. "Slave Castles by the Sea." *Colorado Quarterly* 21 (2): 163–174.

Moravian Periodical Accounts. 1798, 1847, 1862, 1911, 1914. Moravian Archives, Northern Province, Bethlehem, Penn.

Morgan, P. D. 1998. *Slave Counterpoint: Black Culture in the Eighteenth-Century Chesapeake and Lowcountry.* Chapel Hill: University of North Carolina Press.

Moseley, B. 1800. *Medical Tracts.* 2nd ed. London: Red Lion Passage.
Mosk, M. 2000. "Cradle of Slavery: A Maryland Destination." *Washington Post,* 2 October, B1, B9.
Moss, L. W., and S. C. Cappannari. 1976. "*Mal'occio, Ayin ha ra, Oculus fascinus, Judenblick:* The Evil Eye Hovers Above." In *The Evil Eye,* edited by C. Maloney, 1–15. New York: Columbia University Press.
Mouer, I. D., M. E. N. Hodges, S. R. Potter, S. L. H. Renaud, I. Noël Hume, D. J. Pogue, M. W. McCartney, and T. E. Davidson. 1999. "Colonoware Pottery, Chesapeake Pipes, and Uncritical Assumptions." In *I, Too, Am America: Studies in African American Archaeology,* edited by T. Singleton, 83–115. Charlottesville: University Press of Virginia.
Mudimbe, V. Y. 1988. *The Invention of Africa: Gnosis, Philosophy, and the Order of Knowledge.* Bloomington: Indiana University Press.
Muir, E. 2005. *Ritual in Early Modern Europe.* Cambridge: Cambridge University Press.
Müller, W. J. (1676) 1968. *Die Africanische auf der Guineischen Cold-Cust Gelegene Landschafft Fetu.* Harburg: Wilhelm Johan Muller. Reprint Graz, Austria: Akademische Druck-u Verlagsanstalt.
Murphy, B. 2005. "Memory, History and Museums." *Museum International* 57 (3): 70–77.
Murphy, J. M., and M. Sanford, eds. 2001. *Osun across the Waters: A Yoruba Goddess in Africa and the Americas.* Bloomington: Indiana University Press.
Murray, D. 2007. "Three Worships, an Old Warlock and Many Lawless Forces: The Court Trial of an African Doctor Who Practised 'Obeah to Cure,' in Early Nineteenth Century Jamaica." *Journal of Southern African Studies* 33 (4): 811–828.
Myhre, K. C. 2006. "The Truth of Anthropology." *Anthropology Today* 22 (6): 16–19.
National Commission on Culture, Ghana. 1994. Report of the Proceedings of the Conference on Preservation of Elmina and Cape Coast Castles and Fort St. Jago in the Central Region Held in Cape Coast Castle, 11–12 May.
Neuwirth, J. L., and M. D. Cochran. 2000. "In My Father's Kingdom There Are Many Houses: Interior Space and Contested Meanings in Nineteenth Century African-American Annapolis." Paper presented at the annual meeting of the Society for Historical Archaeology, Quebec City, 4–9 January.
New Act of Assembly for the Island of Jamaica, to Repeal Several Acts and Clauses of Acts Respecting Slaves. 1788. London: Stephen Fuller.
Noël Hume, I. 1970. *A Guide to Artifacts of Colonial America.* New York: Knopf.
Nooter Roberts, M. 2000. "Proofs and Promises: Setting Meaning before the Eyes." In *Insight and Artistry in African Divination,* edited by J. Pemberton III, 63–82. Washington, D.C.: Smithsonian Institution Press.
Nora, P. 1989. "Between Memory and History: *Les lieux de mémoire.*" *Representations* 26: 7–24.
Norman, N. L. 2000. Through the Medium of the Vessel: An Ethnoarchaeological Investigation of Ritual Earthenwares in Southern Bénin, West Africa. M.A. thesis, University of South Carolina.
———. 2008. An Archaeology of West African Atlanticization: Regional Analysis of the Huedan Palace Districts and Countryside Bénin, 1650–1727. Ph.D. dissertation, University of Virginia.

———. 2009a. "Hueda Whydah Country and Town: Archaeological Perspectives on the Rise and Collapse of an African Atlantic Kingdom." *International Journal of African Historical Studies* 43 (3): 387–410.

———. 2009b. "Powerful Pots, Humbling Holes, and Regional Ritual Processes: Towards an Archaeology of Huedan Vodun, ca. 1650–1727." *African Archaeological Review* 26: 187–218.

Northrup, D. 2000. "Igbo and Myth Igbo: Culture and Ethnicity in the Atlantic World, 1600–1850." *Slavery and Abolition* 21 (3): 1–20.

———. 2002. *Africa's Discovery of Europe 1450–1850.* New York: Oxford University Press.

Norton, G. 1995. "Ghana's Crumbling Heritage." *History Today* 45 (10): 2–3.

Norton, H. 2012. Estate by Estate: The 1733 St. Jan Slave Rebellion. Ph.D. dissertation, Syracuse University.

NPS Archaeology Program. 2007. African Burial Ground National Monument, New York, http://www.nps.gov/history/nR/travel/cultural_diversity/African_Burial_Ground_National_Monument.html.

Obeah and Myalism Law '92. 1892. 28 September. CO 137/550, National Archives, Kew, England.

"Obeah Case in St. Andrew." 1900. *The Daily Gleaner,* 5 October, 7.

"Obeah in St. Elizabeth." 1891. *The Daily Gleaner,* 11 September, 2.

Odita, E. O. 1973. "Universal Cults and Intra-Diffusion: Igbo Ikenga in Cultural Retrospection." *African Studies Review* 16 (1): 73–82.

Oestigaard, T. 2000. *The Deceased's Life Cycle Rituals in Nepal.* British Archaeological Reports S853. Oxford: Archaeopress.

Ogundiran, A. 2001. "Ceramic Spheres and Historical Process of Regional Networks in Yoruba-Edo Region, Nigeria, A.C. 13th–19th Centuries." *Journal of Field Archaeology* 28 (1–2): 27–43.

———. 2002a. *Archaeology and History in Ilare District Central Yorubaland, 1200–1900 AD.* Oxford: Archaeopress.

———. 2002b. "Of Small Things Remembered: Beads, Cowries, and Cultural Translations of the Atlantic Experience in Yorubaland." *International Journal of African Historical Studies* 35 (2–3): 427–457.

———. 2003. "Chronology, Material Culture, and Pathways to the Cultural History of Yoruba-Edo Region, Nigeria, 500 BC–AD 1800." In *Sources and Methods in African History: Spoken, Written, Unearthed,* edited by T. Falola and C. Jennings, 33–79. Rochester, N.Y.: University of Rochester Press.

———. 2007. "Living in the Shadow of the Atlantic World: History and Material Life in a Yoruba-Edo Hinterland, ca. 1600–1750." In *Archaeology of Atlantic Africa and the African Diaspora,* edited by A. Ogundiran and T. Falola, 77–99. Bloomington: Indiana University Press.

———. 2008. "African Atlantic Archaeology and Africana Studies: A Programmatic Agenda." *African Diaspora Archaeology Network Newsletter,* June, 1–25.

———. 2009. "Material Life and Domestic Economy in a Frontier of Oyo Empire during the Mid-Atlantic Age." *International Journal of African Historical Studies* 43 (2): 351–385.

———. 2012. "The Formation of an Oyo Imperial Colony during the Atlantic Age." In *Power and Landscape in Atlantic West Africa,* edited by C. Monroe and A. Ogundiran, 222–252. Cambridge: Cambridge University Press.

———. 2013a. "The End of Prehistory? An Africanist Comment." *American Historical Review* 118 (3): 788–801.

———. 2013b. "Towns and States in Rainforest West Africa." In *Oxford Handbook of African Archaeology,* edited by P. Mitchell and P. Lane, 855–869. Oxford: Oxford University Press.

Ogundiran, A., and T. Falola. 2007. "Pathways in the Archaeology of Transatlantic Africa." In *Archaeology of the Atlantic Africa and the African Diaspora,* edited by A. Ogundiran and T. Falola, 3–45. Bloomington: Indiana University Press.

Okafor, V. 2004. "Rebuilding Continental-Diaspora African Relations: An Examination of Path-Breaking Trends in Governmental, Pan-African and Educational Linkages." In *Critical Perspectives on Historical and Contemporary Issues about Africa and Black America,* edited by T. Adeleke, 139–165. Lewiston, N.Y.: Edwin Mellen Press.

Okofu, I. N. 1999. *Returning Home Ain't Easy but It Sure Is a Blessing!* Cape Coast, Ghana: One Africa Tours and Specialty Services.

Okpoko, P., and P. Obi-Ani. 2005. "The Making of an Oligarchy in the Bight of Biafra: Perspectives on the Aro Ascendancy." In *Precolonial Nigeria: Essays in Honor of Toyin Falola,* edited by A. Ogundiran, 425–446. Trenton, N.J.: Africa World Press.

Oldendorp, C. G. A. (1777) 1987. *A Caribbean Mission.* Edited by J. J. Bossard. Ann Arbor, Mich.: Karoma Publishers.

Olmos, M. F., and L. Paravisini-Gebert, eds. 1997. *Sacred Possessions: Voodoo, Santeria, Obeah and the Caribbean.* New Brunswick, N.J.: Rutgers University Press.

———. 2003. *Creole Religions of the Caribbean: An Introduction from Voudou and Santeria to Obeah and Espiritismo.* New York: New York University Press.

Olupona, J. K. 1991. *Kingship, Religion, and Rituals in a Nigerian Community.* Stockholm: Almqvist and Wiksell International.

Olupona, J. K., and T. Rey. 2009. *Orisa Devotion as World Religion.* Madison: University of Wisconsin Press.

Olwig, K. 1985. *Cultural Adaptation and Resistance on St. John: Three Centuries of Afro-Caribbean Life.* Gainesville: University of Florida Press.

———. 1994. *The Land Is the Heritage: Land and Community on St. John.* Cruz Bay, St. John: St. John Oral History Association.

Ong, W. (1982) 2002. *Orality and Literacy.* Abingdon, England: Routledge.

Orser, C. E., Jr. 1985. "Artifacts, Documents, and Memories of the Black Tenant Farmer." *Archaeology Magazine* 6: 48–53.

———. 1989. "On Plantations and Patterns." *Historical Archaeology* 23 (2): 28–40.

———. 1994. "The Archaeology of African-American Slave Religion in the Antebellum South." *Cambridge Archaeological Journal* 41: 33–45.

Ortiz, F. 1906. *Hampa Afro-Cubana: Los Negros Brujos.* Madrid: Librería de Fernando Fé.

———. 1940. *Contrapunteo Cubano del Tabaco y Azucar.* Havana: Ediciones Ciencias Sociales.

———. 1995. *Cuban Counterpoint: Tobacco and Sugar.* Translated by Harriet de Onís. Durham, N.C.: Duke University Press.

Ortiz, R. 1989. "Ogum and the Umbandista Religion." In *Africa's Ogun: Old World and New,* edited by S. T. Barnes, 90–102. Bloomington: Indiana University Press.

Ortner, S. B. 1973. "On Key Symbols." *American Anthropologist* 75 (5): 1338–1346.

———. 1984. "Theory in Anthropology since the Sixties." *Comparative Studies in Society and History* 26 (1): 126–166.

Osei-Tutu, B. 2002. "The African American Factor in the Commodification of Ghana's Slave Castles." *Transactions of the Historical Society of Ghana,* new series, 6: 115–133.

———. 2003. "Contested Monuments: Research in Ghana." *West African Research Association Newsletter,* Fall, 16–17.

———. 2004. "African American Reactions to the Restoration of Ghana's 'Slave Castles.'" *Public Archaeology* 3: 195–204.

———. 2006. "Contested Monuments: African Americans and the Commoditisation of Ghana's 'Slave Castles.'" In *African Re-genesis: Confronting Social Issues in the African Diaspora,* edited by J. Haviser and K. MacDonald, 9–19. London: University College Press.

———. 2007. "Ghana's 'Slave Castles,' Tourism, and the Social Memory of the Atlantic Slave Trade." In *Archaeology of Atlantic Africa and the African Diaspora,* edited by A. Ogundiran and T. Falola, 185–195. Bloomington: Indiana University Press.

———. 2009. Slave Castles, African American Activism and Ghana's Memorial Entrepreneurism. Ph.D. dissertation, Syracuse University.

O'Shea, J. M. 1984. *Mortuary Variability.* Orlando, Fla.: Academic Press.

Ottenberg, S. 1983. "Igbo and Yoruba Art Contrasted." *African Arts* 16 (2): 48–55, 97–98.

Painter, N. I. 1976. *Exodusters: Black Migration to Kansas after Reconstruction.* New York: Norton.

Palmié, S. 2002. *Wizards and Scientists: Explorations in Afro-Cuban Modernity and Tradition.* Durham, N.C.: Duke University Press.

———. 2013. *The Cooking of History: How Not to Study Afro-Cuban Religion.* Chicago: University of Chicago Press.

Papenfuse, E. C., A. F. Day, D. W. Jordan, and G. Stiverson. 1979. *A Biographical Dictionary of the Maryland Legislature, 1635–1789.* 2 vols. Baltimore: Johns Hopkins University Press.

Parker Pearson, M. 1999. *The Archaeology of Death and Burial.* College Station: Texas A&M University Press.

Parker Pearson, M., and Ramilsonina. 1998. "Stonehenge for the Ancestors: The Stones Pass on the Message." *Antiquity* 72: 308–326.

Parkin, D. 1992. "Ritual as Spatial Direction and Bodily Division." In *Understanding Rituals,* edited by D. de Coppet, 11–25. London: Routledge.

Parmentier, R. 1987. *The Sacred Remains: Myth, History and Polity in Belau.* Chicago: University of Chicago Press.

Parrinder, G. 1976. *African Traditional Religion.* Wesport, Conn.: Greenwood Press.

Parrington, M., D. G. Roberts, P. Stephanie, and J. C. Wideman. 1989. *The First African Baptist Church Cemetery: Bioarchaeology, Demography and Acculturation of Early 19th Century.* Philadelphia: John Milner Association.

Paton, D. 2009. "Obeah Acts: Producing and Policing the Boundaries of Religion in the Caribbean." *Small Axe* 13 (1): 1–18.

Pauketat, T. R., and S. M. Alt. 2004. "The Making and Meaning of a Mississippian Axe-Head Cache." *Antiquity* 78: 779–797.

———. 2005. "Agency in a Postmold? Physicality and the Archaeology of Culture-Making." *Journal of Archaeological Method and Theory* 12: 213–236.

Payne-Jackson, A., and M. C. Alleyne. 2004. *Jamaican Folk Medicine: A Source of Healing.* Kingston, Jamaica: University of the West Indies Press.

Peek, P. M. 1986. "The Isoko Ethics of Ivri." *African Arts* 20 (1): 42–47, 98.

Peel, J. D. Y. 2002. "Gender in Yoruba Religious Change." *Journal of Religion in Africa* 32 (2): 136–166.

Peirce, C. S. 1998. *The Essential Peirce: Selected Philosophical Writings,* vol. 2, 1883–1913. Edited by N. Hauser. Bloomington: Indiana University Press.

Pemberton, J., III. 1975. "Eshu-Elegba: The Yoruba Trickster God." *African Arts* 9 (1): 20–27.

———, ed. 2000. *Insight and Artistry in African Divination.* Washington, D.C.: Smithsonian Institution Press.

Perry, W., J. Howson, and B. Bianco, eds. 2006. *New York African Burial Ground Archaeology Final Report.* Report prepared for U.S. General Services Administration Northeastern and Caribbean Region by Howard University, Washington, D.C.

Perry, W., and J. Woodruff. 2006. "Coins, Shells, Pipes, and Other Items." In *New York African Burial Ground Archaeology Final Report,* vol. 1, edited by W. Perry, J. Howson, and B. Bianco, 419–443. Report prepared for U.S. General Services Administration Northeastern and Caribbean Region by Howard University, Washington, D.C.

Peter, D., M. Prior, M. M. Green, and V. Claw, eds. 2000. *Freedman's Cemetery: A Legacy of a Pioneer Black Community in Dallas Texas.* Austin: Department of Transportation Environmental Affairs Division Archeology Studies Program.

Pettinger, A. 1998. "Introduction." In *Always Elsewhere: Travels of the Black Atlantic,* edited by A. Pettinger, viii–xix. London: Cassell.

Phillippo, J. 1843. *Jamaica Its Past and Present State.* London: W. Clowes and Sons.

Phillips, C. 2000. *The Atlantic Sound.* New York: Vintage International.

Phillips, T. 1732. "A Journal of a Voyage Made in the Hannibal of London, Ann. 1693, 1694." In *A Collection of Voyages and Travels,* 6 vols., edited by A. Churchill and J. Churchill, vol. 6, 173–239. London: John Walthoe.

Pitts, W. 1989. "'If You Caint Get the Boat, Take a Log': Cultural Reinterpretation in the Afro-Baptist Ritual." *American Ethnologist* 16: 279–292.

Pollard, J. 2001. "The Aesthetics of Depositional Practice." *World Archaeology* 332: 315–333.

———. 2008. "Deposition and Material Agency in the Early Neolithic of Southern Britain." In *Memory Works: Archaeologies of Material Practices,* edited by B. Mills and B. Walker, 41–59. Santa Fe: School for Advanced Research Press.

Pollitzer, W. S. 1999. *The Gullah People and Their African Heritage.* Athens: University of Georgia Press.

Poole, R. 1753. *The Beneficent Bee; or, Travelor's Companion.* London: E. Duncumb.

Postma, J. M. 1992. *The Dutch in the Atlantic Slave Trade 1600–1815.* Cambridge: Cambridge University Press.

Powdermaker, H. (1937) 1993. *After Freedom: A Cultural Study in the Deep South.* Reprint ed. Madison: University of Wisconsin Press.

Poynor R., R. Sieber, and B. B. Bishop. 1995. *African Art at the Harn Museum: Spirit Eyes, Human Hands.* Gainesville: University Press of Florida.

"Practiced Obeah, Sent to Prison." 1902. *The Daily Gleaner,* 20 October, 12.

Preucel, R. 2006. *Archaeological Semiotics.* Malden, Mass.: Blackwell.

Price, C. 2009. *Becoming Rasta: Origins of Rastafari Identity in Jamaica.* New York: New York University Press.

Price, R. 2006. "On the Miracle of Creolization." In *Afro-Atlantic Dialogues: Anthropology in the Diaspora,* edited by K. Yelvington, 115–147. New Mexico: School of American Research Press.

Price, R., and S. Price. 2000. *Maroon Arts.* Boston: Beacon Press.

Price-Mars, J. (1928) 1983. So Spoke the Uncle [Ainsi parla l'oncle]. Translated and introduction by M. W. Shannon. Washington, D.C.: Three Continents Press.

Puckett, N. N. (1926) 2003. *Folk Beliefs of the Southern Negroes.* Chapel Hill: University of North Carolina Press. Reprint Whitefish, Mont.: Kessinger Publishing.

Pulsipher, L., and C. Goodwin. 2001. "'Getting the Essence of It': Galways Plantation, Montserrat, West Indies." In *Island Lives: Historical Archaeologies of the Caribbean,* edited by P. Farnsworth, 165–203. Tuscaloosa: University of Alabama Press.

Queen v. Cunningham et al. 1876. Supreme Court of Judicature of Jamaica, 20 November, Jamaica Archives, Spanish Town.

Raboteau, A. J. 2004. *Slave Religion: The Invisible Institution in the Antebellum South.* New York: Oxford University Press.

Rakita, G. F. M., and J. E. Buikstra. 2005. "Introduction." In *Interacting with the Dead: Perspectives on Mortuary Archaeology for the New Millennium,* edited by G. F. M. Rakita, J. E. Buikstra, L. A. Beck, and S. R. Williams, 1–11. Gainesville: University Press of Florida.

Rakita, G. F. M., J. E. Buikstra, L. A, Beck, and S. R. Williams, eds. 2005. *Interacting with the Dead: Perspectives on Mortuary Archaeology for the New Millennium.* Gainesville: University Press of Florida.

Ramos, A. 1934. *O Negro Brasiliero: Ethnographia, religiosa e psychoanalyse.* Rio de Janeiro: Civilizaçao Brasileria.

———. 1939. *The Negro in Brazil.* Translated by Richard Pattee. Washington, D.C.: Associated Publishers.

Rancière, J. 2003 *The Philosopher and His Poor.* Durham, N.C.: Duke University Press.

Ransdell, E. 1995. "Africa's Cleaned-up Slave Castle." *U.S. News and World Report,* 18 September, 33.

Rappaport, R. 1999. *Ritual and Religion in the Making of Humanity.* Cambridge: Cambridge University Press.

Rashford, J. 1986. "The Cotton Tree and the Spiritual Realm in Jamaica." *Jamaica Journal* 18 (1): 49–57.

Rauschenberg, B. L. 1990. "Coffin Making and Undertaking in Charleston and Its Environs, 1705–1820." *Journal of Early Southern Decorative Arts* 161: 18–64.

Rawick, G. P., ed. 1972. *The American Slave: A Composite Autobiography.* Westport, Conn.: Greenwood Press.

Reed, A. 2004. "Sankofa Site: Cape Coast Castle and Its Museum as Markers of Memory." *Anthropology Museum* 27 (1–2): 13–23.

Reeder, John. 1785. Papers, J16. Devon Record Office, Exeter, England.

Reeves, M. 1996. "'To Vex a Teif': An African-Jamaican Ritual Feature." Poster and text presented at the Society for American Archeology Conference on Historical and Underwater Archaeology, New Orleans, La.

———. 1997. "By Their Own Labor"—Slaves' Survival Strategies on Two Jamaican Plantations. Ph.D. dissertation, Syracuse University.

———. 2011. "Household Market Activities among Early Nineteenth-Century Jamaican Slaves." In *Out of Many, One People: The Historical Archaeology of Colonial Jamaica,* edited by J. Delle, M. Hauser, and D. Armstrong, 183–210. Tuscaloosa: University of Alabama Press.

Regina v. Aaron Mowry. 1865. St. Thomas in the Vale Circuit Court, 1A/5/110, Jamaica Archives, Spanish Town.

Regina v. Maria McKewzie. 1880. Attempting to Feloniously Administer Poison, 23 November, St. James Circuit Court, 1A/5/19, Jamaica Archives, Spanish Town.

Reid, P. A. 2006. Between Slavery and Freedom. Ph.D. dissertation, University of Iowa.

Reinhardt, C. A. 2005. *Claims to Memory: Beyond Slavery and Emancipation in the French Caribbean.* New York: Berghahn Books.

Renee, E. P. 2003. *Population and Progress in a Yoruba Town.* Ann Arbor: University of Michigan Press.

Renfrew, C. 1994. "The Archaeology of Religion." In *The Ancient Mind,* edited by C. Renfrew and E. Zubrow, 47–54. Cambridge: Cambridge University Press.

———. 2007. "The Archaeology of Ritual, of Cult, and of Religion." In *The Archaeology of Ritual,* edited by E. Kyriakidis, 109–122. Los Angeles: Cotsen Institute of Archaeology, University of California at Los Angeles.

Renny, R. 1807. *A History of Jamaica with Observations on the Climate Scenery, Trade, Productions, Negroes, Slave Trade, Diseases of Europeans, Customs, Manners, and Dispositions of the Inhabitants.* London: J. Cawthorn.

"Report of the Inspector General." 1916. *The Daily Gleaner,* 24 August, 6.

Return of Registration of Slaves. 1817–1832. Slave Accounts. National Archives, Spanish Town, Jamaica.

Rex v. Bulgin. 1919. Supreme Court of Judicature of Jamaica, Jamaica Archives, Spanish Town.

Rex v. Chambers. 1901. Supreme Court of Judicature of Jamaica, Jamaica Archives, Spanish Town.

Richards, H. 2007. "Distant Garden: Moravian Missions and the Culture of Slavery in the Danish West Indies, 1732–1848." *Journal of Moravian History* 2: 55–74.

Richards, S. L. 2005. "What Is to Be Remembered? Tourism to Ghana's Slave Castle-Dungeons." *Theatre Journal* 57 (4): 617–637.

Richardson, D. 1989. "Slave Exports from West and West-Central Africa, 1700–1810: New Estimates of Volume and Distribution." *Journal of African History* 30 (1): 1–22.

Richey, S., H. B. Matternes, and J. W. Joseph. 2008. "Old School Cemetery: Mapping, Documentation and Interpretation of a Significant Historic African-American Site,

Washington, Georgia." Report prepared by New South Associates for City of Washington, Stone Mountain, Ga.

Ricouer, P. 1976. *Interpretation Theory: Discourse and the Surplus of Meaning.* Fort Worth: Texas Christian University Press.

Rigaud, M. 1985. *Secrets of Voodoo.* Translated by Robert B. Cross. San Francisco: City Lights.

Robben, A. C. G. M., ed. 2005. *Death, Mourning, and Burial: A Cross-Cultural Reader.* Oxford: Wiley-Blackwell.

Roberts, J. M. 1976. "Belief in the Evil Eye in World Perspective." In *The Evil Eye,* edited by C. Maloney, 221–278. New York: Columbia University Press.

Robinson, C. 1994. "Maroons and Rebels a Dilemma." In *Maroon Heritage: Archaeological, Ethnographic and Historical Perspectives,* edited by E. K. Agorsah, 86–93. Kingston, Jamaica: Canoe Press.

Robinson, I. V. 1994. "Is the Black Man's History Being Whitewashed?" *Uhuru* 9: 48–50.

Robinson, M., and M. Walhouse. 1893. "Obeah Worship in the East and West Indies." *Folklore* 4 (2): 207–281.

Roedinger, D. R. 1981. "And Die in Dixie: Funerals, Death and Heaven in the Slave Community, 1700–1865." *Massachusetts Review* 22 (1): 163–183.

Rorty, R. 1981. *Philosophy and the Mirror of Nature.* Princeton, N.J.: Princeton University Press.

Rouse, J. 2007. "Practice Theory." Division I Faculty Publications, Wesleyan University, Paper 43, http://wesscholar.wesleyan.edu/div1facpubs/43.

Rowlands, M. 2007. "The Politics of Identity in Archaeology." In *The Archaeology of Identities. A Reader,* edited by T. Insoll, 59–71. Abingdon, England: Routledge.

Roy, C. D. 1981. "Mossi Dolls." *African Arts* 14 (4): 47–51.

Rucker, W. 2001. "Conjure, Magic, and Power: The Influence of Afro-Atlantic Religious Practices on Slave Resistance and Rebellion." *Journal of Black Studies* 32 (1): 84–103.

———. 2007. *The River Flows On: Black Resistance, Culture, and Identity Formation in Early America.* Baton Rouge: Louisiana State University Press.

Ruffins, F. D. 1992. "Mythos, Memory, and History: African American Efforts, 1820–1990." In *Museum and Communities: The Politics of Public Culture,* edited by I. Karp, C. Mullen, and S. D. Lavine, 506–611. Washington, D.C.: Smithsonian Institution Press.

———. 1997. "Culture Wars Won and Lost: Ethnic Museums on the Mall, Part I: The National Holocaust Museum and the National Museum of the American Indian." *Radical History Review* 68: 79–100.

———. 1998. "Culture Wars Won and Lost, Part II: The National African-American Museum Project." *Radical History Review* 70: 78–101.

———. 2006. "Revisiting the Old Plantation: Reparations, Reconciliation, and Museumizing American Slavery." In *Museum Frictions: Public Cultures/Global Transformations,* edited by I. Carp, C. A. Kratz, L. Szwaja, and T. Ybarra-Frausto, 394–434. Durham, N.C.: Duke University Press.

Ruppel, T., J. Neuwirth, M. P. Leone, and G. Fry. 2003. "Hidden in View: African Spiritual Spaces in North American Landscapes." *Antiquity* 77: 321–335.

Rush, D. L. 1997. Vodun Vortex: Accumulative Arts, Histories, and Religious Consciousness along Coastal Benin. Ph.D. dissertation, University of Iowa.

———. 1999. "Eternal Potential Chromolithographs in Vodunland." *African Arts* 32 (4): 60–75, 94–96.

———. 2001. "Contemporary Vodun Arts of Ouidah, Benin." *African Arts* 34 (4): 32–47, 94–96.

Russell, A. E. 1997. "Material Culture and African-American Spirituality at the Hermitage." *Historical Archaeology* 31 (2): 63–80.

St. Clair, W. 2006. *The Grand Slave Emporium: Cape Coast Castle and the British Slave Trade*. London: Profile Books.

"The St. Thomas Obeah Case." 1893. *The Daily Gleaner*, 25 September, 2.

Salisbury, S. 2002. "A Protest Today Seeks Memorial to Slaves." *Philadelphia Inquirer*, 3 July, http://www.ushistory.org/presidentshouse/news/inq070302b.htm.

Salkey, A., ed. 1980. *Caribbean Folk Tales and Legends*. London: Bogle-L'Ouverture Publications.

Salm, S. J., and T. Falola. 2002. *Culture and Customs of Ghana*. Westport, Conn.: Greenwood Press.

Samford, P. 1996. "The Archaeology of Slavery and African American Material Culture." *William and Mary Quarterly*, 3rd series, 53 (1): 87–114.

———. 2007. *Subfloor Pits and the Archaeology of Slavery in Colonial Virginia*. Birmingham: University of Alabama Press.

Sansi, L. N., and R. Parés, eds. 2011. *Sorcery in the Black Atlantic*. Chicago: University of Chicago Press.

Saunders, P. 2004. Free and Enslaved African Communities in Buff Bay, Jamaica: Daily Life, Resistance, and Kinship, 1780–1834. Ph.D. dissertation, University of Texas at Austin.

Savary, C. 1970. "Poteries rituelles et autres objets cultuels en usage au Dahomey." *Bulletin Annuel Musée d'Ethnographie, Geneva* 13: 33–57.

Schablitcky, J. 2009. "No Stone Unturned: Expressions of African Spirit Tradition at the Jackson Homestead." Paper presented at the Society for Historical Archaeology, 42nd Annual Conference, 6–11 January.

Schaffer, W., and E. K. Agorsah. 2010. "Bioarchaeological Analysis of Historic Kormantse, Ghana." *African Diaspora Archaeology Newsletter*, March, 1–12.

Schechner, R. 2002. "Ritual and Performance." In *Companion Encyclopedia of Anthropology*, edited by T. Ingold, 613–647. London: Routledge.

Schiffer, M. B. 1983. "Towards the Identification of Formation Processes." *American Antiquity* 48 (4): 675–706.

———. 1987. *Formation Processes of the Archaeological Record*. Albuquerque: University of New Mexico Press.

Schmidt, P. 1978. *Historical Archaeology: A Structural Approach in an African Culture*. Westport, Conn.: Greenwood Press.

———. 1983. "An Alternative to a Strictly Materialist Perspective: A Review of Historical Archaeology, Ethnoarchaeology, and Symbolic Approaches in African Archaeology." *American Antiquity* 48 (1): 62–81.

———. 1996. "Reconfiguring the Barongo: Reproductive Symbolism and Reproduction among a Work Association of Iron Smelters." In *The Culture and Technology of African Iron Production*, edited by P. R. Schmidt, 74–127. Gainesville: University Press of Florida.

———. 1997. *Iron Technology in East Africa: Symbolism, Science, and Archaeology.* Bloomington: Indiana University Press.

———. 2009. "Tropes, Materiality, and Ritual Embodiment of African Iron Smelting Furnaces as Human Figures." *Journal of Archaeological Method and Theory* 16 (3): 262–282.

Schneider, D. M. 1980. *American Kinship: A Cultural Account.* Chicago: University of Chicago Press.

Schramm, K. 2004. "Coming Home to the Motherland: Pilgrimage Tourism in Ghana." In *Reframing Pilgrimage: Cultures in Motion,* edited by S. Coleman and J. Eade, 133–149. London: Routledge.

———. 2005. "The Transatlantic Slave Trade: Contemporary Topographies of Memory in Ghana and the USA." *Transactions of the Historical Society of Ghana,* new series, 9: 125–140.

———. 2010. *African Homecoming: Pan African Ideology and Contested Heritage.* Walnut Creek, Cal.: Left Coast Press.

Schuler, M. 1979. "Myalism and the African Religious Tradition." In *Africa and the Caribbean: The Legacies of a Link,* edited by M. Crahan and F. Knight, 65–79. Baltimore: Johns Hopkins University Press.

Scott, D. 1991. "That Event, This Memory: Notes on the Anthropology of African Diasporas in the New World." *Diaspora* 13: 261–284.

———. 1997. "'An Obscure Miracle of Connection': Discursive Tradition and Black Diaspora Criticism." *Small Axe* 1: 19–38.

Scott, M. 1829. *Tom Cringle's Log.* London: J. M. Dent.

Senior, O. 2003. *Encyclopedia of Jamaican Heritage.* Kingston, Jamaica: Twin Guinep Publishers.

Sensbach, J. 1998. *A Separate Canaan: The Making of an Afro-Moravian World in North Carolina, 1763–1840.* Chapel Hill: University of North Carolina Press.

———. 2000. "Race and the Early Moravian Church: A Comparative Perspective." *Transactions of the Moravian Historical* Society 31: 1–10.

———. 2005. *Rebecca's Revival: Creating Black Christianity in the Atlantic World.* Cambridge, Mass.: Harvard University Press.

"Severe Sentence Passed on St. James Obeahman by R.M." 1932. *The Daily Gleaner,* 25 October, 11.

Shackel, P. A. 1993. *Personal Discipline and Material Culture: An Archaeology of Annapolis, Maryland, 1695–1870.* Knoxville: University of Tennessee Press.

Sharp, L. 2000. "The Commodification of the Body and Its Part." *Annual Review of Anthropology* 29: 287–328.

Sharpe, J. 1880. "Proposals for Erecting a School, Library and Chapel at New York, 1712–1713." In *Collections of the New York Historical Society for the Year 1880, Revolutionary and Miscellaneous Papers (Vol. III),* 341–363. New York: New-York Historical Society.

Shaw, R. 2002. *Memories of the Slave Trade: Ritual and the Historical Imagination in Sierra Leone.* Chicago: University of Chicago Press.

Shaw, T. 1977. *Unearthing Igbo-Ukwu.* Ibadan, Nigeria: Oxford University Press.

Shepard, E. 1888. "Superstitions of the Negro." *Cosmopolitan* 5: 47–50.

"A Shrine to Slaves: Black Americans Restore Ghana's Old Fort Amsterdam." 1972. *Ebony,* January, 88–91.

Sieber, R., and R. A. Walker. 1987. *African Art in the Cycle of Life*. Washington, D.C.: Smithsonian Institution Press.

Silverman, H., and D. Small, eds. 2002. *The Space and Place of Death*. Washington, D.C.: American Anthropological Association.

Simmonds, D. D. 1973. "A Note on the Excavation in Cape Coast Castle." *Transactions of the Historical Society of Ghana* 14 (2): 267–269.

Singleton, T. A. 1991. "The Archaeology of Slave Life." In *Images of the Recent Past: Readings in Historical Archaeology*, edited by C. E. Orser, Jr., 141–165. Walnut Creek, Cal.: AltaMira Press.

———. 2006. "African Diaspora Archaeology in Dialogue." In *Afro-Atlantic Dialogues: Anthropology in the Diaspora*, edited by K. A. Yelvington, 249–287. Santa Fe: School of American Research Press.

Sinou, A. 1994. "Architectural and Urban Heritage: The Example of the City of Ouidah, Benin." In *Culture and Development in Africa: Proceedings of an International Conference Held at the World Bank*, edited by I. Serageldin and J. Taboroff, 289–312. Washington, D.C.: World Bank.

Sloane, D. 1991. *The Last Great Necessity: Cemeteries in American History*. Baltimore: Johns Hopkins University Press.

Smiley, P. 1919. "Folklore of Virginia, South Carolina, Georgia, Alabama and Florida." *Journal of American Folklore* 32: 382–383.

Smith, C. S. 1975. "Metallurgy as a Human Experience." *Metallurgical Transactions* 6A (4): 603–623.

Smith, F. H. 2008. *The Archaeology of Alcohol and Drinking*. Gainesville: University Press of Florida.

Smith, M. G. (1957) 1984. *The Plural Society in the West Indies*. Reprint ed. Berkeley: University of California Press.

Sobel, M. 1979. *Trablin' On: The Slave Journey to an Afro-Baptist Faith*. Westport, Conn.: Greenwood Press.

Sontag, S. 1961. *Against Interpretation and Other Essays*. New York: Farrar, Straus and Giroux.

Stafford, T. A. 1942. *Christian Symbolism in the Evangelical Churches*. New York: Abingdon-Chokesbury Press.

Stahl, A. B. 1999. "The Archaeology of Global Encounters Viewed from Banda, Ghana." *African Archaeological Review* 16 (1): 5–81.

———. 2001. *Making History in Banda: Anthropological Visions of Africa's Past*. Cambridge: Cambridge University Press.

———. 2008. "Dogs, Pythons, Pots, and Beads: The Dynamics of Shrines and Sacrificial Practices in Banda, Ghana, 1400–1900 CE." In *Memory Works: Archaeologies of Material Practices*, edited by B. Mills and B. Walker, 159–186. Santa Fe: School for Advanced Research Press.

Steadman, S. R. 2009. *Archaeology of Religion: Cultures and Their Beliefs in Worldwide Context*. Walnut Creek, Cal.: Left Coast Press.

Steen, C. 2011. "Cosmograms, Crosses, and Xs: Context and Inference." *Historical Archaeology* 45 (2): 166–175.

Stein, J. K. 1987. "Deposits for Archaeologists." Advances in Archaeological Method and Theory 11: 337–395.

Stewart, R. J. 1992. *Religion and Society in Post-Emancipation Jamaica.* Knoxville: University of Tennessee Press.

Stine, L. F., M. A. Cabak, and M. D. Groover. 1996. "Blue Beads as African-American Cultural Symbols." *Historical Archaeology* 30 (3): 49–75.

Strauss, G. 1975. "Success and Failure in the German Reformation." *Past and Present* 67: 30–63.

Stuckey, S. 1987. *Slave Culture: Nationalist Theory and the Foundations of Black America.* New York: Oxford University Press.

Sturken, M. 1991. "The Wall, the Screen, and the Image: The Vietnam Veterans Memorial." *Representations* 35: 118–142.

———. 1997. *Tangled Memories: The Vietnam War, the AIDS Epidemic, and the Politics of Remembering.* Berkeley: University of California Press.

Sundstrom, L. 1974. *The Exchange Economy of Pre-Colonial Tropical Africa.* New York: St. Martin's Press.

Suttles, W. C., Jr. 1971. "African Religious Survivals as Factors in American Slave Revolts." *Journal of Negro History* 56 (2): 97–104.

Sweet, J. H. 2009a. "Mistaken Identities? Oluadah Equiano, Domingos Álvares, and the Methodological Challenges of Studying the African Diaspora." *American Historical Review* 114: 279–306.

———. 2009b. "Slaves, Convicts, and Exiles: African Travelers in the Portuguese Atlantic World, 1720–1750." In *Bridging the Early Modern Atlantic World: People, Products, and Practices on the Move,* edited by C. Williams, 193–202. Farnham, England: Ashgate.

———. 2011. *Domingos Alvares, African Healing, and the Intellectual History of the Atlantic World.* Chapel Hill: University of North Carolina Press.

Szwed, J. 2011. "Alan Lomax, the 'Man Who Recorded the World. Reprint ed. New York: Penguin Books.

Tait, H., ed. 1986. *Jewelry: 7000 Years.* New York: Harry N. Abrams.

Tanna, L. 1984. *Jamaica Folk Tales and Oral Histories.* Kingston: Institute of Jamaica Publications.

Taylor, C. E. 1970. *Leaflets from the Danish West Indies: Descriptive of the Social, Political, and Commercial Conditions of These Islands.* Westport, Conn.: Negro University Press.

Taylor, E. R. 2006. *If We Must Die: Shipboard Insurrections in the Era of the Atlantic Slave Trade.* Baton Rouge: Louisiana State University Press.

Teish, L. 1989. *Jambalaya: The Natural Woman's Book of Personal Charms and Practical Rituals.* San Francisco: Harper and Row.

Teye, V. B., and D. J. Timothy. 2004. "The Varied Colors of Slave Heritage in West Africa: White American Stakeholders." *Space and Culture* 7: 145–155.

Thomas, B. W. 1995. "Source Criticism and the Interpretation of African-American Sites." *Southeastern Archaeology* 14 (2): 149–157.

———. 1998. "Power and Community: The Archaeology of Slavery at the Hermitage Plantation." *American Antiquity* 63 (4): 531–551.

———. 2001. "African-American Tradition and Community in the Antebellum South." In *The Archaeology of Traditions: Agency and History before and after Columbus,* edited by T. Pauketat, 17–33. Gainesville: University Press of Florida.

Thomas, H. 1894. Charms and Implements Seized in Possession of Various Obeah-men, CO 137/561, University of West Indies Special Collections, Kingston, Jamaica.

Thompson, R. F. 1973. "An Aesthetic of the Cool." *African Arts* 7 (1): 40–43, 64–67, 84–91.

———. 1977a. *Black Gods and Kings.* Bloomington: Indiana University Press.

———. 1977b. "Siras Bowens of Sunbury, Georgia, A Tidewater Artist in the Afro-American Visual Tradition." *Massachusetts Review* 18 (3): 490–500.

———. 1983. *Flash of the Spirit: African and Afro-American Art and Philosophy.* New York: Random House.

———. 1989. "The Circle and the Branch: Renascent Kongo-American Art." In *Another Face of the Diamond,* edited by J. McWillie and I. Lockpez, 29–34. New York: INTAR Latin American Gallery.

———. 1993. *Face of the Gods: Art and Altars of Africa and the African Americas.* New York: Museum for African Art.

———. 1997. "Translating the World into Generousness." *Res* 32 (Autumn): 19–36.

———. 2005. "Kongo Influences on African American Artistic Culture." In *Africanisms in American Culture,* edited by J. Holloway, 283–325. Bloomington: Indiana University Press.

Thompson, R. F., and J. Cornet. 1981. *Four Moments of the Sun: Kongo Art in Two Worlds.* Washington, D.C.: National Gallery of Art.

Thornton, J. K. 1977. "Demography and History in the Kingdom of the Kongo, 1550–1750." *Journal of African History* 18 (4): 507–530.

———. 1993. "'I Am the Subject of the King of Congo': African Political Ideology and the Haitian Revolution." *Journal of World History* 4 (2): 181–214.

———. 1995. *Africa and Africans in the Making of the Atlantic World, 1400–1680.* Cambridge: Cambridge University Press.

———. 1998a. *Africa and Africans in the Making of the Atlantic World, 1400–1800.* Cambridge: Cambridge University Press.

———. 1998b. "The Coromantees: An African Cultural Group in Colonial North America and the Caribbean." *Journal of Caribbean History* 32 (1–2): 161–178.

———. 2000. "War, State, and Religious Norms in 'Coromantee' Thought: The Ideology of an African American Nation." In *Possible Pasts: Becoming Colonial in Early America,* edited by R. B. St. George, 181–200. Ithaca, N.Y.: Cornell University Press.

Thornton, L. 1904. "'Obeah' in Jamaica." *Journal of the Society of Comparative Legislation,* new series, 5 (2): 262–270.

Thylefors, M. 2009. "'Our Government Is in Bwa Kayiman': A Vodou Ceremony in 1791 and its Contemporary Significations." *Stockholm Review of Latin American Studies* 4: 73–84.

Tinkham, K., and M. Reeves. 2010. Mansion Cellars Report: Excavations of the Cellar Spaces for the Main Block of the Mansion 2003–2005 Seasons, http://www.montpelier.org/files/mansion-cellars-report.

Tishken, J. E., T. Fálọlá, and A. Akìnyẹmí, eds. 2009. *Sàngó in Africa and the African Diaspora.* Bloomington: Indiana University Press.

Tolliver, D. E. 2000. "Study Abroad in Africa: Learning about Race, Racism, and the Racial Legacy of America." *African Issues* 28 (1–2): 112–116.

Torain, S. H. 1943. "Ante-bellum and War Memories of Mrs. Telfair Hodgson." *Georgia Historical Quarterly* 24 (4): 350–356.

"Trial of the Conspirators at Buff Bay." 1824. *The Daily Gleaner*, 15 March, 7–8.

Trowbridge, A. W. 1896. "Negro Customs and Folk-Stories of Jamaica." *Journal of American Folklore* 9 (35): 279–287.

Turner, V. W. 1969. *The Ritual Process: Structure and Anti-Structure*. Chicago: Aldine Publishing.

———. 1970. *The Forest of Symbols: Aspects of Ndembu Ritual*. 2nd ed. Ithaca, N.Y.: Cornell University Press.

———. 1973. "Symbols in African Ritual." *Science* 179 (4078): 1100–1105.

———. 1982. *From Ritual to Theatre: The Human Seriousness of Play*. New York: Performing Arts Journal.

Turner, V. W., with W. Blogett, S. Kahona, and F. Benwa. 1992. *Experiencing Ritual: A New Experience of African Healing*. Philadelphia: University of Pennsylvania Press.

Ulin, R. C. 2001. *Understanding Cultures: Perspectives in Anthropology and Social Theory*. 2nd ed. Malden: Blackwell.

Valentine, D. 1860. *Manual of the Corporation of the City of New York*. New York: McSpedon and Bakers.

Van Beek, W. 2001. *Dogon: Africa's People of the Cliffs*. New York: Harry N. Abrams.

Van Dantzig, A. 1976. "Castles and Forts of Ghana as a Collective Historical Document." In *Ghana Talks*, edited by M. Dodds, 49–67. Washington, D.C.: Three Continents Press.

———. 1980. *Forts and Castles of Ghana*. Accra: Sedco Publishing.

Van Dongen, B., P. Withers, S. Fraser, T. Insoll, and B. Kankpeyeng. Under review. "Computer Tomography and Organic Geochemistry of Koma Land Figurines." *Journal of Archaeological Science*.

Van Dyke, R. M., and S. E. Alcock, eds. 2003. *Archaeologies of Memory*. Malden, Mass.: Wiley-Blackwell.

Van Gennep, A. (1909) 1960. *The Rites of Passage*. Chicago: University of Chicago Press.

Vansina, J. 1985. *Oral Tradition as History*. London: James Currey.

———. 1990. *Paths in the Rainforests: Toward a History of Political Tradition in Equatorial Africa*. Madison: University of Wisconsin Press.

Van Velzen, T. H. U. E., and W. W. Van Wetering. 1988. *The Great Father and the Danger: Religious Cults, Material Forces, and Collective Fantasies in the World of Surinamese Maroons*. Dordrecht, Netherlands: Foris Publications.

Vázquez de Espinosa, A. 1969. *Compendio y descripción de las Indias occidentales*. Madrid: Atlas.

Verger, P. 1957. *Notes sur le culte des Orisa et Vodun à Bahia, la baie de tous les saints, au Brésil et à l'ancienne Côte des Esclaves en Afrique*. Dakar: Institut Fondamental d'Afrique Noire.

Viveiros de Castro, E. 2012. *Cosmological Perspectivism in Amazonia and Elsewhere*. Manchester, England: HAU Network of Ethnographic Theory.

Vlach, J. M. 1990. *The Afro-American Tradition in Decorative Arts*. Athens: University of Georgia Press.

———. 1991. *By the Work of Their Hands: Studies in Afro-American Folklife*. Charlottesville: University Press of Virginia.

———. 1993. *Back of the Big House: The Architecture of Plantation Slavery*. Chapel Hill: University of North Carolina Press.

Vogel, S. 1974. *Gods of Fortune: The Cult of the Hand in Nigeria*. New York: Museum of Primitive Art.

Von Doering, E. 1895. "Reiseberichte von Premier lieutenant v. Doering aus den Jahren 1893 bis 1895." *Mitteilungen aus den deutsche Schutzgebieten* 8 (4): 231–276.

Von Luschan, F. (1919) 1968. *Die Alterümer von Benin*. Berlin and New York: Hacker Art Books.

Waddell, H. 1863. *Twenty-Nine Years in the West Indies and Central Africa: A Review of Missionary Work and Adventure, 1829–1858*. London: T. Nelson and Sons.

Wagner, R. 1986. *Symbols That Stand for Themselves*. Chicago: University of Chicago Press.

Walker, J. 1998. *The History of Black Business in America: Capitalism, Race, Entrepreneurship*. New York: Macmillan.

Walker, W. H. 2002. "Stratigraphy and Practical Reason." *American Anthropologist* 104 (1): 159–177.

———. 2008. "Practice and Nonhuman Social Actors: The Afterlife Histories of Witches and Dogs in the American Southwest." In *Memory Work: Archaeologies of Material Practices*, edited by B. J. Miller and W. H. Walker, 137–158. Santa Fe: School for Advanced Research Press.

Walsh, L. S. 2001. "The Chesapeake Slave Trade: Regional Patterns, African Origins, and Some Implications." *William and Mary Quarterly*, 3rd series, 58 (1): 139–170.

Walvin, J. 2002. "Slavery and the British." *History Today* 52 (3): 48–54.

Waring, M. A. 1894. "Mortuary Customs and Beliefs of South Carolina Negroes." *Journal of American Folklore* 7: 318–319.

Warner-Lewis, M. 2009. *Trinidad Yoruba: From Mother-Tongue to Memory*. Mobile: University of Alabama Press.

Washington, E. B. 1992. "Land of Gold: Ghana—Cousins." *Essence*, 23 October, 100.

Washington, T. N. 2005. *Our Mothers, Our Powers, Our Texts: Manifestations of Aje in Africana Literature*. Bloomington: Indiana University Press.

Waters, A. M. 1985. *Race, Class, and Political Symbols: Rastafari and Reggae in Jamaican Politics*. New Brunswick, N.J.: Transaction.

Waters, A. W. 2000. *On Jordan's Stormy Banks: Personal Accounts of Slavery in Georgia*. Winston-Salem, N.C.: John Blair Publishers.

Webber, F. R. 1971. *Church Symbolism: An Explanation of the More Important Symbols of the Old Testament and New Testament, the Primitive, the Medieval, and the Modern Church*. Detroit: Gale Research.

Weinlick, J. 1956. *Count Zinzendorf: The Story of His Life and Leadership in the Renewed Moravian Church*. New York: Abingdon Press.

Wesler, K. W. 2012. *An Archaeology of Religion*. Lanham, Md.: University Press of America.

Westmacott, R. 1992. *African-American Gardens: Yards in Rural South*. Knoxville: University of Tennessee Press.

Wheat, D. 2011. "The First Great Waves: African Provenance of the Transatlantic Slave Trade to Cartagena de Indias, 1570–1640." *Journal of African History* 52 (1): 1–22.

White, L. 2000. *Speaking with Vampires: Rumor and History in Colonial Africa.* Berkeley: University of California Press.

Wilberforce, W. 1823. *An Appeal to the Religion, Justice and Humanity of the Inhabitants of the British Empire, in Behalf of Negro Slaves in the West Indies.* London: J. Hatchard.

Wilford, J. N. 2008. "Under Maryland Street, Ties to African Past." *New York Times,* 20 October, http://www.nytimes.com/2008/10/21/science/21arch.html?pagewanted=all&_r=0.

Wilkerson, I. 2010. *The Warmth of Other Suns: The Epic Story of America's Great Migration.* New York: Random House.

Wilkes County Deed Books. 1868–1872, 1890. Vols. 18–22, 57. Wilkes County Courthouse, Washington, Ga.

Wilkes County Wills Book. 1841. Vol. 11. Wilkes County Courthouse, Washington, Ga.

Wilkie, L. A. 1997. "Secret and Sacred: Contextualizing the Artifacts of African-American Magic and Religion." *Historical Archaeology* 31 (4): 81–106.

———. 2000. *Creating Freedom: Material Culture and African American Identity at Oakley Plantation, Louisiana, 1840–1950.* Baton Rouge: Louisiana State University Press.

Wilkie, L. A., and G. Shorter. 2001. *Lucrecia's Well: An Archaeological Glimpse of an African-American Midwife's Household.* Mobile: University of South Alabama.

Willett, F. 1961. "Investigations at Old Oyo, 1956–1957: An Interim Report." *Journal of the Historical Society of Nigeria* 2 (1): 59–77.

Williams, D. 1974. *Icon and Image: A Study of Sacred and Secular Forms of African Classical Art.* London: Allen Lane.

Williams, R. 1973. *The Country and the City.* 2nd ed. New York: Oxford University Press.

Willingham, R. M., Jr. 1969. *A History of Wilkes County Georgia.* Washington, Ga.: Wilkes Publishing.

Wilson, P. J. 1995. *Crab Antics: A Caribbean Study of the Conflict between Reputation and Respectability.* Long Grove, Ill.: Waveland Press.

Winston, A. 1993. "Tracing the Origins of the Rosary: German Vernacular Texts." *Speculum* 68 (3): 619–636.

Wittgenstein, L. 2009. *Philosophical Investigations.* 4th ed. Hoboken, N.J.: Wiley-Blackwell.

Wood, M. 2010. "'Each in Their Allotted Place': Social and Spatial Organization of Moravian Mission Cemeteries in the US Virgin Islands, 1770–1900." Paper presented at the Conference for the Society of Historical Archaeology, Amelia Island, Florida, 6–9 January.

———. 2012. "Mapping the Complexities of Race on the Landscape of the Colonial Caribbean, United States Virgin Islands, 1770–1917." *Historical Archaeology* 46 (4): 112–134.

Wood, P. 1996. *Black Majority: Negroes of Colonial South Carolina from 1670 through the Stono Rebellion.* New York: Norton.

Woolfork, L. 2009. *Embodying American Slavery in Contemporary Culture.* Urbana: University of Illinois Press.

Wright, R., and W. Hughes. 1996. *Lay Down Body—Living History in African American Cemeteries.* Detroit: Visible Ink.

Yai, O. B. 1993. "In Praise of Metonymy: The Concepts of 'Tradition' and 'Creativity' in the Transmission of Yoruba Artistry over Time and Space." Research in African Literatures 24 (4): 29–37.

———. 1999. "Tradition and the Yoruba Artist." *African Arts* 32 (1): 32–93.

Yelvington, K. A., ed. 2006. *Afro-Atlantic Dialogues: Anthropology in the Diaspora.* Santa Fe: School of American Research Press.

Yentsch, A. 1994. *A Chesapeake Family and Their Slaves: A Study in Historical Archaeology.* Cambridge: Cambridge University Press.

Yoder, D. 1990. *Discovering American Folklife: Studies in Ethnic, Religious and Regional Culture.* Ann Arbor, Mich.: UMI Research Press.

Young, J. E. 1993. *The Texture of Memory: Holocaust Memorials and Meaning.* New Haven, Conn.: Yale University Press.

LIST OF CONTRIBUTORS

E. Kofi Agorsah received his Ph.D. from the University of California at Los Angeles. He is professor of black studies and international studies and chair of the Department of Black Studies at Portland State University (PSU), Oregon. He was a former keeper of the Ghana Museums and Monuments Board, and former vice president of the International Association for Caribbean Archaeology (IACA).

Helen C. Blouet is an associate professor of anthropology at Utica College with a Ph.D. from Syracuse University. Her research interests focus on death, burial, and commemoration in Caribbean history.

Danielle N. Boaz earned her Ph.D. in African and African diaspora history at the University of Miami. A practicing attorney, she is an assistant professor in the Law, Politics, and Society program at Drake University, Des Moines, Iowa.

Christopher C. Fennell is an associate professor of law at the University of Illinois, Urbana-Champaign, and visiting professor of law at the University of Chicago. He is the founding editor of Journal of African Diaspora Archaeology and Heritage.

Pablo F. Gómez is an assistant professor in the Department of the History of Science at the University of Wisconsin–Madison. He holds M.A. and Ph.D. degrees in history from Vanderbilt University, and an M.D. from the Universidad CES, with medical residency in Orthopaedic Surgery at the Pontificia Universidad Javeriana, Colombia.

Candice Goucher is a professor of history at Washington State University, Vancouver. A graduate of the University of California at Los Angeles, she has conducted archaeological and historical research in West Africa, the Caribbean, and Mauritius.

Grey Gundaker is Dittman Professor of American Studies and Anthropology at the College of William and Mary. She earned her Ph.D. from Yale University. Her research interests include landscapes, literacies, and theory in the African Diaspora.

Timothy Insoll is a professor of archaeology at the University of Manchester. He obtained his doctorate degree and was a research fellow at the University of Cambridge. He is an Africanist archaeologist with emphasis on religion and ritual.

Benjamin W. Kankpeyeng is an associate professor in the Department of Archaeology and Heritage Studies at the University of Ghana in Accra. He is currently the chair of the department. He holds a Ph.D. in anthropology from Syracuse University.

Jocelyn E. Knauf is an historical archaeologist with a doctoral degree in anthropology from the University of Maryland. She also received a B.A. in anthropology and a B.A. in international studies from American University, as well as a masters of applied anthropology from the University of Maryland.

Cheryl J. LaRoche is a historical and archaeological consultant who earned a Ph.D. in American Studies from the University of Maryland. She specializes in eighteenth- and nineteenth-century black experience in the United States.

Mark P. Leone is an historical archaeologist and professor of anthropology at the University of Maryland, College Park. He has directed archaeological research projects in Annapolis since 1981.

Hugh B. (Matt) Matternes is the director of the Cemetery Studies Program at the New South Associates, where he is responsible for the identification, recovery, and preservation of cemetery sites. He received his M.A. and Ph.D. in anthropology with a focus in physical anthropology and mortuary archaeology from the University of Tennessee, Knoxville.

Neil L. Norman is an assistant professor in the Department of Anthropology at the College of William and Mary. An anthropological archaeologist with interests in issues of social complexity in Atlantic West Africa, he received his Ph.D. from the University of Virginia.

Akinwumi (Akin) Ogundiran is professor of Africana studies, anthropology, and history, and chair of the Africana Studies Department at the University of North Carolina, Charlotte.

Brempong Osei-Tutu is an anthropological archaeologist with interest in heritage management and public policy, social memory, cultural representation, memorial entrepreneurism, tourism, Atlantic Africa, and the African Diaspora. He received his doctorate from Syracuse University. He teaches in the Department of Sociology and Anthropology at the University of Cape Coast, Ghana.

Matthew Reeves is director of archaeology at the Montpelier Foundation. He has conducted archaeological research in the Caribbean and the United States. He obtained his Ph.D. from Syracuse University.

Staci Richey, formerly a historian/architectural historian with New South Associates, is currently a city planner with the city of Columbia's Planning and Development Services in South Carolina. She received a certificate of museum management and a M.A. in public history from the University of South Carolina.

Paula Saunders earned her Ph.D. in anthropology from the University of Texas at Austin. Since 2006, she has been teaching anthropology and history at the Borough of Manhattan Community College, part of the City University of New York.

Amanda Tang is a doctoral candidate in the Department of Anthropology at the University of Maryland with a concentration on historical archaeology and zooarchaeology. She also earned a masters of applied anthropology from the University of Maryland.

INDEX

www.ingramcontent.com/pod-product-compliance
Lightning Source LLC
LaVergne TN
LVHW010347080826
844660LV00003B/212

* 9 7 8 0 2 5 3 0 1 3 8 6 6 *